Holiday, Inc.

Anthony Caruso

&

L. J. Simone

DEDICATION

For my beloved wife, Sarah, who brings magic and light to my life every single day. Also for my parents, Marie and Tom, who instilled in me the everlasting Spirit of Christmas in the first place.

For Aurora – May you always believe in all things magical and mythical.

Table of Contents

Nature's Unfortunate Timing
Pg. 4

Happy Corporate Takeover Day
Pg. 15

Love the One You Are
Pg. 50

How Not to Have an Intervention in 7 Excruciatingly Long Hours
Pg. 82

It Hops
Pg. 122

With Your Hole Heart
Pg. 148

Bill Not Included
Pg. 175

What Not to Do in Case of a Fire
Pg. 195

I Saw Someone Killing Santa Claus
Pg. 214

A Day in the Life of the Tooth Fairy
Pg. 250

Sexy is the New Scary
Pg. 294

Best. Thanksgiving Song. Ever.
Pg. 337

Santa's Last Flight
Pg. 359

Endings and Beginnings
Pg. 430

January

"Clucky says if you can't stand the cold, stay outta the Pole."

The entire carved building is always incredibly cold. After all, it is situated at the center of the North Pole and sculpted from ice, which, as you might assume, is the most easily accessible building material in the area. From afar, it looks like nothing more than a giant block of snow, perched at the edge of a bottomless icy chasm; nothing that passes by, be it a helicopter, bird or one of those pesky satellites, even glances twice at it, let alone discovers that it is occupied.

The inhabitants of this perpetually chilly building have their own methods of keeping their various offices warm (apart from the basement; no matter how hard the employees down there try, they can't retain heat or get the maintenance man to fix their heating systems), but if you were to step out of the elevator and onto the first floor, you would instantly feel as though you had accidentally walked through a wormhole and entered the Sahara.

After getting hit in the face by this wall of heat, you'd find yourself in a seemingly normal office; cubicles line the floor, computers blink and printers buzz. The only odd things about this place are the many clocks lining the walls, filling the space with a constant ticking sound. Clocks of all different shapes and sizes: grandfather clocks, cuckoo clocks, digital clocks, water clocks and even death clocks; all of them are set to different time zones, so that every minute of every day, at least one of them will ring in a new hour with their chimes, or their gongs, or their chirping birds. It drives most people crazy, and it certainly ensures that this particular floor doesn't receive many long-term visitors, even though the man in charge here finds the constant noise incredibly soothing.

Though it is well after five p.m., the employees who handle New Year's are still slouched over their keyboards, sipping at cold coffee and trying to ignore the distant sounds of celebration from above. For them, it is officially January first, but until New Year's Eve ends in every time zone, their boss is going to keep them working, tracking numbers and monitoring losses until that final stroke of midnight.

Father Time strokes his long gray beard as he surveys his employees through the open door of his own private office. Midnight is fast approaching the Eastern Seaboard of continental North America and he figures that once it hits, he'll let them go and handle the remaining time zones himself. After all, the majority of their revenue comes from Times Square, so every time zone that follows this spectacle is merely gravy.

Taking a sip from his third glass of champagne, dribbling some down his beard and onto his ancient gray robes, the old man glances at his giant computer screen once more. "The final numbers from Newfoundland have arrived! There's been a five percent increase from last year! Probably a lot more savvy underage kids finding new ways to trick the system. Remember the days when you didn't need an I.D. to get into a bar?" He glances at a man sitting in the corner of the office who appears even older than himself (though this is obviously impossible).

This man is thin and hunched, and his skin – covered in liver spots – is stretched so tightly over his bones, that he appears little more than a skeleton. He stares vaguely into the distance, drool hanging from his mouth, and it takes him almost a full minute to even turn his head and stare when Father Time addresses him.

"Well?" Father Time prompts, sounding annoyed.

In response to the question, the skeletal man lets out a low, painful sounding moan, causing Father Time to smirk.

"I didn't think so," he replies, glancing at the large hourglass resting on the center of his desk. The bottom bulb is about halfway filled with sand, while the top bulb looks as though it isn't emptying at all despite the steady stream of tiny white particles falling into the lower one. "That was a *long* time ago."

Father Time glances out of the window behind his desk at the small village below, which is, as always, decked out for Christmas. After downing the rest of his champagne, he turns back toward his computers. "The East Coast numbers should be coming in any second," he mutters to himself as he hits a button on his keyboard. "And they are – *what the fuck?*"

His eyes widen as he stares at the overwhelming amount of negative numbers filling up his computer screen. New York, New Jersey, Florida, Toronto – all dropping rapidly. Not one city situated in the Eastern Standard time zone has earned a single penny more than last year. In fact, for the first time in its very long history, New Year's Eve is *losing* money.

"How is this possible?" Father Time demands, ignoring the nervous looks that his three employees are throwing his way through his open office door. "How does New York City put us in a *deficit*?"

The old man sitting in the corner lets out a low moan again, causing Father Time to roll his eyes.

"Oh, why don't you go ahead and just *die* already?" he snaps. "Come back as a woman so you can distract me with a blowjob at times like these!"

Standing up, Father Time grabs his long wooden staff and marches out of his office.

"How does New York City put us into a *deficit*?" he repeats to his office at large. "What happened to the Times Square celebration, don't they *do* that anymore?"

"They do," begins a timid woman with pointed features named Clotho. "But--"

"Then what the *hell* happened?" Father Time interrupts. "How do we lose money *now*? The East Coast is supposed to be the home stretch! The *easy* part of the night!"

"It seems there was a freak blizzard," another woman, Lachesis, pipes up with some hesitation. "It hit the entire East Coast."

"Worst this world's ever seen," Atropos adds. "The mortals are calling it *Frankenstorm*."

"Over eighty-five mortals confirmed dead so far, and--"

"How is this *my* problem?" Father Time demands. A phone rings on the other side of the room, which Lachesis hurries to answer.

"Well," Clotho continues. "Most people didn't want to risk life and limb just to celebrate a holiday."

"How did we not know about this storm?" Father Time asks. "Where's our weather guy?"

"We don't have one. He was transferred to the South American branch in 1603, remember? Normally, Mother Nature--"

Father Time holds up a hand, stopping Atropos mid-sentence as he tightens the grip on his staff. It was all her fault – Mother. Nature. That plant obsessed bitch.

"Where are you going?" Lachesis calls as Father Time hurries across the floor toward the elevator bay, his long robes trailing behind him.

"To deal with this."

"Sir," Lachesis continues hurriedly. "Corporate is on the phone. They want to talk to you about--"

"Stall them!" he barks at the three sisters.

Father Time jabs at the up button and steps into the brightly lit elevator. None of the buttons are numbered but are all different shapes and sizes instead. Pressing the one resembling a Christmas tree, the elevator doors close and Father Time begins to rise, fuming as he tries to block out the sound of *Auld Lang Syne* playing on the overhead speakers. The last time the numbers had been close to this bad the Black Death had been to blame. Corporate hadn't even accepted carts of bodies in the streets as a good excuse for bad sales – now he has to try and blame a little frozen water? Up at the Pole they are buried in the white stuff from January to December and *they* manage just fine. Well, most of the time. There was that one questionable Christmas before Rudolph was born, but that was a freak accident. The fact is, these mortals get lazier, fatter and dumber every year.

When the elevator comes to a stop on the twelfth floor, the doors open again and Father Time finds himself in the middle of a raging celebration. Normally empty space most of the year, the company hosts all of their holiday parties up here, for the enormous floor to ceiling windows offer a panoramic view of the North Pole and the Aurora Borealis. The cosmic light display used to awe and inspire those who were forced to move to the Pole when the fat man in red refused to move away, but now the once breathtaking view had become little more than a decoration to most of them.

Christmas trees are spaced every few feet throughout the room and tables full of food and liquor are surrounded by people and various creatures, most of whom already look drunk. In one corner of the room, Father Time notices a small bearded elf with a beer gut passed out cold, being ignored by everyone around him. On a shabbily erected stage against one of the back windows, a stumbling vampire and two tiny muscled men sporting tutus are howling into a microphone, singing Prince's *1999* completely out of tune.

"Boo! You *suck*!" an old crone screeches, throwing her empty wine glass at the stage, which nearly knocks one of the pixie men from the air as it zooms past. The glass misses all three singers and hits the window behind them, causing the windowpane to spider. The vampire and the winged men, however, continue their song undeterred, ignoring the faint whistling of the wind now drifting into the room behind them. "It's not even nineteen ninety-nine! You're *stupid*! You *suck* and you're *stupid*! *Stupid*!"

Father Time next passes by an enormous rabbit on the dance floor, wearing a Christmas wreath atop his head, surrounded by fuzzy yellow chicks. Nearby, an oversized turkey with beautiful feathers seems to be in the middle of a drunken dance off with a bald eagle. Father Time tries to ignore everyone he rushes past, even as they call out his name merrily. His eyes are too busy darting around the room for the woman he is angrily searching for.

He hurries by a tall, amazingly gorgeous, curvy brunette woman with pointed ears locked in a passionate embrace with a young, dark-haired, handsome man wearing an Armani suit. Just a few steps away, behind an old man lying fast asleep on the dance floor, stands a wiry man with glasses and the same pointed ears, watching them jealously as he feigns interest in a conversation that he is in the middle of with an overly hyper groundhog and a perpetually happy moose.

Finally, after pushing past a boyish young man with platinum blonde hair spinning an old white-haired woman wearing a long red dress with a white apron, Father Time finds the focus of his wrath. She is talking with a tall pale man in long black robes, with long dark hair and entirely black eyes, and an attractive, strawberry blonde woman tightly clutching a large purse. His target is a thin old woman with messy gray curls and a patchwork green dress, currently taking a sip of punch. Clearly it isn't her first cup, for her dirt-covered cheeks are a bright red and when she speaks, her words come out slurred.

"I'm tellin' you," she says. "That naughty leprechaun came in here and *stole* half of our booze! That table over there," she points unsteadily in the direction of three separate tables. "Was *stacked* with vodka before and now it's all gone! Gone I tell you! Sigh-ya-horah!"

"Are you sure it's not coursing through your veins right now?" the frightening looking man asks in a charming British accent.

"I've barely touched--" the old woman hiccups. "Oops, pardon me! I've barely touched any alcohol. I've been drinking this children's punch all night!"

"You do know there's alcohol *in* the punch, right?" the pretty strawberry blonde asks slowly, an eyebrow raised. "And there aren't any children here."

The old woman stares down at her glass perplexed, her eyes unfocused.

"Mother Nature!" Father Time calls from ten feet away, causing all of those in the immediate vicinity to turn and look at him.

Mother Nature glances up and turns unsteadily. "Father Time!" she says loudly, her voice cheery. "Happy New Year!"

"Is it? Is it *really*?" he growls.

"So glad you could join the party!"

"You bitch, why didn't you tell me?" Father Time demands, deciding to cut straight to the chase.

"What are you talking about?" the younger, pretty woman furrows her eyebrows, as Mother Nature hiccups again, scandalized.

"Well, Regina, I'm glad you ask," Father Time says, forcing politeness into his voice. "New Years has been ruined. Mother *Nature* here thought it would be a good idea to send a blizzard, one so bad that the mortals have dubbed it *Frankenstorm,* down to North America this evening. On New Year's Eve," he points out, shaking with anger. "Causing *my* holiday to *lose* money for the first time since its *inception!*"

Regina blinks, taken aback, as Mother Nature's mouth drops open, her expression one of mingled rage and shock. Beside them, the frightening man puts one of his long-fingered hands to his head and shakes it, annoyed.

"They *always* get this wrong," he laments. "Frankenstein was the *man, not* the *monster!* Naming it *Frankenstorm* makes no sense! Ugh, where's Agatha?" he stands on tiptoe, craning his neck as he stares over the heads of the partygoers. "I'll put her on damage control – we can still save the names of the good doctor and his monster."

"How many times do I have to tell you," Mother Nature begins, her voice rising rapidly, causing even more people to turn and watch their conversation. "That I don't control the weather! I *can't!*"

"*You're* Mother Nature! *I'm* Father Time!" Father Time yells, furious. "If I can control *fucking* time, you can control the *fucking* weather!"

"It doesn't work like that, Father Dumbass!"

Father Time snorts in derision as the teenage looking boy and the woman in the long red dress saunter over to join them.

"Would you guys keep it down and *chillax*, please?" the young man requests. "We're trying to enjoy the party."

"Not to mention my husband's asleep next door," the white-haired woman adds. "You know how he gets if he's woken before January second."

"Mrs. Claus," Father Time begins with a weary laugh. "I could hear this party from the first floor. A little shouting isn't going to make a difference."

"What's all the shouting about anyway?"

"Tempus, here," Mother Nature begins to yell at the top of her lungs, her voice trembling, bringing the music to a grinding stop as everyone in the room turns to stare. "Is blaming *me* because *he* fucked up!"

"Because of the weather that *you* caused, *bitch*!"

"I DON'T CAUSE THE WEATHER!" Mother Nature shouts, glancing around the room for support before her eyes find the platinum-haired young man. "If you're going to blame anyone, blame *Slack* Frost! It was a blizzard! He announces winter!"

Father Time rounds on the boy, who holds up his hands defensively.

"I *herald* winter," he clarifies. "I don't create it. The seasons are a force of *nature*." He glances at Mother Nature stubbornly.

"Well if you *herald* it, why didn't you let someone in my department know about this damn blizzard?" Father Time demands.

"Nobody asked me!" Jack Frost replies defensively. "And it's not my *job*. Maybe you should put one of *your* people on weather duty! There's a little thing called the *internet* that you could have used to track the storm. Weather dot com. It's not that hard."

"Just like his dick, I presume," Mother Nature mutters spitefully to Regina, who stifles a giggle.

Father Time sighs heavily, turning to face the drunk woman once again. "Corporate isn't going to be very happy with you, Gaia."

—

11

"Why not?" the pale man with completely black eyes asks sardonically. "It's *your* holiday that lost money. It's *you* who screwed up. If anybody's going to get punished for this, it's *you*." He smirks, showing off his pointed, shark-like teeth. "That's what you get for naming last year's Baby New Year *Damien*, I suppose. You should have known that name would be a bad *omen*."

Father Time gapes at the Boogeyman, but before he can articulate a response, a wall phone beside the elevators begins to ring.

Everybody freezes as their eyes find the dreaded phone, which rings yet again. When it becomes clear that nobody else is going to answer it, the large rabbit with the Christmas wreath atop his head hops over and puts the receiver to one of his long ears.

"Hello?" he answers. After a moment of listening, he lowers it from his head and looks at Father Time. "It's for you."

"Damn it, Francis!" Father Time swears as he marches across the room and takes the phone from the rabbit.

"Hello?" he speaks into the receiver, trying to keep his voice calm. "Yes…yes, I understand…absolutely not, it was Mother…but she…no, it wasn't Jack…yes, I know North America's supposed to be a cakewalk."

Everyone watching waits with bated breath for Father Time to finish his conversation. Only the snores of the Sandman fill the silence as the man in charge of New Year's Eve listens to the unheard voice on the other end of the line.

"No," he exclaims, panicked. "There's no need to…right…yes…yes, I understand….absolutely. Thank you."

And without another word, Father Time slowly hangs up the phone, staring at it with blank shock on his face.

"Well?" the groundhog prompts from the other side of the room. "Who was it?"

"Corporate," Father Time replies softly, turning to face the crowd of employees. "They're sending two supervisors down next Monday to do an extended evaluation of the company."

At these words, the spidered window behind the stage shatters completely, causing a loud wind to whistle around the floor as a concerned murmuring immediately breaks out among the crowd. Only the voice of Matilda the moose seems cheerful and unconcerned.

"Oh, that's nice of them, eh?"

Before anyone can even bother trying to explain to her why this isn't good news, the doors of one of the elevators slide open and the old man who had been sitting in the corner of Father Time's office hobbles out, moaning loudly as though he is in incredible pain.

"What is it?" Father Time asks exasperatedly, staring at his comrade.

The man turns to face him, ever so slowly, before bursting into flames, eliciting cries of shock from those standing nearest.

"My eyes!" Francis shouts, covering his eyes with his long ears as a stray spark catches the wreath around his head, causing it to instantly catch on fire.

When the smoke finally clears, the old man is gone, leaving behind a large pile of sand, from which the sounds of a crying baby can faintly be heard. Jack Frost casually strides over to the Easter Bunny and puts out the flames around his head with a quick touch, as Father Time sighs exasperatedly.

"Fuck me," he moans as he stares down at the pile of sand.

"I *think* that Corporate is going to do exactly that to *all* of us because of you."

Father Time exchanges a glance with the Boogeyman, who has sidled up silently beside him. Around them, there is nothing but complete silence apart from the whistling of wind, the cries of the unseen baby and the cooing of that perpetually happy moose somewhere in the crowd.

"Ooh, a baby! Who doesn't love a baby?"

"What the fuck is this shit?"

The two figures standing in the lobby of the North American Headquarters do not arrive by train, plane, bike, boat, car or sleigh. Instead, they simply appear without warning, clipboards in hand, ready to tear the place apart. With their preferred mode of transportation, they don't need jackets to protect themselves from the weather.

They look as though they're in their mid-twenties, with tan skin and dark hair. Some people might mistakenly assume they're related, but they'd both be quick to inform you that they most definitely are not. The man has movie star good looks, including the chiseled jaw of some silent era matinée idol. He's casually dressed in a dress shirt, the long sleeves rolled up to his elbows, his tie hanging neat and wrinkle free. He looks professional, if not completely polished - the top button of his shirt remains undone.

It is his female counterpart, in her curve-hugging suit and tightly pulled ponytail, who speaks first, only seconds after taking in the scenery. She's staring at a painted portrait of a happy looking moose wearing a pink polka-dotted hair bow between her antlers. The lobby is lined with such portraits, all attractive likenesses of the various employees they have arrived to take charge of.

"What is this fucking shit?" she asks again, with more disgust this time. The moose and its vacantly dopey eyes still have her attention.

Her companion shrugs. "They're just portraits."

"Who the hell paid for this garbage?" she spits, turning away from the moose at last. Her delicate features would probably convey great beauty if she didn't look so angry. "Honestly. Some people are so fucking full of themselves." She fondles the cornucopia charm hanging on a silver chain around her neck and strides forward confidently on her stilettos. "Nobody can even bother to greet us? Corporate told these morons we were coming, right?"

"Of course. I'm sure someone will be right--"

He can't even finish the sentence before the elevator doors open, revealing a hesitant looking middle-aged man with little hair in a cheaply made short-sleeved shirt. His pants are too big and his battered shoes are barely tied. Around his neck dangles a string that looks like it holds glasses, although none are attached. He is already sweating profusely.

"Who are *you*?" the woman asks with a sneer.

"Uh, I'm Bill, sir - er - ma'am."

"Has anyone ever told you you're disgusting, Bill?"

"I…uh…um…"

She ignores his attempt at an answer. "My name is Pia. This is Russ--"

"Tuss," the other man corrects kindly with a small wave hello.

"Gather everyone up and take us to your conference room immediately."

"We…um…we thought you might like a tour of our facility first."

Even her smile, a tight-lipped formation created out of pity, is frightening. "Gather everyone up," she repeats in a slow, careful tone, like she is speaking to the dumbest horse on the planet. "And take us to your conference room. Immediately, you disgusting moron."

"S-sure. Right this way." His shoes slip as he hastily starts back for the elevator.

"No wonder this place is tanking," Pia mutters, following.

Tuss shakes his head sadly but says nothing. As he drags his feet after her, he regrets volunteering for this. It had seemed like such a good opportunity for a change of scenery at the time.

The trip to the sixth floor is a quick one, and Pia leads the way into the conference room as though she has been there a million times before.

Arranged around the large table are a variety of elaborate chairs: one has a cushion patterned like the Mexican flag, yet another is made up to resemble a shiny pile of gold, and one is an oversized armchair done up like a cushy Christmas tree and draped with a candy cane patterned blanket. There are also two seats of the barely comfortable, standard office variety, clearly meant for the Corporate visitors, but Pia bypasses these and goes to a chair that is painted like an American flag that has the name 'Bill' stenciled right across its back. She stands in front of it, leaving the chair's owner to stand awkwardly behind her.

Other than them and the variety of creative furniture, the room is empty.

"Where the fuck is everyone?"

"Well…uh…we *really* thought you'd like a tour, so it's going to be a few minutes. If you just wanna have a seat…" Bill tries to gesture to the plain chairs, but Pia sits in the chair with his name on it anyway, crossing her arms over her chest and glaring at the door as she reluctantly waits.

It is a good five minutes of terribly awkward silence before the first few faces pass through the doorway. There are no hellos, no words of greeting. Each of the holiday heads immediately see Pia's venomous eyes and proceed directly to their thrones. Most of the seats are filled quickly, but three remain empty as each uncomfortable minute continues to tick away.

"I don't think anyone else is coming," Bill mutters to her, eyeing the chairs themed after gold, Christmas and Mexico.

"Fine." Pia stands and immediately addresses the figures before her, not wasting any more time. "So. I see you sent this personification of failure to greet us. That's about what I expected from this sorry excuse for a branch. That's why Corporate sent me here to fix you. I am here to make changes, to make things right and to stop this branch from sliding into the shitter. And it's in *your* best interest to just shut the hell up and do what I tell you, because no branch under *my* control is going to take a loss like you morons just caused with New Year's Eve."

"With all due respect," Father Time speaks up icily from his clock-themed throne. "It wasn't my fault the blizzard--"

Pia is already rolling her eyes. "Save it, grandpa. Your whole holiday shouldn't burn like the damn Roman Empire because of a few little flurries. You were lazy. And now we're starting the year in the red because of you and the dementia you're suffering from."

"How dare you! I don't know what your name is, *missy--*"

"Pia. This is Puss--"

"Tuss."

"And you can cram your little comeback down your wrinkly old throat, you dusty fucking corpse. For the laughing stock you made out of New Year's, Corporate has agreed you need to be punished. For the next year, every clock, watch and timepiece in this building will always show the wrong time to you and only you."

The color drains from Father Time's face instantly. "You cannot be serious."

"Completely." She seems to enjoy his misery.

"No! You cannot do such a thing--"

"Enough. I don't have time to listen to losers." Pia glances around the table at the faces - among the expected fear and shock are a few satisfied smirks, glad to see someone else get torn apart. This is not acceptable and requires immediate correction. "None of you should feel satisfied with the shitty job you've been doing. Every single one of you morons should be so embarrassed by your pathetic, miserable, miniscule profits that you shouldn't physically be able to look me in the eye."

"I resent that!" gobbles a large turkey that has made a nest for itself in a seat shaped like a pilgrim's hat. The name 'Tom' is carved into the side. "No one takes more pride in their holiday than *I* do. My father was served at the very first Thanksgiving all the way back in 1621! He gave

---

18

his *life* for this holiday! I do my best every year to make Thanksgiving-"

"Do you? Then what kind of merchandise are the mortals buying come November? Thanksgiving trees? Turkey canes? Dancing, singing birds that shit overpriced, tasteless chocolates that constantly need to be replenished? No. If it wasn't for grocery sales and that dumb parade we invented, you'd have been a sandwich years ago. A dry, boring little sandwich. You think that's fucking funny?"

Pia's attention turns to the groundhog across the room, who is struggling to suppress a nervous smile. He's sitting on a large tree stump that bears his name, 'Ted', on a small plaque across the front. "W-w-who, me? N-no! Not at all, not at all, m-m-m'am--"

"You've got nothing to grin about, you borderline rat. If it was up to *me*, Groundhog's Day wouldn't even be a fucking holiday. All it does is depress people. You furry, brainless cowards piss yourselves over a harmless little shadow, declare six more weeks of winter and the mortals whine about it for a week. Why your useless corpses don't show up on dinner plates, I have no damn idea."

"Hey, Pia--"

She ignores Tuss' attempt to corral her and instead starts pointing to other people in the room, many of whom are wishing they could disappear or at the very least hide under the conference table. Pia begins with the moose from the portrait she hated downstairs. The cheerful mammal is wearing a floppy hair bow and has to sit on a cushion on the floor due to her size. "You--"

"Matilda!" the moose interrupts, her voice chipper. "Tilly for short!"

"I don't care what your fucking name is, nor do I give a shit about any national holiday they celebrate in that country of hockey obsessed freaks. You - and *it* - are irrelevant and a waste of perfectly good space."

"Well, you know what they say, eh? Honesty is the best policy!"

Next is an oversized white rabbit donning a mint green bow tie and occupying a chair that resembles a misshapen, painted egg. 'Francis' is visible in a pretty script near the bottom. "Easter Bunny - you have no excuse for your holiday not being Spring's fucking Christmas. You've got baskets of presents, tons of tooth rotting candy and some mouth-breathing moron in a rabbit costume in every mall across the damn continent! Even Jesus himself comes back from the dead for it! No excuse!"

Her subsequent target is a handsome bald eagle resting atop a shiny gold perch. An official looking nameplate on the front reads 'Thomas Jefferson'. "Independence Day - you may have those fireworks that the brainless mortals can't get enough of - because clearly lights in the sky are very impressive to the simpleminded - but how many states are they still illegal in? I can go down there and buy an assault rifle but not a fucking Roman candle? Unacceptable!"

Sitting on a throne of bones is the Boogeyman, a shadowy figure who gives even most adults nightmares but can't seem to scare away Pia's accusatory gaze. "Halloween - scary is dead. Kids don't want scary anymore. Kids are pansies. They don't want to be the devil, they want to paint themselves with fucking glitter and call themselves vampires."

Unlike the others, he is brave enough to fire back a reply, but Pia doesn't give him a chance before she rounds on her next victim - a pretty, youthful woman in a chair curved like a giant cushy tooth. "Tooth Fairy - we are pumping sugar into everything. Kids should be losing their adult teeth before they're fucking twelve. Something is wrong there. Work on it!"

Her next target, lounging in a plush velvet chair, doesn't look frightened at all. In fact, he is smiling -*widely*. His perfect teeth only enhance his nearly impossible good looks. "Me next?"

Pia may be looking in his direction, but she makes no attempt to meet his eyes. "Your holiday is a mess. We've given you internet dating, singles cruises - even speed dating - and tons of these losers still can't find a date one day a year."

"Somebody needs to get laid. *Badly*."

Instead of tearing into him for his grossly unprofessional comment, Pia turns to the still empty seat shaped like a pot of gold. "Where the fuck is *he*?"

Everybody shrugs, clueless.

"Well that about sums up that degenerate midget."

"There's another chair empty," Tom the turkey mutters bitterly, glancing sideways at the empty Christmas-themed seat beside him with his beady bird eyes.

"Santa doesn't need to be here," Pia says. "I don't give a shit if he never shows up as long as he's still going down chimneys with sacks stuffed full of toys to put under expensive trees decorated with tons of pointless junk! Santa could puke in every stocking and still outperform every single one of you assholes. I wasn't forced to come all the way down here from Corporate because Santa can't do his fucking job. I'm here because this is supposed to be our most successful branch and all of you are incompetent morons!"

There is silence. Is it possible that she is finally finished talking? Hesitant glances are exchanged around the table. Then Mother Nature breathes a sigh of relief that can just barely be heard in the otherwise silent room.

And it's clear within a moment that Pia is actually nowhere close to finished. "And you..." She turns to the older woman as Francis trembles and covers his eyes with his ears in the next seat. "I don't know what brainiac put you in charge of the family holidays. Just because the word *mother* happens to be part of your name doesn't mean you're in any way at all qualified to run those holidays. This email and Facebook garbage has practically killed card sales entirely and what have you, Mother Worthless, done about it? Nothing. Nothing but watch your holiday sales shrivel and die just like your usefulness to this company. You're a bigger fucking embarrassment than that degenerate midget who didn't even bother to show up today. You're fired."

Gasps escape the lips of several of the figures seated around the table as Pia finally sits in the chair clearly marked for Bill. "Questions?"

"What's Facebook?" Tilly asks, genuinely confused. No one even bothers to look at her. Mother Nature looks blankly ahead, her jaw slack.

"Um..." Bill creeps forward a step from where he has been standing this whole time, his hand raised partway in the air like a kid who's unsure of their answer.

"What?" she snaps.

"I'm sorry, but...um...where's Miguel?"

"Miguel? Who the fuck's Miguel?"

Bill's unsteady hand points to the empty chair bearing the Mexican flag. "He...uh...he ran the Mexican national holidays?"

"Oh, no. Fuck that guy. It's bad enough I'm stuck with *Canada*. I transferred him to the South American office. Let him be with his *own* kind."

"But he was my best friend..."

"Don't pretend you have friends, Bill. Now, sit your ass down."

"Um...but...you're...kind of in my seat..."

Pia doesn't even look back. She simply reaches behind her and touches the American flag print that bears Bill's name. Instantaneously it's gone, replaced by a cornucopia and her own name in an elegant script.

Bill trudges over and takes Miguel's former seat with a frown.

"Questions?" Pia asks again, though it sounds more like a challenge.

The bald eagle angrily squawks, flapping his large wings and adjusting his pointy looking talons on his perch.

Pia stares at him with a blank expression and waits, but it's quickly clear that this is the bird's only means of communication. "Are you kidding me? I don't speak bird. Do I look like I have a pair of sissy wings?"

"I'm T.J.'s translator."

Rubbing her temples, Pia sinks back into her stolen chair with a sigh. "Of course you are, Bill. Because the last thing I want to hear again is your fucking voice."

"What did he say?" Tuss speaks up, attempting to neutralize Pia's nasty tone.

"He…uh…it's not really…nice? I'd rather not--"

"You fucking bird!" Pia snaps. "I'll make you the next meal every fucking household in America is carving into tiny little pieces by next Thanksgiving!"

"Over my dead body!"

"I don't think now's really the time, Tom," Francis says timidly.

"If any of you have a problem with the way I run things, too fucking bad," Pia states. "File a complaint with *Fuss* over here."

"It's Tuss, everyone. *Tuss,*" he says, firmly this time, addressing Pia directly. The kind lines have vanished from his face. "You *know* it's Tuss. You've known it for years. Don't act like we just met yesterday." He turns to face the room as a whole before he can catch her rolling her eyes. "Corporate has sent us down to make sure that there are no more… *incidents* like what happened on New Year's Eve. She may have been a little…*rough* explaining it, but it's true that we can't afford to take a hit like that again. I'm sure you see us as intruders. I mean, no one likes the boss breathing down their neck. But we are here to help, first and foremost. We want you to succeed. So please, if you need anything, or have any questions at all, please see me or…" He hesitates, glancing sideways at his partner. "Or Pia." She snorts in response and crosses her arms over her chest as Tuss continues. "I'd be happy to answer any questions."

Mother Nature slowly lets her hand go into the air. "So I'm not fired?"

—

"No, I'm afraid you're really fired."

"What?! But why?"

"Our orders come straight from Corporate," Tuss explains sadly.

"They made the decision after reviewing last year's numbers. I'm sorry, but I'm sure we can find something for you to do."

"Who will handle Mother's Day and Father's Day then?" she questions.

Tuss softly clears his throat and simply glances at Pia, who looks quite smug.

Going around the table, there are a lot of dissatisfied expressions. But before there can be any further inappropriate bird shrieking, Tuss speaks up again, "I think we'll take that tour now, if you'd all like to return to your offices. I'm sure we'd both like to see how things work around here."

"I wouldn't have chosen any of those words."

Ignoring Pia's comment, Tuss smiles hopefully at Bill. "Where to first?"

Bill seems reluctant to lead them back to the elevator, but he manages to put on a smile anyway. Instead of pressing one of the colorful buttons at the top, he taps the boring little circle at the very bottom simply labeled 'SB'.

"Let's start at the bottom and work our way up!"

"What does 'SB' stand for?" asks Tuss, trying to make conversation while Pia crosses her arms and glares from the corner.

"Sub-basement."

"Why are you wasting my time with the basement?" Pia sneers.

"*Sub*-basement," Bill corrects. "And that's where my office is."

"Of course it is."

The sub-basement doesn't look like the type of place where anyone would have an office, let alone spend any time willingly. With its drab concrete floor and flickering fluorescent lighting, it more closely resembles the setting of a horror movie where some skank is murdered by a man with a hook for a hand than any kind of legitimate office space. Just a few steps from the elevator, Bill shows off a closet-sized room covered with pictures of flags and a huge chart titled 'United States Holidays'. "This is my office!"

"This is even sadder than what I pictured," Pia remarks. "I honestly didn't even think that was possible."

"Who else has offices on this floor?" Even Tuss is glancing around with disgust, rubbing his arms with a shiver.

"Just Ted, the Sandman, Regina, Tilly and, well, Miguel *did*."

"Fake holidays get fake offices," shrugs Pia.

"Memorial Day and Labor Day inspire a lot of barbecues," Bill insists.

Pia is already walking back to the elevator.

Bill looks pleadingly at Tuss. "They really do."

"Let's get on with the tour." Tuss tries to sound upbeat but doesn't quite pull it off.

They skip over the basement (storage) and lobby ("Do you have a portrait, Bill? Did the artist cry the whole time they were forced to fucking look at you?") and head straight to the first floor. There, Bill's sweatiness increases fifty percent as Father Time glowers at them through his office window. Pia and Tuss can't help looking at all of the different clocks lining the walls as they approach the three fates. The sisters are huddled around Lachesis' desk, smiling and pointing at something.

"I wouldn't be smiling at anything if my sales were in the toilet." With that warm greeting, Pia stomps over and snatches the object they are fawning over. It's a small device with a video screen on which a blonde, fair-skinned baby can be seen dozing in a crib. "What the hell is this?"

"That's Baby New Year!" Clotho explains. "Little Caleb. Isn't he adorable?"

"Much cuter than last year's model," Artropos agrees with a nod.

"Back to work," Pia snaps. "Is this what you old crones are used to doing all day? No wonder this department is such a disaster. Maybe if you spent more time trying to actually do your jobs and less time gossiping, I wouldn't have to be here yelling at you right now."

The women don't seem to enjoy being spoken to in this manner and who can blame them? But before one of them can open their mouth to retaliate, Tuss steps forward with a charming smile. "What an absolutely adorable child." He gently takes the baby monitor from Pia and hands it back to Lachesis. "Thank you for all your hard work. We're sure you're working on lots of good ideas for next year and we can't *wait* to see what you've come up with."

"Stop saying *we* like you speak for both of us."

Tuss ignores Pia and gives Father Time a friendly wave on the trip back to the elevator. In return, he gets the finger.

A heart-shaped button leads to the next office on the tour. The three of them step off of the elevator and into air heavy with the scent of perfume and chocolate, as well as the melodious bass of a Barry White love song.

Pia's expression instantly sours further and she seems reluctant to journey from the elevator. "I've seen enough. Let's get out of here before I hurl."

Tuss is trying to see down the hallway but a few cherubs going about their assigned duties obstruct the view. "Is his office nothing but a heart-shaped bed?"

"Let's get out of here before I fucking hurl!" Pia turns abruptly, only to find the manager of this department standing directly behind her.

"Why, hello."

Pia steps back quickly, putting plenty of space between them. "Your breath smells terrible."

"That is *absolutely* not true," he contradicts with a gorgeous grin, closing the little space between them. "It smells amazing."

"Get out of my way."

"Are my dazzling good looks hurting your eyes? Happens all the time."

Gritting her teeth, Pia slides by, being careful to avoid any accidental contact. "Delusional and an asshole."

"Nice ass by the way!" Cupid calls after her, waving until the doors finally block him from view.

Back in the safety of the elevator, Bill punches the button shaped like a four-leaf clover. "I don't think the next floor will make you feel any better," he warns.

"I'll be nauseous as long as I'm stuck looking at you, so what's the damn difference?" Pia snaps.

Bill takes a lightly stained handkerchief out of his pocket and mops his face with it. At this point, even Tuss has to look away from him.

But Bill *was* right about the state of the third floor. If you didn't know that it is supposed to be a functioning office, you would think the place had to be evacuated. *Suddenly.* After a very large party where most of the people mistook the hallway for the bathroom.

There's not a soul in sight. A banner reading 'Happy St. Patrick's Day' is half trailing on the floor, the tape on one side having long since given up. Numerous liquor bottles lie empty and broken, the glass strewn across the dirty, sticky tile floor. The wall of odor that engulfs them is

---

27

repulsive - so repulsive, in fact, that Pia takes one breath before shoving Tuss and Bill back into the elevator and slamming the egg-shaped button for the next floor multiple times herself.

"When was the last time anyone was on that fucking floor? Last St. Patrick's Day?!"

"Probably?"

"When was the last time that itty-bitty asshole showed up for a meeting?" Pia demands.

"Uh… "

"That useless little dwarf better pray his neck is too short for me to get my hands around."

"That was…not good," Tuss has to agree. "Someone really needs to clean it. It's not sanitary."

"Not sanitary? I'm pretty sure I saw actual shit on the floor. And unless they have some super big rats - which I'll admit might be possible - somebody shit on the floor! In an *office*! I bet when we get to the floor that's full of fucking *birds* we don't find any shit on the floor!"

"The Thanksgiving floor does have a…*unique* odor though."

"Shut the fuck up, Bill!"

"Who's in charge of cleaning?" Tuss asks.

"Jack Frost. But good luck getting *him* to do anything."

"I can get anyone to do anything I want, Bill. I'm not a complete loser like you," Pia says. "I'm surprised you can even get your own disgusting body out of bed every morning."

Luckily the next floor greets them with the pleasing scent of a freshly mowed lawn as they step off the elevator onto a floor of grass. The walls are painted a soft pastel blue, and tiny chicks and fluffy bunnies scurry past, clutching newly painted eggs and wrapped chocolate rabbits in the image of their boss.

Tuss takes it all in with a smile and nod. "At least things seem to be running smoothly here."

Pia tries to avoid stepping on a happily chirping chick with her overly expensive shoe as she complains, "I'm still sick to my stomach."

Bill leads them quickly around the floor and they are able to peek in on several areas where the employee animals are busy at their conveyor belts cheerfully making all sorts of Easter basket goodies. Lastly, they pass by Francis' office, but the big rabbit is too busy stressing over the phone with someone named Daisy to notice them.

"Women troubles," Bill explains as they return to the elevator.

"Was that his wife?"

Bill snorts. "Wife? He's a rabbit! He has at least a *hundred* wives that I know of. He's on the phone with them half the day."

"Wouldn't want to be him on Valentine's Day!" Tuss comments with a pleasant chuckle.

They are ready to leave when Francis sticks his head out of his office. "Butters!" he calls to a passing bird. "Can you get me an updated jelly bean count?" He then notices the Corporate visitors and is visibly startled. "Oh! Uh, hello!" he calls out uncertainly, trying to casually loosen his bow tie. "Welcome to the Easter floor. I think you'll agree things are running pretty smoothly here…right?"

"Very smoothly," Tuss agrees, trying to instill some confidence in the jumpy rabbit.

"I hear you make quite a few personal calls," Pia accuses, undoing all of Tuss' effort.

"Personal…calls?"

"Bill-the-tattletale here tells me you spend most of your time talking to your wives!"

Francis clears his throat uneasily, shooting Bill a barely noticeable glare. "I do speak to my wives a bit. But some of them head up the Easter branches in the other headquarters."

"So it's business," Tuss clarifies.

"Yes." Francis fidgets in the silence that follows, trying to avoid looking at Pia's still unhappy face. "Would you like to see some of my kids?" Bill shakes his head no, but the large rabbit takes out his wallet anyway. A long roll of photos spills out as he opens it, and he begins pointing at photos of one bunny after another. Most of them are white, brown or some mixture of the two colors. "This is Sprinkles, and this is Chester. This one is Merry, and over here we have Pippin. Here's Jumpy Twelve, and behind him is Clover Seventeen…or is it Clover Fourteen? Or maybe it's Poppy. Or Hoppity Twenty-six."

"Oh, fuck this." Pia starts stomping back to the elevator, Bill quick on her heels.

"Sorry," Tuss apologizes, hurrying after them. "Another time! You have beautiful children!" He leaves the flustered rabbit behind and catches up with the rest of his tour group at the elevator. "That was rude," he chides his counterpart.

"If you want to go back there and see the rest of that sick display, go right ahead," Pia replies coldly.

"So boring," Bill pipes up.

"You're boring. Shut up."

Sighing, Tuss watches the numbers above the elevator light up as it makes its way back to them. "Fine. What's next?"

Pia just glares at him. "Next is our new floor. Take notes on anything that needs changing."

The next button on the elevator is shaped like a flower. Sure, flowers are a popular gift for Mother's Day, but when the doors open it's clear as to why the floor is marked with this particular symbol.

All they can see are plants.

Various types of vegetation line the hallway from beginning to end. There are dozens of distinct varieties visible, some with beautiful blossoms and others that look and smell terrible. There are vines with large leaves as well as a curious, tiny specimen that seems to tremble as they pass. There are pitcher plants, mushrooms of all shapes and sizes, cacti and flowers in almost every color of the rainbow. All of them are neatly maintained, keeping to their area against the wall. But there is no dirt or any sign of roots. Everything just seems to be part of the walls and floor.

Tuss looks rather amazed as he steps into the corridor, stopping to take a look at each new type of plant. Unfortunately, his enjoyment is quickly ruined by his counterpart who stomps into the middle of the hallway becoming increasingly enraged the more she looks around.

"What the hell is all this?" She looks at Bill for a response.

"Well, this was Mother Nature's floor," Bill explains. "She kind of likes plants."

"It's not hers anymore. That stupid bitch is gone. This is my domain now--"

"*Ours*," Tuss tries to pointlessly remind Pia.

"I want all this shit out of here! Now!

"I don't think that's possible…" Bill seems very reluctant to say.

"Not possible?" Pia demands. "How is it not possible? They're stupid fucking plants! Get me a shovel, I'll dig them up myself!"

"But there's no dirt," Bill points out. "I'm not sure where these plants come from."

Pia studies the floor and surrounding area and sees that he is indeed speaking the truth. "The office isn't full of this Garden of Eden crap, is it?"

"Uh..." Bill hesitates

Hurrying down the hallway, Pia only finds additional plants: Venus Flytraps, tulips, jasmine, sunflowers, basil, oleanders and a bunch of other stuff she doesn't bother to identify. "This place is like a fucking hedge maze!" Mother Nature's nameplate is still on the door to her former office but Pia takes a moment to snatch it off before entering the room, instantly dismayed at what she discovers. "That crazy bitch! What the fuck am I going to do?"

Tuss glances around and sees the entire room is covered in vines. Vines with thorns. "Interesting design choice."

"This shit has to go. I don't know what I'm going to do, but I know I can't work like this." She glares at the vines as though she would tear them from the walls herself if they weren't covered in sharp little points.

"Shall we move on?" Bill speaks up hesitantly.

"Probably for the best," Tuss agrees.

They skip the sixth floor, having already seen the ridiculous chairs of the conference room, and head to the seventh. Its elevator button is a flag and as soon as the doors slide open, it's clear that if you don't like flags this floor is not for you.

American flags from all eras line the walls, floor to ceiling. It's overwhelming - a red, white and blue assault to the eyes. Overhead, *Stars and Stripes Forever* seems to play on an endless loop. The two Corporate visitors grimace and restrain themselves from covering their ears.

Bill smiles widely, spreading his arms. "Welcome to my domain."

"Just because you translate for the fucking duck doesn't mean you belong here."

Bill's smile melts like ice cream in a microwave.

Tuss speaks up quickly, trying to negate the impact of Pia once again. "What exactly do you do here, Bill? Besides serve as translator?"

"I handle many United States holidays," he begins proudly. "Such--"

"Yeah, the shitty ones. Memorial Day? Labor Day? Who cares?" Pia asks. "President's Day and Veteran's Day? Even worse."

"I…uh…I also handle Dr. Martin Luther King Jr. Day and Flag Day."

"Are those even holidays? I've never even heard of them and it's my job."

"Maybe Flag Day could be made profitable with the right marketing," Tuss offers hopefully, but Pia is already rolling her eyes and walking away.

Once she is finally out of view, Bill lets out an exceedingly long breath. "She is certainly..."

"Terrible?" Tuss finishes. "I know. We're from different departments, so we've never really worked together before. It's...going to be a...year. It's going to be a whole year," he sighs deeply. Maybe it's his own fault for not bothering to ask who he'd be paired with before volunteering for this job.

"Let me show you the rest of the floor."

Aside from the loud music, the floor is quiet. They find Pia waiting for them near an office marked 'Thomas Jefferson, Office Manager'.

"This is the worst tour I've ever been on, and I was visiting Pompeii when the damn volcano exploded! Congratulations, Bill. I'm sure you don't need me to remind you that you're terrible, but that doesn't mean I won't."

Bill tries to ignore Pia and leads them past T.J.'s office. The large, regal bird is busy at work, pecking at his computer. The walls behind him are covered in motivational posters, all of which feature bald eagles, many of them sweeping down over large expanses of water. "Hey, buddy!" he calls in happily.

Beak snapping up, the bird screeches angrily, yellow eyes narrowing. Bill frowns and plods on while his tiny tour group follows.

Pia is grinning ear to ear. "I'm no duck translator, but I'm pretty sure he just told you to go fuck yourself."

"He's an eagle," Tuss corrects.

"Does it have feathers and a beak? Then what the hell does it matter? They're all the same."

They get in the elevator and Tuss gives up as Bill presses a button shaped like a hamburger.

"The cafeteria is only open from twelve to two," he explains. "Jack writes the daily menu on a board right outside."

Sure enough, the doors slide open and they find a whiteboard with the words 'Fruitcake and Marshmallow Bunnies' scrawled on it in handwriting that is only borderline readable.

"Ugh, fruitcake again?" Bill hangs his head, disappointed.

"Fruitcake ever?" Pia leads the way, stomping inside, her heels clicking on the tile floor. Inside, the cafeteria is only a counter and about a dozen tables with chairs that make up the small seating area. Behind the counter is the young, light-haired maintenance man/janitor/food server/security guard who heralds winter on the side. Jack Frost has a line of customers: a nerdy looking elf, a grumpy looking shorter elf, and Regina, also known as the Tooth Fairy. None of them look happy.

"Fruitcake again?" Regina complains. "Is it the same one from yesterday?"

"No one ate it yesterday," Jack explains. "What else am I supposed to do with it?"

"These marshmallow things are rock hard!" grumbles the shorter elf.

"What do you expect?" Jack asks. "They're almost a year old."

Regina collects her meager slice of fruitcake and turns to leave, nearly bumping into Tuss who is standing right behind her. He had been staring at her reddish-blonde hair, which reminds him of a sunset over the Aegean Sea.

"Sorry!"

"Completely my fault. Enjoy your lunch." He steps aside with a smile.

Regina smiles back. Her teeth, as you would imagine, are perfect; bright white, not a single one out of place and practically shining. "That's impossible, but thanks. Nice teeth."

"Uh, thanks." Tuss intends to watch her go, but his attention is quickly drawn back to Pia, who has stepped up to the counter to bitch at Jack. He braces himself.

"You there, Frost. You're the one in charge of cleaning this fucking building, aren't you?"

Jack stares at her with ice blue eyes. "Who are you?"

"Your fucking boss."

Here we go, Tuss thinks wearily.

"Hey, I'm trying to order here," the short elf exclaims angrily.

"Can it, pipsqueak. Adults are talking," Pia snaps.

"I fucking hate this place," the elf mumbles before muttering something about never trusting his father again.

35

"Do you or do you not do the cleaning? Because that's what this disgusting moron told me." Pia jerks her head at Bill.

Jack shrugs. "Sometimes."

"Sometimes? Have you seen the state of the third floor? Because the rats have, and I think they believe it's home."

Jack shrugs again and slaps some fruitcake on a plate. "I'll get to it."

"You'll *get* to it?" Pia repeats. "St. Patrick's Day was almost a fucking year ago! It's unacceptable."

Jack slides the plate over to the shorter elf and stares blank-faced at Pia with his cold eyes. "I'll. Get to it. Bitch."

Pia's face turns a shade of red that a tomato would envy. Tuss quickly steps in, grabbing her arm and guiding her back to the elevator. "Thank you!" he calls to Jack. "Later I'd like to discuss security with you - whenever you have some free time!"

"Are you fucking kidding me?" she snarls, fighting back. Despite her strength, Tuss is stronger and she can't break his grip. "Corporate will hear about this, you little shit!"

"Corporate can't touch him," Tuss reminds Pia as he finally lets her go.

"Then *I'll* fucking touch him!" she rages, slamming her palm so hard against the wall that the entire cab seems to vibrate. "I'll beat the living shit out of him!"

"You can't do that. I'm sure he'll get to it like he said." Bill snorts from his forgotten corner of the elevator and Tuss shoots him a nasty look. "Calm down," he adds firmly. "Why don't you have a seat and we can have some lunch?"

"You actually want to eat here?" Bill asks in surprise.

"Of course we do," says Tuss definitively.

"Stop speaking for both of us!" Pia snaps. "I refuse to eat anything that fucking scumbag touched."

"Then just sit down and join us for lunch." Tuss could ask for better company than the constantly sweaty Bill and generally unpleasant Pia, but unfortunately, no other company is available.

Pia chooses the table farthest from Jack Frost's counter while making sure she's still in his line of sight and therefore able to glare at him. Bill and Tuss collect their meager meals and join her at the table. Bill actually attempts to sit next to Pia before she violently kicks the chair out from under him and he winds up falling to the floor. He tries to pick himself up with some dignity and chooses the chair across from her instead.

"So." Tuss takes a bite of fruitcake and immediately regrets it — it tastes like sawdust mixed with congealed hard candy. "What do people do for fun around here?"

"Work very hard," Bill responds, eyeing Pia.

"I meant when you're off the clock," Tuss says gently, trying to ignore the intense glowering match going on between Jack Frost and Pia. "Are there any restaurants? Any bars? We know nothing about the village."

"There are two restaurants. One bar. We also have a bakery and a general store."

"Ooh, a general store," Pia begins with enough sarcasm to fill Santa's workshop. "I hope I can buy buttons and soap by the pound."

"Well, they do sell soap and buttons," says Bill, sounding confused. "But they're all Christmas-themed. Everyone around here either smells like pine or gingerbread."

"Fan-fucking-tastic."

"I'm glad you have a store," Tuss says with a nod. "With all the snow out there, I'm going to need some boots."

"They don't carry any," Bill tells him bluntly. "You'll have to ask Corporate for a pair."

Tuss is obviously caught off guard at this news. "Really? Why?"

"They only carry elf shoes."

"Huh. That's interesting."

"That's not interesting, that's horrible," Pia interrupts.

But Tuss continues, undeterred. "What else do they carry?"

"The store sells mostly necessities," Bill explains. "Like food, toiletries, cleaning products – that sort of thing. They have clothing, but it's all elf stuff. If you're lucky, you'll find holiday items on clearance a few times a year. Anything else you have to fill out a form and send away to Corporate for. And I suggest you do that in advance – they're pretty slow. I waited three months for my Snuggy."

"We can leave whenever we want to go back to Corporate and shop in decent stores," Pia pipes up condescendingly.

"Technically, but we're not supposed to keep going back and forth while we're on assignment," Tuss reminds her as she rolls her eyes. "I guess I'll have to get one of those forms so I can ask for some boots."

"Like *you* won't be able to get what you want immediately," Pia mutters to herself.

"What about live music?" Tuss asks, trying to continue the conversation despite his partner's best efforts to end it.

"Only if you like Christmas music," Bill says. "The elf choir's *always* putting on a show. The director's a nutcase though and they do *not* take requests."

"This place is sounding better and better," mutters Pia.

Tuss gives up and lets chewing fill the next few minutes. During this time, Jack Frost hangs a closed sign and disappears, ending the undeclared glaring contest - a winner could not be determined.

Finally, Tuss puts down his napkin, unable to swallow another bite. His throat hurts from trying to choke down stale marshmallows coated in rock hard sugar. "Why don't we finish the tour? Then we can see where we're staying and do a little unpacking." He addresses Bill directly. "Do you know where we'll be staying? Corporate was a little fuzzy on the details."

"Santa's judge, jury and executioner when it comes to that village," Bill informs them with some obvious bitterness. "He'll have to tell you."

The elevator doors open as soon as the button is pressed to head upstairs and Tuss can't help but let out an exclamation of surprise when he sees that it is not empty.

"What the hell is this?" Pia demands

A skinny old man with a long white beard and wearing an old fashioned nightcap lies on the floor of the elevator. His navy blue nightshirt matches his hat and his bunny slippers are threadbare with holes in the soles.

"Get up, you lazy ass!" scolds Bill, kicking the old man's legs with more force than is necessary.

The old man sits up slowly, rubbing his eyes.

"This is the Sandman, in case it isn't obvious," Bill explains. "He's responsible for keeping the mortals asleep when Santa, the Easter Bunny and the Tooth Fairy come to visit."

"Where am I?" the Sandman asks groggily.

"The cafeteria," Tuss clarifies kindly.

"Oh good! I'm hungry!"

"It just closed, you lazy good for nothing!" snaps Bill. "Now get out of

---

39

our elevator! I'm in the middle of a tour!"

Looking extremely disappointed, the Sandman shuffles out of the elevator.

"He's still better than you," Pia tells Bill as the crestfallen man disappears behind the closing elevator doors.

Bill slams the weight-shaped button and they start their journey up to the next floor. "The gym is next! Wait till you see it! You're gonna love it!"

The gym is a boring white room with a few treadmills and a busted looking stair climber. Tilly the Canadian moose is taking up two of the treadmills, wearing a sweatband and some leg warmers.

"Hello!" she calls warmly.

"Bill, this place is as pathetic as your face," Pia states.

"But we have two different kinds of machines now!"

"That stair climber looks broken."

"Well, Santa thought he'd take a few pounds off last spring. It still works though. We've got it taped up real good," Bill says proudly.

"The gym at headquarters has more than a dozen different kinds of equipment," Pia sneers. "Weight machines...an Olympic-sized pool..."

"We have weights!" Bill points to a few discarded hand weights in the corner. A spider has made itself a cozy home between them.

Pia just shakes her head

"Maybe you sweeties from Corporate can help me," Tilly pipes up, breaking up their conversation. "I've been sending in request forms but I haven't heard back from the fulfillment department! I'm trying to get my hooves on a copy of *D2: The Mighty Ducks*. I saw the first one a few months ago and I just *have* to know what happens next!" Pia stares at her with dead eyes as the moose babbles on. "It's the heartwarming tale of this delightful peewee hockey team--"

Pia turns and simply starts walking away. Bill hurries to follow her, but Tuss lingers behind, looking apologetic. "I'll see what I can do."

"Thanks so much! I'll see you around, eh?" Tilly calls merrily.

Tuss feels compelled to wave goodbye.

As they wait for the elevator to arrive, Pia impatiently taps her foot and scowls at her own reflection in the shiny door. "Can you believe that shit? This place is in worse shape than I thought."

"I've never really watched hockey, but it seems like it's really popular."

Pia glares at Tuss as the elevator finally arrives.

"It's not that great."

"Nobody asked *you*, Bill," Pia snaps.

Cupid steps off the elevator in tight fitting workout clothes, wearing his usual devilish grin. "We meet again," he says to Pia. "Must be fate."

"Well, they *are* right downstairs," Tuss jokes awkwardly.

Grumbling something incomprehensible, Pia charges into the elevator, the others right behind her.

"See you again soon!" Cupid calls cheerfully as the doors shut.

"Do you know him or something?" Bill dares to ask Pia.

If looks could kill, well, Bill would have been dead an hour ago at least. But this look definitely would have set his corpse on fire.

"Uh…Halloween's next," Bill announces, clearing his throat uncomfortably. His hand hovers over a button shaped like a pumpkin. "Watch your step."

Considering the lack of light on the next floor, Bill's warning makes sense. Spiders scurry along the corridors, slinging from web to web. More than once even Pia is startled by small shadowy figures with spindly arms and legs that materialize from the floor. The Boogeyman himself is lurking in one such hallway, surrounded by his entourage. There's a witch with a crooked, wart-covered nose and wild, frizzy, gray cat-lady hair, a long nosed, pointy-eared vampire with sharp teeth and deadly fingernails, and a brown, furry werewolf in a tracksuit.

"We need ideas for a new kind of horror movie," the Boogeyman is explaining to his captivated inner circle. "I'd like to do another one where we take a popular holiday and ruin it for everyone. Christmas, Valentine's Day, St. Patrick's Day and Halloween, obviously, have already been covered. Ideas?"

His own Shadow, which stretches to the ceiling and shouldn't even be visible in the current lighting conditions, takes the form of a firecracker.

The Boogeyman shakes his head. "That won't sell in Canada."

"What about Easter?" the werewolf suggests. "It's already about someone rising from the dead and zombies *are* hot right now."

"Excellent thinking. Poster - graveyard scene. Tagline: In three days they're all coming back." The Boogeyman finally catches sight of Bill and his tour group and pushes his greasy black hair out of his face. "Ah. I see Corporate has come to inspect us. Meet my faithful assistants." He waves vaguely in their direction.

Agatha the witch, Maxwell the vampire and Howie the werewolf briefly introduce themselves. Pia and Tuss have met their kind before, although it's been awhile since they've actually encountered one. Near extinction after being hunted by mortals, the remaining few were given jobs and safety in locations like these around the world.

"Perhaps I could call on you sometime?" Maxwell croons, baring his fangs with a twisted smile. He casually takes a long swig from a bottle filled with a dark red liquid.

"Fuck no," Pia replies flatly.

A spider crawls down the wall over Bill's head, frantically spinning an intricate web that spells out 'Call' when it's finally finished.

"It seems I have a phone call. Please excuse me," the Boogeyman apologizes.

One of the little shadowy figures jumps onto Bill's shoulder, causing him to emit a terrified scream, much to Agatha's delight.

"Let's go," Bill grumbles, hugging himself and looking around cautiously for any other scary surprises on their journey back to the elevator. Once inside, he quickly punches the turkey-shaped button for the eleventh floor.

Bill may be spooked by shadows, be fashion challenged and run subpar holidays - but he *is* right about one thing. The unique odor of the Thanksgiving floor hits them as soon as the doors open. At first it's the comforting aroma of sweet potatoes and pumpkin, mixed with spices and gravy. There's even the hint of roasting turkey, which, considering the line of birds loudly gobbling past them, is a little disturbing. But then, as they venture into the corridor, they begin to detect a gamey, stinky undertone beneath the pleasant aroma of corn and baking biscuits. Nothing, no matter how delicious smelling, can completely cover up the fact that a bunch of birds live here *or* that they use hay for a toilet and don't love to bathe.

At least the visuals are interesting. Besides the line of birds parading the halls like a group of kindergarten students on their way to recess, the walls are brightly painted with murals featuring various scenes of the traditional first Thanksgiving. Besides featuring the standard Pilgrims and Native Americans, each scene depicts a turkey in various states of slaughter, from being hunted all the way to being served at the dinner table. Again, considering the loud gobbling that's impossible to ignore, it's a little disturbing.

They decide not to bother Tom, who's on the phone yelling about cranberries, and return to the elevator for the last stop of their tour.

43

"Can you imagine if you were afraid of birds?" Tuss tries to joke on their way to the twelfth floor.

"I can't imagine being afraid of anything," comes Pia's cold reply.

The twelfth floor is marked with a Christmas tree but unlike the floors below, there is no office for its head honcho and no production is done here. (The village down below is much more than a quaint little town in the middle of nowhere, after all.) It's mostly used for choir practice or parties, like it was most recently. In fact, the place is still a bit of a mess and an assortment of elves are scurrying around shoving dirty plates and crushed plastic cups into trash bags.

"They should get to work on the third floor when they're done," Tuss remarks jokingly. He turns to look at Pia, figuring this is one thing they might actually agree on, even if he isn't completely serious, but she's already halfway across the room.

"Good work, everyone!" a booming voice calls out from the far side of the floor. Clad all in red, the large man is not exactly difficult to spot and Pia is headed right for him. Shaking his head, Tuss starts in that direction.

"Santa!" Tuss has to look twice for the source of the voice before he realizes it's Pia. She is even smiling brightly. "How are you?"

"Ho, ho, ho! Pia! I thought I heard rumors about someone joining us from Corporate! And who is this young man?"

"The name's Tuss. It's nice to meet you."

"It's good to meet you too, son!"

"You're looking well, sir!" Pia interrupts, ignoring her coworker's existence. "And congratulations are in order! This was the most successful Christmas season yet!"

"I did work extra hard this year!" Santa says, while the nerdy looking elf from earlier stands beside him, typing on his tablet. He has dark hair, glasses and a headset in his ear.

"Santa, I found some leftover candy canes for you!" A pretty elf with curly dark hair tucked behind her pointed ears comes over. She is one of the taller ones, slim and curvy in her red uniform. By elf standards, she is as gorgeous as a supermodel and the men tend to flock to her like children to presents. She holds out the aforementioned candy with a sparkling smile.

"Thank you, Holly! I don't know why we can't make these year round. We should start earlier than September!" Santa takes the treats and tucks them away in his pocket for later. "Let me introduce some of my team! This is Holly, my personal assistant. This is Wally, my head elf!" He claps the elf with the glasses on the shoulder before pointing to several others working around the room. "Then we have Jolly, Polly, Tully, Sally, Golly, Nelly, Billy, Bobby and Elly! Oh, and this is Frank!" He motions to an elf who is on the floor shining his boots and has gone unnoticed by everyone until this moment. It's the same short, grumpy elf they encountered earlier in the cafeteria. "Frank is my intern!"

Frank grumbles unhappily as he continues his work.

"I am *very* excited to be able to work so closely with you this year, Santa," Pia practically swoons, batting her long eyelashes. "I'd love to help you make this Christmas season even more profitable than last year."

"I plan to make this the best Christmas season ever!" Santa bellows. "My last and greatest ride of all time!"

Tuss' eyes snap in Pia's direction. She meets his gaze before turning back to the much beloved Christmas icon, momentarily lost for words.

"Your...last?"

"I plan on retiring after this year. Hang up the old coat, take the missus somewhere warm." Santa pulls on his suspenders and rocks back and forth on his feet with a twinkle in his eye. "Yup. It's about time I pass the torch."

Retiring? How can he be retiring? Bill is suddenly grinning like a doofus but Pia has to plaster a smile back on her face. "It's going to be the best Christmas ever!" she says again, making no mention of this sudden news.

Wally pulls a phone from his pocket. "The house for our visitors is ready, Santa."

"Excellent! I apologize, but it's all we have to offer you at the moment. We have so many homes being repaired right now. We had so much snow this year, a bunch of roofs just went and collapsed!"

Pia's smile never wavers. "I'm sure it will be more than satisfactory, Santa."

"Wally will lead the way. And if you need anything, just let me know!"

"Thank you so much for your generous hospitality, Santa," Pia gushes as Tuss stares at her, wondering if she's possessed.

Bill follows them back to the elevators. "Hope you enjoyed the tour!"

"Are you still here, you fucking parasite?" Pia snaps. As Bill falls back, his head hanging low, she rounds on Tuss. "Did you hear that?"

Tuss is almost relieved to see her acting like her normal self. He isn't sure which side of her is more unsettling. "I did," he confirms with a nod. "We're going to have to call Corporate about it right away. They certainly aren't going to be happy." He pauses for a moment, unsure. "I could do it…unless *you* want to."

Pia pulls at the charm on her necklace as she turns to face the arriving elevator. "I'm not calling them."

Before Tuss can say another word about the subject, Cupid steps out of the elevator, still in his gym clothes. "Fate!" he cries when he sees Pia.

"What the hell are you doing here?" Pia demands. "I thought you were pretending to work out. Or trying to fuck that llama."

"Stair climber broke again, so I thought I'd come up here to see if anyone found my cock ring. Pretty sure I left it at the party the other night!"

"You disgust me beyond words."

"You turn me on beyond words. Which is why I need to find that cock ring."

"Ugh! I don't have time for this!" This time Pia shoves him out of her way so she can step into the sanctity of the elevator. She's hitting the button for the lobby so quickly that the doors try to close on Tuss as he tries to get inside.

Cupid waves at them until the doors finally shut.

They ride in silence most of the way until Wally gathers all the courage in his body, clears his throat, and asks, "Don't you want to get your coats?"

"We don't need coats," Pia replies snottily.

Wally looks like he wants to reply, but keeps his mouth shut.

As soon as they step out of the lobby doors and into the freezing, snowy air beyond, it is clear that Pia was very wrong. The cold seems to swallow them whole and Pia finds herself unable to stop her teeth from chattering as she automatically wraps her arms around herself. Tuss sticks his hands into his pockets as far as he can but it does little good. Both of them are too blinded by the overwhelming below zero temperature to notice the quaint, storybook-like town they are being led through. Neither of them notice the line of shops draped with holly and garland or the bright neon sign of the village pub. They don't see the dozens of happy elves bringing home their packages, singing carols and throwing snow, or see the puffin directing traffic by the gazebo in the town square.

Tuss swears the first thing he is going to do when he gets settled is ask Corporate for the warmest coat in existence. Pia is thinking the same, although despite her chattering teeth and oncoming frostbite, would never admit she was cold, even under torture.

Luckily for them, the village is small and the walk is not long.

"Here we are," the elf says proudly as they trudge up the freshly shoveled pathway to what will be their residence for the next eleven and a half months.

The two bedroom home has two bathrooms, a kitchen and even a fireplace in the living room. It would have certainly been more than satisfactory if it hadn't been built with persons of a smaller stature in mind.

Standing in the living room, fireplace blazing and ready for their arrival, both Pia and Tuss have to slouch so they don't hit their heads on the ceiling.

"It's built for midgets!"

"They prefer elves."

"I don't give a shit what they prefer! I prefer a fucking ceiling I don't hit my head on!"

"It's only temporary," Tuss reminds her as gently as he can. "Besides, we can make do."

Pia touches the fireplace and the fire increases twofold, sparks shooting onto the hearth. "I know."

"Clucky's heard that expression about letting something go if you love it. But if that thing has wings, it ain't never comin' back."

"Ted, I've told you before how I think Groundhog's Day is a waste of fucking money."

"Yes. Every day."

"That's because there's no merchandise or decorations; no seasonal food or beverages. The majority of the profit comes from tourism to a handful of backwater American towns." Pia pauses to smile widely, although her expression appears more triumphant than happy. "But I've changed all of that."

"So the articles did well then?" Ted asks excitedly. He's sitting on his stump in the conference room facing both Tuss and Pia, although the former hasn't said much of anything. In fact, right now Tuss appears rather perplexed by Ted's giddiness.

"Absolutely. Thanks to them, we sold lots of costumes and other creepy as hell groundhog related fetish paraphernalia."

Ted's smile wavers for a moment before finally collapsing. "Wait...I... uh...*what?*"

"If you're looking for the fucking specifics, I don't know and I don't want to know. But I'm sure that pervert Cupid knows all about that sort of shit." Pia glances at the clock. "We have to meet with that freak next, by the way," she tells Tuss.

"Um…" Ted begins tentatively. "I'm really glad you're happy, but I'm confused."

"About what?" Pia huffs impatiently.

Ted shrinks back in his chair but presses onward, his voice trembling. "Well, w-what do you mean by costumes? A-and f-f-fetish stuff?"

Tuss turns to Pia angrily. "You didn't tell him?"

"Tell me what?" the groundhog whimpers.

Pia stubbornly crosses her arms over her chest. "I told him the articles were for furry magazines!"

"You said they were for animal lovers," Ted reminds her timidly.

"Right. Animal *lovers*."

Ted blinks in confusion, still not catching on.

Sighing deeply, Tuss resigns himself to having to explain to this poor, innocent mammal what he actually consented to. "These magazines are for people who like to dress-up as animals and...*fornicate*."

Ted gasps in horror. "Is that why I was asked so many questions about our mating habits?!"

"I made myself perfectly clear," Pia maintains.

"I never would have consented to that!" Ted frantically insists to Tuss. "Never!"

"I know. I'm sorry."

"You're not sorry!" Pia corrects Tuss. "He's not sorry!" she snarls at the groundhog. "The fucking holiday actually made decent money! *You* should be sorry for complaining about it!"

Before Ted can respond, the door to the conference room bursts open and Regina strides in purposefully.

"We need to talk," she says firmly, staring at Pia and Tuss.

"Can this wait?" Ted asks meekly, turning to glance up at the woman. "We're in the middle of--"

"Get out, rodent," Pia orders.

And without another word, Ted hurries from the room on the verge of tears, throwing a handful of anti-depressants in his mouth as Regina sits down on her tooth-shaped throne.

"What the hell do you want?" Pia demands. "What is so damn important that you have to barge in here when we're in the middle of a fucking--"

"I want Mother Nature's office," Regina cuts across Pia smoothly.

Both Pia and Tuss widen their eyes in surprise before the former asks, "Why the hell should we give Mother Nature's old office to *you*, Tooth Fairy? You don't even represent a holiday! Even *Bill* has more so-called *holidays* than *you*!"

"I thought that perhaps you could relate to me a bit," Regina replies, ignoring the appraising looks of Tuss out of the corner of her eye and choosing to focus her attention fully on Pia instead. "We both know how hard it is to be a woman in today's business world--"

"I don't find anything hard," Pia snaps. "If you're finding it hard running a department and being a woman at the same time, we have much bigger problems to discuss. You're not using that feminist bullshit on me."

"Pia," Tuss begins wearily. "Why don't you just give her a minute to explain why--"

"Do you know how old I am?" Pia continues. "I've been around a lot longer than you have, *sweetie*. I know how hard it *used* to be for women. We used to get stoned to death for even *looking* at a man the wrong way. It's a cakewalk for us nowadays compared to how it was back then."

"That aside, I still think I'm the most deserving of Mother Nature's old office," Regina replies calmly, leaning back in her seat.

"*Newsflash*, you prissy ballerina. Russ--"

"Tuss."

"--Here isn't even important enough to set up camp in her office. He's taken the closet next to it."

"You have?" Regina asks, surprised.

"I don't mind," Tuss shrugs. "It's the only space clear of plants on the entire floor! Besides, Pia wanted--"

"You won't be in there forever though," Regina points out to Pia, as Tuss frowns at being interrupted. "Your assignment is only temporary."

"Yeah, and do you know how many other fucking losers are vying for that office? Every damn one who works down in that hellish dungeon with you!" Pia begins to count them off on her fingers. "The narcoleptic. The glorified rat. *Bill.*" She drops the name with acid dripping from her tongue. "And you want me to give it to you? At least some of them run actual holidays!"

"I bring in more money than the three of them combined," Regina points out. "I'm the *Tooth Fairy*! I work seven days a week, all year long, not just one day per year."

"And if it were up to me," Pia begins. "You'd be out of a job too."

"But it's not," Regina replies smugly. "We all know that people much higher than you at Corporate have the final say on firing."

Tuss sighs wearily as he watches this verbal sparring match and is very surprised when Pia actually allows it to come to an end.

"We don't have time for this shit." She stands up and stares down at Tuss imperiously. "We have to go meet with Don Juan downstairs about last quarter's chocolate sales. And as for *you*," she glares at the Tooth Fairy. "Don't your little tutued minions need babysitting?"

Regina opens her mouth to reply but Tuss cuts her off. "You can handle Cupid alone. I'll handle this. It should be dealt with now."

"Considering we're stuck here for a whole fucking year, I don't see why it's such a big deal to name a successor to that damn office right this second."

53

"Maybe *you* don't, but *I* do." Tuss forces a smile onto his face.

"And what makes you think--"

"The longer you stand here arguing with me," Tuss cuts Pia off quickly. "The more time you're wasting. What?" he asks innocently, as she stares at him angrily. "You can't handle Cupid alone?"

"Of course I can," Pia snaps. "I'm not incompetent like the rest of the women in this company."

She throws Regina one last scathing look before storming out of the conference room without another word, leaving Tuss alone with the annoyed Tooth Fairy. "I'm sorry about her," he laughs.

"Don't be sorry." Regina flashes him a bright smile that makes his heart flutter. "I feel sorry for you having to deal with her constantly. Where did Santa put the two of you up?"

"Some tiny - and I mean *tiny* - place down on Santa Claus Lane."

"Well, if you ever want to get away from that bitch for a little while," Regina jerks her head at the door that Pia had just left through. "My door is always open. My place is cozy but it's big enough for the two of us."

Tuss blinks in surprise. Is it his imagination or is there a hint of flirtation in her voice?

"Uh…thanks," he clears his throat. "That's very kind of you. Living with Pia's not exactly easy. It's like living with someone you've been married to for twenty years. Except without the sex," he adds with a nervous laugh.

"Well…maybe I could…help you with that," Regina smiles nervously. "*Maybe.*"

She leans forward ever so slightly, giving Tuss a direct view of her considerable cleavage. As the blood rushes away from his head, Tuss realizes what's going on.

—

54

"Are you trying to get Mother Nature's office by flirting with me?" he asks, trying to ignore the throbbing of both his heart and the straining appendage in his pants.

Regina lets out a coquettish giggle and asks, "Is it working?"

"This…uh…" Tuss clears his throat as he pushes his chair back from the table. "This is very unprofessional."

"You have *gorgeous* teeth," Regina notes, surprising herself when she realizes that she's actually being genuine.

"Thank you," Tuss breathes shallowly. "But this – um – that is to say that uh…this is wrong. Corporate has a lot of rules against this sort of behavior."

"I'm sorry," the Tooth Fairy gets to her feet and places her hands splayed on the table in front of her. "I'm being inappropriate. Sometimes, I can be a bit of a naughty girl." She leans forward so that her face is mere inches away from Tuss' and lowers her voice to a sexy purr. "Sometimes I'm so naughty, I feel like I just need a good *spanking*."

"I have to go," Tuss says, standing up so quickly that he knocks his chair over in the process. "I forgot that I have to check on Mother Nature. You know," he laughs as he starts making his way toward the door. "She's been filing complaints with HR claiming she was wrongfully terminated, so I gave her a coffee cart to run in the lobby. I was hoping it would make her happy, but unfortunately it doesn't seem to be working, so I have to try and figure something else out. I'll see you later!"

And much to Regina's surprise and disappointment, Tuss practically runs from the room, leaving her alone.

"Well, that didn't go the way that I thought it would."

♥ ♥ ♥ ♥ ♥

Meanwhile, downstairs, Cupid is lying on the giant heart-shaped bed in his office trying to be an attentive listener. Ted the groundhog sits awkwardly across from him chattering away.

"I just don't understand!"

"What's so hard to understand?"

"Why would the mortals be *into* anything like that? It's disturbing!"

"When you think about some of the other stuff they're into, putting on an animal suit to get busy in seems super tame." Cupid looks up at poor little Ted who is wringing his paws atop the office's only chair. "I mean, do you even know what a golden shower is?"

"No…but it sounds like something Cormac might like. He loves anything having to do with gold."

"Yeah, I can see him on the giving end." Cupid nods his agreement. "But the point is, buddy, you need to keep an open mind. It made a lot of money for your holiday, right? For once Corporate paid attention to you! You've been complaining for years that they didn't care. Embrace it, my friend. Enjoy the attention. Besides, you shouldn't judge people based on what they do in the bedroom."

"I'm not judgmental!" Ted insists. "Would I be here right now talking to you if I was?"

"True. If you knew half of what went on in this bed…" A mischievous grin pops up on Cupid's face. "Not to mention the chair."

"What?"

"Nothing. Just promise me you won't reject this furry thing without learning more about it. I've got some magazines in that pile if you wanna borrow them." He points to one of the many stacks of porn and sex related reading material scattered throughout the messy office. Even the walls are covered with photos and drawings of naked people, many of them doodled by Cupid himself.

___

56

"Maybe…some other time," frets Ted, eyeing the pile with disgust. He considers Cupid a friend but he wouldn't even accept a piece of candy he touched, never mind some sketchy magazine.

"Gotta admit, I'm pretty surprised that tight bitch from Corporate even came up with that idea." Cupid rolls onto his back and stares up at the ceiling, which is also plastered with inappropriate images. It's exclusively dedicated to various couples (and a few groups) engaged in the act of fornication. He likes to jokingly refer to it as the 'real' Creation of Adam. "She is full of surprises."

The groundhog opens his mouth when there is a knock on the door and the tall, dark-haired, nerdy elf with glasses pokes his head into the room. "Got a minute?"

"Wally!" Cupid exclaims brightly. "Come in, come in. Take a seat."

"Uh…" Wally looks pointedly at Ted who is occupying the only chair in the room.

"I guess I'll get going," Ted says, jumping off the coveted seat.

"What's the rush?" Cupid calls after the groundhog as he scurries from the office and passes a cherub carrying a giant stack of chocolates. "There's plenty of room for Wally right next to me!" He pats the bed seductively.

"I don't…uh…I don't really…um…swing that way," Wally says awkwardly, as he sits down in the now vacated chair.

"Honey, *everyone* swings that way a little bit." Cupid lies down on his side and stares at the elf intensely. "Five minutes with me--"

"Is kind of all I have time for," Wally laughs nervously, checking his watch. "Santa needs me back at the workshop to give the bouncing balls a good testing."

"We can make it fast."

"I actually came here to talk to you about Holly," Wally says, nervously biting his lower lip.

"Who?" Cupid asks blankly.

"I couldn't help but notice that you two got – uh – *cozy* at the New Year's party."

"Wait, which one was she?" Cupid furrows his brow as he tries to remember. "Was she the one with the tongue ring? Or the pierced va-"

"She's the one with the really long legs," Wally says quickly, staring off into space and smiling at the pretty elf's image in his mind's eye. "Curly brown hair--"

"Nice firm ass?" Cupid interrupts with a reminiscing smile.

"I guess?" Wally swallows hard, going red in the face.

"Aw, is that what this is about?" Cupid asks. "You're jealous?"

"Yes."

"Well then, hop on!" Cupid lies back down and thrusts his pelvis out seductively.

"What? Ew, no!" Wally stands up, frightened. "I'm jealous that Holly chose you and not me!"

"Well, what do you want me to do about it?" Cupid asks. "Me and her aren't together. It was a one-time thing. No one's tying me down unless it's to a bed."

"I just – hold that thought." Wally pushes a button on the headset stuck inside of his ear. "What is it?" he barks into the phone. "What? Frank, just calm down, what do you mean the bakery's on fire?...No, I'll be right down!" He sighs deeply, pushing the button in his ear again before looking up at Cupid and asking, "Is there anything you can do to help me?"

"What, get Holly?" Cupid laughs. "I can't make you magically grow a pair of balls."

"I meant something more akin to shooting us with one of your arrows?"

He stares pointedly at the wall over Cupid's bed where a gold crossbow is mounted beside a quiver of arrows.

"My magic doesn't work on our kind," Cupid explains. "Sorry, kiddo. Believe me, if it did, I would have shot myself in the ass a hundred years ago. Don't look so down," he adds quickly, climbing onto his hands and knees as Wally hangs his head in disappointment. "I can show you a special move or two that's *sure* to get the pretty young thing coming back to you begging for more!"

"What the fuck is going on in here?"

Pia appears in the doorway, glancing from Wally's horrified face to Cupid's seductive stance on the bed.

"Pia!" Cupid exclaims, his smile growing wider at the sight of the woman who, for the first time since she's appeared at headquarters, looks slightly out of her element. "Always good to see you and those perky tits of yours."

"Get out," she barks at Wally, without turning to look at the elf directly.

"Why are you kicking him out?" Cupid demands. "There's plenty of room in here for the three of us."

"I said get the fuck out!" Pia snaps angrily, and — not needing to be told for a third time — Wally hurries from the office without a backwards glance.

"I'm sensing a lot of pent up frustration." Cupid stares at her as he climbs out of bed. "Getting laid could help release some of it."

"That's no way to talk to your boss," Pia says curtly, sticking her arm out to block Cupid from closing the door.

59

"I don't believe in titles," Cupid replies, shooting her an amused look. "But if you want to get technical, I *think* I may be slightly higher up on the food chain than you."

"Well, I don't believe in technicalities," Pia quips, causing Cupid to laugh.

"Very good," he replies, eyeing how stiff she looks. "Would you relax? Loosen up! Don't you trust me?"

"Absolutely not," Pia says matter-of-factly.

"I could help you with that, you know." He steps closer, staring down at her sexily. "Are you as tight as you look? Because that could be a *lot* of fun."

"Get away from me," Pia gags, backing away from the stunningly handsome man. "Your cologne is making me want to puke."

"It's Calvin Klein."

"It's fucking disgusting," Pia replies harshly. "It's almost as bad as the songs you have playing throughout this floor all damn day and night!"

"They're classics."

"They're horrible! Is Eric Clapton even alive anymore?"

"Is there a reason you came to see me?" Cupid asks pointedly, dragging his chair over to a desk in the corner. His computer is well hidden behind various colognes, boxes of condoms and stacks of porn.

"I wanted to go over your candy sales from last quarter," Pia replies, snapping her fingers. Immediately, a large black folder stuffed with paper appears in her hand.

"Can we make it quick?" Cupid asks casually without turning to face her as she begins to rifle through the binder; he's too busy stuffing condoms into his pockets and spraying multiple colognes onto his neck. "I have an appointment in Venice in about half-an-hour."

—

"*Excuse me?*" Pia looks up from her folder, her eyes narrowed.

"Yeah, I put an ad on Craigslist a few days ago," Cupid explains. "Looking for a quick lay. Well, *apparently*, the woman who answered wants me to fuck her in front of her husband."

"*What?*"

"I know," Cupid says excitedly, mistaking Pia's tone of voice for enthusiasm. "That's crazy, right? Humans get more and more fucked up with each passing year. Back in the day, a woman could get stoned to death for cheating on her husband! Now there's a whole fetish devoted to *cuckolding*. Most of the husbands actually *enjoy* watching too!"

"You can't go down to Venice," Pia states through gritted teeth. "You need permission from Corporate to leave the Pole and you don't have it."

"I need permission?" Cupid raises an eyebrow.

"You know the rules," Pia snaps. "Don't play dumb."

"Who's going to stop me?" Cupid asks mischievously, backing up toward his office door. "*You?*"

"I could."

"I'd like to see you try," Cupid laughs. "You don't have the power."

"But my bosses do," Pia says, her voice rising loudly as she follows Cupid out of his office and down the hall, passing tiny cherubs flying back and forth, manning conveyor belts full of chocolates and bouquets of roses.

"They should be more worried about Baby New Year! Talk about the terrible twos," Cupid replies without looking over his shoulder. "Did you hear what he did to Father Time the other day? Pushed him down one of the elevator shafts! Thankfully, he didn't fall that far."

"*Thankfully?* That old crank would have deserved it!"

When they reach the elevator bay at the end of the hall, Cupid pushes the down button before spinning to face Pia again. "Just gonna grab some coffee from the lobby so I'll have plenty of energy for banging."

"I'm not letting you leave," she says.

"Sweetie, I know you'll miss me, but you had your chance."

"Fuck you."

"Yes, please."

Pia rolls her eyes but before she can speak, Cupid cuts her off. "Shouldn't you be more concerned with Santa's retirement than my comings and goings?"

"Santa's not retiring," Pia says firmly.

"He changed his mind?"

"He's going to."

"He should," Cupid agrees. "I would if I were him. I didn't even think retirement was allowed."

"He's not going to retire," Pia insists. "Even if he *was*, him and the Mrs. are a special case – they get to live on."

"More perks for the old man. Don't let Tom get wind of that," Cupid advises as the elevator doors open with a loud ping. Stepping inside, he adds, "See you later, sweetheart!"

"Valentine's Day is less than a week away!" Pia snaps, placing her arm inside of the elevator to stop the doors from closing and slow his escape. "You have work to do! Work that doesn't involve your dick!"

"I'll be back in an hour! *Two* tops," Cupid replies.

———

"The damn chocolates still need to be filled and boxed--"

"And my employees will do that," Cupid interrupts her. "Agatha's going to supervise them."

"*Agatha?*" Pia repeats. "The hag from the fucking Halloween department?"

"The Boogeyman's letting me borrow her for a few hours so stop worrying," Cupid insists, pushing Pia out of the elevator. "I'll be back later."

And Pia can do nothing but watch as the elevator doors close, obscuring Cupid from her view.

She stands still, fuming, clenching her hands into tight fists before spinning around quickly to see a bunch of Cupid's winged workers staring at her, their innocent eyes wide with fright.

"GET THE FUCK BACK TO WORK!"

❤ ❤ ❤ ❤ ❤

"You want to talk about next year? Already?" Ted sits atop his stump in the conference room, fidgeting. A one-on-one meeting with Pia is bad enough without it being about *that* interview in *that* magazine. And considering it has only been a few days since their previous meeting, the nervous mammal was hoping to avoid her toxic gaze for at least a week since their last chat ended rather unpleasantly.

"Yes, *already*," she shoots back. "Unlike the rest of you lazy asses who only get your shit together the month before your holidays, I'm *always* thinking about next year. And next year we're going to have one of you weasels on the cover of every single one of these freak magazines. Plus, these weirdoes have conventions. I want booths promoting you and your stupid holiday at every last one. Maybe the costumes will even catch on for Halloween. Although, they'd probably need to make some adjustments to the design...get rid of those access panels or whatever those perverts requested. I'm getting off topic. The point is, we are in the sexy groundhog business now and I don't want to hear you complain a single damn word about it."

Ted swallows hard, trying to keep Cupid's advice in mind. "I'd be happy to do whatever you need."

Pia blinks, obviously surprised by his change of attitude. "As you damn well should. You should be on the ground kissing my feet and thanking me for saving your shitty holiday. Do you know that half of America thinks you're a fucking beaver? I can't imagine you're happy being mistaken for a buck-toothed tree murderer. But one thing at a time. First, we need to get all of the sick freaks to want to dress up like you and bang each other. Then, we'll worry about the rest of those morons down there in that stupid country of fat, dumb, lazy idiots." She slides a magazine across the table. "Here's the issue they featured you in – hopefully it will help you come up with some new shit to say next year about mating rituals or whatever these weirdoes wanna hear about."

Ted stares at the happy groundhog featured on the cover of *Furry & Friends* magazine, too scared to touch it. The top article is titled: *Discover Your Inner Groundhog and See More Than Your Shadow This Year.*

"We'll talk more about this later. Right now I have a specific pervert and a bunch of sappy, chocolate hearts to check on."

It's not until the click of her heels are safely out of earshot that Ted tentatively reaches across the table and picks up the magazine, flipping through it with a frown. He doesn't see anything terrible inside, just a lot of articles and animal pictures. A stupid person might even mistake it for *National Geographic.* He is starting to think that maybe Cupid was right after all when he flips to the back and finds a section featuring personal ads. His eyes immediately come to rest on one ad at the top, which reads:

Lonely? S/W/M ISO LT Pen Pal. WE, into B&D and S&M. Will Answer All!

Ted stares at this ad, unable to turn the page. He *is* lonely and *would* like a pen pal. Writing to someone would give him something to do besides try and get his paws on more medication. He isn't *exactly* sure what any of the many abbreviations mean, but he feels confident in assuming B&D stands for burrowing and digging and S&M is short for sleeping and meals. Who didn't love all of those things? He feels he has a lot in common with this other lonely person already.

Keeping Cupid's words in mind, he decides to go ahead and write a letter. It would help him get to know these kinds of people better. Pia would like that. Besides, a letter was harmless. Nothing bad had ever come from a simple little letter.

Ted excitedly bounds from the conference room in search of a pen, a piece of paper and an envelope.

❤ ❤ ❤ ❤ ❤

Cupid is in his office, sitting at his desk (for once). It's the day before Valentine's Day and he figures he needs to put in some actual work before the fourteenth – especially with those two wet blankets from Corporate hanging around. He's not scared of them, but their bosses are another story. If he messes up his holiday as badly as Father Time screwed up New Year's, he will get into huge trouble. He doesn't even want to think about what kind of punishment would be in store for him if his holiday doesn't make money.

"What do you want?" he asks, hitting the speakerphone button on his phone the moment it rings.

"I *told* you not to fucking leave!" Pia's voice echoes loudly around his office, causing the furniture to shake.

"It's been three days and you're *still* going on about this?" Cupid asks, rubbing his temples, exasperated. "For the last time, I don't give a shit about policy. I can come and go as I please. And believe me, I came *plenty* that day. Do you know how much of a turn on it is to fuck a woman while berating her loser of a husband as he jerks off in the corner?"

"Shut the fuck up, you STD-riddled pervert!" Pia snarls, taking Cupid by surprise. "I don't want to hear about your secret life as a moonlighting gigolo!"

"Then why did you call?"

"To tell you to get your ass upstairs to the conference room! *Now!*"

Before Cupid can reply, he hears the sound of Pia slamming down the phone.

"This day just keeps getting worse and worse," Cupid mumbles as he stands up. Grabbing a bottle of Aspirin, he walks out of his office and calls over to his employees on the way to the elevator. "I'll be back in a few minutes! Keep at it! We can still get our last shipment of chocolates to the stores before midnight! Maybe a few last minute sales will help that bitch relax and get off my back until she's laying on hers beneath me."

♥ ♥ ♥ ♥ ♥

"You fucked up!" are the first words out of Pia's mouth as Cupid strolls into the conference room.

"I *should* be fucking *you*," Cupid flashes her a smile, somewhat surprised to see that they are not alone. Tuss is seated beside Pia, looking serious, and the Boogeyman is leaning back on his throne of bones, looking bored. Beside him, sitting in Tom the turkey's empty seat, Agatha fiddles nervously, her black hat slightly askew on top of her head. "Whatever this is all about," Cupid continues, as he falls into his own chair. "Can we make it quick? I have a killer hangover."

"We have a serious issue to discuss, you unbelievable embarrassment," Pia snaps.

"Is it the fact that you haven't been laid since the Elizabethan Era?" Cupid raises an eyebrow, adding as the Boogeyman snorts, "Or has it been longer than that?"

Tuss lets out a small laugh that he quickly tries to cover with a cough

———

66

when Pia throws him a dirty look.

"It's about the fact that you ruined Valentine's Day!" Pia says through gritted teeth, as she turns to face Cupid again, her face growing steadily redder with each passing second. "Because you couldn't keep your dick in your pants and you left this old crone," she jerks her head at Agatha, "In charge of overseeing chocolate production - all so you could go down to Venice and fuck some slut!"

"Do we still have to be here?" the Boogeyman interjects. "You tore my employee a new one already--"

"I haven't even begun to tear her a new one!" Pia shouts, staring at Agatha who shrivels under her glare.

"You already kidnapped her cat!"

"Mr. Meow-Meow!" Agatha whines, tears springing to her eyes.

"Can somebody just tell me what happened?" Cupid demands impatiently, staring around at each face in the room.

"Aggie, here," Tuss begins calmly. "Thought that she would - uh – try to *improve* the love potion that you put into your chocolates by working some of her own magic on the mixture."

Cupid, who had been listening calmly, whips his head around, panicked, to face the old witch.

"I was only trying to help," Agatha replies defensively. "I--"

"If you want to help, go upstairs and pack up your desk, you're fired!" Pia yells, throwing her pen down in frustration.

Horrified, Agatha turns to the Boogeyman who shakes his head reassuringly. "Don't worry, you're not going anywhere."

"On whose authority?" Pia demands.

"*Mine*," the Boogeyman snarls, baring his shark-like teeth as his

---

Shadow triples in size behind him, baring sharp teeth of its own.

"I'm the one in charge here," Pia snaps. "Not you, you decomposing corpse!"

"Pia, you know we don't have the authority to fire someone without Corporate's permission. Can we get back to the point?" Tuss interjects before his colleague can reply. "Cupid," he turns to stare at the man in question. "The chocolates were shipped – nobody caught Agatha's mistake. They were distributed all throughout Los Angeles."

"It's having the opposite effect on people," Pia explains. "Making people fight, argue and break up! I'm sure even *you*, with a brain tinier than your dick, can gather what that means? It means we're losing money! One of the biggest cities in the world is going to be down an alarming amount of couples for *your* fucking holiday!"

"It's not my fault," Cupid says smoothly, glancing at Agatha.

"You left the Pole! How is it not your fault?" Pia is on her feet now and as her voice reverberates around the room, the ground beneath their feet begins to shake and the lights overhead flicker ominously.

"Calm down," Tuss warns her before firmly addressing Cupid. "You need to fix this."

"And how am I supposed to do that?" Cupid asks. "The chocolates went out. That's it. Even if I send whatever we produce today down to L.A., it's not going to make up for the amount that's already gone out. We're just going to have to take the loss this year."

"We can't afford the fucking loss, you colossal moron," Pia breathes deeply. "You know what happens if our profits go down."

"You get in trouble from your boss?"

"We'll *all* get into far more serious trouble than even *my* boss can dish out," Pia replies ominously.

A tense silence settles over the room for the briefest of moments before Cupid asks, "Well? What do you want me to do?"

"You're going to have to go down to L.A. and fix this mess you caused," Pia says curtly. "The old-fashioned way," she adds with the slightest hint of a smile.

"Oh no," Cupid moans, sensing the implication. "Don't tell me. Not the--"

"The bow and arrows," Tuss nods. "You're going to have to shoot as many people as you can and make as many love matches as possible in the next," he checks his watch. "Thirty-five hours."

"Put as many fucking people together as you can," Pia demands. "I don't give a shit if they're compatible or not."

"You haven't in years," Cupid points out. "No one at Corporate has. That's why we switched to mass distribution instead of sending me down to make *true* love matches. Besides, could you imagine if I had to do it one-by-one *these* days? Talk about overpopulation! It would take me *forever!* Those mortals don't need my help making sexual connections anymore."

"I mean it," Pia continues, as though Cupid hadn't interrupted her. "Put *anyone* and *anything* together that you can manage! Thank God homosexuality is actually accepted nowadays - that's double the amount of matches right there!"

"Fine, but I'm not wearing the diaper," Cupid insists, folding his arms across his chest. "I won't."

"Why not? You're practically a man-child as it is," Pia points out.

"The mortals won't think it's cute seeing a grown man in a diaper with fluffy white wings flying above their heads with a bow and arrow like they did in the old days," Cupid insists.

"Improvise," Tuss suggests. "Just get down there and fix this."

As Cupid sighs in resignation, the Boogeyman speaks up. "You don't still need me and Agatha here, do you?"

Tuss leans back in his chair, exhausted, as Pia launches into speech, lecturing about how she'll tell him when they're not needed anymore.

♥ ♥ ♥ ♥ ♥

Twenty-four hours later, Cupid is sitting in his dark office watching live news coverage from Los Angeles, a glass of scotch in hand. The floor that he presides over is completely empty – he gave his cherubs the rest of the night off since Valentine's Day is coming to an end in Earth's remaining time zones.

"I'm standing outside of the Los Angeles Convention Center, where earlier today Valentine's Day fever settled over all of the attendees."

Cupid eyes the blonde news reporter with interest – if he wasn't so depressed, he would make his way down to California that instant and seduce her. He has a strong suspicion that the carpet doesn't match the drapes and he would love to prove himself right.

"Men and women of all ages who were inside attending a science fiction convention were struck by Cupid's arrows – literally."

Cupid downs the rest of his scotch in embarrassment as stock footage from earlier that day plays on the screen under the woman's voiceover. He's standing there, in nothing but a pair of white briefs (which, he's at least happy to see shows off his considerable package and his firm ass), trusty crossbow in hand. From his back, two giant, feathery wings are protruding; those gathered around him on the screen, however, barely look twice at him. Why? Because they are all dressed as various characters from *Star Wars*, *Star Trek*, *Battlestar Gallactica* and a variety of other geeky franchises that Cupid can no longer keep track of.

He watches himself on-screen firing arrow after arrow at random people. Once struck, each person instantly begins to flirt and seduce whoever is standing closest to them.

"A fan dressed as the legendary Roman God of Love took his role a little too seriously, somehow sneaking his crossbow past security and into the convention center where he began to shoot people at random. Rather than complaining and reporting the overzealous stranger, other convention-goers decided to play along - often veering into inappropriate territory."

Cupid raises an eyebrow as he watches a gray-haired man dressed as Dr. Who lift a young girl, who barely looks eighteen, off of the ground and push her against a wall where they begin to make out passionately.

"Donald Strong, a fifty-five year old history teacher at a local high school, was arrested for engaging in sexually explicit activity with a sixteen-year-old student. When questioned about the incident, the teenage girl insisted the two were soul mates and madly in love. An investigation is currently underway as to how long the two have been seeing one another outside of class."

Cupid feels slightly guilty listening to the news report, but at least the cops wouldn't be able to dig up anything on the pair – he had only randomly put them together hours ago.

"Meanwhile, one teenage boy, whose name is being withheld at the request of his parents, came out of the closet in a very public way."

News footage quickly switches to a shaking closet door. Under the newscaster's voiceover, Cupid can distinctly make out the sounds of Darth Vader's voice asking through the closed door, "Who's your daddy now, bitch? Who's your daddy?"

"How is that appropriate for TV?" Cupid mutters, pouring himself more scotch.

"When the boy's parents were called to the police station to pick up their son for public indecency, his self-proclaimed Christian mother insisted that her son was straight, while his father had to be rushed to the hospital after having heart palpitations at the news."

Cupid grimaces at the story, feeling bad for the boy – but Pia had instructed him to put as many people together as he could, so who cared if they were compatible? Or not of the same sexual proclivity? He hadn't been paying attention. He was just trying to get it over with.

"And these two pairings were far from the only ones struck by Cupid's arrows today."

Suddenly, the news footage begins to flash quickly across the computer screen, depicting various scenes from the convention center earlier that day. Men and women making out; men and men; women and women; one man and his dog – all falling instantly in love with one another while Cupid himself stands in the middle of the crowd, robotically shooting arrow after arrow from his crossbow. He sees Princess Leias undoing their gold bikinis for Captain Kirks, Supermen being straddled by Catwomen and even two men dressed as Batman and Robin kissing awkwardly around their masks.

"Police are still unsure why hundreds of people decided to play along with this man dressed as Cupid, but they are launching an official investigation and asking if anyone has any information on him to please contact the authorities immediately. Meanwhile, a spokesperson for the Los Angeles Convention Center has confirmed that they are launching an investigation of their own, looking for gas leaks or contaminated water that could have possibly caused all of these people to temporarily lose their minds."

Cupid has had enough of the news report and turns his computer off just as a voice behind him asks, "Admiring yourself on the computer now? What, a mirror isn't enough for you anymore? Or has your repulsive face cracked them all?"

Cupid spins around in his chair to find Pia standing in the doorway of his office, her arms folded across her chest.

"What are you still doing here?" he asks. "It's late."

"I had to wait for the final numbers to come in," she says, stepping into his office without waiting for an invitation.

"But it's Valentine's Day."

"Exactly," Pia replies simply, staring around the room. "Fucking hell, don't you have any money in the budget to get some more chairs in here?"

"Feel free to lie on the bed," Cupid waves his arm at the heart-shaped mattress. "I can lie down with you – it's probably the closest you'll come to getting laid tonight. Unless, you know, you actually *want* to have sex, in which case I can help you with that too."

"Fuck off," Pia snaps. "It's never going to happen."

"We'll see about that," Cupid smirks.

"I just came to inform you that despite your laziness and insubordination the other day, you have successfully rectified your mistakes. Shocking, I know." She snaps her fingers and a clipboard immediately appears in her hands. "Valentine's Day sales are through the roof. Especially in that disgusting, smog-filled city full of talentless people who get paid ten times more than they should. So congratulations. I guess your brain is functional after all. At least partially."

"I guess this just shows that I can slack off all I want because in the end, I get the work done," Cupid says plainly.

"It means that you shouldn't slack off in the first place so you don't have to make an eleventh hour play in your fucking *underwear* to save the day," Pia insists. When Cupid stares at her, confused, she rolls her eyes. "It's a sports metaphor. Don't fucking look at me like that," she snaps. "People in my position need to be able to relate to their employees on some level."

"I'm pretty sure you don't need to know any sports metaphors to relate to anyone up here," Cupid snorts. "Shows how much you know about *us*. Such a Corporate drone."

"All I need to know is that *I'm* in charge and *you* have to do what I say," Pia smiles smugly.

"Just like you ordered me to put together as many people as I could just to increase profits, right?" Cupid asks as he stands up.

"Exactly."

"It's one thing putting love potions into chocolates," Cupid explains. "People who buy them are normally in relationships or going on dates, so it enhances their feelings for the person they want to be with. But shooting people at random to create some kind of…of…*obsession*? It's…it's *wrong*."

"Since when do you give a shit about what's right and wrong?" Pia demands, unable to keep the surprise completely from her voice.

Cupid glances at his dark computer screen before answering. "Did you see the news reports?"

Pia rolls her eyes. "Who cares about any of that crap?"

"I might have ruined peoples' lives!"

"The effects are only temporary," Pia reminds him. "The police won't find anything on any of them – or *you*, for that matter. They think you were just some freak in a costume. Which, to be honest, isn't that far off," she adds with a snort.

"Yeah, but don't you remember the days when we actually wanted to help people?" Cupid asks. "*Genuinely* help them? Put care and thought into our work? Now all we care about is profit!"

"Profit's fucking important and you know that better than anyone else in this wasteland," Pia says. "We need to keep profits on the rise, or you know what will happen. The times are changing and you need to change with them. *Otherwise*, you'll never move up and you'll be stuck in this position - in this *hell* hole - for a long time."

"The difference between you and I, Pia," Cupid begins seriously, leaning down so that their faces are inches apart now. "Is that I like my position in life. It's what I chose. I don't need to please other people to make myself happy."

"You have some fucking nerve," Pia spits.

"I have some fucking cock too." Cupid smiles, standing up straight. "I can show you if you want. We can work out some of our issues by having angry sex. Come on – you know you want to. How long's it been for you? Seriously, can I guess? A hundred years? Two hundred? Don't tell me it's been longer than two hundred! That's a sexual emergency!"

Rolling her eyes, Pia storms out of the office without another word. In the hallway, Caleb – now a two-year-old boy spending his days hobbling around the building in-between attempting to playfully kill his Father – is being handed a box of Valentine cards, the type that children hand out to their friends in grade school, by a plump cherub fluttering in midair. As Caleb gleefully takes the box, Clotho fusses over him, trying to wipe his chocolate-stained face with a baby wipe.

"Caleb, stand still." The Fate pushes a strand of hair behind her head. "Let me clean you up."

As Pia passes by, she realizes this is the first time she's seen the kid since he was a baby a mere month ago. Feeling a small bit of her annoyance with Cupid ebb away at the sight of the child who had tried to kill the old man who had colossally fucked up New Year's Eve, she smirks to herself and tousles his hair as she passes, refusing to slow down.

"Good job, kid," she mutters, still staring straight ahead at the elevators at the end of the hall. "That old fuck deserves more than the broken legs you gave him."

Clotho stares after Pia as she passes, scandalized by the woman's words. Caleb, however, feels no such horror. The blonde, fair-skinned child stares around at the woman and smiles happily at the small compliment she had just given him. Cooing in delight, he hobbles after her, waving his box of Valentines through the air, determined to give her one.

"Caleb, wait!" Clotho exclaims in exasperation, hurrying after the boy. "Where are you going?"

Watching the scene through his office door, Cupid can't help smirking to himself as his phone rings. Falling into his chair, he picks up the receiver before it can ring a second time and places it to his ear. "What is it?"

"I've been doing everything you've told me to do." The Tooth Fairy is sitting in her own closet-like office, her phone to one ear and a finger in another, trying in vain to block out the bickering sounds of Hugh and Hugo from their tiny desks on the shelves above her. "And it's not working."

"Really?" Cupid's voice replies. "You tried the spanking thing?"

"Yes, I tried the spanking thing!" Regina snaps, ignoring the now curious looks from her two protégées above. "Three days ago!"

"And you're just calling me now?" Cupid asks, perplexed.

"I've been busy collecting teeth! There's been a lot of peewee hockey games going on! The point is, it was degrading! How the hell did I let you talk me into doing that? It didn't even work! That's the worst part!"

"Maybe he's gay?" Cupid suggests into the phone. "Because you have a spectacular ass, my darling. Given the chance, I'd give you an office in order to slap it in return."

"I'll keep that in mind the next time you have a spare office to give," Regina says, annoyed. "Do you have any other ideas I could try?"

"I don't know," Cupid says, frustrated. "Just…be yourself."

"What?" Regina asks, taken aback as Hugh and Hugo resume their arguing above her. "Are you high?"

"Only on life, my dear."

"Since when is being yourself enough for you?"

"It's not good enough for me," Cupid says quickly. "I prefer a nice pair

——
76

tits, a big round ass, a landing strip--"

"You're disgusting."

"Look," Cupid begins. "Don't turn into a slut to get the office. There are tons of better reasons to turn into a slut. That's *definitely* not what Pia or Tuss want to see. Just show them you're good at your job and why you deserve that office. That's all those Corporate drones care about. In fairness," he laughs. "You don't have much competition. Ted needs to be somewhere small and dark so he doesn't accidentally see his shadow, and they're not going to give the place to the Sandman just so he has somewhere bigger to sleep. And as for Bill? Pia would rather perform a lobotomy on herself than give that guy more power!"

Regina bites her lower lip as she mulls over Cupid's new advice. Finally, she asks, "Are you sure you're okay?"

"I'm fine."

"Well, something must have happened," Regina insists. "I haven't heard you speak this much sense in fifty years."

"I don't know what you're talking about. I'm *always* speaking sense," Cupid replies.

Before Regina can respond, there's a knock on her office door and she looks up to see Tuss standing in the doorway, his enormous frame blocking the dank hallway beyond. When they lock eyes, he flashes his perfect smile and Regina feels her heart skip a beat.

"I have to go," she says quickly into the phone, watching as Tuss glances around her tiny office, unable to hide the disgusted look on his face. "We'll talk later." She slams the phone down and looks up at Hugh and Hugo in their bright pink tutus. "Get out!" she snaps, rising to her feet.

As the two muscular pixies fly out of her office, Regina crosses to the door in three steps, squeezing past Tuss, and shuts it.

"Hi," she breathes, looking up at Tuss who notices that their bodies are inches from touching.

"Hi," he says nervously, diverting his eyes from her as he looks around her office again. "Nice digs you've got here."

The Tooth Fairy's office is barely bigger than a linen closet. Windowless, her giant desk is pushed against the back wall, on top of which a large jar of teeth sits. Shelves line the surrounding walls; two of the highest ones have two tiny desks situated on them, at which Hugh and Hugo normally sit conducting their work. Because the space is so small, the stacks of papers, file folders and books placed around the room wherever they can fit make the area seem overly crowded and messy.

"What's that noise?" Tuss asks as the office walls shake every few seconds in tune with a loud rumbling sound.

"The Sandman's office is next door," Regina shrugs as she sits on the edge of her desk and stares up at her boss. "The walls down here are pretty thin, I can usually hear when he falls asleep."

"Ah," Tuss says with a slight nod of his head. "Yeah, I…uh…I passed his office and saw he had his head down on his keyboard."

"That's why he's the Sandman." Regina smiles, studying the man's strong face, trying to tell what he's thinking.

"That was after I spent half an hour with Bill trying to get Tilly's antlers unstuck from her office doorway before tripping into a hole in the ground."

"Sounds like Ted's work," Regina laughs. "All normal occurrences down here in the sub-basement. What are you doing down here anyway?"

"I…uh…" He clears his throat. "I came to see *you*, actually."

"Really?" she raises an eyebrow.

"To apologize," Tuss explains, noticing a bunch of old black and white photos on the Tooth Fairy's desk. "For running out on you the other day. It was unprofessional."

"Don't worry about it," Regina says. "If I recall, I was the one being unprofessional first."

"I have to admit, I kind of liked it," Tuss laughs nervously, avoiding her eyes.

"Did you?" Regina asks, her tone seductive as she leans back slightly on her desk. "So the real reason for your visit comes out."

"I really did just want to apologize," Tuss says, turning to stare at her. "And to tell you that I'm going to talk to Pia...see what I can do about getting you that office when we leave."

"Really?" Regina asks, sitting up straight.

"Yeah." Tuss nods. "Really. I think you deserve it. Besides, if Ted burrowed too deep up there, he'd fall through to the Easter floor."

"I definitely deserve it," Regina says with a smile. "But wow, I – uh - I don't know what to say. Thank you!"

"Don't thank me yet," Tuss warns. "It's going to take a long time to convince Pia, if I can even do it at all."

"You can do it," Regina says with confidence. "I'm sure you can. A strong, handsome guy like yourself shouldn't find it too hard to persuade a woman to do anything."

Tuss smiles. "Well, I should...you know, get going. It's getting late." Regina nods. "I'll see you tomorrow."

Tuss turns and opens the office door, but before he can walk out, Regina calls, "Oh, and Tuss?"

"Yeah?" he asks, turning around, surprised to see her standing nose-to-nose with him.

"Happy Valentine's Day," she says softly, standing on her tiptoes to kiss the man on his cheek.

"Happy Valentine's Day," Tuss mumbles, red-faced.

As the Tooth Fairy flashes him a wide smile, he turns and hurries out of her office and into the dingy, dimly-lit hallway beyond, trying to suppress a smirk of his own as he gently feels the cheek that her lips just touched.

Cupid ended up turning them a giant profit and he got a flirtatious little kiss from Regina – all in all, Tuss can't help but think it was a great Valentine's Day. And he won't be the last one to get a nice surprise before the day is over either.

In fact, down in Santa's workshop at that very moment, Wally is overseeing production of a new line of toy bouncy balls when his headset beeps insistently.

"Hello?" he asks, after pushing the button to answer it.

"Wally? It's Cupid. I've changed my mind. I'm going to try and help you win over Holly."

Wally widens his eyes, taken aback by the man's voice, before a smile unfolds on his face and he finds the pretty brunette elf across the room, handing Santa a mug of hot chocolate. "Really?"

"Really," Cupid replies. "Consider it a gift. Happy Valentine's Day."

March

"Clucky made the mistake of going to the third floor once...now Clucky has to live with that decision *forever*."

"This place is absolutely miserable."

Pia is standing at a window in the conference room watching the snow outside fall steadily, as it always does.

"I think it's okay," Tuss replies with a shrug from where he is sitting at the table. "A bit dark maybe, but the Aurora Borealis is pretty--"

"Pretty boring," Pia says harshly as she steps away from the window and begins to pace the room. "What time is it?"

"See for yourself," Tuss mumbles under his breath, drumming his fingertips on the tabletop.

"What?" Pia demands, spinning around to face him.

"Uh, five-fifteen," Tuss sits up straight after glancing at the clock hanging in plain view on the wall.

"Just wait until I get my hands on that incompetent dwarf!"

"Leprechaun," Tuss replies, deadpan.

"Whatever the fuck he is," Pia snaps. "It's his damn holiday and he's *still* not showing up for fucking work!"

"He'll show up," Tuss reasons, avoiding her eyes as he scratches his ear. "Don't worry about it. The early numbers coming in are all great, so clearly he's getting things done--"

"From home?" Pia scoffs. "We don't pay him to work from home!" Then, stopping dead in her tracks, she turns to face her colleague and asks, "Do you think he even goes home? He never answers his door down in midgetville when I knock."

"He's probably always passed out cold when you knock." Tuss smirks. "Do you ever check the bar?"

"I don't go to bars! I don't remember the last time I even stepped foot in a damn bar," Pia answers automatically. Tuss raises an eyebrow at the response and Pia silently berates herself for her honest answer. "Forget I said anything."

"When was the last time you even went on a date?" Tuss asks.

"I said fucking forget it!" Pia glances at the clock on the wall. "What time are they calling?"

"They should have called five minutes ago." Tuss checks his watch before staring at the speakerphone situated in the center of the conference room table. "Would you relax?"

"Don't tell me what to do! You're not my boss, asshole."

"And *you're* not *mine*," Tuss reminds her sternly. "Stop stressing. They're only calling to instruct us on how they want Cormac dealt with when he *does* come in."

"*If* he comes in! Besides, I don't need them to tell me how to deal with Irish Napoleon," Pia says, falling into Bill's chair with a huff. "I'll strangle him! And I'll like it!"

"I *think* that's what they're probably trying to avoid," Tuss points out. "He gets the job done, he just needs to be more professional and--"

"Show up for fucking work?" Pia interrupts.

"Exactly."

"Well, let's see what they have to say," Pia says curtly. "Hopefully this doesn't take long."

"Hopefully it does," Tuss mutters nervously under his breath, glancing at the wall clock again as the phone finally rings.

☘ ☘ ☘ ☘ ☘

Up on the twelfth floor, the Christmas trees in the corner of the room sparkle brightly, lighting up the drafty, empty space as Regina arranges chairs in a semi-circle in the center. Around her, the other holiday heads are talking amongst themselves; notably absent are Bill, Tom, Father Time and, of course, Cormac, who nobody's seen in a year.

"Do you know what time he's supposed to show up?" Francis asks, straightening his green bow tie. "I'm pretty busy, you know."

"We're all busy, *Franny*," the Boogeyman replies as he folds his arms across his chest.

"Yes, but Easter's only a few weeks away!" Francis' whiskers twitch nervously. "I should be downstairs overseeing egg production! The purple dye chute got clogged last week and it took my chicks three days to get it running again! Half of them are still dyed purple! Clucky spends all his free time in the bath trying to wash the color out of his feathers!"

Regina bends down over her large purse and begins to pull out a giant easel, on which a large pad of paper is resting.

"Did you hide the body of Mary Poppins in her magical bag after you killed her for it?" Cupid asks with a raised eyebrow.

"Bite me," Regina says, carefully placing the easel so it can be viewed from every chair.

"I'd love to," Cupid replies. "On your earlobe…your neck…your--"

"Say another word and I'll pull out your teeth the next time I'm working on them." Regina whips around, her face serious.

"Touchy." Cupid throws his hands up in mock-surrender as he falls into one of the chairs and jerks his head at the bag. "Need to bend over and pull anything else out of there? That was a nice view."

"Not while you're sitting behind me," Regina quips. "I'm afraid that you may try to stick something inside of--"

"Ho, ho, ho," Santa laughs nervously, walking over to join the feisty pair. "Don't make me put both of you on the naughty list."

"That's the only list worth being on," Cupid quips.

"Regina," Santa begins. "Perhaps we should get started?"

"Excellent idea," Regina says, before calling out to the others. "Can you all take a seat, please? Thank you."

As her colleagues begin to settle into their seats, the Sandman beginning to snore instantaneously upon sitting, Regina just rolls her eyes as the elevator doors open behind them.

"What time is it?" Father Time demands as he rushes from the elevator with Caleb, now ten-years-old, tucked under his arm. "What time was our meeting supposed to be?"

Mother Nature snorts in derision as Regina says, "Don't worry. You're not that late. We're just about to get started."

"I'm late?" Father Time demands, trying to catch his breath as he falls into a seat with Caleb. "I spent the last week fixing all the clocks in this building! I consider this punishment cruel and unusual!"

"Hearing you bitch about it constantly is cruel and unusual," Mother Nature grunts, folding her arms across her chest.

"Who else is missing?" Regina asks pointedly, noticing there are still three empty seats.

"Besides the obvious one?" the Boogeyman replies. "Bill and that *insufferable* turkey."

"Where are they?"

T.J. screeches and caws in something akin to exasperation from the chair on which he is perched, shaking his head.

"Uh…what was that?" Santa asks politely.

—
85

T.J. screeches louder this time, more frustrated.

"What's he saying?" Santa asks the room at large.

"Nobody speaks eagle except for Bill," Francis points out. As T.J. screeches again, he adds hurriedly, "Maybe I can get one of the chicks from the Easter department to come up and translate? But their dialect sounds pretty different. Though I do recall Clucky telling me once that he could speak twenty other types of bird--"

"Ugh, not *Clucky*! Get one of the hot chicks to come up," Cupid winks.

"You're disgusting."

"Maybe we should get down to business, eh?" Tilly suggests brightly.

"I'd love to, but Regina refuses to," Cupid smiles.

Regina rolls her eyes once more. "You know," she begins, but she is cut off as the elevator doors ping open again and Bill and Tom come spilling out, both out of breath and the former extremely sweaty.

"Sorry I'm late," Tom exclaims, waddling toward his peers. "I had a Thanksgiving emergency to deal with! Can you believe the mortals have invented something called turducken? It's a deboned chicken stuffed into a deboned duck stuffed into a deboned turkey!" He clucks disapprovingly. "How dare they! How dare they soil perfectly good turkeys with those other filthy birds! It's an insult to turkeys everywhere! This will not stand! We're the only birds that are supposed to be eaten on the most sacred of days."

"Maybe we should just eat him this year then," the Boogeyman leans toward Cupid, hissing in an undertone. "So we don't have to listen to any more of his crap for the next half a millennia."

"I'll drink to that," Cupid replies, pulling a flask from inside of his Armani blazer and taking a long swig from it.

"Did we miss anything?" Tom asks, settling into an empty chair between Tilly and Ted.

"We were just about to get started," Regina replies, slightly annoyed, before turning toward Bill. "What's your excuse, stink breath?"

"Ha, a teeth joke, how clever," Bill replies, pushing his glasses farther up the bridge of his nose as he steps up beside the Tooth Fairy, cradling a large, rolled up piece of paper in his arms. "I was just finishing this banner!"

And with a flourish, Bill unrolls it in the center of the circle, revealing the word 'Surpise!' sloppily painted in large green letters.

"What the heck is that?" Regina asks.

"It's a banner!" Bill exclaims brightly. "For Cormac!"

"I don't think that *surprise* was the word you were looking for," Ted points out kindly.

"Neither was *surpise*." the Boogeyman grins maliciously.

"Wait, what?" Bill glances at the banner and, noticing he misspelled the word, sighs with heavy disappointment. "Oh man, I worked for five hours on that."

"Why do we need a banner at all?" Mrs. Claus asks, confused.

"To make Cormac feel better about the intervention," Bill replies. "It'll make him relax a bit!"

"At the very least it'll test his spelling skills," Cupid smirks.

"Um…" Francis raises a hand timidly. "An intervention? I thought we were here to celebrate St. Patrick's Day! I wore my favorite green bow tie and everything!"

"Damn it, Francis," Regina rolls her eyes. "That's not why we're here! Didn't you get my memo?"

"I didn't get *any* memo," Francis replies defensively, his whiskers quivering. "Mother Nature just grabbed me on her way up!"

"I knew I shouldn't have trusted those two tutued twits," grumbles Regina, trying to remain calm.

"I have a question," Jack Frost raises his hand, balancing his chair on two legs. "Why do we have to be here if Cormac's not even here yet? I could be--"

"Not doing your job?" Father Time spits, trying to restrain Caleb on his knee. "But that *is* an excellent question, I'll admit."

"Father, I'm thirsty," Baby New Year whines. "I want juice!"

"And I want Damien back as Baby New Year," Father Time replies bitterly. "He knew how to be seen, but not heard. Would you let go of my robes? They're ancient, you know! And not replaceable! Unlike *you*."

"Don't mind your father, dear," Mother Nature says loftily. "He's an old curmudgeon. Doesn't care much for anybody – even somebody he's been *friends* with since the *dawn of time*."

"Are we still on this?" Father Time groans.

"I've known you since we were saplings!" Mother Nature shouts. "And now because of *you* I'm stuck running a coffee cart in the lobby!"

"Oh dear," Tilly mutters, shaking her antlered head. "I hate confrontation."

"I guess even Canadians have to hate something," Jack Frost snorts. "You're the only one who never complains about the lunch menu."

"What *is* for lunch this week, anyway?" Santa interjects, patting his belly.

"I think we all need to remember that we're here for Cormac's benefit today," Ted speaks up, nervously combing his fur with his paws. "Not to fight."

"Excellent point, Ted," Regina says brightly. "Thank you! Bill, get rid of that thing," she snaps decisively, waving at the banner on the floor.

Hanging his head, Bill gets on his hands and knees and begins to sadly roll up his precious banner as Regina snaps her fingers and pulls a long pink and silver wand from thin air.

"Right then. Let's get started." Slapping the easel with her wand, the word 'Intervention' appears instantaneously on the blank notebook page. The Boogeyman and Cupid exchange a wary look as the Tooth Fairy launches into her presentation. "*Webster's Dictionary* defines intervention…"

☘ ☘ ☘ ☘ ☘

Down in the conference room, Pia and Tuss are leaning close to the speakerphone in the center of the table, listening to the clipped, cool voice emanating from it.

"I understand that you both have your own ways of dealing with personnel, but we can't fire Cormac. You know this."

Pia, who is drumming her pencil on the table in annoyance, speaks up. "I'm not talking about firing him," she says, forcing patience into her voice. "But we can't just let him get away with slacking off three hundred and sixty-four days a--"

"Lyra," the voice interrupts firmly.

"Pia," Pia corrects, glaring at Tuss as he stifles a giggle.

"St. Patrick's Day is right about level with Easter and Valentine's Day as far as relevance based on profit," the voice explains. "Right after Christmas and Halloween. In fact, Cormac probably scrapes in a tiny bit more for his holiday than Cupid or the Easter Bunny do for theirs! In liquor alone," the voice adds. "Then once you throw in all of the campy green decorations…"

Pia stares across the table at Tuss pointedly, who sighs in resignation before speaking up himself.

"So what's protocol on this?" he asks. "What do you want us to do?"

"When the fucking midget even decides to show up," Pia mutters under her breath, so low that even Tuss can barely hear her.

"We want you to deal with it, Tuss. *Alone*."

"Excuse me?" Pia demands, snapping her pencil as Tuss blinks in surprise.

"We need to keep Cormac happy,' the voice explains calmly.

"But--"

"You're hotheaded," the voice interrupts her. "I'm sure you're great at what you do, Mia--"

"Pia."

"But we want Tuss to take the lead on this one. He's talented. He knows how to deal with subordinates, if not his equals." Tuss shifts uncomfortably at the statement. "I'm sorry, Tia--"

"*Pia.*"

"That's my final word on the matter."

And before either Pia or Tuss can say anything more, the line goes dead as the person on the other end of the line hangs up on them.

"Can you believe this fucking shit?" Pia exclaims angrily. "The damn leprechaun's escaping trouble and they're letting *you* take the lead? *You?* You can't even keep your *hair* in line!"

"I can handle it," Tuss says as he stands up, casually running a hand through his tousled hair. "It's not rocket science."

"I'm surprised you can even handle getting ready in the morning without any help from your mommy," Pia continues bitterly, getting to her feet. "This is bullshit! If I were running Corporate--"

———

"That's never going to happen," Tuss interrupts quickly.

"Maybe not, but if I *did*, all of these worthless employees would take their jobs a lot more seriously."

"Or choose to quit."

"Don't be ridiculous. They can't quit! Not unless they want to--"

"I'd want to. What?" he asks defensively in response to Pia's annoyed look. "I'm just saying--"

"Save it for the fucking leprechaun." Pia crosses her arms across her chest as she jerks her head at the conference room door. "Let's go see if the dumbass munchkin is even here yet. I can't wait to see you crash and burn. Too bad there isn't time to make popcorn."

As she makes her way toward the door, Tuss glances nervously at the clock. The conference call was a lot shorter than expected – he doubts that the planned intervention for Cormac is even close to being over yet. If it has even started at all, that is; who knew if the leprechaun had even shown up for work yet? When Regina had come to him earlier in the day with the plan she and the other holiday heads had for throwing the intervention, Tuss agreed immediately to keep Pia distracted for as long as he could during it. After all, who would ever want her at an event so sensitive? He had expected their conference call to take up the majority of the time, but now it looks as though he has to improvise to keep her away (and to keep impressing the lovely Tooth Fairy).

"Uh, Pia, wait!" Tuss calls out urgently.

"What is it?" She stops dead in her tracks and turns to face her partner right before she's about to walk out of the room.

"Let's not go down there yet," Tuss says brightly, sitting back down in one of the chairs at the table.

"Why the hell not?" Pia demands.

"Because…because…" Tuss takes a deep breath and plunges on

through gritted teeth. "I could use a bit of help coming up with what to say to Cormac."

"And why should I help you when I'm so looking forward to seeing you fail, *Mr. Talented*?"

"Because I think…you're – uh – *better*," he swallows hard, a bitter taste in his mouth at the word. "At this sort of stuff than I am. No matter what Corporate thinks. They don't know what they're talking about," he adds as an afterthought, knowing how to stroke her ego.

Pia considers him for a moment before smiling widely and taking a seat at the conference table again. "Of course I am," she says forcefully. "I'm glad you're finally fucking admitting it. Though if I were you, I'd latch onto that compliment from Corporate and use it as a ladder to climb up in the company."

"I don't want to climb up in the company," Tuss says quickly. "I'm happy where I am right now."

"Then you're an even bigger idiot than I thought you were," Pia notes.

And Tuss, knowing he's going to regret this, settles in and prepares himself to be berated.

✼ ✼ ✼ ✼ ✼

"And remember." The Tooth Fairy takes a deep breath as she points with her wand to a large piece of paper labeled 'Step 14' now propped up on the easel. "Anyone can be an addict, including any of us, so let's try to be sympathetic when talking to Cormac, alright?"

"I have a question." The Boogeyman raises his hand, trying to stifle a smirk at Francis diligently taking notes. "Where did you get this information?"

"Santa found it for me," Regina answers, pointing her wand at the fat man in the red suit.

"And Wally found it for me," Santa replies jovially. "On some website called...uh..." He digs around in his pocket and pulls out a piece of crumpled paper. "wikiHOW."

"Wikipedia?" Tilly asks, confused.

"What the hell is Wikipedia?" Father Time asks, trying to hold Caleb in place as he squirms restlessly in his lap.

"An offset of Wikipedia," Mrs. Claus clarifies.

"Because that makes it *so* much better," Cupid grins.

"It *is* better." Santa nods, not sensing the sarcasm in Cupid's voice. "Anybody, anywhere in the world can edit any page so you *know* you're getting the best possible information available."

"Not *any* page," Tom clucks. "Nobody can edit the page on Santa Claus unless they're a premium member, and even then it's monitored for accuracy." He pauses awkwardly, his eyes darting around the room. "Not that I've tried."

"Can we get back on topic please?" Regina asks, exasperated, just as the elevator doors ping open again. "Ugh, now what?"

Hugh and Hugo fly into the room, shoving one another through the air, arguing in their deep voices. Judging from the state of their ripped tutus, they've been fighting for a while.

"I want to go."

"No, I do! It's my turn!"

"You're on secretary duty this week!"

"It's not fair, the last time a celebrity lost a tooth--"

"Would you both shut up and explain to me why you're interrupting our meeting?" Regina snaps loudly, bringing the two pixies to a fluttering halt in midair in front of her. As they both begin to speak over one another, she rolls her eyes. "You." She points at Hugo. "Speak."

"Betty White lost a tooth."

"She's over ninety-fucking-years-old, she should have lost them all by now," Cupid says.

"One of her adult teeth," Regina explains with a loud sigh. "It happens to most people her age, jackass. This is good news," she addresses her employees again. "Celebrity teeth bring in more money. Why are you fighting about it?"

"Because it's my turn to collect!" Hugo whines. "When Clint Eastwood lost one a few weeks ago, Hugh got to go and get it."

"It's not my fault that celebrities tend to lose their teeth on my weeks," Hugh smirks smugly.

"Seriously?" Regina asks, an eyebrow raised. "Honestly, just because you're *dressed* like little girls, doesn't mean you have to *act* like little girls."

"We only dress this way because you make us," Hugh replies automatically, realizing instantly it was the wrong thing to say.

"Exactly! I'm your boss, don't ever forget it!" Regina snaps as she swats them away like flies. "Hugh, you're on secretary duty for the next month."

"But--"

"No *buts*!" Regina cuts across him. "Hugo, you're on collection duty. Starting now. Go get Betty White's tooth."

"Yes!"

"Now get out of my sight."

"But Regina - I mean, Tooth Fairy," Hugh stutters.

———

"*Out!*" Regina yells.

Hugh and Hugo flutter away quickly, not wanting to incur her wrath, and disappear into the elevator, shoving one another as they continue to argue in low voices. The minute the doors close on them, Regina turns to the room at large again.

"Sorry about that. Where were we?"

"*We* were just leaving," Father Time states as he climbs to his feet, throwing Caleb under one arm with more strength than one would think possible for someone his age.

"But Cormac's not here yet!"

"He'll probably never be here," Cupid says, taking another long swig from his flask.

"Seriously?" Mother Nature eyes him. "Alcohol at an intervention being thrown for an alcoholic?"

"I'm not the one who has the drinking problem," Cupid replies with a shrug.

"Father, I'm thirsty!" Caleb whines as Father Time carries him toward the elevators. "I want juice! Make Cupid share his juice with me!"

"I'd be happy to," Cupid smiles, holding out his flask.

"No one can leave yet!" Regina yells, stamping her foot hard on the ground. "Cormac will be here any moment--"

"Don't hold your breath," the Boogeyman mutters.

"And I thought we could role-play a bit before he gets here. You know, practice what we're going to say."

"Role-play? I love role-play," Cupid pipes up eagerly.

"Good," Regina smirks. "You can be Cormac."

"Impossible," Cupid replies. "I never get the whiskey dick."

"You're playing Cormac," Regina says with an air of finality. "Father Time - sit back down, you're not going anywhere."

"Who died and made you boss?" Father Time grumbles, dragging Caleb back to the circle and sitting down with a huff.

"Unfortunately not you," Mother Nature spits.

"Everyone, please," Santa raises his voice slightly. "Let's all wind up on the nice list this year by giving Regina our full attention."

"Thank you, Santa." Regina flashes the old man her perfect smile. "Now, Francis - ugh, what are you doing?" she asks Cupid, as he takes another swig from his flask.

"Getting into character."

"Cormac's not going to be drunk at his own intervention," Regina insists.

"Wanna bet?" Cupid raises his eyebrow. "I'll bet a night of hot, steamy, passionate sex with you that he's going to show up drunk and pee in the corner like one of those obnoxious turkeys."

"I'd rather kill myself," Regina decides, as Tom makes a noise of outrage.

"Well then, if you're going to force me to be here," Cupid says with the air of explaining something simple to a five-year-old. "Shut up and let me play the part my way."

"Can I play Cupid since he's playing Cormac?" Ted requests a bit too eagerly, raising a paw into the air.

"Do you realize how sad that sounds?" the Boogeyman smirks.

"Why can't we all just be ourselves?" Mrs. Claus asks, confused.

"We *can* be," Regina replies, fighting to keep a note of patience in her tone of voice. "Except for Cupid, who's going to pretend he's Cormac."

Behind the Boogeyman, his Shadow stretches out and forms its hand into the shape of a handgun, which it points at its head before pulling the trigger, causing little bits of Shadow to go flying around the room.

"My thoughts exactly," the Boogeyman mutters.

"Dude, *nice*," Jack Frost exclaims, holding up a hand to high-five the Boogeyman who merely stares at it in disgust.

"By nice do you mean morbid?" Tom asks.

"You're one to talk," Jack replies. "We've all seen the murals."

"Would everyone shut the hell up for one minute *please*?" Regina demands loudly, setting firecrackers off in the air with her wand to bring attention to the group once more.

As everyone settles down, T.J. ruffles his feathers in an annoyed fashion and Tilly trembles nervously.

"Oh dear," she mutters. "I hate loud noises."

"Wow, a Canadian admitting they hate two things in one day," Jack says in mock-amazement. "It's a new record! Next thing you know you'll be admitting you hate hockey!"

Tilly gasps in horror as Regina rolls her eyes. "Shut up! Both of you! *Now*," She rounds on the Easter Bunny, whose large ears are covering his wide eyes in fright. "Francis. When Cormac comes in, after we explain to him why we're doing this and how it's in his best interest, you can start by telling him how his drinking has negatively affected you in the past. So...go."

She motions at Cupid, who takes another long swig from his flask as the Easter Bunny stares at him, his mouth slightly open. "Uh…"

"Role-playing?" Pia spits at Tuss. "Why the hell would I role-play with you? That sounds like the kind of sick shit that Cupid would suggest."

"Just to make sure I've absorbed everything you've told me," Tuss suggests wildly. "I need to make sure I can reply to anything that Cormac throws at me on the fly."

"You also need to make sure you actually talk to the moronic leprechaun before he leaves for the year. You know that, right?"

"I know, just - just humor me." Tuss smiles at his colleague, throwing the clock on the wall a quick glance, trying to figure out how much longer he has to keep her distracted for.

"I've been humoring you for the last hour! Do you need me to draw you a fucking picture?"

"That would be great, actually! Do you need a pen?"

✤ ✤ ✤ ✤ ✤

"I honestly think you're a great guy, Cupi-Cormac," Francis says awkwardly.

"Do you really, Franny?" Cupid asks.

The Easter Bunny blinks, confused, before looking around the circle for help. When no one comes to his aid, he asks, "Are you – are you asking me as Cormac or as Cupid?"

"As myself," Cupid smirks.

"You're supposed to be Cormac," Regina points out.

"I'm genuinely curious!" Cupid shrugs. "I've never met anyone who likes the guy besides me."

"You only like him because you're both creeps," Jack Frost points out.

"Doesn't change the fact that I like him," Cupid replies with a small shrug as he takes another sip from his flask.

"Could you take this seriously, please?" Regina asks, annoyed. "He's going to be here any minute--"

"Let's hope so," Mother Nature cuts across her. "I'm getting tired. And who knows how much longer Tuss can keep Pia distracted for."

"I'd keep her distracted for a long time," Cupid says wistfully. "Over, and over, and over again."

"Oh Cupid, would you stop? She's such a nice girl," Mrs. Claus scolds before leaning in close to her husband and whispering, twirling her hair. "Maybe you should take some lessons from him, Nicky."

"If by *nice* you mean practically a born again virgin, then I'd have to agree with you," Cupid states.

"Ted, why don't you take a turn?" Regina turns to the groundhog pointedly, giving him an encouraging smile. "Say something to Cupid and he'll reply as Cormac *if he values his molars at all.*"

"Uh...okay." Ted clears his throat, sitting up straight in his chair. "Cormac. We've always been great friends--"

"Have we?" Cupid asks in a thick Irish brogue that causes chuckles around the circle, before drinking deeply from his flask.

"I like to think we have," Ted replies, disheartened. "And I feel like your drinking problem is causing a rift in our friendship."

"Eh, who cares?" Cupid slurs his words, causing Regina to eye him closely, trying to figure out whether or not he's acting. "I never really wanted to be friends with a rat anyway."

"Groundhog," Ted corrects sadly, hanging his head.

99

"Cupid!" Regina widens her eyes.

"So I'm back to being *myself* now?" Cupid exclaims. "This is very confusing."

"You know he's sensitive," the Tooth Fairy speaks through gritted teeth, jerking her head at the groundhog.

"Hey, Ted, buddy," Cupid drops the Irish accent. "I'm just joking with you, you know that, right? Remember what we talked about?"

Ted nods and takes a bottle of pills labeled with a giant smiling face from his pocket. As he throws three uppers into his mouth, Cupid smiles to himself and takes a swig of whatever alcohol is inside of his flask.

"Cupid," Regina starts like a stern mother.

"What?" he asks, innocently. "This is my own version of happy pills!" He waves his flask through the air.

"I think Ted needs his own intervention for popping so many pills," Tom notes. "And Santa needs one for being a fatass."

Before the Tooth Fairy can respond, the elevator doors ping open once again. Holly and Wally step out, staring around as they make their way toward Santa.

"Ugh, another interruption. We're never going to get through this!" Regina throws up her hands in defeat.

"Is everything okay?" Santa asks his elves, concerned. "How's the workshop? Did you finally get those toy dogs to stop yapping? We don't want any complaints from parents this year. Not after the *My Pet Bigfoot* fiasco."

"Yes, everything's fine," Wally assures him. "Frank's down there right now keeping an eye on things."

"Ah, excellent!" Santa booms. "Remind me, which one is Frank

---

again?"

Wally and Holly exchange a look as the Boogeyman rolls his eyes.

"The...uh..." Wally clears his throat. "The intern you hired at the beginning of the year?"

"Oh, right, right, right, right, right," Santa nods. "I remember. Good work."

"We've been looking for you," Wally continues. "We tried the St. Patrick's Day floor, but--"

"We couldn't have the intervention down there," Regina explains. "Too disgusting. *Jackass* Frost over here still needs to get around to cleaning it up."

"I'm not paid nearly enough to clean up literal piles of shit," Jack Frost replies defensively.

"Holly, make a note to get Frank in there at some point and clean it up, would you?" Santa asks. As the elf nods her head and scribbles a note on her notepad, Santa smiles at his circle of colleagues. "He loves cleaning."

Wally and Holly exchange an amused look, before Wally continues. "Anyway, like I was saying, we looked everywhere for you--"

"Have you turned on the TV?" Tom asks, sarcasm dripping from his voice. "It's already March! Shouldn't this year's Christmas commercials start airing soon?"

"Here we go," the Boogeyman sighs, exasperated. "How many times do we have to listen to this rant?"

"December!" Tom clucks. "Not November! *December!* But what happens the day after Halloween?"

"The radio starts playing Christmas music," the entire circle drones.

"Shut the fuck up, Tom. We're already suffering enough sitting through this meeting," Jack Frost snaps.

"Anyway," Holly says, leaning toward Santa with her clipboard, gently brushing a strand of dark hair away from her elegant face. "I just need your signature really quickly, and then we'll be out of your hair--"

"You know, you two are actually just in time!" Santa says jovially. "We were just going around the circle telling Cormac how his drinking negatively impacts all of us. Why don't you have a go?"

As he motions at Cupid, whose cheeks are turning bright red from drinking so much, Holly raises an eyebrow before asking, "You uh…you know that's Cupid, right?"

"Ho, ho, ho, it's called *role-playing*, my dear," Santa winks at her. "Go on then, show the rest of us how it's done."

"What?" Holly asks, as every eye turns to her expectantly. "Uh…" She leans closer to Santa and whispers. "You know, I just – uh – I just really need your signature. That's all I came for."

"Not until you say something to Cormac," Santa says, his voice resolute.

Holly, embarrassed, straightens up and clears her throat as she locks eyes with Cupid. "I don't uh…" she stammers. "I don't really know you that well, but I think your drinking causes a lot more unnecessary work for all of us. You've disrupted the workshop on more than one occasion, especially the time you relieved yourself in the apple cider…and due to your short stature and green clothes, a lot of mortals probably confuse you for an elf so…you're giving my whole race a bad name. Also, my eyes are up here, please," she adds sternly.

Cupid, who is staring at her breasts, replies, "I know," without meeting them, as Wally looks on angrily.

Fuming, Holly crosses her arms across her ample chest and turns to Wally. "Why don't *you* take a turn?"

"Excellent idea, Holly!" Santa exclaims. "Go on, Wally," he urges. "We'd all love to hear what you have to say."

Wally looks sideways at Holly, who is trying to suppress an amused smile, before finding Cupid, who winks at him.

"I…uh…think that you make things a lot more complicated than they need to be," Wally stammers. "If you didn't drink as much, we wouldn't spend so much time cleaning up your messes. And you *are* pretty small. You look like an elf, so you're really ruining our reputation as well as your own, but you don't seem to care."

Santa blinks, confused, before looking up at Wally as Cupid claps an exasperated hand to his forehead.

"You're just repeating what Holly said," Santa says.

"I'm…uh…" Wally stammers, looking sideways at the elf of his dreams who is staring at him with a raised eyebrow.

"When I said to try personality mirroring, I didn't mean literally repeat every word that comes out of her mouth," Cupid mutters under his breath as the Boogeyman laughs in his usual creepy way.

"Okay then," Santa sighs, disappointed, as he grabs Holly's clipboard and signs his signature. "I'll see you two later."

As the two elves hurry back toward the elevator, Holly can distinctly be heard asking, "Personality mirroring? Really?"

"Just – don't," Wally mumbles as the doors close, obscuring them from view. Unfortunately the doors of the elevator adjacent to it open immediately, depositing yet another interruption.

"*Now* what?" Regina exclaims, pulling at her hair in frustration as Maxwell hurries out of the elevator, wringing his hands nervously as he approaches his boss.

"Master?"

"Not now, can't you see we're busy?" the Boogeyman hisses. He seems not to be looking at the vampire, but with his fully black eyes, no one can really tell for sure.

"But Master, it's urgent," Maxwell stammers with trepidation, licking his fangs. "The spiders are threatening to go on strike."

"*What?*" the Boogeyman demands.

"They say it's too cold up here for any insects besides themselves to live for very long. They claim they're starving," Maxwell explains. "They want--"

"They're going to want to talk to Pia and Tuss," the Boogeyman cuts him off. "They're up here to improve efficiencies, maybe they can do something about employee morale too. Why do *I* need to be bothered with this?"

"But--"

"Maxwell, please," the Boogeyman replies, rubbing his temples as his Shadow rises up threateningly behind him. "We're in the middle of a *very* tedious exercise here," he gestures around the room, ignoring the dirty look Regina is throwing at him. "Leave us alone so that we can get through it faster and I can be freed from this ridiculous waste of time. Thank you."

Maxwell hesitates for the briefest of moments as though he wants to argue with his boss, but after catching one glimpse of the Boogeyman's Shadow, which looks ready to pounce, he bows low and hurries back to the elevators.

"Well, this is turning out even *lamer* than I thought it would," Cupid comments nonchalantly, taking another swig from his flask as the vampire disappears behind the metal doors.

"*Enough* with the drinking!" Regina yells, snatching the flask out of Cupid's hands and throwing it to Father Time. He catches it and places it on his lap beside Caleb, who eyes it with excitement. "You're ruining everything!"

"I'm only trying to help, just like you wanted," Cupid replies sardonically. "I'm playing Cormac!"

"*Help*," Regina scoffs. "You're purposefully making things difficult. You don't know how to help anyone. You're the definition of selfish."

"Oh, really?" Cupid asks, raising an eyebrow, surprised to find that he's actually offended. "If I don't know how to help anyone, why did you ask me for advice on how to get Corporate to give you Mother Nature's old office?"

"You bitch!" Mother Nature exclaims. "I thought we were friends!"

"We are!" Regina insists, angry now that she's lost all control of her intervention seminar. "But you got fired! You got kicked out of it! No point in letting it go to waste. Anything to get me out of the sub-basement and away from tweedle-dee and tweedle-*dumbass* over there." She jerks her head at Bill and the still unconscious form of the Sandman, who's mumbling something about flapjacks in his sleep.

"I didn't know you were applying for the office too," Tilly says. "I guess I wasn't the only one then, eh?"

"I went for it too," Ted says awkwardly as he pops another three anti-depressants into his mouth. "I didn't think that anybody else would."

"Well, *I* obviously did," Bill says haughtily. "I'm more deserving of it than any of *you*."

"Right," Regina snorts. "In your dreams, Bill."

"And speaking of helping people," Bill continues. "Why do we want to help the drunk, anyway? He doesn't deserve his own holiday! He's putting us all at risk! I'd be happy to take over running it--"

"Are you going to joint market it with *Flag Day*?" Jack Frost laughs.

"Flag Day is extremely relevant!" Bill counters angrily. "All of my holidays are! And I'd run St. Patrick's Day like a well-oiled machine! We should just let Cormac crash and burn."

"We're not like *your* kind, Bill," Regina points out. "We don't like seeing people failing and burning."

"Speak for yourself," the Boogeyman smiles, bearing his shark-like teeth.

"Ugh, this whole thing is a disaster," Regina groans.

"I couldn't agree more," Father Time crankily agrees, as Caleb drinks from Cupid's flask on his lap, unnoticed by anyone.

Before the Tooth Fairy can even attempt to take some form of control over her meeting again, the elevator doors once again ping with a new arrival. But this time it's not elves, vampires or tiny men in tutus – it's turkeys. Six turkeys marching in matching step out of the elevator in a tightly packed two-by-two formation. There are multiple groans from the various holiday heads as soon as they are spotted, but their disappointment is drowned out , for when the gobbling birds spot their similarly feathered leader seated amongst the group, they all begin to speak at once.

"I hear this bird hybrid mixture actually tastes pretty good!"

"Are you having a party? I forgot my dancing shoes!"

"Mortals also have tofu turkeys! I don't even think that's meat!"

"You know what's a fun word to say? Mongolian!"

"I ordered some of the turkey hybrid for tasting!"

"I think it'll taste good! But maybe I'm just clueless!"

Tom blinks. "What? One at a time!"

"We won't have any to taste until May!"

"I hope my dancing shoes didn't get lost! How will I do my *Teach Yourself Salsa* lessons?"

___
106

"We also have platters of tofu turkeys on order!"

"Mongolian, Mongolian, Mongolian! So fun!"

"All this talk of other types of turkeys makes me angry."

"It has to taste better than haggis!"

"*What?*" Tom demands.

"You can talk later!" the Boogeyman snaps impatiently as his Shadow sweeps the turkeys back into the waiting elevator and slams the button to take them downstairs.

"Hey! That could have been important!" Tom protests.

"It'll be next St. Patrick's Day before you figure out what the hell they were talking about," the Boogeyman says through gritted teeth.

"Not true! Not true at all," Tom says, eyeing the Boogeyman's sharp teeth nervously. "There's just a lot of background noise in here, that's all! I normally understand them perfectly!"

"Look, I don't think Cormac's showing up anytime soon," Francis sighs wearily. "Maybe we should just go. I don't want to get in trouble from Corporate for being here when I should be downstairs preparing for Easter."

"We've been here for *hours*," Mother Nature throws her head back impatiently. "The day's almost over!"

"We can't just *leave*," Regina insists. "When Cormac *does* show up, we have to help him! We have to practice what we're going to say. If this *asshole* would just cooperate…" She motions at Cupid, who rolls his eyes.

"You want me to cooperate? Fine," Cupid says in a clipped voice as he stands up in the center of the circle and begins to address all of them in his fake Irish brogue. "I may drink a lot, lads, but is it really a problem if I'm still pulling in a higher profit than most of your holidays combined? Has it ever occurred to any of you that I drink so much because it's what the people want?"

"Is that actually why you do it?" Mrs. Claus asks, playing along.

"Fuck no!" Cupid replies, still in character. "But since you want to point out my character flaws, why don't we talk about some of *yours*, shall we?" He rounds on Regina. "Tooth Fairy! You're obsessed with teeth! *Teeth*! Do you realize how weird that is? Who cares how clean, or dirty, or perfectly shaped everybody else's are? Worry about your own!"

"I'll have you know my teeth are perfect," Regina replies as she flashes her perfectly white smile, offended. "And also, oral hygiene is very--"

"I don't care," Cupid replies. "*Because they're teeth*! You can always get dentures! You," he rounds on Santa. "You're a copious overeater and a giant pervert. You watch kids when they're sleeping for fuck's sake! Why? How naughty can a ten-year-old kid be in their sleep?"

"Preach!" Tom flaps his wings excitedly. "Finally somebody's speaking the truth!"

Mrs. Claus opens her mouth to defend her husband but Cupid shuts her up before she can.

"And don't you say a word, lady! You're an enabler. Why don't you try getting your husband a fucking treadmill as a gift this Christmas! Unless you think he's going to break it like he broke the stair climber in the gym! Tom," Cupid rounds on the turkey. "You're angry because Christmas always overshadows your holiday, but have you ever stopped and realized that it may be because your holiday glorifies a bunch of English people murdering Native Americans? Let go of the rage, my brother! And get some help for your cannibalistic thoughts – we all know you've tasted yourself!"

Tom's mouth drops at the statement, but before he can reply, Cupid turns to the bald eagle.

"T.J.!" Cupid barks. "You're the national symbol for the United States of America, *an English speaking country*, but you can't speak English yourself! You just squawk in some Spanish bird-like accent!"

"I'm so glad I'm not the only one who hears a hint of Spanish in there," Jack Frost mutters to the Boogeyman, who nods his agreement.

"It's bad enough that we have to press two for Spanish as it is, but you're going to have us pressing three for *eagle* soon enough!"

T.J. squawks loudly, outraged.

"What did he say?" Tom asks the room at large, but before Bill can translate for them, Cupid rounds on Tom once more.

"And another thing about you! YOU ARE A *BIRD*! LEARN THE LANGUAGE!"

"I'm a *turkey*, okay?" Tom demands. "Not an *eagle*. All birds do *not* speak the same language! How racist of you to assume that we do! I am sick and tired of--"

"I don't care," Cupid says before turning to Bill. "As for you, *Mr. Translator*, where the fuck do I begin? You're useless, you're pathetic, you're a self-obsessed loser who thinks he's as important as the people he surrounds himself with even though he's around the likes of fucking *Santa Claus and the Easter Bunny*! Also, you can't spell," he adds as an afterthought.

Bill, who looks as though he's about to cry, straightens his glasses and chokes, "With all due respect, I don't--"

"Ted, you're a pill popper," Cupid states as the groundhog throws another one into his mouth. "And your pen pal is a freak of nature!"

"Takes one to know one," Ted laughs feebly, fishing around inside of his near-empty pill bottle for another small capsule to pop into his mouth.

"Tilly, you're impossibly happy all the time. You must have so much rage bottled up, you're going to literally *explode* one day if you don't let it out!"

"I politely disagree," Tilly shrugs her broad shoulders. "I really am just this happy."

"Sandman!" Cupid snaps, rounding on the old man who is still snoring in his seat. He considers him for a moment before muttering, "Why waste my time? Jack!" He rounds on Jack Frost. "Stop telling me to *chillax*, okay? You're the only one who thinks it's funny! *And* everybody always complains about what you serve for lunch because your cooking sucks! Not to mention, just because you have the body of a teenager doesn't mean you have to be as lazy as one! Start doing your job and keeping this place clean!"

"*Chillax*, man. I'll think about it," Jack Frost winks, leaning back casually in his chair.

"Francis," Cupid turns toward the Easter Bunny who is trembling nervously in his seat. "How many wives and kids do you have around the world? You're a borderline deadbeat dad and husband – spend more time with them! How often do you see them? If you don't want them in your life, stop being such a nymphomaniac and having more kids!"

The Easter Bunny covers his eyes with his ears and shakes his head back and forth, muttering, "I'm not listening, I'm not listening, I'm not listening."

"Mother Nature," Cupid rounds on the old woman. "This isn't the sixties anymore, you fucking hippy! You need to learn to trim your bush!"

"But what's wrong with letting my plants grow out?" Mother Nature asks, her brow furrowed as the Boogeyman shakes his head and Jack Frost laughs.

"Boogeyman!" He rounds on the pale figure and stares into his black eyes. "You're grotesque, you invade peoples' dreams, you - what *isn't* wrong with you?"

"A fair question," the Boogeyman replies as his Shadow looms over him protectively.

"And *you*," Cupid turns to Father Time. "You're O.C.D. about *time* of all things! *Time*! I mean, if somebody's a minute early or a minute late, they'll never hear the end of it! Some people have actual lives and don't sit around staring at a clock all day! *And* you bring your *kid* to an intervention!"

"Pia has the fates taking inventory of the stockroom," Father Time replies defensively.

"That doesn't excuse the fact that you let your *kid* get *drunk* at an *intervention*!"

"*What?*" Father Time exclaims, staring down at Caleb who is swaying back and forth giggling on his lap. His face is beat red, his eyes droopy and the scent of alcohol is covering his entire body. "Caleb!"

"Father, I want more juice," Caleb burps, slurring his words as he waves Cupid's now empty flask through the air.

"Great," Father Time groans. "Thanks for that," he snaps at Cupid.

"Typical parent," Cupid replies. "Blaming everybody else for your failure in raising your child. But you're not even the worst of us! Cupid is! Who, me?" Cupid asks himself in his normal accent now, jumping to the side and staring at the empty space where he stood just a second ago. "Yes, you!" he says, jumping back to his previous spot and donning the fake brogue again. "You'll fuck anything with a pulse! *Anything!* Man, woman, animal. What's your record for people fucked in one day? Thirty-six? That is disgusting, sir!" He jumps back again, using his regular voice once more. "Why, yes! But orgies were very popular in those days!" Donning the accent again, he continues. "You don't give a shit about anyone but yourself half the time, and you can't take anything fucking seriously!" Using his regular voice, he replies. "How dare you, sir! That is uncalled for!" He jumps back to his original spot, donning the accent one final time as everybody in the circle watches, confused. "It's true! We all have our problems! But who cares? Nobody's perfect! So I like to drink, big deal? We need to do what makes us happy in life!"

"Hear, hear!" Ted agrees in a daze, falling from his chair and throwing another anti-depressant into his mouth.

"And....*scene*." Cupid bows, out of breath, his voice normal once more.

Everybody stares open-mouthed at the exceedingly handsome man for a moment, before the Boogeyman and his Shadow begin to sarcastically applaud him, with Jack Frost and Ted joining in enthusiastically. Regina stares at Cupid for a moment before clasping a hand to her face and shaking her head.

🍀 🍀 🍀 🍀 🍀

"Enough wasting time," Pia says angrily as she stands up once more. "If you still don't know what to say to the leprechaun, then you're beyond help. Let's go deal with this shithead!"

As she storms toward the door, Tuss jumps up, panicked. Throwing caution to the wind, he yells the first thing that he can think of to distract the woman. "I'm in love with you!"

Pia comes to a complete standstill and whips around disgusted, at a loss for words. She stares at Tuss who appears as though he has just swallowed a lemon.

"I didn't want to admit it to anyone at first, even to myself, but the truth is," he starts, stepping closer to her. "Being forced to work so closely with you, it's made me realize how fucking amazing you are and how *crazy* I feel about you. The things I think when we're around one another – the things I want to say to you and do to you...I can barely control myself sometimes." He shakes his head, trembling now that their faces are inches apart. "You're gorgeous...smart...funny...I love you, Pia. I say, let's forget about the fucking degenerate midget for a few minutes because I just want to throw you over this table and...and..." As he stares into her eyes, he bites his lips and shakes his head, backing up quickly. "Nope. No. Absolutely not." He lets out a long sigh. "Not worth it. Can't do it."

"What the *fuck* are you talking about?" Pia asks, breathless.

"I'm not in love with you or sexually attracted to you in any way."

"Thank *fuck* for that!" Pia exclaims, letting out her own sigh of relief. "I would have either had to kill myself or you – probably you, as I'm actually *important* to this whole operation."

Tuss laughs as Pia's eyes darken.

"Why are you wasting my time with shit like that? Trying to be *funny*?"

"I was uh…" he glances at the clock, out of excuses. "Well, I *have* been stalling for a few hours."

"What the fuck are you talking about?"

"I was trying to distract you," Tuss admits guiltily. "The holiday heads wanted to have an intervention for Cormac, and they asked me to keep you busy so you wouldn't interrupt them."

"They *what*?"

The room shakes as Pia explodes with anger, causing Tuss to stumble backwards a few steps.

"Now, don't be angry at me," Tuss says hurriedly. "You can't really blame them for not wanting you around for something like that – you're not exactly good in certain situations like--"

Pia lets out a strangled yell that makes the lights overhead flicker, before storming out of the room in a huff. Tuss gives her a head start of about two minutes before hurrying after her.

"She might kill them. She's *actually* might kill them."

☘ ☘ ☘ ☘ ☘

The holiday heads sit around the twelfth floor in silence, avoiding one another's eyes. Finally, Francis looks at his watch. "St. Patrick's Day just ended five minutes ago," he says.

"Five *minutes* ago?" Father Time demands. "Are you sure it wasn't five *hours* ago? It feels like we've been sitting here forever!" He rolls up his sleeve and glances at his arm, which has ten wristwatches wrapped around it. "According to one of my watches it *was* five hours ago!"

"I think it's official - Cormac's definitely not going to show up," Francis continues somberly.

"I don't get it," Regina laughs humorlessly. "He should have been in today of all days at the very least." She sighs. "I just wanted to try and help him."

"Maybe we can help him some other way," Santa suggests. "Maybe we should just institute a rule making St. Patrick's Day an alcohol free holiday?"

Santa's suggestion is met by loud groans from the room.

"You can't be serious?" The Boogeyman lets out a derisive laugh. "All because of one alcoholic leprechaun, you want to ban booze from the entire holiday? See how much money we lose when *that* happens. Corporate would never--"

"Cormac!"

The elevator doors ping open, and everybody braces themselves for more turkeys before realizing it's Pia rushing toward the circle, red in the face, causing the ground to shake beneath them.

They all would have preferred the turkeys.

"Bloody hell, calm down woman," the Boogeyman says. "You're going to give yourself a heart attack."

"I don't have a heart!" Pia snaps. "Where's Cormac?"

"He never showed up," Ted replies hazily from where he is shaking on the ground, trying in vain to shove another anti-depressant into his mouth as Tilly looks down at him with concern.

"What the *fuck* is wrong with you?" Pia spits at the groundhog before shaking her head. "It doesn't matter. Of *course* Cormac didn't show up. He doesn't show up for work on his own holiday, why would he show up for a *fucking* intervention?" She spins around, noticing the Easter Bunny. "What the hell are you doing here, *Watership Down*? Easter's right around the corner! You should be working overtime, not taking extended breaks to indulge the rest of these pathetic losers!"

Francis, terrified, covers his eyes with his ears and mutters a hasty apology. Beside him, Bill breathes in and out deeply.

"Go to your happy place," he mutters to himself. "Happy place."

"*You*! You pathetic waste of space! You are worth nothing to this company! Do you understand that? *Nothing*! Next time something like this happens again and you're involved, you either inform me or you're fucking fired!"

"Y-yes, sir. Uh, ma'am. Sir ma'am. Just ma'am, I meant ma'am," Bill stammers.

"What's all the noise about?" the Sandman groans from his seat, keeping his eyes resolutely shut tight. "I'm exhausted! Some of us are trying to sleep here, you know! I only got twenty-three hours last night!"

"That's all you do, you lazy lump of crap!" Pia yells, spinning around in the center of the circle. "Whose bright idea was it to throw this fucking intervention?"

"Regina's," Mother Nature points out quickly.

"Mother Nature!" Regina widens her eyes, annoyed.

"Shouldn't be going for my office, bitch."

"Of course it was," Pia snaps, rounding on the Tooth Fairy. "You little--"

"Pia!"

115

Pia spins around as the elevator doors ping open again to reveal Tuss, who emerges confidently and hurries toward the group. At the sight of him, Regina's relieved heart skips a beat.

"What the hell do *you* want, Benedict Arnold?"

"To show you the final numbers for St. Patrick's Day," Tuss says calmly, waving a piece of paper in her face. "It was our highest grossing one yet."

"Let me see that," Pia demands, snatching the piece of paper from Tuss and reading it quickly. "Impossible! The fucking midget didn't even show up for work today! How could he get numbers like *this*?"

"I guess alcohol sells with or without his help," Tuss shrugs. "The holiday's as big as ever! He must do promoting year round that we don't know about." He pauses for a moment before conceding. "Or maybe the holiday just about runs itself."

"Hear that?" Jack Frost asks Santa. "Alcohol sells. Honestly, suggesting that we ban booze from the holiday--"

"What moron suggested that stupid idea?" Pia asks, looking up immediately.

"That would be me," Santa replies coolly.

"Oh! Santa!" Pia says, the anger gone from her voice as her face turns pink with embarrassment. "I didn't even see you there."

"How could you? You were too busy storming in and belittling people to take notice of your surroundings."

"Ah, yes, about that--" Pia begins, but Santa cuts her off.

"Getting mad at us for trying to help our friend?"

"I wouldn't exactly call him a friend," Tom points out.

"Santa, you have to understand the position I'm in," Pia laughs nervously, but Santa cuts her off.

"St. Patrick's Day is officially over, Pia," Santa states. "And I just realized I didn't even have one drink to celebrate the occasion. If anyone wants to join me, I'm going down to the Decked Halls Pub in the village for a pint!"

Murmurs of approval break out amongst the various figures standing around the room, and they all slowly begin to make their way toward the elevators, talking amongst themselves.

"Five minutes ago he wanted to ban booze from the holiday," Jack Frost mutters, shaking his head with a small smile. "Talk about going senile."

"That sounds like a great idea!" Pia calls after Santa. "I'll meet you down there!" The minute he's out of earshot, she rounds on Tuss, punching him hard in the shoulder. "What the fuck?"

"What the fuck was *that* for?" Tuss demands, rubbing his shoulder.

"The leprechaun didn't show up for work!" Pia snaps. "How did he pull it off?"

"Beats me," Tuss shrugs.

"Well, congratulations," Pia sneers. "You didn't have to play bad cop after all and you'll *still* get praised by Corporate."

"That's the last thing I want," Tuss says grimly. "But I think congratulations are in order for *you*." He smiles. "You're going to a bar tonight for the first time in years!"

"Go fuck yourself."

"You're very pretty, lady."

Tuss and Pia look down, surprised to see Caleb staring up at Pia, bleary-eyed, swaying on the spot unsteadily.

"Are you *drunk*?" Pia demands, staring from Tuss to Father Time, who hurries over quickly. "Is this kid fucking *drunk*?"

"Not my fault," Father Time insists as he picks the kid up off the floor. "If you want to blame anyone, blame Cupid."

As he carries Caleb toward the elevators, Pia follows after them.

"I should have known that something as sick as a drunk child could be attributed to you," Pia says as Cupid hurries to catch up with her.

"You have never been more attractive to me than you were just now," Cupid remarks. "Yelling at us? Berating us? I love a woman with a filthy mouth."

"Oh, go blow yourself."

"Why would I do that when I'm pretty sure you want do it for me?"

"What the hell happened here?" she demands, smelling the alcohol on Cupid's breath. "Is *everybody* drunk?"

"Not everybody," Cupid answers. "But I'm pretty sure Ted is high."

They glance over to where Ted is still lying on the floor, his pill bottle clutched tight to his chest. Hovering above him, Tilly keeps asking, "Are you alright? Ted? Are you okay? I'm really worried about you!"

Rolling her eyes, Pia storms away with Cupid following close behind. Tuss laughs as he watches their retreating backs.

"I thought you were going to keep her distracted?"

Tuss turns around to see the Tooth Fairy standing behind him, smiling wide with an eyebrow raised.

"I did my best," he says, as the remaining holiday file past them. "How did the - uh – *non-intervention* go?"

"As you'd probably expect," Regina laughs. "I'm glad you showed up when you did. I'm pretty sure Pia was ready to punch me in the face for organizing it."

"I have good timing," he replies, rubbing the spot where Pia just punched him.

"I bet."

Tuss laughs as he places his hand on the small of Regina's back and begins to guide her toward the elevators.

"Come on. Let's go get a drink."

"Sounds good to me," Regina sighs. "I could use a nice stiff one."

Tuss smirks as they step into an empty elevator. "I bet you could."

✿ ✿ ✿ ✿ ✿

Pia stares up at the green and red lettering of the Decked Halls sign hanging over the bar door and mentally steels herself before going in – she hates social interaction. The place looks tacky on the outside, but it is even worse than she imagined on the inside. Brightly lit with Christmas lights, Christmas songs blaring overhead, elves everywhere - Santa and the Boogeyman are laughing at a joke Francis is telling, while Regina and Tuss are standing close at the crowded bar watching as Cupid shamelessly hits on the bartender. Pia considers walking out before any of the holiday heads, enjoying one another's company, spot her, when she catches movement in the corner of her eye.

Turning around, she sees a small man sitting alone in a booth, dressed entirely in green and sporting a fiery red head of hair and matching beard. The top hat on his head is lopsided and if his drunken, green appearance wasn't enough of a giveaway, the fifty empty glasses in front of him clearly indicate who this person is.

"Cormac?" Pia asks dangerously, sliding into the empty seat across from him.

The leprechaun stares at her through bleary eyes, trying to keep her in focus.

"Who the bloody fuck are you?" he slurs.

"Your worst fucking nightmare," Pia snarls angrily, a thrill of joy coursing through her body. "I'm your boss, you asshole."

And as she begins to rip Cormac apart for his poor attendance and lack of work ethic, Pia can't help but smile to herself. This was shaping up to be the best St. Patrick's Day she has ever celebrated – maybe she should allow herself time to socialize more often.

Over at the bar, Santa turns around and nudges the Boogeyman in his side, smirking slightly.

"What is it?" the Boogeyman asks.

"Look." Santa jerks his head at the corner booth. "I think Pia's starting to loosen up. She's sitting down with Cormac without even trying to strangle – oh…oh dear."

"Spoke too soon," the Boogeyman smirks. "Now *this* is entertainment."

And as they watch Tuss rush forward to pry Pia's hands off of Cormac's neck, the holiday heads begin to down their drinks as fast as they can, wanting to get out of the bar before Pia really starts to get angry. After all, elf–built-walls are only so strong.

"Clucky saw way scarier things during the Great Chick War of 1543."

It Hops

"After reviewing the St. Patrick's Day numbers, Corporate wants every last one of you fucking rejects to come up with more ways to push liquor on your holidays. Apparently, alcohol is the only thing that's easy to sell anymore. Probably because it's the only way those mortals can forget their sad, fragile, pathetic, meaningless lives. Bill, you can probably relate. I mean, if a tiny drunk dwarf can sell booze by doing absolutely nothing whatsoever, I think even you amazingly stupid morons can handle it." Pia overlooks her audience. Father Time, T.J., Bill, Cupid and Tom all look stoic, although Cupid seems more preoccupied with checking his phone than listening to what she has to say. If she took her top off, she'd have his full attention, but it would be a cold day in hell before that idea even sprang into her mind.

"Most of the sales for my holiday revolve around alcohol to begin with," Father Time speaks up after Pia has drilled her eyes into him for more time than he is comfortable with. He is already on her bad side for being thirteen minutes late to the meeting and then complaining about that fact for another four. "No holiday moves more champagne than New Year's. How am I supposed to increase that?"

"By dusting the damn cobwebs off your shriveled old brain and actually thinking, you impotent old asshole!" Pia snaps. "And learn to control your kid! He's been following me around, leaving me love letters like some kind of demented stalker. Last night he somehow got into my house and was watching me sleep!"

"Sounds like Santa's a bad influence..." Tom mutters, his beady bird eyes shifting.

"Bird brain!" Pia snarls. "Booze sales for your holiday suck! How do you plan to fix that, you overstuffed glob of giblets?"

"That's not true! The night before Thanksgiving is the busiest bar day of the year!"

"Is the night *before* Thanksgiving actually Thanksgiving?"

Tom deflates slightly. "Well, no, but--"

"Then it doesn't fucking count!"

"It isn't fair!" Tom exclaims. "Christmas gets an Eve! Why not Thanksgiving? We demand equality!"

"Here we go..." mutters Cupid.

"No," Pia snaps. "I am not going to listen to your whining about what Christmas gets that your inferior holiday doesn't. Do better and shut the hell up."

"It's only a matter of finding something that compliments the succulent, robust flavor of turkey," Tom speaks up with confidence. "I will conduct a focus group."

"Please eat yourself," Cupid murmurs so only he and Pia can hear, but she ignores his comment.

She turns to her next victim. "What about you?"

"Well, Memorial Day barbecues are the perfect time--" Bill begins.

"I was talking to the bird! No one cares about your sad little holidays! They're beyond help!"

Bill swallows nervously. "But barbecue and beer--"

T.J. screeches loud enough to make everybody wince, and since his beak is practically pointed in Bill's ear, it's a wonder his eardrum doesn't rupture.

"But that's what I--"

"What did the quail say, Bill?"

"He just said what I--"

"What did the fucking quail say, Bill?!"

"That Independence Day barbecues are a great time to push beer sales," Bill reports sheepishly.

"Then get started on that now." Pia next turns to Cupid, who is still very involved with his phone and paying zero attention to the meeting. "What the hell are you doing? No cell phones!"

"But I love sexting! These college girls are filthy! Hold on - this one wants a picture." He reaches for his fly.

Pia slaps the phone from his hand, a move she immediately regrets because who knows where it's been. "Be a sick pervert on your own time! We're discussing an important issue here!"

Cupid shrugs. "I think booze sales for my holiday are fine. Alcohol helps people get together and then, down the road, helps them forget why they hate each other. We even put liquor in the chocolate!"

"There has to be something you've overlooked," Pia grumbles. "What about something you don't even have to ingest? Like an alcoholic perfume?"

Cupid rubs his chin thoughtfully but before he can respond, Maxwell bursts in waving around a piece of paper. "Fax for you from Corporate. Apparently it's urgent."

"Using other people's minions as your bitches, huh?" Cupid comments with a smirk. "I bet the Boogeyman loves that."

Pia snatches the paper from the vampire's twisted hand. "Says the moron who let that witch screw up his holiday." Her eyes fly over the words as her face grows increasingly red with rage. Around the table, the holiday heads begin to brace themselves like they're in a spaceship that's about to crash. Father Time slides away from the table as Bill closes his eyes and holds onto his seat, just as she erupts. "Where is that *damn* Easter Bunny?!"

$$🥚🥚🥚🥚🥚$$

"So you know how I told you about the substance Violet found in

Skippy Four's room last week? Well, it was just as bad as we had suspected. Alfalfa. He was selling it and everything. We put him in rehab, but who knows if it will take. It didn't help Bouncy Seven. This is going to drive my already out of control child support payments through the roof." Francis sighs and slinks further into his seat at Mother Nature's coffee cart in the lobby, his whiskers wilting.

"More espresso?" asks Mother Nature kindly, showing off a fresh pot of the stuff.

"Please." Francis drops his head into his paws, ears drooping. "After dealing with all of that, I was on the phone half the night with Mitten trying to convince him no one was going to come in the middle of the night and cut off his foot to use for luck. Who tells a bunny that humans do that?"

"A sick, sick person." Mother Nature turns to Caleb, now a young teenager, completely engrossed in a notebook he is scribbling in. "More iced tea, dear?"

"No, thanks!" he replies happily.

"I'll have some more, please," Wally requests. He is seated a few stools down from Caleb but has been mostly quiet, deep in thought as he sips his iced tea and occasionally asks about flowers. "What about daffodils?"

Mother Nature shakes her head. "I wouldn't go there, dear."

"Enough about me," Francis sighs as the old woman refills Wally's glass. "Did Corporate get the last letter you sent?"

"Oh, they got it - the bastards." Mother Nature scowls. "They're ignoring me! I've sent one every month and not one peep from HR! Not one! But if they think I'm going to give up, they're going to be in for a shock when they get next month's letter! And the one after that! At some point they're going to have to acknowledge me or they'll have a personnel file a mile long!"

"How about peonies?" Wally asks.

"Oh, honey, goodness no."

"But roses are so cliché!"

The elevator arrives and the doors are barely open before Pia comes storming out, trying to shake off Tuss, who is close on her heels.

"*You!*" She points an accusatory finger and heads right for the Easter Bunny, whose whiskers instantly begin to tremble.

"Pia! You look extra beautiful today!" Caleb leaps in front of her, clutching a sheet of paper he has freshly ripped from his notebook. "Is that a new shade of lipstick? It compliments your eyes - which are already as rich and shiny as the world's most beautiful emeralds. I wrote this for you!"

Since hitting his teenage years, Caleb had been spending every waking second professing his love to Pia and she was convinced it was all because she had been stupid enough to pay him one fucking compliment when he was a mere two years old. Each day she was forced to endure some new, pathetic attempt to win her affections. There had been the terrible morning when he rigged a tape of him singing horribly outdated love songs way off-key to play at full volume in her office. Another time, he bought her a Christmas-themed negligee that was clearly meant for one of the shorter elves. It was covered in green and red glitter and was extremely tacky. It even said 'Definitely Naughty' across the lower back. Now, he apparently thinks he's a poet.

In one swift motion, Pia grabs Caleb's latest work and rips it in half, letting the ruined pieces flutter sadly to the floor. "Out of my way, you stupid fucking brat!" She shoves him hard enough to send him flying into the wall as her heels quickly close the distance between her and the overgrown lagomorph. "What. The *fuck*. Is *this*?"

With those words, she slams down the slightly crinkled fax she received upstairs not five minutes ago. Printed there is a photo of a screaming child with a rabbit - a rabbit with black, soulless eyes, a misshapen, lumpy skull and sharp teeth that look perfect for ripping supple young flesh from bone. Everyone in the vicinity leans in to take a look before backing away in disgust.

"Um…uh…er…" Francis stammers.

"*This* is the costume you approved for this year's mall photo-ops?" Pia demands. "This unholy *nightmare*! Kids are too afraid to go the hell near it! There has been an unprecedented amount of pants wetting! Photo sales are almost nonexistent - and it's not hard to see why! What parent would let their spawn near this damn thing? This is a fucking monster that will break into their house in the middle of the night and gnaw their fucking brains out! *Tell me* you didn't approve this. *Tell me* this isn't your signature on the paperwork, and that some idiot like Bill forged it, hoping I would fucking kill you and he could take your holiday."

"I…did approve that," Francis mumbles.

"You unbelievable moron--"

"But…Bill did do the design."

"*What?*"

Francis can't bear to look at Pia. As his eyes remain focused on the counter, he imagines her face rivals the terrifying rabbit in the picture with the screaming child. "I was busy with some personal issues and he was kind enough to volunteer, so--"

"*Please* don't tell me you let that complete fucking moron design the costume!" Pia's face is so red, it looks ready to explode.

In response to the question screamed right into his sensitive eardrums, Francis cowers, his eyes falling to the floor as he nervously runs his paws down his ears.

"Pia…" Tuss makes a move like he's going to put a hand on her shoulder but thinks better of it. He's rather attached to his appendages and would rather not lose any of them. "Let's try and handle this calmly. At least it doesn't look like Pinhead."

"Did he know he was supposed to design a costume for a *rabbit* and not a fucking serial killer?" she goes on, ignoring Tuss' advice. In the background, Cupid saunters unnoticed off of the elevator. When he sees the scene at the coffee cart, he smiles like he's stumbled across some pleasing street theater. "This is supposed to be some stupid, cuddly, googley-eyed forest creature that kids want to visit and get their damn picture taken with! Their parents are supposed to order lots of copies to give to grandma, and grandpa, and Uncle Bob, and Aunt-Go-Fuck-Yourself and whoever else those dimwits give a shit about!" She continues to shove the disturbing picture in the Easter Bunny's face as Cupid starts to make himself a cappuccino, Mother Nature being too involved in the performance to do anything but continuously wipe the same glass with the same rag. "No one's going to take a picture of this unless they plan on giving it to the news after it murders a bunch of fucking kids! Which is all it looks like it's going to do!"

"It didn't look so bad on paper!" Francis says.

"*This* is on paper! Does it look bad *now*?"

Tuss finally snatches the fax, which at this point is practically touching the Easter Bunny's quivering nose, away. "I think he gets the point."

"Wait until I get my hands on that basement dwelling, flag pushing, pig sweating, son of a bitch," Pia seethes, backing off at last. "If I didn't have to deal with this disaster, I'd be getting on that fucking elevator and--"

"What Pia *means* to say is that we need to deal with this problem immediately," Tuss interrupts, before she can go off on another lengthy rant.

"We need to go down there and see how bad it is for ourselves," Pia says. "The mortals are probably too busy shoving hot dogs and beer into their faces to notice a giant rabbit in their midst. We'll just put a hat on you."

"I don't think so, Pia," Tuss speaks up reasonably. "The people will notice a giant rabbit walking around. I don't care what kind of hat you put on Francis. This isn't a sporting event where he can pass as some kind of mascot. Have you seen some of those? They're quite...uh… *interesting*."

"Well, who's going to go then?" Pia demands.

"I'll go!" At the mere sound of Caleb's voice, Pia is rolling her eyes. He comes running around the cart so he is as close to Pia as he can get, while still remaining outside of striking distance. "I can film everything for Francis on my new camera! Plus, I can go undercover and get up close to the costume with the rest of the kids."

"Down there I think you're technically called a teenager," Mother Nature says.

"You can be like my mom," Caleb continues hopefully, smiling dreamily at Pia.

"No," Pia insists. "That is beyond creepy."

"And I can be daddy. I love being called *daddy*. You can call me daddy anytime!"

Pia glares at Cupid, who is smiling behind his cup of coffee. "I'd rather call you a--"

"That *would* make you blend in down there," Tuss once again interrupts with a shrug. "Pretending to be a normal nuclear family. It's not a bad idea."

"I'm full of good ideas," grins Cupid, with a wink in Pia's direction.

Pia's return gaze gives the impression that she's thinking about ripping that eye right out of its pretty little socket. "That's not why he wants to go down there. He just wants to find some brainless bimbo to stick his dick in."

"I'm insulted that you think I wouldn't want to help."

"Oh, please. The only thing you care about is getting yourself off."

"I'd care about getting *you* off, if you'd only give me the chance," Cupid insists.

"I wouldn't give you the chance if it was between you and that repulsive disgrace who designed the zombie bunny costume."

"Enough. You're wasting time, Pia," Tuss speaks up firmly. "Every minute that goes by is another minute that costume is sitting in a mall with no kids clambering to take a picture with it."

"I am aware of the situation. Don't tell me how to do my damn job," Pia snarls in reply, glaring at the smug smile on Cupid's face. "It's bad enough I have to take my borderline stalker, I don't want to have to take *this* disgusting pervert too."

"Well, I'm not taking no for an answer," Cupid states.

"Time is ticking, Pia," Tuss adds.

"Thanks, Father Time Junior," she snaps at Tuss, as she stomps toward the door. "Let's just go and get this over with."

"You heard your mother, son," Cupid says in a playful voice to Caleb. "Get a move on."

"You – rabbit – go down to the workshop and watch us on Santa's naughty or nice globe," Pia orders Francis as she heads out. "I want you to see the terror you created."

"This is going to be so much fun!" Caleb exclaims. "I can't wait to see what mortals are like! And malls sound so cool! Do mortal kids still use that word? *Cool*?"

Pia gives Francis one last debilitating glare, her green eyes practically forming snake-like slits. "I should have your foot for this, rabbit. *Both* of them."

🥚 🥚 🥚 🥚 🥚

"*Ooh*, what's that?"

"Shut up."

"It's an escalator."

"And what's that thing?"

"Shut *up*."

"It's a pretzel."

"And what's that? It's beautiful!"

"Shut the fuck--"

"That's a fountain."

Caleb, dressed in jeans that are two inches too short and a flannel shirt three sizes too big, goes running over to this new wonder, leaving Pia and Cupid milling around with a bunch of shoppers in Middle America.

"We don't have time for this shit," Pia grumbles, watching with a shake of her head as Caleb runs excitedly around the fountain, trying to touch the water. In her black pencil skirt and jewel-toned blouse, she looks like she should be on her way to a business lunch, not at the mall with her alleged son.

Even Cupid, although he wears no tie and his shirt isn't even tucked in, is dressed too nicely to blend into the crowd. "Leave him alone, he's never seen one before. We can't have fountains at the Pole, they'll just freeze." Hands shoved in the pockets of his blazer, Cupid rocks back on his heels as he glances around at the crowd, approvingly. "It's like a MILF bonanza in here."

"I don't know what that is, and I don't want to know." They start heading over to Caleb, who has seated himself on the edge of the fountain, peering into the water in innocent amazement.

Cupid gives a suggestive wink to a passing blonde in a halter top causing Pia to hit him hard in the ribs. "That girl is like *fourteen*, you sicko."

"I remember when girls used to be married by fourteen. Do you remember those days, Pia?"

"Hardly." She walks over to Caleb and slaps his hand away before he can touch the pool of water. "What are you doing?"

"There are shiny things in the water!"

"That's money," Cupid explains. "They call them coins."

"Wow! That's a lot different from ours! Why do they drop their money in the fountain?"

"To make a wish," Cupid says at the same time Pia snottily answers, "Because the mortals are morons."

"What do they wish for?"

"Can we stop talking about stupid crap and do our jobs?" Pia snarls, trying to keep her voice low. They are already getting some curious looks from a mother and her preteen daughter sitting nearby. "This isn't fucking playtime."

"Can we at least get some of those shoes first?" Caleb asks, pointing to a shoe store across the way that has a display of colorful sneakers in the window. "Those are *cool*."

"No!" Pia scolds. "You can't just take what you want here, you have to pay money!"

"But there's plenty of money in the fountain--"

"I am going to lose my fucking mind if we don't get over to this Easter Bunny in two seconds." Pia turns to find Cupid winking at the staring mother with a devilish smile. She hits him in the ribs again. "Stop it! I *knew* you'd do this. This is why I didn't want you to come."

"I don't know what you're talking about. I'm just being friendly." Cupid waves at the mother, who can't help smiling back.

"Mentally undressing every woman you see is not being *friendly*!"

"Not *every* one." Cupid points to an old woman wobbling by with a cane. "Even *I* wouldn't hit *that*." He pauses and cocks his head. "Probably not."

"I'm going to punch you in the balls if you don't knock it off."

"Pretty sure that's considered assault here," Cupid teases. "And you wouldn't want to end up in jail. Corporate wouldn't like having to bail you out and dealing with all of that paperwork."

"You wouldn't press charges," Pia snorts. "You'd like it."

"You're right." He shrugs.

"Is that a store?" Caleb asks.

"Yes. They're *all* fucking stores," Pia replies.

"Then why does it say 'Gap'? How is it a store if it's a gap?"

"It's not a fucking gap. It's a *fucking store* called the *fucking Gap*."

"That sells gaps? Why would you want to buy a gap?" Caleb asks, confused.

"It doesn't sell gaps, it sells clothes," Cupid tries to explain before Pia completely loses it in front of all the mortals. "See what's in the window?"

"Fascinating," Caleb breathes.

"Yeah, it's miraculous," mutters Pia with another roll of the eyes.

A young man with several gold teeth wanders over to Pia, wearing a smarmy smile. "Hey there, gorgeous."

"Go fuck yourself," Pia snarls in the nastiest possible tone. The look she fixes him with sends him practically running away.

"So charming," Cupid teases her.

"Is that a car?" asks Caleb, pointing to a display vehicle parked near the Gap.

"Yes."

"It's so shiny!" the teenager beams. "But not as shiny as Santa's sleigh! Why is it parked inside? I thought mortals drive them outside."

"I don't know."

"Can I go inside of it?"

"No! We need to figure out where this demon bunny is scaring the hell out of kids!"

"I think the Easter Bunny is probably in that direction," Caleb speaks up suddenly.

"And what makes you think that?"

"Because I've seen at least a dozen kids run crying from over there," he clarifies.

"That sounds like our bunny," Cupid agrees.

🥚 🥚 🥚 🥚 🥚

During all of this, back at the Pole, Santa's workshop is buzzing with activity, which is making it difficult for Francis to concentrate on the giant globe before him. Looking like a crystal ball filled with smoke, it is three times his height and five times his width. He knows he should be paying attention to the smoky images of Pia, Cupid and Caleb investigating the terrifying costume he allowed to exist, but it's hard to concentrate when there's so much going on around him. In the brief time he has been standing here, he has already heard an impromptu performance of *Silver Bells*, nearly had a tray of snowflake-shaped cookies dumped on him by a clumsy elf named Jolly and watched at least a hundred rocking horses be painted from head to hoof in a matter of minutes. Considering how they were always scrambling to paint tons of eggs the night before Easter, Francis was beginning to think he had recruited his employees from the wrong gene pool.

"Ho, ho, ho - what are you watching?" Santa comes striding over, Holly sashaying right behind him. "Is this one of those *CSI* programs? I love that show! I think that little puny one there is going to be murdered by that crazy looking woman with the ponytail!"

"I'm not watching TV, that's Caleb and Pia," Francis explains.

Santa squints, leaning closer to the giant images of people he is very familiar with. "So it is! I guess the globe does add ten pounds!" he chuckles. "Maybe those American kids aren't as fat as Knobby thinks they are!"

"Pia told me I had to watch, but there's so much--"

"Excuse me, Santa? Can I talk to you for a minute?"

The big man in red and the Easter Bunny both turn around to find a burly, ruggedly handsome elf standing behind them.

"Hi, Bobby," Holly swoons immediately.

"Oh, hey there, Holly," replies Bobby, flashing a dashing smile.

"Of course you can talk to me!" Santa bellows merrily. "What's on your mind, son?"

"Well, ever since Gully transferred to wardrobe, it hasn't been easy managing the sleigh and taking care of all the reindeer by myself. I could really use some help to clean--"

"Clean?" Santa repeats. "You need some cleaning help? Why, I have just the elf for you! He absolutely loves to clean! He cleaned all the hair out of my shower drain just last night!" Chuckling, he strokes his beard and turns to the oversized rabbit. "You probably know a thing or two about shedding yourself, I'll bet!" He then turns to Holly. "Why don't

135

you help Bobby find Frank? I'm sure he'd love to help. He was in my office sweeping up my toenail clippings last I checked!"

"Of course." Holly smiles at Bobby, tossing some stray strands of dark, curly hair over her shoulder in a way she considers flirtatious. "Right this way."

With the elves gone, Francis turns back to the globe and tries to concentrate. At least until the picture dramatically decreases in size.

He turns to find Santa fiddling with a remote control. "Sorry! But I need to do my hourly check-in!" The other half of the screen is now focused on a little girl jumping rope. "Nice!" Santa decides, before flipping to the next child, who he also considers nice. So is the next child, and the next child, and the child after that.

While this is going on, an older elf hobbles up on a cane, a grumpy expression on his old, wrinkled face. His white hair and long beard are neatly trimmed, but his uniform, although clean and freshly pressed from the tip of his hat to the toe of his curly shoes, has clearly not been standard issue for many years. "Santa," the older elf huffs, tapping his gnarled wooden cane on the floor. "We have an issue."

"Nice, nice, nice - what's the problem, Knobby?"

"Moths have somehow gotten into the wardrobe archives," the old elf complains. "I'm sure it has something to do with Mother Nature again. It was her fault we had that caterpillar problem back in 1623!"

"Nice, nice, nice - get yourself some mothballs! Holly can order some from Corporate for you! I just sent her back to my office."

Knobby stands there and watches Santa declare ten other children nice, even one who pushes another child to the ground right before their eyes.

"Nice?" Knobby sneers. "He just hurt that other child."

"Oh, it's just a little harmless sibling squabble!" Santa assures him. "Kids will be kids!"

Knobby goes off grumbling about how kids these days get away with everything.

Francis turns back to his tiny screen, vowing to pay attention to the important mission at hand.

He watches for a good two seconds before his sensitive ears picks up the conversation between Wally and Frank, who are passing by at that moment.

"It's a crystal vase," Wally is saying with excitement. "You wouldn't believe what it cost me. And that was *before* I paid for the flowers. It's worth it though. *She's* worth it. Holly's amazing."

Frank snorts. "I think she's a whore."

"There you are, Frank!" Santa declares, turning away from the globe. "Bobby's looking for you! He needs some help cleaning up reindeer droppings, so I volunteered you for the job."

"Oh, crap," Frank groans.

"I knew you'd be excited! Get a move on, now! Those reindeer do *not* like to smell their own feces!"

Frank goes off grumbling as Wally heads off in another direction, his face buried in his tablet.

Santa sighs and switches channels again. Only this time, instead of tuning in to a child that needs to be judged, it's the opening credits of *Law & Order*. "It just started!" he declares happily.

Francis sighs to himself, accepting the fact that Pia will know he didn't watch and he'll be in even more trouble.

🍬 🍬 🍬 🍬 🍬

Pia, Cupid and Caleb quickly head off in the direction of the crying children. As they grow closer to the rabbit hole themed area, they pass

———

137

dozens of hysterically crying children, some of which are still standing in puddles of fresh...well...their bladders just couldn't handle it. Kids are running away from the entrance area, screaming in terror as their frantic parents attempt to chase after them.

The three of them break into a jog as they come around the front of the exhibit, which is decorated with brightly painted cardboard cutouts of giant carrots, fluffy yellow chicks and an assortment of jeweled eggs. And there, beneath a banner enthusiastically announcing 'Meet the Easter Bunny Here' is a fluffy purple chair upon which the abomination of nature is seated.

Even Pia can't help but step back in disgust.

"It looks even worse in person," Cupid mutters.

"Get up there, Caleb." Pia gives him a shove.

Wordlessly, Caleb shakes his head and takes a terrified step back.

"Get up there, you brat," Pia snaps, trying to force him to walk forward. He's surprisingly strong for a slip of a kid. "You said you would! You know it's just a guy in a suit!"

But Caleb just continues to shake his head and keeps his feet planted firmly on the floor.

"You said you'd film it and you're not even doing that!"

"It's repulsive," Cupid decides. "It even looks like it's drooling blood. What *is* that?"

"I think it's supposed to be the tongue," Pia squints. "That's what you get when you let a moron with a barely functioning brain design something. I swear, I'm going to take that drawing and shove it up his ass."

"Ooh. Me first, please," Cupid says eagerly.

"Can you believe that thing?"

Instead of responding to Cupid's latest off-color remark, Pia turns toward the source of that comment - a father whose young son is cowering behind his legs. He is talking with a group of women dealing with similarly terrorized children.

"I can't believe they're calling that *thing* the Easter Bunny," one of the mothers agrees. She has a child in a stroller who is holding a blanket over their face.

"You can't even call it a Halloween costume!" another agrees. "It's *heinous*!"

"If this is what passes as the Easter Bunny these days, then I am *never* taking my kids to see him again. I wouldn't send my kids up there even if they *did* want to go."

The other parents nod and mutter in agreement as yet another child screams bloody murder and flees from the vicinity of the monstrous bunny.

Pia turns to Cupid, her face white. "*Never* again?"

Even Cupid looks serious. "This is even worse than we thought."

"There are tens of thousands of malls in this country. If we lose all those photography sales--"

"We've gotta fix this. *Fast.*"

"No shit! But how? There isn't time to remake thousands of rabbit costumes!" Pia looks at the still frozen Caleb and starts snapping her fingers in front of his face. "Would you take the damn video already?"

"I don't want it on my camera!"

"Are you fucking kidding me? That's the only reason you're here, you little shit! Now get to fucking work!" Noticing she has drawn the attention of a nearby group of parents, Pia pats Caleb on the head with a nervous laugh and a forced, awkward smile. "*Honey.*"

"Ow," Caleb complains. But after another series of nasty looks, he does manage to produce the promised video. While he films, Pia turns her back to the parents while Cupid asks if any of them are single.

"Let's get out of here," Pia proclaims as Caleb tucks the camera away. She stops Cupid from getting a number from an apparently divorced dad just in time. The Easter Bunny is leaving his area to go on break, causing a sea of children to run screaming, more than one shrieking about how it is coming to eat them.

Caleb is one of them. "Gladly!"

🥚 🥚 🥚 🥚 🥚

The camera shakes violently. Children flee, screaming and crying for their mommies and daddies at the very glimpse of something - something yet to be seen. Suddenly, the camera zooms in, focusing on vacant black eyes, a lumpy, potato sack-like skull, floppy, frayed ears, vampire-like teeth, razor-like whiskers and lips and paws stained red, like it was recently feasting on the sweet, sweet blood of the innocent.

Somebody in the room cries out in terror as the television freezes on this horrifying image. Pia steps closer to the screen, remote in hand, as she overlooks the group around the conference table. "What. The fuck. Are we supposed to do. About *this*?"

Francis, Tuss, Caleb, Cupid and Bill sit in silence, working to avoid her venomous gaze.

"*You*." Bill knows she's pointing at him, even though he's still staring at the candy cane and corn printed carpet. "*You* scream at the sight of that thing? You *created* that abomination!"

"That's not what I drew!"

"You lying son of a bitch. Are you trying to destroy Easter? Because I will go straight to Corporate and--"

"No!" Bill cries desperately. "That's not what I drew!" He digs a mostly crumpled piece of computer paper out of his pocket and starts smoothing it out on the table. "What I drew was cute! And cuddly!"

Everyone crowds around to look before unanimously calling out in disgust. "Ugh!"

"What's wrong with it?"

"Why are the ears like that?"

"Because he's a lop bunny!" Bill explains.

"Why do his whiskers look like tiny knife blades?"

"I wanted them to stand out! They don't look like - well, maybe in this light..." Bill's face falls.

"Why is he bleeding from the mouth?"

"That's his tongue!"

"I told you," Cupid smirks at Pia.

"He's happy!" Bill insists.

"Happy he just murdered some kids and put their severed fingers in the eggs for the others to find. Happy Easter!" Cupid smirks sarcastically.

He is shot with a trio of dirty looks as Pia finally snatches the disturbing drawing off of the table and crumples it back up. "If you *ever* even *think* about volunteering to help another holiday again, I will chop off the fucking balls you barely have to begin with and feed them to the spiders upstairs!"

"Did you hear about their complaint, by the way?" Tuss puts in hesitantly. "We really should talk about that later."

Pia turns to Francis who sits in his brightly colored seat like a clump of boneless white fur. "Since you're the one who let bizarro Michelangelo ruin your profits, you better have a damn good idea of how to fix this!

The mortals are threatening to never bring their spawn to see the bunny again! Even Caleb was afraid of it!"

"I was just trying to fit in with all the other kids," Caleb insists unsuccessfully.

Pia's cutting green eyes remain focused on the bunny. "*Well?*"

Francis shrugs, looking fully defeated, and says nothing.

"*Useless!* What about the rest of you imbeciles? Peewee? Hyper Dick? *Puss?* Most Useless Piece of Pathetic Shit in the Universe?"

"I guess that's me," Bill mumbles.

"Of course it's you! Was that really not fucking clear? You're a category of failure all by yourself!"

"I think you're going a little far, Pia."

"Can it, *Wuss*. Unless you want a detailed explanation of how fucking useless *you* are."

Tuss angrily starts to say something about how their focus should be on a solution and not disparaging people, but he is interrupted by the cheery sound of a cell phone ringing to the tune of *Here Comes Peter Cottontail.*

There is no mystery as to who that cell phone belongs to. Everybody looks at Francis as he sheepishly answers the call.

"What?...I'm in a meeting...No...No...No...Well what did your mother say?...No she didn't. If you got a job...fine. Do whatever you want." Hanging up, Francis massages his forehead with his ears. "Those kids are gonna be the death of me. Did you know a female rabbit can get pregnant with a second litter while she's already pregnant? *Why?* Just *why* is that possible?"

"Francis - your stupid kids - are they giant rabbits like you?" Pia asks.

"Yes," he sighs lifelessly.

"And what the hell are they doing with their lives?" she demands.

"Well, Clover's pretty active on some *Harry Potter* message board. And Squeakers has a one-man band. Other than that, spending my money. Online shopping. Racking up my phone bill. Rehab. Pyramid schemes. Reality shows. Lots of naps. So, nothing really."

"Not anymore. They're all hired." Pia says.

"Excuse me?"

"They're going to be our new mall Easter Bunnies."

"Are you crazy, Pia?" Tuss pipes up. "You can't do that! They're real rabbits! Mortals will know it's not a costume!"

"Not if we're smart! I'll talk to Corporate and get them some handlers - this is what the Emergency Response Team is for! Those stupid mortals will think they're some really elaborate costumes that put the shit at Disney to shame!" She starts heading for the door with even more conviction in her step than usual. "Easter will not fail on my watch!"

"I love her," Caleb sighs dreamily, while everyone else looks at him like he's crazy.

But Pia isn't done just yet. A moment later she returns, an angry finger pointed at Bill. "And you find a use for your terrifying murder costumes! Or the cost of them is coming out of your paycheck!"

Bill frets and sweats, stuttering but getting out no actual words.

"Oh, and by the way," Pia continues, with a smile that makes Francis immediately uneasy. "You should go down to your office. You have a few guests waiting for you."

"G-guests?" the rabbit stammers, bracing himself for the answer.

"Fifteen to be exact. I would have invited more, but unfortunately I couldn't squeeze any more of your wives into your office."

"Fifteen? Of my wives? In my office?" his voice is barely a squeak.

"I figured I'd lock you in there for a good three hours of private time," she continues with a look of sick pleasure. "I think you all need time to talk. They certainly have a lot to say, and most of them look angry."

Francis swallows, the sweat building under his fur.

"Now, hop the hell on down there!" Pia declares, slapping the table hard enough to make him jump. "Don't wanna keep the ladies waiting! Oh, and if you screw up like this again, I'll maroon you with *all* of your wives on an island for a fucking *week*!"

Slowly, the Easter Bunny forces himself out of his seat, bracing for what will be the longest and worst three hours of his life.

🥚 🥚 🥚 🥚 🥚

"Most photo sales ever, can you believe it? My kids were a hit! They enjoyed themselves too. I think we'll do this every year from now on. I personally got a call from Corporate thanking me for all my hard work!"

"I thought using your kids as free labor was that bitch Pia's idea."

Francis' happiness fades as he frowns at Mother Nature from his seat at her coffee cart.

"I'm sorry, Francis," she apologizes immediately, arranging a lovely assortment of lilies and roses in a crystal vase. "You work very hard and you deserve all the praise. I don't suppose you asked Corporate if they plan on responding to my letters any time within the next century?"

"Still haven't heard anything, huh?"

"I think I may have to try something a little different with next month's letter."

The front doors open and Holly shimmies inside, shaking the snow from the hood of her parka. She spots the flowers and her face lights up like the Christmas star. "Those are for me?"

"They certainly are, honey!" Mother Nature beams.

Holly hurries over and admires the blooms, touching the delicate petals carefully. "No one's ever gotten me non-Christmas flowers before! Are these roses?"

"And lilies!"

"Easter lilies!" Francis puts in eagerly.

"They're beautiful!" Holly buries her face in the petals, inhaling the pleasant scent of both flowers. But a moment later she jerks back, a look of disgust of her face. "What's that?"

"What's what, dear?"

"Those little crawly things!"

"Oh! Just some aphids." When Mother Nature notices the elf's bemused stare, she continues. "They're bugs. They love roses. They're harmless."

Holly hesitates before picking up the vase, holding it as far from her body as her arms will allow. The look of disgust doesn't leave her face. "Lovely."

"Make sure they get plenty of sunlight!" Mother Nature calls, as Holly heads back out into the snow without a backwards glance.

"I think next year I should let the kids choose their own bow tie color," Francis ponders aloud.

"You take that leap, dearie."

The front doors groan open again, but this time the first thing through them are cardboard boxes. Cardboard boxes pushing small mounds of snow and torn flower petals into the lobby.

"What's all this?" Mother Nature asks.

The doors close behind Maxwell and Howie, who shakes himself off like a dog.

"Hey! I'm serving food here!" Mother Nature protests, shielding herself from the flying droplets of water.

"Sorry," Howie apologizes. "It's really coming down out there."

"I guess we have to go back for the rest," Maxwell says, sounding tired. He takes a sip from the bottle of red stuff strapped to his belt.

"The rest of what?" Francis asks, eyeing the boxes curiously.

"Not sure," admits Howie. "Corporate just dropped them off. The boss told us to get them and put them in storage."

"Let's go get the rest and get this over with," Maxwell urges.

As soon as they are out the door and out of sight, Francis hops over to one of the boxes and tears off the tape in one smooth motion.

"What do you think is in there?" asks Mother Nature. "Not more bats, I hope. They destroyed all my plants last time!"

"I know exactly what's in here." The Easter Bunny reaches into the box and fishes out one of the misshapen, demon-eyed faces that had already successfully frightened millions of children across America. "Thoroughly tested Halloween costumes."

"Clucky's mother always said that once the egg breaks, there's no putting it back together."

Every seat in the conference room has a body in it except for the one made of gold coins covered in dust and the chair that formerly belonged to Bill that now belongs to Pia. That's because she is at the head of the room looking over three large mock-ups of some print advertising for the upcoming holiday that will soon be seen in every magazine, newspaper, bus station, bathroom and smart phone game pop-up across the United States.

"It's brilliant. Fucking brilliant." She walks back and forth between them, nodding her head with approval. "You know why it's brilliant?" She turns to the others at last, smiling in a way that manages to make everyone uncomfortable. "Because someone who isn't a complete moron came up with it. *Me*."

More than a few people roll their eyes, but Pia either doesn't notice or doesn't care.

"Since this holiday was so badly managed for years," she goes on, making sure to look pointedly at Mother Nature, "I have a lot of ground to make up. Unlike some people, I won't be sitting back and watering my obnoxious, pointlessly pointy plants while the mortals use email - or *Facebook* - to wish their mothers a happy Mother's Day. No. I'm going to make sure they understand just how fragile and unpredictable their sad, little, meaningless lives are." She points to the first ad, which is simple white text on a black background that reads: 'Life can change in an instant. Buy your mom a great Mother's Day gift today at [store]'. "We can charge retailers to display their logo in this ad, which is beneficial to them *and* us. I'm targeting department stores, but obviously I'll accept any interested company."

"Even an adult video store? Best Mother's Day ever! I'm serious! We can run a MILF campaign!"

Pia chooses to simply glare at Cupid as she continues her presentation, pointing to the center ad, which features several lovely flower arrangements on a pleasant pink background. In elegant script it says: 'This year, send your mom a bouquet of flowers to say I love you. Because this may be your last chance'. "This one should push flower sales, which you would think old mommy dearest would actually have been good at, but no. Can she fill a fucking office with horrible thorny vines that stab me at every available opportunity? Sure. Can she push a bunch of actually pretty, overpriced roses on some brainless, last minute shopper who is so desperate for something they will literally purchase the next thing they see? No. That is why I am here and she's still, and forever will be, *fired*."

"She pushed them on Wally," Cupid mutters.

"I don't appreciate being spoken of like I'm not here!"

Pia ignores them both and moves on to her last ad. "This one is my personal favorite. It's going to push card sales through the roof!" The ad reads: 'Don't you wish you had purchased that Mother's Day Card?' Behind the text is a young man crying in a graveyard, kneeling at a headstone that bears the simple legend: R.I.P. Mommy. Pia admires this creation with an especially pleased grin. "Fantastic."

Behind her, a lot of uneasy looks are exchanged.

"This is going to be the most successful Mother's Day ever!" Pia brags, turning to the group again. "This campaign I've come up with is going to sell more cards, flowers, gifts and other sappy crap in one month than that last piece of shit made in the last ten years she ran it."

"Did you invite me to this meeting just to throw all of this in my face?" huffs Mother Nature.

"Why else would I bother? Unless I wanted you to bring me some coffee."

"We get it, Pia," Tuss speaks up, sounding tired of the whole thing.

The Boogeyman is looking at the graveyard scene, nodding his head. "I like it."

"Bottom line - prey on their stupid emotions and their ability to die easily and suddenly. This campaign practically wrote itself. *What* is your damn problem?"

Pia has been able to ignore the Sandman's snoring, Tom's gobbling, Father Time's clock checking, Bill's very existence and Cupid's variety of lewd gestures this entire time, but she can no longer overlook the glaring, sighing and obvious discontent of the Tooth Fairy. The two women glower at one another as more than one witness starts to silently hope for a catfight.

"I don't like it," Regina says plainly.

"Because you're ignorant."

"Maybe you haven't heard, but--"

"Nobody gives a shit what you think. You collect teeth. *Bill* could do that."

"I don't think Mother's Day should be about--"

"Nobody. Gives. A shit."

"It's completely morbid--" Regina continues, louder.

"You don't know anything about this," Pia seethes, her voice surprisingly low as the floor trembles slightly. The intensity of her glare is enough to send Ted scurrying under the table, but Regina does not flinch. "*Nothing.* So shut your mouth and keep your worthless opinion to yourself."

Before anyone can say another word, Pia throws open the conference room door, startling Caleb who has been kneeling outside, listening.

"Your idea is brilliant, Pia! You're so smart! You're the smartest, most beautiful woman I've ever met!" He hurries after her, but the elevator doors at the end of the hall have swallowed her up by the time he even gets to his feet.

"Ted? It's okay, buddy. You can come out now. She's gone."

The groundhog cautiously peeks out from beneath the table at Cupid's words, letting out a giant sigh of relief. "Thank goodness."

Father Time rushes into the hall, slapping twenty-year-old Caleb's hand away from the elevator button he is frantically smashing. "Stop it! You're too old to be acting this way!"

"But I love her! She *needs* me!"

"The only thing she *needs* is a personality adjustment! You're coming downstairs with me to help the Fates turn next year's number into some novelty glasses."

"No! That's boring! I wanna help Pia!" Caleb whines, but Father Time shoves him into the elevator and presses the button for the first floor anyway.

Everyone else is meandering out of the conference room rather slowly in the aftermath of that mostly unpleasant meeting. Bill is muttering obscenities under his breath, as T.J. takes off, soaring over everyone's head. Tom complains to Santa to move his fat ass, as Mother Nature drags the still snoozing Sandman out the door. Ted scurries through everyone's legs to escape the Boogeyman and his Shadow, while Cupid and Francis strike up a conversation about fur. Regina, however, remains in her chair, staring at Pia's advertisements with a frown. Tilly comes over, gently nudging her arm with her muzzle.

"I agree with you," the moose says kindly. "I think these ads are terrible!"

"Then why didn't you say anything?" Regina asks.

"Because," Tilly begins, as though it should be obvious. "She's terrifying."

Once the Canadian leaves the room, Regina assumes she is alone and is surprised when she turns to find Tuss standing there, shuffling the same stack of papers over and over. "Hey."

"Yeah?" he asks, looking up.

"Can't *you* do anything?"

"About what?"

"About *that*?" She gestures vaguely to the ads without looking at them; she's seen enough. "Is this really how she plans to market Mother's Day? It's morbid and disgusting and...just...*wrong*. That's not what Mother's Day is about! Not at all!"

"That *is* her plan," Tuss admits with a sigh. "And you know Pia. Even if I try to talk to her about it...once she's made up her mind, she's impossible."

"But can't you go over her head? Go to Corporate?"

Tuss simply shakes his head. "I wish I could, but they've already approved everything. They seem to love the idea."

"Hard to believe," Regina mutters.

"It still surprises me that she got this holiday to handle. I mean, if you'd associate Pia with any holiday it would have to be Halloween, right?" he tries to chuckle, but as his joke falls flat he quickly adds, "If there was anything I could do..."

"Yeah. I'm sure," says the Tooth Fairy shortly, stomping toward the door without looking back. "Thanks anyway."

"You called for me?" Wally approaches Cupid's office to find him lounging on his heart-shaped bed flipping through a porn magazine called *Jugz*. The elf swallows uneasily and tries not to look at the scantily clad redhead on the cover.

"Yes!" Cupid smiles brightly, tossing the magazine over his shoulder as he springs to his feet. He snatches a box of chocolates off of his desk and holds it out excitedly. "This is for you."

"Uh, thanks? But I don't really--"

"It's not for *you*, you! It's for *you* to give to *Holly*! Success is guaranteed." He winks suggestively.

Wally takes the box and turns it over in his hands. "What does it do?"

"It will get her in the mood for love, of course." Cupid smirks.

"Does she have to eat the whole box?"

"Probably not." Cupid shrugs.

"*Probably* not?"

"Look, just give to her, okay? She'll have some and then you'll *get* some. Get it?"

"Yeah, but I don't just want--"

"Trust me," Cupid assures the nervous elf, slinging an arm around his shoulder and leading him back to the door. "It'll work. I promise."

"*How* does it work?" Wally asks. "It's not a drug or something is it?"

But the only answer he receives is the click of a door. Wally turns around to find Cupid is gone and his office door is closed. Considering what he had just been reading with the door open, Wally doesn't want to know what he does when the door is actually shut. Frowning, he looks down at the heart-shaped box in his hands. "Well...he *promised*..."

"Of course I came to you, Santa! No one knows more about running a successful holiday than you do!"

Santa leans back in his plush office chair surrounded by his vast collection of snow globes. The various landscapes beneath each tiny dome continuously experience a steady fall of glittery snow, no shaking necessary. "I'm flattered you came to me, Pia, but I'm not sure what kind of advice you're expecting!"

"You've been running the most profitable holiday in the world for hundreds of years," Pia gushes like a groupie interviewing their favorite singer. "There must be *something* you can tell me. I know Mother's Day isn't Christmas - it's basically a shameless cash grab - but I need it to be as successful as possible."

Tucking his hands under his suspenders, Santa ponders her question for a few moments. "Passion. You need to have *passion*. If you have that, everything else will come."

"Passion," Pia mutters, trying her best not to frown in front of the illustrious man in red. "Great..."

"I love Christmas," Santa continues, getting to his feet. He stares at a snow globe featuring a miniature version of himself commanding his team of reindeer through the sky. "There's nothing like seeing the joy on a child's face when they get exactly what they asked for. You can send all the cards, bake all the cookies and buy all the trinkets you want - that's not what makes my Christmas. It's the joy in their eyes. The smiles. Making memories. *Those* last all year long. That's what's been getting me in that sleigh year after year and *that's* what I'll miss the most when I retire."

Pia visibly bristles at that last word. She abruptly rises to her feet, lips pursed. "Thanks for your help," she says curtly, turning to the door.

"Going already?" Santa asks, surprised. "Would you like to take a few gingerbread men with you? They're fresh off the line!"

"No, thanks." Opening the door, Pia nearly trips over Caleb, who bounds in front of her with a plate of fruitcake, cranberry sauce and a headless chocolate rabbit. "What the fuck--"

"Hi, Pia! I figured you hadn't eaten yet, so I brought you some lunch! This was all the cafeteria had. Well, they had some turkey too, but Bill got the last piece. Stupid Bill, right? Also, I got a little hungry and ate the rabbit's head, but I figured you wouldn't mind. Get it? *Mind?* Because I ate his head?" He smiles with enough hope to power a Christmas tree.

"Get out of my way, you annoying brat!" She gives his outstretched arms a shove, sending the plate and all of its contents crashing to the floor. Caleb stands there in the mess, looking like he's about to cry, as Pia stomps away, her heels angrily clicking with every step.

Santa emerges from his office and sees the spilled cranberry sauce, smashed fruitcake and cracked chocolate bunny parts. "Oh dear. What happened here? Frank? Frank? Clean up in the aisle outside my office!" He chuckles at his joke before giving the crestfallen Caleb a firm pat on the back. "Cheer up, son! No use crying over spilled cranberry sauce!" He then frowns, searching around for the elf whose name he's been calling. "Frank? Frank? Wally - where's Frank?"

Wally is standing only steps away from the employee of the month wall. He's in the middle of handing Holly the box of chocolates and is quite flustered by the interruption. "Uh, I'll find him for you in a minute, Santa." To Holly, he rushes, "Enjoy them, okay?"

"Okay, Wally." Holly sighs deeply, plastering a forced smile onto her face. "I'll save them for a special occasion."

Her smile makes Wally smile, then he's rushing off to find Frank.

Santa takes Caleb into his office and Holly follows them, shutting the door behind her. Seconds later, Frank walks by, sees the mess, and steps right over it.

"Fuck this. I'm gonna go get drunk."

Regina is sitting in her office silently fuming as she stares at one of the black and white photographs on her desk. How could Corporate have approved Pia's Mother's Day campaign? Did they honestly think it was appropriate? There were so many people out there who grew up without mothers for one reason or another and she was making light of that situation! Surely there was no way that the mortals would go for it...

"Ma'am?"

"What is it, Hugo?" Regina asks without looking up. Even with their identical voices, she can tell the two pixies apart without needing to look at their almost identical faces.

"It's just...it's Mother's Day tomorrow," Hugo says gently.

"I had no idea," Regina says sarcastically, glancing up at the pixie near the ceiling in time to see his look of surprise. "I'm sorry," she sighs. "It's just been a...*bad* few days."

Hugo laughs nervously before continuing. "It's just...you see, our mother's on vacation right now." He looks across the room to see Hugh staring at him darkly from his desk. "She's in Australia visiting some family. But she gets back next weekend and I was wondering if Hugh and I could have it off to go and visit her for the holiday?"

Before Regina can reply, Hugh snorts in derision. "Count me out," he says firmly. "I don't want to see that bitch."

"Hugh!" Hugo gasps.

"Why not?" Regina asks curiously, despite knowing better than to insert herself into the personal lives of the two brothers.

"She was *horrible* when we were growing up!" Hugh insists. "To *me*, anyway."

"She was not," Hugo protests.

"Of course you won't say anything bad about her," Hugh snaps. "You were always the favorite! Why can't you be more like your brother? He's an *angel*. Why are you such a little terror? You fucking demon! And did dad ever stick up for me? *No*, of course not. He was never home!" He looks down at Regina. "He was always in South America trying to save the rainforest like he was one of those stupid fairies from *Ferngully* or something."

"It was his *job*!" Hugo cries out. "And what do you mean he was never

---

156

home? He came home every night!"

"Semantics," Hugh brushes his brother off before continuing. "All I wanted was to grow up to be somebody's fairy godfather--"

"Because *Cinderella* was your favorite bedtime story growing up." Hugo smiles despite himself. "Which isn't gay at all--"

"Coming from the guy wearing the tutu!" Hugh snaps.

"You're wearing one too!"

"And besides, plenty of boys like *Cinderella!*"

"Straight ones?"

"Boys..." Regina sighs, exasperated. "Can we please not fight?"

"But *no*," Hugh continues. "I *couldn't* be a fairy godfather and do you know why? Because mom just wanted me to work at Stonehenge and tease the mortals like any respectable fairy would do. She was never proud of me *once* until I got this job." He crosses his arms over his chest as he stares at his brother. "And you want me to go visit her for Mother's Day?"

Before Hugo can answer his brother, Regina speaks up. "You're going to visit her."

"*What?*" Hugh demands as Hugo beams down at his boss.

"She's your mother!" Regina states sternly. "She just wants what's best for you. Don't you get that, you twit? No matter how much you resent her, you should still respect her...still love her...never forget her..." She intakes a sharp breath of air as she blinks back tears. "*Appreciate* her. Say *thank you* every now and then. Always--"

"Regina? Are you alright?" Hugo asks after exchanging a confused look with Hugh.

"Fine," Regina manages, clearing her throat haughtily. "Just fine.

Allergies, you know," she adds as she wipes her eyes. "Why don't you two start vacation now? Have the entire week off."

"Really?" Hugo asks as Hugh pumps his fist into the air.

"Yes!" he exclaims. "You don't need to ask me twice!"

"It's to visit your mother!" Regina calls after Hugh as he flies quickly from the office. Hugo hurries off too after an ecstatic "Thanks!" to his boss over his shoulder. The moment Regina is alone, she picks her wand up off of her desk and waves the door shut. Sighing deeply, she places her head down on the desk in front of her and mumbles to herself, "This week just keeps getting worse and worse."

"Get out of here, you little shit! I don't want a damn foot massage!"

"But I just figured that since today is finally Mother's Day--"

"I'm not your mother, you creepy little fuck! I'm never going to let you put your grabby little hands on me. *Ever*!"

"But--"

"*Out*!"

Accepting defeat at last, Caleb departs Pia's office. Despite the numerous attempts she has made to stop them, the plants have taken over all of the walls and are working on the area beneath her desk. She has searched the internet for 'how to poison thorny vines' so many times that her browser now suggests that phrase every time she goes to type anything into the search box.

But those bothersome plants are the least of her concerns today. Today is it. Her day had finally arrived. Mother's Day. Right now the mortals were down there snapping up those last minute sappy cards and gaudy charm bracelets. They were fighting over the last wilted bouquet of grocery store carnations. They were treating those who bore them to expensive brunches, lunches and dinners. Gift wrap had been purchased and perhaps even a cake had been special ordered. Every dime mattered. Every penny was important. If someone bought a bone for their pet bitch in honor of the holiday, Corporate got a cut; it didn't matter how those stupid mortals spent their money. All that mattered was that they spent it. A *lot* of it.

Her ads have been running relentlessly for the past few weeks. If ad space was available, Pia bought it: magazines, benches, buses, mall directories, even in the background of several revenue desperate television programs. Her goal was to get her ads in front of every pair of human eyes in North America at least once every day. It was an almost impossible task, but she feels she has done her best.

But would the numbers show it?

Pia taps her fingers on her desk, watching the last minute sales figures tick in. There's a steady rise, but she can't get excited; since it's a busy day for restaurants, the final numbers won't be in until well after midnight. Sitting here watching the totals when there's so many hours to go is silly and she knows it.

But she can't help herself.

If the numbers keep looking like this, she'd be on track for the most successful Mother's Day in...well...she doesn't want to say *all time* and jinx herself.

Even if it doesn't reach that, even if it falls short, she is definitely on track to beat last year and every year that crazy, plant-hoarding bitch ran things in recent memory.

Corporate is going to be pleased.

They definitely will be, she insists to herself.

Pia leans back in her chair, staring at the computer screen until her eyes burn, but she ignores the pain. She doesn't dare look away.

"It's a bad day for both of us, dear." Mother Nature pours another cup of boiling water for Regina, who is currently her only customer. The Tooth Fairy sits glumly, staring down at the dull countertop, her head resting in her palm. "Another cup of peppermint?"

"Yes, please."

The older woman complies, adding the tea bag and carefully setting the cup down in front of her.

"Thanks."

"You're very welcome." With a sigh, Mother Nature rests for a moment, leaning on her sparkling clean prep counter. "She won't even let me see my plants, you know. My poor babies. Luckily they can take care of themselves."

"Tuss says she's been trying to kill them," Regina says.

"I know," Mother Nature responds with a little smile. "He's not so bad, that one. For one of *them*, anyway. Those bastards *still* won't acknowledge my letters."

"I thought about contacting them too," Regina admits. "About her advertising."

"Why didn't you, dearie?"

"I think it's pretty obvious."

"You should always make an effort to have your voice heard," Mother Nature says wisely. "Even if you don't think anyone will listen. Watch the world run you over otherwise, honey."

Before Regina can respond, Tuss comes through the front doors, rubbing his bare hands together. "Coffee, please, Mother Nature? Black and to go, thanks."

"Sure thing, hon. Do you want some carrot cake with it? Just baked this morning!" She points to a tray of pastries next to a small chalkboard that reads: 'Easter Bunny Recommends!'

"No, thanks. Just the coffee." Tuss comes to a stop beside Regina as Mother Nature busies herself with his order. The Tooth Fairy's position and disposition have not changed. "Everything okay?" he asks her.

"Fine," she responds in that way where it's obvious that everything is clearly not fine.

Frowning, Tuss seems to ponder his next words carefully. "You...don't seem fine."

"Fine."

Tuss accepts his coffee with a thankful smile and waits for Mother Nature to go clean the coffee pot before speaking again. "What's wrong? Too many kids still not flossing?"

Regina only gives him a half-smile, which still seems forced.

Tuss doesn't like how sad she looks and he feels an overwhelming urge to do something - anything - to cheer her up. There's no way he can walk away and leave her like this. He blurts out the first thing that comes to mind. "This coffee is really hot."

Regina blinks. "Well...it *is* coffee."

He then blurts out the second thing that comes to mind because that first thing was downright terrible. "You wanna go for a walk?"

"A walk?" the Tooth Fairy repeats.

"It's not that cold out. Well, it's cold, but considering...it's not even snowing." He doesn't want to stay here. Not in front of so many potential sets of eyes. Besides, exercise helps fight sadness. Endorphins and all that good stuff.

Regina considers his offer for so long that Tuss worries she may turn him down. But at last she nods her head, a cascade of her shampoo-commercial-worthy hair spilling over her shoulders. "Why not? Lead the way."

Conveyor belts are running around the perimeter of the factory, laden with toys for the elves to paint, as the aroma of gingerbread and peppermint drifts into the large space from the hallway connecting the factory to Mrs. Claus' bakery. The majority of one wall is covered with wreaths and sparkly garland, while another hosts an enormous 'Countdown to Christmas' clock. The third is dedicated solely to the wall of 'Employee of the Month' photos, all featuring Santa himself striking various poses. The fourth wall and workshop ceiling are made of glass so that the Aurora Borealis fills the building with its beautiful light display every hour, of every day, of every year.

Their eyes are shiny, their variously colored bow ties are all tied perfectly and each heart stitched onto the bottoms of their feet are expertly sewn. Wally makes a mark on his clipboard and waves this shipment on its way. "These bears are perfect - keep up the good work." He turns around expecting to check the paint job on the remote control cars, not to be smacked in the face very hard by a very angry hand.

"How dare you!"

Wally touches his burning cheek and stares numbly at Holly as she finally comes into focus. "Wait, what?"

"How dare you!" she yells again, drawing the attention of all the elves in the vicinity. Despite their legendary work ethic, they can't help glancing over. "That was the worst chocolate I've ever had!"

"It was?" Wally blinks. "But--"

"They were terrible! Disgusting! Just like your face! Those glasses don't even fit your disgusting face! You look like a string bean trying to look smart! And you need a haircut! And a nose hair trimmer! And you probably have earwax! All because you're a workaholic!" And with those parting words, Holly throws the empty box of chocolates from Cupid at his feet and stalks away, disappearing behind a stack of wooden blocks.

All around him, the other elves are already giggling and whispering. He'll be the talk of the workshop for at least a week. *Again*. But right now, Wally is too stunned to care, or think, or even pick up the trash still lying at his feet.

"What just happened here?" he asks himself, dumbfounded.

The air is chilly and the conversation, unfortunately, is no different. As the wind rushes between them, Tuss shivers, unable to draw any warmth from the Tooth Fairy.

"Believe it or not, I'm still not used to this cold weather," Tuss admits.

"Neither am I. And I've been here a lot longer than you."

Tuss once again searches his brain frantically for something else to say. "Are all of the roads here named after candy?"

"Not all of them," Regina replies.

Tuss matches Regina's stride as they turn down Spearmint Circle. "Between the street names and these candy cane lamp posts, I almost feel like they should rename this place Candy Land." Regina sort of smiles but says nothing. Tuss feels compelled to press on and keep the conversation moving. "That would be ironic, wouldn't it? The Tooth Fairy living in Candy Land? I bet watching all this candy be made all around you all year long drives you crazy." Tuss tries his best to put on a feminine sounding voice as he continues, "Those poor little teeth! Oh, the humanity!"

"I don't appreciate it, no," Regina responds flatly.

"Have you tried suggesting healthier holiday treats?"

"Of course. But that went over about as well as my Mother's Day suggestion."

Tuss has been forcing the conversation along the entire length of their walk. He has said far too many silly and obvious things. (Such as, "It's cold", which had come out of his mouth at least five times.) He can't keep this up. If he says another word about the weather, even *he's* not going to want to hear another word come out of his mouth. Stopping in the middle of the quiet residential street, he says, "You look depressed. That's why I suggested this walk. Exercise is good for cheering people up, supposedly."

Regina stops a few yards away, twirling her faux fur muff uneasily. Although she looks like she wants to speak, her lips remain closed and motionless.

"It wasn't just about the exercise. I also don't like seeing you sad." Tuss admits, cautiously closing some of the space between them. "I understand if you don't want to talk, but...you're one of the few things I like about this place. When Pia's bitching at me, or Corporate is giving me a hard time, or somebody like Tom is whining about Santa getting an extra piece of fruitcake at lunch...just picturing your smile cheers me up. So now I'm trying to return the favor. Doesn't seem like I'm doing a very good job though."

About a step separates them as their footprints begin to disappear under the suddenly falling snow. The only sound is the brush of the wind between the houses, but neither of them hear it.

The smile on Regina's face is small but visible. "I really didn't want to be alone today, so thanks. I've been up here a long time and for the most part I love it, but...it gets lonely. Sometimes I feel like the only one up here."

Maybe it's the snow on her eyelashes or the drift of her minty fresh breath; maybe it's just the cold and the silence. But Tuss has an overwhelming urge to act - an urge that overpowers any vague attempt to reason. An urge that he cannot shove back down into a safe place because it feels like it could level a skyscraper.

He kisses her. He absolutely has to.

The chill disappears completely.

After their lips mutually part, they remain there close together, enjoying the warmth, neither sure of what to do next.

It is a lovely, fleeting moment that is over too soon.

"Oh." Regina steps back suddenly, her eyes glancing over Tuss' shoulder.

"What?" But Tuss answers his own question the second he turns to find the Boogeyman loitering on the sidewalk, leaning against one of the candy cane lamp posts.

No one moves for some time. Tuss' heart is now pounding against his chest for a different reason.

"That…uh…we…" Tuss stutters, frantically searching for any reasonable, business related explanation for this very precarious situation.

"No need to fear," smirks the sinister looking figure, beginning to retreat back into the shadows. "I'm great at secrets." And he seems to disappear right before their eyes, dissolving into the snow.

"Where did *he* come from?" Tuss demands.

"I don't know," Regina replies.

"I thought we…I never would have…" Tuss turns back to the woman again but avoids her stare. "This is not good."

"If you're worried about him going to Pia, he won't," Regina says. "I promise you. He hates her. And he's not a rat like Bill. He may not seem like the most trustworthy guy, but--"

"But what if it *was* Bill?" Tuss frets. "Or Pia herself? I was sure we were alone and we weren't."

"*Feeling* alone and *being* alone are two different things."

"If Pia finds out, she'll go straight to Corporate," Tuss continues, as though the Tooth Fairy hadn't spoken. "And they wouldn't be happy. This goes against so many policies. I'm your boss. It's not professional."

"Is policy the only thing you're worried about breaking?" Regina raises an eyebrow.

Tuss ignores this. "We can be friends, but we can't... I can't take the risk. I'm sorry."

"Who even said I wanted anything more than friendship?"

"Do you?" Tuss wonders, despite himself.

"It doesn't matter, does it?"

"I guess not. I'm sorry."

"It's fine. I understand." The Tooth Fairy's face is as cold as the sudden rush of wind that blows between them. "Let's go inside. I'm freezing."

"The numbers are acceptable."

Pia smiles. Once all of the numbers were tallied, the call came. There were no pleasantries exchanged. Not even a hello. They got straight to business. "I've nearly doubled the profits from the past three years."

"I said your numbers are acceptable. *Unfortunately*, your advertising campaign was not."

Her smile dissolves. "What do you mean? I had it approved. And I think even *you* can agree it was incredibly effective--"

"Maybe so." She is interrupted by the measured voice on the other end of the line. "But the mortal response to it on the internet was incredibly negative."

"Those mortals don't know what they want--"

"We have decided not to rerun this campaign again next year. That's money out of your profits."

Pia runs her nails down the side of her face, leaving angry, red marks. Her next words are said with great difficulty. "I apologize."

"We expected better. Maybe *I* didn't, but the *others* did. And they are disappointed."

"A, let me rework the campaign for next year. The ads can easily be salvaged and--"

"And what, Pia? We edit out the graveyard?" the voice asks sarcastically. "Change the slogans? We might as well start over. They are useless. Completely useless."

Pia thinks about attempting another protest, but knowing her boss, she chooses to shut down instead. "I understand."

"Manipulating the emotions of the mortals may work in the short term, but they are not as dumb as you would like to believe. Maybe someday you will learn that, but I'm not counting on it. If you haven't grasped such a simple concept by *now*, there's probably no hope for you. After all, there are many simple things you seem incapable of understanding." Pia listens to the voice coming from the speaker with her hands pressed against the sides of her head, like she's trying to hold her skull together. "Put your energy toward the next holiday and maybe the next time we speak, I won't be as disappointed."

Pia is not surprised by the click that follows. For about a minute she sits unmoving, listening to the cruel drone of the dial tone. Then her fist suddenly comes down on the keypad, silencing the last memory of the phone call and causing the light bulb in her lamp to shatter, sending broken, fragile bits sprinkling to the ground as the office goes dark.

Rubbing his baggy eyes, the Sandman stumbles into Bill's office. If one didn't know he was tired, they'd probably think he was drunk by the way he crashes into the door frame and then stares at it curiously like he's not sure how it got there. Bill is too engrossed in writing something on a long sheet of white paper with a crayon to notice him until he actually speaks. "Did you know the cafeteria is closed? It's lunch time!"

Without looking up from his project, Bill chooses a purple crayon and replies snidely, "It's not lunch time. It's past four."

The Sandman reaches under his nightcap and rubs his head, confused. "But I only had my morning nap...and my *other* morning nap...and my *third* morning nap." He frowns. "Maybe I overslept."

"Yeah. Maybe that's what you did," says Bill, his voice dripping with sarcasm. "You do that all the time! And then you come in here complaining you're hungry! The cafeteria hours are clear! Set an alarm or something!"

"I tried that, but I slept through it." He is thoughtful for a moment. "Maybe you could wake me."

"I'm way too busy for that!" Bill proclaims, scrutinizing his color options before choosing a green crayon.

Jack Frost comes by, clutching a giant roll of duct tape. "Damn stair climber broke again! Somebody tell Santa if he breaks it one more time, he's buying a new one!"

"Can you open the cafeteria again? I'm hungry," the Sandman kindly requests.

"No way! Last week I told you no, the week before that, and before that and a hundred *years* before that!" Jack exclaims, exasperated. "Stop asking! Besides, I'm outta chocolate eggs and haggis."

As he disappears into the elevator, the Sandman turns back to Bill, a frown still across his face. "Do you have any food?"

"I can't keep food here! The rats will get it!" There is an angry knocking on the wall, which causes Bill to shout, "I don't mean you, Ted!" He then mumbles, "Leave me alone, you fucking rat."

"So hungry," the Sandman grumbles sadly, patting his growling stomach.

"Can you leave? I'm in the middle of something," Bill responds testily.

But the Sandman has noticed someone else stepping off the elevator. Somebody who looks like she's stuck in a bad mood she just can't shake. "Tooth Fairy! Do you have any food? They closed the cafeteria early again."

"It's nearly dinner," a confused Regina remarks.

"Please?" he requests again.

She sighs with some annoyance. "I have some apples in my office."

"Oh, thank you! Thank you!"

"But you better not fall asleep eating again," she warns sternly. "I *will* just let you die this time."

"That's never happened."

"It happened last week."

"I don't remember that..."

"Can everyone please *leave*?" Bill complains. "I'm in the middle of a very important project!"

"With *crayons*?" Regina comments with disdain.

"Out!"

"Come on, Sandman," she mutters, retreating toward her office. The Sandman follows, dragging his slippers on the concrete floor.

It's quiet in her little corner of the building with Hugh and Hugo still taking advantage of their time off. Regina goes straight to her desk and digs out a shiny and perfectly ripe granny smith apple, which she rubs on her sleeve before handing it to the perpetually sleepy man before her.

"Thank you. You're the only one who helped me." He smiles gratefully before yawning. "You're like a dream come true."

Despite the day that she's had, Regina finds herself sinking into her chair with a smile. "Thanks," she mutters. "I needed that today."

"Tuss, Tuss, Tuss! Why are you not in your closet? Where are you hiding?" Cupid darkens the doorway of Pia's already dark office only an hour after the phone call from Corporate. "Are you two playing hide and seek? Because that's a *terrible* hiding place."

She's seated at her desk, her glare coming across with its usual potency despite the dim lighting. "Tuss isn't here."

"What's with the vampire routine? Getting ready for Halloween already?" Cupid smirks. "I think Independence Day is next, although Bill may have a holiday or two in there..."

"My lamp is broken," Pia says through gritted teeth.

"Did the vines do it? Are they becoming sentient? I knew it was only a matter of time."

"Leave."

"Hey, now! Why are you so cranky? Called my mother today, figured I'd be a good son, and she mentioned Mother's Day brought in some big money."

"Of course it did," Pia snaps.

"Then why do you look so grumpy? Shouldn't you be downstairs throwing it in Mother Nature's face?" Cupid asks. "Or you could at least put on a smile for the occasion. I'm also available for celebratory sex."

"Leave."

But Cupid refuses to listen, as usual. "Something go wrong?"

"No. My plan went perfectly."

"Something went wrong. Did Bill steal your thunder? Did he volunteer to take credit for your brilliant advertising campaign?"

"Why won't you fucking leave?"

"Because I don't want to," Cupid says plainly. "I'll stay here guessing all night unless you tell me what's wrong. Does it have anything to do with Tilly getting stuck in the elevator the other day and Jack refusing to help her get out? Can't exactly blame the guy, she gets herself trapped at least once a month."

"Yes. That's exactly it," Pia replies flatly.

"Don't lie just to get me to go away."

"Is there any other way?"

"You *could* show me your tits…nah, that would have the opposite effect." Cupid steps into the room being careful to avoid stepping on any vines. "If it's not any of those other things…I'm going to have to assume you heard from A."

Pia crosses her arms over her chest and looks away.

"I'm guessing she said something bad." Cupid continues.

No words, no reaction from Pia.

"What did she say? Did she bring up--"

"The mortals didn't like my ad campaign." Pia says, her voice as icy as the howling wind currently blowing in a blizzard right outside of her window.

"Well, it *was* a little harsh," Cupid admits. "Who wants to hear their mother's gonna die?"

"It's the truth," Pia snaps, rising to her feet. "Those puny mortals can drop dead at any moment. *My* mother did. They completely deserve to have their mortality shoved in their weak, pathetic faces."

Cupid stares at her, only a shadowy form in the darkness and hesitates to respond. "Don't dwell on that."

"I don't *dwell* on anything."

Seeing a dead line of conversation before him, Cupid wisely decides to change the subject. "I have something that will cheer you up! Remember that batch of Valentine's candy that Agatha screwed up? I gave a box to Wally by accident. I hope he didn't give it to Holly. Or she didn't eat it. Because if she did...he is *not* going to be happy with me. Come to think of it, maybe I should call him…"

"Well, that would make two of us not happy with you." Pia pushes past Cupid on her way out the door, leaving him behind in her dark office. "I'm going home."

"Fucking tiny ass door piece of shit!" Pia enters the living room of the miniature house her and Tuss are unfortunately still sharing, rubbing her forehead and looking ready to destroy the next thing that even slightly irritates her. She sees Tuss sitting on the couch, slouching in front of the fireplace like a sack of flesh. "What the hell is wrong with *you?*"

"Nothing." He sits up, clearing his throat. "Heard Mother's Day did well."

"Yeah, you and everybody else." A knock at the door interrupts any further conversation. "What the fuck *now?*" Stomping back over to the door, Pia throws it open with a bang to find Caleb standing there, a thick coat of snow covering his head and shoulders. The blizzard is really starting to come in and the cold, white stuff is falling so thickly it's already impossible to see the houses across the street, even with their lights on. "You again? I told you to leave me the hell alone!"

She goes to slam the door shut, but Caleb sticks his foot in the way, not even flinching as Pia continues to try and close it anyway. "Please, Pia! I just want to be near you! I'll do anything!"

Pia is about to tell him to fuck off and continue trying to crush his foot, but then Caleb's last word dances through her mind. "*Anything?*"

"Yes! Anything! I'll do anything for you, Pia! I love you! I love you more than the angels--"

"Would you dig a hole ten feet deep over there?"

"Yes! Yeah! Yes! You bet I will! Let me just get a shovel!" He runs away to do so, tripping and sliding on the ice and slush.

Tuss has appeared in the doorway besides her. "Why'd you ask him to do that? We don't need any holes."

Pia smiles, watching as the snow quickly swallows up Caleb's footprints. "Because I could."

"Nobody laughs at Clucky unless they don't value their fingers."

"So...uh...you definitely should *not* engage in sexual relations with your coworkers because it could lead to problems if the relationship ends badly." Tuss nervously shuffles the paperwork he's been reading from and looks up at his audience. "Are there any questions?"

There probably aren't, but no one gets a chance to raise their hand before the door opens and Pia charges in, carrying a sheet of paper. "I need to talk to you. *Now.*"

"Can it wait? I'm in the middle of this Corporate mandated sexual harassment seminar."

"Are you fucking kidding me?" She turns to see Ted, Bill, Tom, T.J., Frank and Tilly staring blankly at them. The Sandman is there as well, but he is anything but attentive and is muttering something about goat butter in his sleep. "Who the hell are these morons going to sexually harass? Themselves? Where's everybody else?"

"They...didn't show up."

"Hallway. *Now.*"

Tuss gives up the fight, but only because he's not too excited about the next segment of the presentation: 'Fondling. It's Not Always Fun for Everyone'. "I'll be right back," he informs the group.

"Take your time!" Tilly calls cheerfully. "We can busy ourselves with this helpful literature you handed out!"

"What do you mean you're out of goat butter?" murmurs the Sandman.

Once they're alone in the hall with the conference room door closed, Pia shoves the important looking piece of paper at Tuss, which turns out to be an email from Corporate. "Get a load of this crap."

Tuss scans it quickly. "Are they serious?"

"No, it's a fake email that I sent from A's account," Pia snaps sarcastically, snatching the paper back. "Of *course* they are. When aren't they? They want us to call a meeting about it."

"But we already have so much going on."

"I know! I hate the idea! They're already down my throat about Halloween *and* they're making *you* give a lecture about *sex* to a bunch of *animals* and a *dwarf*!"

"He's an elf," Tuss corrects her. "And don't forget the Sandman. Or Bill."

"The only women that sleepy sack of shit is harassing are in his own sick dreams," Pia spits. "And Bill couldn't get laid at Mardi Gras by the most desperate, drunken hooker around!"

"The lecture is about sexual harassment. Not actually *having* sex."

"The one person who needs to hear this garbage isn't even in there! Cupid harasses me and everybody else in this office a million times a day!"

"Actually, I'm surprised no one has complained about him to Corporate," Tuss points out.

"Like they'd ever touch a precious hair on his head." Pia's face darkens. "Look. We have to have a meeting about these changes and you--"

Before she can continue, the conference room door opens again and Bill timidly sticks his head out. "Can I talk to you both for a teeny, tiny second?"

Pia shoots him a cutting glare. "What is *so* damn important that you need to interrupt our *obviously* private conversation?"

"It'll just take a second."

"Is it about someone sexually harassing you?" Pia snorts. "Because they should just kill themselves."

"It's…uh…about Flag Day."

"*What* day?"

"Flag Day!" Bill says enthusiastically. "It's an American holiday celebrating their highly recognizable and *very* marketable flag. I have a lot of great ideas for this year, starting with a parade that…features… ponies..." He trails off as the look he is getting from Pia seems volatile enough to set him on fire.

"Bill," Pia begins dangerously. "Get your sorry, disgusting ass back in that conference room before I beat the ever living shit out of you and string your battered, scrawny little body up in the lobby as a warning to others."

"I…uh…just thought that…uh...since you won't take my calls--"

"*Now!*"

All color gone from his face, Bill pops back into the conference room without another word.

Pia rubs her forehead. "I can't *believe* what they're making us do. This is the second to last *fucking* thing I want to deal with. After whatever the hell Bill was talking about."

"I've never heard of Flag Day," Tuss remarks thoughtfully.

"Tell everyone there's a meeting tomorrow and they better show up. I better not get a turnout of the office sad sacks like you have in there."

"I probably should have lied about what the seminar was about," Tuss admits. "Or maybe promised food."

"Lie, drug, beat, whatever. Just get their asses in their seats. This is *everyone's* problem."

177

"So Corporate has decided, since these countries we handle will take in any dumb piece of shit and whatever crazy garbage they celebrate, that we have to be *inclusive* and run a ton of other *stupid* religious holidays from now on." Pia strides before her captive and almost complete audience in the conference room with her usual look of displeasure. (What's-his-face who runs St. Patrick's Day is the only one missing, as usual.)

"These holidays have been handled for years by our other offices around the world, but since they now have a sizeable following in North America, Corporate wants a piece of those profits as well." Tuss clears his throat. "Also, for those of you who missed my sexual harassment seminar yesterday, I have some pamphlets for you to take when you leave."

"These dumbass holidays are all religion and no substance," Pia complains. "Some of them last for days, some for a whole damn month! They involve terrible things like *fasting*! And *charity*! I mean, what the hell are we supposed to sell then? *Air*? Invent a phony charity?" She pauses thoughtfully for a moment. "Actually, that's not a bad idea..."

"I fail to see how this involves us," drones the Boogeyman, as his Shadow stifles a yawn behind him.

"It involves you because someone has to handle all this shit! So start volunteering!"

Bill's hand shoots up immediately.

"How about someone who's not a total loser?" Pia states.

No other hands go up.

Pia glares around the table like a robot assassin scanning targets for weaknesses. A lot of people suddenly find the surface of the table extremely interesting and Ted even dives behind his stump, but still not one of them speaks up. "If no one wants to volunteer, I'll be happy to assign these dumbass holidays based on the time of year." She pulls a list out of her pocket and starts barking out orders. "Looks like Ash

Wednesday falls closest to Valentine's Day. That would make it *yours*, you disgusting asshole."

Cupid's head snaps up and he stops doodling breasts on the pad of paper that Ted brought into the meeting. "What? No! I'm not taking that holiday! People don't do anything but go to church! And I think they give things up too! That *totally* goes against my moral code!" The Boogeyman snorts, but Cupid continues. "Dump that on Francis. That's part of the lead up to his holiday, isn't it?"

"I have enough to do!" protests Francis. "Those beautifully painted eggs we churn out every year are extremely time consuming! We barely finished this year's batch as it is! I don't have time to take on another holiday!"

"Shut it, Cupid. And you shut it too, *rabbit*." Pia glares. "I was already planning to dump Passover on your ass."

"Passover?" Francis' whiskers twitch. "Never heard of it!"

"It's one of the Jewish pilgrim festivals!" pipes up Bill. "It celebrates the Exodus from--"

"Bill! Adults are talking!" Pia snaps.

"I'm not taking that holiday." Cupid crosses his arms stubbornly.

"Me either!" Francis insists.

The Boogeyman chuckles and sits back to enjoy the bickering with his hands behind his head, his Shadow imitating the movement on the wall behind him. "This is *quite* amusing."

"Is it?" snaps Pia, turning on him and giving the frazzled bunny and the perverted doodler a breather. "Because I have two on the list for *you* - Rosh Hashanah and Yom Kippur."

The color drains from the Boogeyman's already pale face. "I absolutely refuse. And I'm fairly sure you made both of those up."

179

"Actually, Rosh Hashanah is the Jewish New Year and Yom Kippur is one of the Jewish High Holy days where--"

"Bill! Nobody gives a shit!" Pia yells.

"I will not take any further holidays and you can't force me to," the Boogeyman says definitively, crossing his arms over his chest. Behind him, his Shadow does the same, even nodding its black, faceless head in agreement. "If it's a New Year's thing, give it to the clock-obsessed old man."

"Absolutely not! I have a *baby* to take care of!" Father Time groans.

"You're not being inclusive!" Pia shouts. "I don't see what the damn problem is if you're *all* going to suffer! T.J. will take Ramadan--"

"The ninth month of the Islamic calendar!" Bill explains.

"And Santa can take on Kwanzaa and Chan-u-kah," Pia continues.

"That's not the correct pronunciation," Bill raises his voice. "It's actually pronounced--"

"Shut. The. *Fuck*. Up. Bill!"

Santa has been smiling in his usual jolly way this entire time, but his famous grin has quickly faded from his face. "Pia, I know you're just doing your job, but I'm afraid we have enough on our plate at the workshop as it is. I simply don't have time to take on and Chanukah and...that other holiday you mentioned."

"I am one *hundred* percent sure Kwanzaa is made up," Cupid insists.

"Actually--"

"Bill! If you talk again, I'm going to staple your fucking mouth shut!" Pia snarls.

"But I know all of these holidays," he whines. "If you'd just give me a chance--"

"Why don't we just hire someone new to handle these holidays?" Tuss suggests. "Clearly no one wants them and frankly, I don't blame them. It's a lot of extra work and added stress."

"But I--"

"I second that idea!" Cupid speaks up immediately.

"Me too," the Boogeyman nods curtly.

"Me three," Francis concurs. "Or...four."

T.J. lets out a loud screech.

"I think that sounds like a splendid plan!" Santa beams.

"But I would be happy to--"

"Fine." Pia grumpily plops down into the chair that once belonged to Bill, cutting him off in the process. "Because I have *tons* of time to find someone to handle these holidays that no one gives a crap about."

"That's the spirit!" Santa says cheerily, not noticing the sarcasm.

"Speaking of underappreciated holidays," begins Bill, trying to speak with confidence. "Flag Day is almost here and I'd like to announce--"

"Meeting adjourned," Pia states.

"But I'd just like to say real quick--"

"I said meeting adjourned!" Pia repeats loudly. "Everybody get the hell out - *especially* Bill!"

Everyone is all too happy to leave the conference room and get back to their many pending tasks, which include sampling a fresh batch of holiday gravy, filling some fake blood capsules and jerking off to some internet porn.

But Bill does not leave the chair that once belonged to his best friend

181

Miguel. Instead, he sits in the empty conference room and collects his thoughts for a moment. "I'll show them. This is going to be the best Flag Day ever," he grumbles to himself. Out in the hallway, he can hear everyone trying - and failing - to pronounce Chanukah. "And once they see what an amazing job I've done, Corporate'll be so impressed they'll give me *all* those other holidays. I'll earn them! Just wait! I *will* earn those holiday's fair and square."

Suddenly, Cupid ducks back into the room, quickly grabbing the pad of paper Ted left behind. "Don't want to forget this," he says with a grin. "I did some good work here."

"What's that?" Wally enters the toy factory's modest break area and takes a fresh sugar cookie from the snack tray; one of the perks of being an elf.

Frank snorts and puts down the pamphlet he's been reading at the small table in the corner. Other than the two of them, the area is empty. Elves - well, most of them anyway - have a very strong work ethic and never, *ever* take unscheduled breaks. "Some dumb brochure I got at that stupid sexual harassment seminar yesterday."

"Frank! Frankie? Where are you, son?" Santa's booming voice seems to seize Frank like a sudden case of diarrhea. "My long underwear needs scrubbing! Some of these stains are just so stubborn! Like this chocolate one that's all over the back…at least I *think* it's chocolate…"

"I better go," Frank grumbles unhappily, dragging himself out of the break area and leaving the pamphlet behind.
Wally picks up the pamphlet and flips through it with interest. On the first page it reads: 'Female employees need to be treated the same as men in the workplace, from wages to benefits to uniforms'.

"Hey, Wally."

At the sight of Holly, Wally hastily shoves the pamphlet into his back pocket. "Uh, hi! How's it going?"

"I went on a terrible date last night." She begins to pour herself a mug of hot chocolate, more rich and delicious than anything humans could ever replicate. "Can you believe he didn't pick up the check right away?"

"That's horrible." Wally adjusts his glasses as his eyes glide over her legs, which are generously exposed thanks to the short skirt that she and the rest of the female elves wear.

Then he realizes something.

"You shouldn't have to wear that."

"Huh?" Holly is adding marshmallows to her cocoa.

"A skirt," Wally points out. "You should get to wear pants like the male elves. Skirts are sexist," he adds definitively.

Holly can't help smirking as she glances at the nearly skin tight green pants Wally is wearing; they're standard issue and only a few inches more forgiving than tights. "I like my skirt, thanks."

"You do?" Wally stutters, thrown off balance by this information. "B-but they're so short and....it must be hard to...you know...bend over."

"They're super easy to move in, actually. *And* we wear shorts underneath." She smirks. "You didn't know that? You're hilarious." Completed cocoa in hand, she returns to work.

With a frown, Wally reaches into his pocket, pulls out the pamphlet and keeps reading.

"What about that guy Merc suggested?"

"No way. I already have to deal with *one* drunken fucktard who never shows up to work, I don't wanna go for *two*." Pia is sitting besides Tuss at Mother Nature's coffee cart while the old woman glares at them, continuously cleaning the same cup.

"I didn't think the guy looked that bad," Tuss replies with a shrug.

"I know Merc better than you, so trust me. He does *not* run with anyone I'd ever wanna hire."

The door to the nearby restroom opens and out trips Caleb, trying to model a pair of fiery red stilettos. It's the tenth pair he's put on. "What about these, Pia?"

She glances over briefly. "Put those in the maybe pile."

"You got it!" Caleb wobbles his way back into the bathroom.

"Why don't you try on the shoes yourself?" Tuss asks wearily.

"It's more fun this way," Pia shrugs.

"Why do you make him try them on in the bathroom? He could sit here."

"It's. More. Fun. This. Way. Besides," Pia reasons. "I'm too busy trying to find some asshole to do this job to do anything else."

Behind them, the elevator doors slide open. Bill quickly pushes out a big box and then goes back inside, leaving the box unattended. No one even looks at it.

"What about that golem you interviewed?" Tuss asks.

"No way. Total yes man."

Caleb clops out of the restroom once more in a pair of bright green peep toe pumps. "These match your eyes!"

"They're hideous," Pia says without even looking at them. "Reject pile."

"Are you sure?" Caleb asks, crestfallen. "They're pretty comfortable. Well, kind of."

"Reject pile!"

Caleb returns to the bathroom as if he is headed for the reject pile himself.

Again, the elevator doors open and again, Bill shoves out a big cardboard box. Still nobody notices.

"Maybe we should split them up between a few new hires," Tuss suggests. "We're probably not getting any applications because no one wants to take on so many holidays."

"I would hardly call these *annoyances* we have to deal with *holidays*," Pia says. "They're pains in my ass, that's what they are. No one gives a shit about them."

"You know that's not true." Tuss takes a long sip of coffee. "They won't recruit anybody?"

"For crappy little holidays like these? Never. Besides, they're trying to get away from doing that."

This time when the elevator doors open, Bill slides yet another box out, sweating more than usual. "Only one more!" he announces joyfully.

No one even turns around.

"What about--"

Tuss cuts himself off as Caleb comes stumbling out of the restroom in zebra patterned pumps with heels so high they clearly belong around a stripper pole. He has a very hard time even taking a step in them. "I'm not sure about these..."

"Come closer," Pia instructs.

With great difficulty, Caleb makes his way over, having to lean heavily on the chairs just to stay on his feet. He's barely come to a stop in front of Pia before she's shaking her head, not even taking another glance at the shoes. "Reject."

With a frown, Caleb begins the return trip, relying on the chairs again and nearly falling on his face as one of the chairs slips on the floor from his weight.

Tuss can't take it anymore. "Take them off! Please! Just take the damn shoes off!"

Before Pia can object, Caleb hops out of the shoes and scurries into the sanctity of the bathroom.

"How dare he listen to you!"

"He was going to kill himself in those things! I can't believe you even considered wearing them!"

"I didn't. I just wanted to see him fall on his face. Now I'm disappointed."

Mother Nature's eyes have practically narrowed to slits by the time the elevator arrives again. And this time as the doors open, Bill pushes out a box but doesn't rush back inside. Instead, he leans on the box to catch his breath, smiling despite his exhaustion. "Homemade flags!" he announces to absolutely no one. "I'm taking them to the shipping center right now! Been making them all year! They're gonna sell like candy canes at Christmas! Best Flag Day ever!" With those words, he puts his weight behind one of the boxes and pushes it out the front doors of the building.

Tuss turns around. "Was someone just here?"

"Nope," Pia answers. "And what the hell are you glaring at, bitch?" she barks at Mother Nature.

Santa stands in the doll production area, nodding his head as Wally reads the daily numbers from his tablet. Holly stands just behind her rotund employer, typing intently on her phone. Around them are about twenty female elves stitching buttons, spinning yarn for hair and painting tiny eyes and tiny mouths with equally tiny brushes. "Ho, ho, ho! Excellent work, everyone! Keep it up!"

"Of course, Santa!" replies a chorus of high-pitched voices.

"Now, where's Frank? I have some bunions that need some attention. Frank!"

Santa goes wandering off, but Holly stays where she is, still typing. Wally sees this as an opportunity to redeem himself in her eyes, but he can't think of a conversation starter. Frantically, he scans the area, but all he can see are female elves busy at work on their dolls as per usual.

Then it hits him.

"It's pretty sexist that only the female elves make dolls, don't you think?" he speaks up, feeling as though he is making a brilliant observation.

But Holly only shakes her head with a bit of a smile and follows after Santa.

Wally frowns.

"We like making dolls!" A nearby elf named Ally pipes up, her voice chipper. "It's way more interesting than painting trucks or carving blocks!"

"Of course it is," grumbles Wally. He stomps off in the opposite direction, knowing that he'll once again be the talk of every cocoa break.

"So then he comes into the doll area, and says 'I think it's sexist that only female elves make dolls'."

Pia gives Holly and Regina a dirty look as they giggle over their lunch conversation. She is sitting with Tuss and Caleb, who is happily filling a fork with another scoop of slop. Despite the fact that Jack Frost is serving up a questionable mash of turkey, chocolate, hot dog and fruitcake that he is calling holiday hash, the cafeteria is crowded and every table is taken.

"Should she even be in here?" Pia grumbles as the elf and the Tooth Fairy laugh again. "Shouldn't she be with her *own* kind?"

"That's not very inclusive..." Tuss mutters as he eyes Regina longingly across the room.

"Here you go, Pia!" Caleb proudly holds up the full fork and aims it at her mouth.

"Not now!" she snaps, waving him away. "I'll tell you when I want it." She frowns at the brown goo she is being offered. "Which may be never, by the look of that sludge. It's disturbing."

"Not as disturbing as Tom encouraging everyone to pick out the turkey bits to eat first," Tuss notes.

Pia glances over to where Tom is seated nearby with a couple of other turkeys. "He's not actually *eating* this stuff, is he? That bird is fucked in the head!"

"Not as fucked as we'll be if we don't find someone to take these holidays," Tuss points out. "I got three calls from Corporate this morning. From the same person."

"Big deal! I got seven! Why do they care so much about these useless holidays? I don't get it! Are they that damn desperate for money? The *yak* probably brings in more with her holidays and I'm pretty sure only five people live in that forgettable, pointless excuse for a country! Isn't their currency snow?"

"She's a moose and none of that is true," Tuss says patiently. "By the way, have you forwarded Tilly's emails to Corporate? She seems to *really* want that *Mighty Ducks* DVD."

"Are you fucking kidding me right now?" Pia demands.

Before Tuss can respond, Caleb asks, "Are you ready yet, Pia?"

"I said I'll tell you when I'm ready, Caleb!" Pia angrily rubs her temples. "I swear, if there was an *actual* holiday this month, I would not be spending one damn *second* on these pointless, useless, forgettable second-rate excuses for holidays!"

"Good afternoon, all!"

Everyone turns their attention to the entrance of the cafeteria, where Bill is standing, having just entered the room. He is dressed in full late eighteenth century American clothing. *Women's* clothing.

"What the hell?!"

"I am dressed as Betsy Ross, the maker of the first American flag. Well, arguably. Most historians agree--" The laughter that follows drowns out everything else he's trying to say. Bill frowns, clears his throat and speaks louder. "I'm here to announce that this year we will see the best Flag Day parade ever!"

"Ooh! There's a parade?" Tilly asks excitedly.

"There most certainly is!" Bill goes on proudly. "Except unlike boring old Thanksgiving, there's actually more than one!"

"There is? Where are they?" the moose asks.

"Uh...*towns*..."

"Really?" Tilly asks, genuinely interested. "Which ones?"

"Ones...you've never...heard of," Bill flushes.

A fresh crop of laughter pops up from Tom's table, led by the head turkey himself. "Hey, Bill!" he calls condescendingly. "How many people watch your parades? Seven, give or take a couple of squirrels?"

"The only parade you should be going to in that ridiculous getup is for gay pride."

Tuss frowns at Pia, even though the rest of the room is chuckling at her remark. "That's not politically correct at all."

Ignoring that comment, Pia snaps her fingers at Caleb, indicating that she finally wants her food. She takes a mouthful from the fork Caleb offers as Bill speaks up again.

"As I was trying to say, my costume symbolizes--"

But he's interrupted again when Pia stops abruptly, her eyes bulging slightly. She grabs for her throat with both hands.

"She's choking! She's dying!" Caleb cries hysterically, leaping to his feet so quickly he overturns his chair. "Do *something*! Somebody do *something*!"

Tuss sighs and slowly puts down his napkin. "She'll be fine. *Relax.*" He slowly ambles to his feet and calmly performs the Heimlich maneuver. A chunk of chewed up brown sludge comes flying out of her mouth and lands on the floor by Bill's feet.

Jack Frost shrugs from where he is watching in the kitchen. "No different from the shit usually coming out of her mouth."

Getting her breath back, Pia turns on Caleb like a leopard locating its prey in the grass. "You little *shit*! You practically killed me!"

"No he didn't," mumbles Tuss with a roll of his eyes.

"It was an accident!" Caleb has tears in his eyes.

"Are you so *damn* stupid that you can't even pick up food with a fucking fork? It's not that hard! Even the fucking *yak* can do it!" She jerks her head at Tilly.

"I'm a moose and I use a specialized fork that I can pick up with my hoof!" Tilly cheerfully explains.

"Shut the fuck up, *yak*! You're not helping my point!"

As all eyes are now on the show Pia is putting on starring a deeply embarrassed Caleb, a dejected looking Bill is able to slink unseen out the door, bonnet and all.

Here We Come A-wassailing?" Willy, the elf choir director, demands.

"Do you even know what wassailing is?" Wally asks. "I think it sounds sexual."

"I'm pretty sure it means caroling!" Willy insists.

"*Allegedly.*"

"Well, what's wrong with *Up On the Rooftop*?" Willy asks. "It's about Santa delivering gifts!"

"The word *ho* is used a disturbing amount of times in that song," Wally explains.

"Because it's Santa laughing!" Willy complains, waving the list that Wally gave him through the air. "I don't believe this!"

"Well, I'm sorry," says Wally loudly. They are standing in the workshop break room and it's not a particularly noisy location. With Willy standing so close, there's really no obvious reason for him to speak at his current volume. "But some of these songs might make the female elves uncomfortable. And as respected members of the team, we want them to have a safe workplace." Except that Holly happens to be standing nearby, refilling the napkins.

"What are you two talking about?" she asks finally, finishing her task and walking over to join them.

"Wally gave me this list of Christmas songs he thinks are sexist!" Willy says, outraged. "He doesn't want the choir to perform them anymore!"

Holly takes the list and looks it over. "Why is *O Christmas Tree* on here?"

"How lovely are thy branches? That's not something you should say...to a tree...in the workplace," Wally blushes.

Holly shakes her head and hands the list back. "You're weird."

"I'm going to have to change our whole summer concert series!" Willy complains, as Wally watches Holly walk away with a frown. "Not to mention regionals! The penguins at the South Pole are going to wipe the ice with us! What about *Deck the Halls*? Is that one okay, or is *fa la la la la* street slang for a hand job?"

Wally takes the list from the choir director and tears it in two with a crestfallen mumble of "Forget it."

The ceiling is dripping again and the smell is unidentifiable as usual. The Sandman's snoring shakes the room as it echoes up and down the concrete halls, rattling the framed picture of himself and Miguel resting on his desk – the only evidence that he has a personal life at all. Or *had* a personal life, anyway. Also, the last bulb he had for his only lamp just died. Just another day in Bill's office.

At least the banner hanging over his desk - the one the reads 'Best Flag Day Ever!' – is adding some color to the place. He had to steal every last crayon from the Easter floor, but it was worth it. Despite the fact that the holiday is almost over and went entirely ignored by Corporate - *again* - the banner is making him happy.

Well, not quite happy maybe, but slightly less miserable at the very least. Bill places his head in his hands and figures he better start thinking about Labor Day.

"This is the worst place on Earth and I've been to fucking New Jersey."

Bill's head snaps up in surprise to find Pia standing in his doorway. Pia never comes down here. *Ever.* Having her here is like a holiday in itself. "P-P-Pia! What are you doing here?"

"I came to this hell hole of a floor to find some plant poison, which is not here. Stupid Caleb. He told me he ordered it," Pia sighs deeply. "Anyway, since I was already torturing myself, I decided to come tell you that we've decided to give you those extra pointless holidays that we couldn't dump on anybody better."

"Really? All of them?" cries Bill excitedly, joyfully leaping to his feet.

"All except Kwanzaa," Pia explains. "Tuss found somebody Corporate was willing to hire for that dead weight."

"Is this because this year's Flag Day was so successful?" Bill asks with a wide smile. "I sold seventy-two flags! A new record!"

"Hell no!" Pia spits. "I'm giving them to you because they're as useless as you are! And what the fuck is Flag Day?"

"Jack Frost tried to cook Clucky one day. Clucky didn't like that."

"You should know *exactly* why I'm here."

"If it's about your shriveled up dick not working, I can't help you. But Cupid probably has some kind of pill that can help with that."

Father Time frowns at Pia as he bats another rogue vine out of his face. The thorny nuisances that happily snag the hair of any average-sized visitor have overrun the office ceiling. It's one of the many problems the entire floor is having with the plant life Mother Nature once treasured. "You could at least stop making impotent jokes if you insist on mocking me every time we speak. You know damn well I'm here about Caleb."

"What about the little moron?"

Visibly bristling at her words, Father Time frowns and makes his point clear. "I object to how you've been using him. He - for some unknown, unexplainable and *insane* reason - thinks he's in love with you. And you treat him like a slave!"

"I haven't forced him to do *anything* against his will," Pia remarks.

"You had him chase down a polar bear for your amusement!" Father Time yells.

"It's not like he was going to catch up with it," Pia shrugs.

"He was lost for three days!"

"It's not like he was going to *die*," Pia rolls her eyes. "Besides, Santa had his people find him."

"After they found him, you immediately had him *cleaning the toilets on your floor*!"

"Bill used one! It was a fucking emergency! And it's not like *Jack Off Frost* was going to do it anytime this century! Pretty sure he hasn't even been to that disgusting third floor since Cormac's people had that potato famine! Besides, Caleb's still being punished for the time he almost choked me to death."

"Something we've *all* dreamed about," Father Time mutters under his breath.

Pia gives the old man a particularly venomous stare. "He's like a forty-year-old man. He can make his own decisions."

"He's only forty *physically*!," Father Time stresses. "Not *emotionally*! He's not even *close*! Why doesn't *anyone* understand that?"

At that moment, Caleb stumbles into the office, looking like he just lost a very rough fight with a plant. There are leaves tangled in his hair, burrs clinging to his clothes and pollen dotting his face. His hands are streaked with angry red scratches and his skin is coated with various sticky mixtures, all of which smell terrible. "Pia, my love, I really don't think those plants want to go!" he reports breathlessly. "Oh, hello, Father."

"Of course they do! You're just not trying hard enough!" Pia snaps. "Those satanic fuckers have to have roots somewhere! Destroy the floor if you have to! You can fix it later!"

"Okay..." Caleb does not seem very enthusiastic as he trudges back into the hallway.

Before Father Time can object, T.J. comes soaring into the office, landing expertly on the edge of Pia's desk after dropping a rolled up piece of paper in front of her. A breathless Bill hurries in moments later, already wiping his forehead with his stained handkerchief.

"What the hell does everybody think this is?" Pia complains, unfurling the paper. "A damn open house?" She reads the memo with a frown. "*More* garbage from Corporate?"

"Not more holidays, I hope," frets Father Time. "I have no affiliation with Chinese New Year and I plan to keep it that way."

T.J. lets out a derisive cry and Bill smirks as he translates. "You're afraid of dragons?"

"They are terrifying creatures!" Father Time says defensively.

"Relax, limp dick." Pia rolls her eyes. "Apparently Corporate is concerned because American Independence Day is the holiday with the most accidental fires. And since you can't spend money if you're dead, they want us to spread fire awareness this year."

"I was surprised it has the most," Bill comments.

"How can you be surprised?" counters Father Time. "Half the profits are based off of illegally purchased fireworks! And with all the drinking that goes on, I doubt they're set off safely."

"Can you go now, you ugly old piece of shit?" Pia snaps.

"No! I haven't finished what I came to say!"

Pia rolls her eyes and turns to the eagle. "Why are you wasting my time with this?"

T.J. screeches loudly.

"He wants you to come to his office tomorrow so that he can test out the fire safety tips he prepared on an audience. I offered to read them-" Bill gets an angry screech right in his face. "But...he doesn't want me to do it."

"Fine," Pia sighs, staring at the eagle. "Whatever. Anything to prevent Bill from saying another *damn* word. Are you done now? Can you leave?" She turns her glare on Father Time as she continues. "Or is your rickety old back keeping you from hobbling back to the fucking elevator?"

"Help!" Caleb's voice drifts in clearly from the hallway. "Pia! Help! I'm being eaten by a plant!"

Pia rolls her eyes. "*Again?*"

197

T.J.'s office is the perfect size for a bird with a large wingspan, but it's not an ideal place for a meeting. Aside from the eagle himself, Tuss, Bill, Jack Frost, Cupid, Francis, Regina, Father Time, Santa and the Boogeyman have already gathered inside by the time Pia arrives the next afternoon, yelling into her cell phone.

"I just left you five fucking seconds ago!" she snaps. "I don't care if you don't see the point of it! Someone has to trim those things! I can barely see my damn monitor! I was nice enough to get you the gloves you wanted, so just shut up and get it done!" She is already annoyed when she hangs up and is only further irritated to find Bill is blocking the door. "Out of my damn way."

"Um…T.J. has requested that everyone leave their cell phones outside so they don't interrupt the meeting." He points to a table nearby where a bunch of other phones are sitting, abandoned. One is ringing to the tune of *I'm Your Boogie Man* by K.C. and the Sunshine Band and three of them have Cupid's name spelled out in sparkling jewels.

"This is ridiculous," Pia grumbles, as she reluctantly places her phone besides the others. "Let's get this over with."

Inside the office, everyone is a little impatient. Jack Frost sneezes without bothering to cover his mouth, earning a disgusted look from Regina. "That's really unsanitary."

"Well, *sorry* that I'm sick," he shoots back. "It's bad enough that it's throwing off everything."

"You mean sexually?"

"No!" Jack glares at Cupid. "I mean my powers."

"You mean your power of avoidance so that you don't have to clean anything?"

"You're fucking hysterical," Jack grumbles, glaring at the Boogeyman.

"Can we get started please?" Father Time complains. "I feel like I've been here *forever.*"

"That's because you got here two hours ago," Bill shoots back. "We *told* you that you were early."

"The clock said I was on time!" Father Time snaps. "And I just fixed them all! Again!"

"Where's Kwanzaa?" Francis is asking Bill as Pia takes the pamphlet on fire safety from T.J.'s claw. "I told him to come."

"He started already?" Bill asks, surprised. "I haven't even met him!"

"I'm glad he's not here," Cupid states.

"Why?" Bill asks.

"Shut up, Bill. Why are you always fucking talking when I'm trying to run a meeting?" Pia stands beside T.J.'s perch, ready to go. "I can't be the only one who wants to get this over with so that I can get back to doing actual work. *Some* of us have *actual* work." She glares at Jack as she says this, but he's just leaning against the wall staring up at the ceiling, oblivious. "Bill! Go somewhere where I don't have to see your ugly face!"

Bill quietly closes the door in order to muffle the patriotic music playing loudly in the hallway, before stepping behind Francis.

Pia turns to the pamphlet and begins to read aloud the tips T.J. spent about five minutes putting together after a single internet search. His favorite part was finding clip art to match each one. "The duck wants some feedback on this crap, so pay attention. Tip number one. Fire drills should be held at least once every three months."

"What's a fire drill?"

The Boogeyman's question brings the room to an immediate halt. Everyone looks at everybody else, waiting for an explanation, but even Pia seems without an answer.

"That's…uh…when you practice making a fire?" Francis guesses.

"No it isn't," Regina speaks up in a motherly tone. "This is for fire *safety*. The idea is to *avoid* fire, not cause one. I think."

T.J. yells something.

"It means practicing leaving the building in case of a fire," Bill translates.

"*Oh*," everybody choruses with an understanding nod.

"They should call it a fire *escape* and not a fire *drill*," Father Time decides. "To make it more clear."

"Tip number two," Pia continues. "Never use the elevator during a fire. Only use the stairs."

"We don't *have* stairs," Cupid points out.

"Well, we're not delicate little mortals who have to worry about being murdered by some stupid fire," Pia counters, as Regina shoots her a dirty look.

"What's the point of standing here listening to this stuff if it doesn't even apply to us?" Cupid shoots back.

T.J. gives an angry screech that silences the room.

"Because the angry bird wants it that way!" yells Pia, not even bothering to wait for the translation. "Can I get on with it? Tip number three. Never put cigarettes out in trash cans. Always use an ashtray."

"What about lit Jack-o'-lanterns?" the Boogeyman calls out. "Is that frowned upon?"

Why wouldn't you just put out the candle before tossing it?" asks Tuss.

The Boogeyman shrugs, bored. "I don't actually do that, I was just wondering if I could."

"Keep all of your stupid comments and questions to yourself!" Pia interrupts. "I would be done with this crap already if you morons didn't keep interrupting me! Tip number four! All exits should be clearly marked so they can be located easily in an emergency."

Cupid raises his hand. "Is a boring meeting an emergency?"

Pia ignores him and keeps talking. "Tip number five. Fire extinguishers need to be available and regularly checked to make sure they are in working order. Everyone should also understand how to use one in case of an emergency."

"At least we have those." Santa points to a closet that bears a small sticker indicating that there's a fire extinguisher inside.

"I don't know how to use one though," admits Regina.

"It's not important, despite what this garbage says," snarls Pia, her patience still remarkably intact, but teetering dangerously on the borderline "No one here will ever need to use one."

"I repeat what I said earlier about needing to be here," Cupid says.

"Tip six!" Pia raises her voice. "Make sure all fire alarms are working and have batteries. Tip *seven*! If you suspect there's a fire, feel all doors before opening them to make sure they're not hot."

"I know a thing or two about being hot." Cupid winks at Regina and Tuss. "He doesn't." He points to Jack Frost.

"Shut up," Jack sneezes.

"Tip eight," Pia hurries on. "If there is smoke coming under a door, use a towel or your clothing to block it."

"Uh..." Francis begins, his nose twitching.

"Tip nine--"

"Excuse me?"

"What did I say about stupid questions and comments, Bill?" Pia barks.

"Actually...it was me," the Easter Bunny gulps

Pia's eyes find Francis, who is running a paw nervously over his right ear. "What is it?"

"I...think I smell *smoke*."

Pia rolls her eyes with such force, her whole head moves. "Sure you do."

"I think somebody's a little paranoid," chuckles Santa.

"I do smell it!" Francis insists.

"You just *think* you do because we're talking about smoke and fire," reasons Tuss kindly.

"You're crazy," the Boogeyman adds bluntly.

"I'm not crazy!" the large rabbit protests. "I'm the only animal here!"

T.J.'s loud cry seems to protest this, but Francis continues unaffected. "My sense of smell is better than yours! I'm telling you, I smell smoke! It's faint, but it's definitely there."

"You've been wrong before," the Boogeyman points out. "You bet me good money Amelia Earhart would make it."

"I know what I smell!" Francis insists.

"Too bad we never had any fire escapes then," Father Time mumbles, giving his many watches a glance. "We're all doomed. Now can we hurry this along, *please*? For once, I agree with the demon woman. I have a stack of party hat designs to go through!"

"What did you just fucking call me?" Pia snarls.

"You heard me, demon woman," Father Time repeats coldly.

Bill gasps.

"You old, wrinkled, shriveled piece of--"

"I smell it too!"

"Smell what?" Tuss asks Regina, hoping to stop Pia's latest tirade before it really gets going.

"Smoke!" she cries. "I think Francis is right!"

"I told you!" The rabbit is too busy fretting about the situation to enjoy the validation. "There's a fire in the building!"

"There *can't* be a fire," Father Time insists logically. "If there was, one of the fire alarms would have sounded. We *do* have those, correct?"

He addresses Jack Frost with that last question, but he doesn't look like he's about to give any sort of reassuring answer as he nervously scratches the back of his head. "Yeah...about that...they don't have batteries. Never did."

"*What?*" the old man yells. "How do they not have batteries?"

"Everybody keeps needing them for their TV remotes! Corporate never sends me enough!" Jacks says defensively.

"Also, I stole a bunch once for some...*personal* items," Cupid admits with a grin.

"I smell the smoke too," Santa speaks up, sounding worried.

"That's because it's coming under the door!" shrieks Bill, running as far away from it as he can. "There's a fire! There's a fire! There's a fire in the building!"

"Calm down!" Regina shouts, attempting to take charge. "Yelling and getting worked up isn't--"

"Where do we go?" Bill continues, ignoring the Tooth Fairy completely. "There's no marked exit! How are we gonna get outta here?"

"There's only one door! There doesn't *need* to be a marked exit!"

"Yeah, but the pamphlet said we can't take the elevator," Cupid points out. "We're trapped on this floor anyway."

"We are going to die!"

"Not permanently," the Boogeyman unhelpfully reminds everyone. "There will be immense pain and suffering, but eventually we will revive ourselves, so stop worrying."

Bill starts to pound frantically on the windows. "We are going to *die*!"

"Calm down!" Regina shouts again in her stern, motherly voice. "We need to put some clothing under the door to block the smoke. Everybody take something off!" Within seconds, there is an assortment of clothing tossed at her, including Francis' bow tie, Santa's hat and the sash from Father Time's robe. Jack Frost hops around on one foot as he struggles to get his socks off and Tuss contributes his shirt as Regina adds her sweater to the pile. "Ew, Bill. Is that your handkerchief? And who put their *pants* in here?"

"Yours truly," grins Cupid, proudly standing naked from the waist down.

"Don't you at least wear *underwear*?" Pia demands.

"It just gets in the way."

"You are disgusting."

"Where's *your* contribution?" counters Cupid.

With a great sigh, Pia slowly removes one of her heels and reluctantly hands it to Regina.

"Really?" Regina can't help asking, taking the red sparkly shoe by the heel.

"It's all I can spare," Pia replies.

"You're no fun."

"This isn't a joke, Cupid!" yells Bill. "If that smoke gets in here, we are *dead*!"

"Smoke doesn't kill people, the *fire* does."

"Yes it does! You breathe it in and it suffocates you before the fire even gets a chance to burn you to a crisp! I know! I'm the one who proofread the pamphlet! That bird is a typo machine!"

Cupid goes a little pale. "Oh. Maybe I actually should have listened to the presentation."

"Get that stuff under the door! Hurry!" Santa encourages.

"It's not enough!"

"You didn't contribute anything!" accuses Bill, pointing at the Boogeyman.

"Contribute what? I have nothing to take off!"

"You selfish bastard! You probably want to die, but I've gone several millennia without having to experience it and today will *not* be the day!" With those words, Father Time leaps at the Boogeyman, tearing the hood from his robe in one quick motion.

"You crazy old man! You owe me a new robe!"

Regina adds the new piece to the pile of randomness at the bottom of the door and the smoke stops drifting in, at least for the time being.

"Now what?"

"*Now what?*"

"Shouldn't we call for help?"

"Great idea, Tuss. Too bad there's no phone in here and all of our fucking cell phones are in the *hall!*"

"Yeah, burning!"

"Why is there no phone in here?"

"T.J.….can't really use the phone. He can't really talk to anyone."

"You stupid buzzard! This is all *your* fault!"

"Father Time, *calm down!*"

"Who doesn't have a phone in their damn office?"

"You know, Pia...since we're going to die and all, we might as well get it over with and give everybody a thrill while we're at it," Cupid suggests.

"Get. The fuck. *Away* from me. I'm not *dying* anywhere."

"CAN ANYBODY USE TELEPATHY?! "

"Deep breaths, everybody. Has anyone felt the door to see if it's hot?"

"I have!" Francis informs Regina. "It's definitely hot!"

"The fire is bearing down on us!"

"Our cell phones are *gone!* GONE!"

"We should get the fire extinguisher!" Tuss flings open the closet door, ready to be a hero, but the only thing sitting there is a thick coat of dust.

"What the hell?"

"Oh yeah. I was supposed to order those."

Father Time rounds on the man supposedly in charge of building maintenance. "Fix this, Jack *Frost!* Much of this is because of *your* negligence!"

There is much agreement, but Jack only shakes his head. "I can't *do* anything, okay? I've got this...*issue*...and it's throwing my powers out of whack!"

"Are you trying to tell me Jack Frost can't do anything because he has a *cold?*"

"Yeah, that's what I'm telling you, you old geezer!" Jack snaps.

"So you're useless as usual! Of *course!*" Father Time exclaims, exasperated.

"WE'RE ALL GONNA DIE!"

"What about the windows?" Tuss asks, running over.

"They don't open! None of them open!"

"Why do we have windows that don't open?"

"THIS ENTIRE BUILDING IS A DEATH TRAP!"

"On Dasher, on Dancer!" Santa cries, pounding on the glass and peering out into the snowy nothingness outside. "On Prancer and Vixen! COMET AND CUPID! DONNER AND BLITZEN! SAVE ME! SAVE SANTA!"

T.J. has started to peck feverishly at the glass too, but even his strong beak doesn't even make a scratch on the surface.

"WHAT ARE THESE WINDOWS *MADE* OF? *TITANIUM?*"

"ON DASHER! ON DANCER!"

"What do you think death will feel like?"

"PRANCER! VIXEN!"

"I imagine it will be pleasant," the Boogeyman guesses.

"COMET! CUPID!"

"You *would* say that."

"ANYBODY!"

"Is there anything lying about that we can bash the window with?"

"Start looking!"

As Father Time and Regina take on this new task, Pia shakes her head and grabs Tuss' arm before he can join the search. "Are you kidding me? Let's just get the hell out of here!"

"Just *leave* everybody?" Tuss asks.

"Yeah, just *leave* everybody." Pia rolls her eyes. "Let's get the fuck out of here."

Cupid joins them. "You guys talking about teleporting?"

"*She* is," Tuss says, throwing Pia a sideways glance.

"It's not a bad idea," Cupid shrugs. "At least we could get some help."

"Sure, whatever." Pia agrees with a half-hearted shrug. "Either way, I'm leaving with or without you losers."

"YOU LAZY REINDEER! I KNOW YOU CAN HEAR ME!" roars Santa, pounding both fists on the glass while Bill sobs beside him and Francis begins to tear out clumps of his own fur.

"Yup. I'm outta here," Pia nods her head.

"Everybody stop!" But since everybody does not stop, the Boogeyman has to repeat his order a second time. "Everybody stop right *now*! There *is* no fire!"

That does indeed get everyone to stop in their tracks. Father Time even freezes, holding a bronze bust of America's third president over his head, hell bent on chucking it at the allegedly titanium windows.

"What do you mean there's no fire?" asks Bill shakily, tears and sweat pouring down his colorless face.

The Boogeyman gestures to his Shadow, which fills up the wall behind him, shaking its head slowly. "I sent him to check. There's no fire."

"But Francis said the door was hot," Regina reminds everyone, walking over to it herself. Hesitantly, she gives the handle a quick touch with the tip of her finger. She frowns and touches it with her whole finger, then her whole hand. "It's not hot at all!"

"Damn it, Francis!" cries Father Time, putting the bust down with much difficulty.

"I thought it felt hot!" the rabbit says defensively.

"Probably because you're practically hyperventilating!"

"There may not be a fire, but there's definitely smoke coming from somewhere." Tuss opens the door and a gush of black, meaty smelling smoke rushes into the room. Coughing and shooing it out of their faces, everyone follows the trail of smoke to an air vent close to the doorway. "It's coming from upstairs."

"So there's a fire *upstairs*?" Father Time asks.

"We should check it out," Tuss decides.

"Do you think it's okay to take the elevator?" worries Francis. "The pamphlet said--"

T.J. nastily screeches something that seems to speak for everyone.

Wordlessly, everyone piles into the elevator and proceeds upstairs to the cafeteria. There, they find no fire, but more smoke, which leads them to the kitchen where Wally is standing with a very burnt roast.

"*Wally?*" cries Santa in surprise.

"Santa?" blinks Wally, taking off his candy-striped oven mitts. "What are you...why is Cupid not wearing pants?"

"Like what you see?" Cupid winks.

"What are you doing here? And what *was* that?" Regina asks, pointing to the smoldering remains of something that *had* once resembled meat.

"I was trying to make dinner for Holly," Wally admits with a frown. "I guess I'll be ordering take out. I hope she likes walrus."

"Why the hell were you cooking in here?" demands Pia.

"He said I could," Wally points at Jack.

"Oh. Right. I forgot I told you that you could use the kitchen," Jack Frost says in response. "Sorry."

"Sorry? *Sorry?* After all of that, all you have to say is *sorry?*" screams Father Time, as red in the face as Santa's coat.

"Yup," shrugs Jack.

"I don't believe this! I'm going downstairs to have a bath and a good, strong drink!" Father Time huffs.

"I like your thinking! Care to join me, Pia?" Cupid asks.

"Go fuck yourself." Pia says, as she and several of the others turn to leave.

"I think you wet your pants, Bill," Regina points out.

"Oh...uh...I...uh...thought they felt a little damp," mutters Bill, stepping away from Regina delicately.

"What *happened?*" Wally asks.

"Don't ask," mutters the Boogeyman, turning to leave.

Francis sniffs the air. "I think something else is burning."

"My carrots!" shrieks Wally and without another word, he lunges for the stove.

"Yeah, but it *didn't* eat your finger, so I don't see what the problem is!" Pia says.

"It's just...uh...it's...I don't...uh...some of those plants are mean," Caleb replies lamely.

"Those plants are going to have nothing on me if *you* don't get rid of them! Now get out of my office - I'm sick of your face!"

"Okay, got it!" Caleb hurries out of Pia's office, calling squeakily over his shoulder. "You're still beautiful!"

Tuss has a confused look on his face as he enters. "What was that about?"

"Incompetence, what else?" Pia rubs her forehead and glowers at him. "What do you want? Are the Independence Day numbers in?"

"Yup. They're great! But..." Tuss hesitates. "Unfortunately, this year had the most fires ever."

"*What?* After all *that?*"

"Yup."

"The *most* fires?"

"Yup."

"How is that *possible*?" Pia exclaims, falling back into her office chair and accidentally letting the vines get their thorny teeth into her tightly pulled ponytail. "We sent out all of those fucking pamphlets!"

"Uh…actually, those were never sent out," Tuss explains.

"*What?* Why the hell not?"

Tuss pauses for a long moment, knowing his partner won't find the humor in the irony like he does, before saying, "They were destroyed in a fire."

"Clucky's ideal retreat would involve a bunch of chicks fresh outta the shell."

"Santa?" Pia pauses to politely knock on the open office door before entering. "Did someone upset you?" She and Tuss observe the open suitcase thrown upon the desk, which is overflowing with a variety of red clothing. Poor Frank is currently sitting on top of it, trying to get it to close, but his weight is not enough to compress the contents more than an inch or two. "Was it that little clucker Tom? Because that puny neck of his is long overdue for a good--"

Santa laughs in his usual warm way. "Everything is fine, my child! Why do you ask?"

"We heard you were packing," Tuss admits, pointing to the suitcase. "Pia assumed the worst."

"Don't worry, you two! I'm not retiring just yet! Why, I still have my last ride to look forward to!" With a chuckle, he tries pushing down on the suitcase himself, but it still doesn't come close to closing.

"You have too much crap in here," complains Frank.

"I suppose I can leave the gingerbread house lamp behind, but I _need_ my framed pictures of the reindeer _and_ my kazoo. Sinterklaas will not win the talent competition this year!"

"So...where are you going?" Tuss asks at last.

"Oh! I'm going to the yearly convention! Me and a bunch of my fellow Christmas figureheads get together in Greenland this time every year. We discuss Christmas issues, share tips and tricks, and generally have a good old time! It's one hundred percent Corporate approved!" Santa assures them with a wink. "I'll only be gone a few days. Wally will make sure the workshop runs smoothly, although I will be taking Holly and Frank with me! My nose hairs can't trim themselves!" He pats Frank on the back with a laugh, but the elf doesn't even attempt to smile.

"Sounds like fun," says Pia, sucking up like usual. "I wish I could go with you, Santa."

"Why don't you come along? There's plenty of room in the cabin!"

Pia is momentarily tongue-tied. This comes as a complete surprise - she was just trying to show an interest in the trip, not actually get herself invited. "I...that's very nice of you, Santa, but I don't think I should be leaving the Pole right now."

"Why not?" Tuss speaks up in a rush, seeing an opportunity he simply cannot let pass by. "There are no major holidays coming up and it's only for a few days. I can handle anything that might come up around here."

Pia turns to him with a subtle glare - the type of look that silently chides him for daring to try and get rid of her. "Oh, is that so?"

Tuss leans in, quickly whispering in her ear, "Maybe you can talk him into not retiring while you're away."

It's a good idea that even Pia can't deny. "Well then...why not? I'd be honored to join you, Santa."

"Wonderful!" Santa cries. "Better get packing! We leave at dawn! But would you mind sitting on my suitcase before you go? Maybe with the three of you, plus a few other elves, we can get this thing to close! Wally!" he calls, walking over to open the door of his office. "Holly! We have a code mistletoe! Get up here! And bring at least half the choir!"

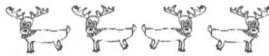

If Corporate only paid attention to all the things Pia does for this company, she would be earning medals at every single one of those end of year banquets. The entire ride to the convention site (which was not via sleigh, due to a virus contracted by Rudolph), she was forced to sit next to Holly and listen to her prattle on and on about how some other elf was constantly sending her gifts, and complimenting her, and otherwise trying to impress her. "Oh, he's so nice but I don't think I could ever see him as more than a friend," she had said at least a dozen times. Was it because Pia was a woman that this girl thought she'd want to listen to this garbage for two hours straight? If Santa wasn't within earshot, she'd have told her straight out where she could take her pointless boy problems. But since she was trapped traveling like some low level being (because none of them could travel anywhere they wanted in a split second like she could), she was forced to sit there and listen to every single worthless word the bitch said for over two hours. *Two fucking hours.*

When they finally arrive in Greenland (which was decidedly misnamed), Pia is more than happy to trade her warmth in order to get away from the annoying elf.

After arriving, Santa eyes the pile of luggage, which includes twelve well-wrapped snow globes, eleven plastic containers, ten books of kazoo songs, nine reindeer portraits, eight giant snowshoes, seven oatmeal cookies, six pairs of long johns, five golden goblets, four fluffy pillows, three different beard trimmers, two curling irons and, for some odd reason, a partridge in a pear tree. He turns to Frank. "You can handle all of this, right, Frankie? We'll meet you at the cabin!"

Ignoring the small elf's loud protest, Pia, Santa and Holly walk a little ways from the icy, rocky beach to a clearing where there are several cabins arranged around a blazing fire pit. The cabins are surrounded by dense forest and there aren't any mortals for hundreds of miles. It's the perfect place for this sort of gathering and as the group approaches, they can make out over half a dozen figures clustered around the inviting fire.

"Well, well, well! Look what the reindeer dragged in!" cackles an old woman holding a broomstick.

"I'm not the last one here, am I?" booms Santa, hugging her warmly.

"No, Sinterklaas is late as usual. You know him - has to arrive in style!"

She may come from the Corporate office, but Pia has only ever handled North American affairs and she has little idea who these other figureheads are. They do make a strange group, and any mortal who did manage to stumble upon this clearing would definitely be terrified for their life.

"Pia, meet La Befana, mother to all the children of Italy." Santa wraps an arm around the old woman fondly.

"Nice to meet you," Pia says warmly, shaking hands. After all, any friend of Santa is a friend of hers. Good thing Santa and Bill are not friends.

"Pia is from Corporate!" Santa announces.

"Oh, is that so?" asks La Befana. "Do you have any children, dear?"

"No."

"Well, do you like pasta at least? I make mine from scratch! I promise you've never tasted anything like it!"

"Sounds wonderful," Pia says, wishing the old woman would let go of her hand already.

"And this is Krampus!"

Despite the fact that Pia has spent a lot of time around odd looking characters, she is still startled by the next figurehead Santa introduces. Hairy, with goat-like hooves and horns, Krampus has a long, pointed tongue dangling from his mouth. He wears many chains and has a dirty sack strapped to his back that seems large enough to hold a naughty child or twenty. He definitely looks like he was assigned to the wrong holiday.

"Um, hello," Pia says uncertainly.

"Krampus deals with the naughty children of Austria and Germany," Santa explains, instantly clearing up many of Pia's questions.

"I see," Pia nods.

"Belsnickel couldn't make it this year," says Krampus. His low, gravelly voice would sound sinister even if he was giving you a hug and wishing you Happy Birthday. "Gryla either. I'm on my own this year."

"That's a shame," Santa laments. Turning to Pia he adds, "They do a *wonderful* job of keeping naughty children in line."

"I bet."

Next, Santa introduces her to another bearded man in a similar red coat. The only major difference between the two is that this one is noticeably less round in the middle. "This is my French counterpart, Pere Noel, and his assistant, Le Pere Fouettard!"

Le Pere Fouettard also has a beard, but it is long, neglected and flicked with soot. His face is creased with the lines of a long unhappy man and his morose expression certainly matches his dark and dirty robes. An obviously well used whip with initials carved into the handle hangs from his belt. Pia declines to shake his hand and manages to get by with only a polite wave.

"How are things in France? Did you bring me any cheese?" Santa asks.

"Did you bring me any of those gooey Easter candies?"

"Oh, I forgot!"

"You always forget!" scolds Pere Noel, while his assistant stands there glaring like an angry gargoyle.

"You shouldn't eat those things anyway! You don't want to end up like little old me!" Santa pats his large belly with a chuckle.

"It's true!"

"One of these days you have to share your diet secret with me!"

"I'll never tell!"

Fouettard continues to stand there glaring as they move on to greet the next pair.

"Ded Moroz handles Russia and that general area of the world," Santa explains as they approach a large man with a blue coat, fur hat and a long staff. He is accompanied by a beautiful young woman in sparkling blue robes and a crown made to resemble a cluster of snowflakes. "And this is his granddaughter!"

"Snegurochka," says the girl with a warm smile.

"Uh, we just call her Snow Maiden; Snowy for short," Santa breaks in.

"Wait till you see my sleigh," brags Ded Moroz. "Put a new coat of paint on it! My lovely granddaughter even painted a mural of Russia in winter on the side!"

"So it's all white then?" The two of them laugh loudly at this apparently hysterical joke.

"I like your coat," Snowy says to Pia, while the men exchange some more small talk.

Pia cannot remember the last time another woman complimented her on anything. Momentarily stunned, it takes her a few moments to remember how to respond. "Thank you."

"And look who decided to show this year!" Pia goes with Santa to the last figurehead currently present. "He really only covers a small part of Spain, because I guess his brand of Christmas fun never caught on like decorated trees did! Pia, meet Tio de Nadal, also known as the Pooping Log!"

A little log-like creature with a carved face stands there crankily, a blanket thrown around its wooden shoulders.

"I'm sorry, Santa. I don't think I heard you correctly," Pia says.

"You heard him correctly," snaps Tio. "They call me the Pooping Log."

Santa has been laughing so hard this whole time that he is wiping tears from his eyes. "Families make their own at the beginning of December and then feed it every night until Christmas Eve. The next morning they beat it with sticks and order it to poop! There's a song and everything! Then it drops candy, nuts and other goodies. It's a pooping

219

Christmas piñata!"

The wooden creature is not amused and stands there with its stick-like arms crossed. "Do you have to laugh like that *every* time we speak?"

Santa is laughing too hard to respond.

"Nice to meet you," Pia says insincerely.

"Yeah, sure it is," grumbles Tio.

Santa finally collects himself, wiping yet more tears from his face. "I think that's everyone! Everyone who's here, anyway. You already know Cupid."

Pia has to do a double take. But indeed, there is the head of Valentine's Day himself, standing by the fire, feeding it sticks.

"What is he doing here?" But Pia's question goes unanswered as Santa has gone back to chat with Ded Moroz and Pere Noel. She takes this opportunity to stalk over to Cupid and demand he answer her question himself.

"Well, hello to you too," he replies with his usual dashing grin. "What does it look like I'm doing? I'm making sure this fire doesn't go out."

"You know what I mean," she replies icily. "Last time I checked, you didn't run Christmas."

"Last I checked neither did you."

"Santa invited me," Pia replies proudly.

"Well, Snow Maiden invited me. We're dating. Well, I'm trying to fuck her." Cupid smiles and waves over to the pretty blonde. "It's gonna be awesome."

"You *would* come to a place like this to do something like *that*," Pia says with disgust.

"You *would* come to a place like this to do something like suck up to Santa," Cupid shoots back. "What, do you think you're going to talk him out of retiring or something? Corporate does know about that yet, right?"

Pia ignores the question and turns to watch Fouettard glare at Krampus as he passes by to talk to Tio. "At least the company looks entertaining. Although I don't know who the hell is scarier - nightmare goat man or Pere Noel's assistant. *Our* Santa has elves. *That* creep looks like a damn child molester!"

"Close, but not quite. You don't know his backstory?" When Pia shakes her head no, Cupid continues. "He captured, robbed and killed three boys on their way to boarding school. Cut them into pieces and put them in a barrel."

"What the *fuck*? And he was recruited?" Pia demands in disbelief.

"Well, the children were resurrected and he supposedly repented," Cupid shrugs. "But his punishment was to be Pere Noel's assistant for eternity."

"That is the worst fucking backstory I have ever heard."

"Merry Christmas!" Cupid says with a cheery smile.

"I'm surprised all the parents in France don't board up their chimneys with that freak running around," Pia shudders.

"I'd rather celebrate with the shitting log any day," Cupid agrees.

Suddenly, there is screaming and yelling heard from down at the beach. Behind the heat of the fire, Pia has a hard time making out what is going on at the shoreline.

"It's Sinterklaas!" Snowy cries, running over to her grandfather. "His boat! It's sinking!"

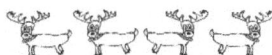

Everyone rushes to the shore to find an old man with the standard white beard and a soaking wet red cape panting beside a half inflated life raft. He is dressed more like a Catholic bishop than your standard Santa Claus. Beside him, in their poor excuse for a lifeboat, is a dark-skinned young man dressed in a Renaissance Page costume - pantaloons, feathered cap and all. He is dripping wet and shivering.

"Sinterklaas! Zwarte Piet!" Santa cries in alarm as Holly and Frank rush over with heavy wool blankets. "What happened?"

"Mines! Someone put mines in the water! They sunk my steamboat!" Sinterklaas blurts out between chattering teeth. He takes the offered blanket and wraps it tightly around his shoulders.

"What? That's impossible!" says La Befana with a gasp.

"It's true! We saw them from the raft!" gasps Zwarte Piet.

Pia looks out into the water, but all she can make out is the faint outline of a sinking boat.

"But there are no mortals around here," La Befana insists. "How can there be mines in the water?"

"I know what I saw!" Sinterklaas barks angrily. He allows Santa to help him to his feet. "Mines! Like someone was trying to target my ship!"

"That's preposterous!" Pere Noel huffs. "Who would want to target you?"

"I don't know." The Dutch Santa seems to lose some of his steam as he accepts the hot cup of tea Snowy comes running over with. Behind him, Krampus and Cupid help Zwarte Piet out of the deflating raft. "But is there another explanation?"

"They are probably left over from some mortal war!" grunts Fouettard from where he stands behind the rest of the group. "You know how violent they are."

"*You* would know," Krampus shoots back.

"Now, now," Pere Noel interjects. "Now is not the time for wild speculation. Let's get these two inside and warmed up."

"Someone tried to kill me," Sinterklaas keeps insisting as he is helped toward the cabins. "And I wouldn't be surprised if they strike again!"

Everyone starts heading back to the warm roar of the fire, but Pia stays behind, looking over the beach. Aside from the abandoned life raft, however, nothing looks out of place.

"Trying to crack the case?" Cupid teases. He had started back with the others but turned back at the start of the path. "Old murder face is probably right. Probably leftover from some war."

"But don't they come here every year? Why wouldn't the ship have hit them before?"

Cupid shrugs. "Currents pushed them over here or something. Who knows. Nature is complicated. You know that, you deal with her on a daily basis. It has to be something stupid like that, Pia. I mean, come on. Who would want to kill a *Santa Claus*?"

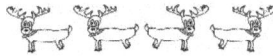

The mood is somber following the boat incident. After getting Sinterklaas and Zwarte Piet warm and settled, everyone retires to their own cabins for dinner and bed. But between Santa's snoring, Frank's angry muttering and the incident at the shoreline, Pia finds herself unable to sleep. Slipping into her parka, she walks back down to the beach, treading carefully on the uneven path. The full moon reflects generously off of the crashing ocean, but it's still hard to see much of anything. If there even *is* anything worth seeing.

Standing alone with only the moon and the waves for company, Pia finds that she almost doesn't mind the cold.

Then her cell phone rings. Rolling her eyes, she answers it angrily. "What is it, Caleb? …No, you spray the poison *onto* the leaves…Spray it everywhere then!…I don't care if it's burning your eyes! That probably means it's finally working!...Well, then just get a machete and cut it all down!...Look it up, *moron*! I don't have time for this! It better not look like a fucking jungle when I get back!" Shaking her head, she hangs up and stuffs the device back into her pocket.

"You just can't take a break, can you?"

Pia turns to find Cupid strolling up behind her. "What are *you* doing here? Shouldn't you be doing *somebody* else?"

"She's playing hard to get," he admits with a shrug. "No worries, I like a challenge."

"Maybe she's too smart for your ridiculous games."

Cupid laughs. "That would be a first!"

"You're not as charming as you think you are."

Cupid takes a casual step closer to Pia. "I'm impossibly charming. Also gorgeous. I'm practically irresistible. Surely you've noticed." He shoots her a smile that looks even more dazzling in the moonlight.

Pia turns to the ocean, her eyes focused on the dark horizon. She tugs at the cornucopia charm that hangs around her neck. "Yeah, I've noticed what a fucking asshole you are."

"I don't know what's colder - the air or *you*. I know you never used to be this way. You used to enjoy a bit of *male company*, from what I've heard."

Pia looks to find him standing alarmingly close. "Who the hell told you that?"

"Come on, Pia. You know how gossip gets around that place. You know A didn't keep her mouth shut. But I don't care. Actually, I find it kind of sexy."

His breath on her skin is the only warmth she can feel. "I don't know what you're talking about."

Before he can say another word or move another inch, a scream pierces the night, sending a flock of birds into the sky and both of them running back toward the camp. Everyone seems to be rushing into La Befana's cabin, so Pia and Cupid follow the crowd. Pia maneuvers her way through a bunch of overweight bearded men in nightshirts and finds a stunned La Befana sitting at the rustic wooden kitchen table, an unfinished bowl of pasta in front of her.

"I was dead!" she cries.

"What?" The word rises generally from the group gathered around her.

"I was *dead!*" she repeats. "I was just revived! Someone killed me!"

"What do you *mean* you were *dead?*" Ded Moroz pronounces the latter word like he doesn't even understand the concept.

"I was dead!" the old woman screeches. "Gone! Deceased! Morta!"

"I told you they would strike again!" Sinterklaas cries. "Someone is out to get us!"

"What is the last thing you remember?" asks Pere Noel.

"Just sitting down to dinner!"

Everyone's attention turns to the cold bowl of pasta. Holly takes a deep whiff and makes a disgusted face. "Smells like arsenic."

"I don't smell anything!" La Befana says.

"Elves have an excellent sense of smell," Santa informs the old woman. "Someone must have poisoned you."

"But who would *do* such a thing?"

"And why?" Cupid mutters, mostly to himself.

"Look!" shrieks Sinterklaas suddenly, pointing a horrified finger at the ground. "Look at the floor!"

Pia looks down and, under a smattering of broken glass and a scattering of nuts, are some very clear hoofprints.

Everyone immediately looks at Krampus.

"I didn't do anything!" the beast cries defensively, holding up his hairy hands and baring his sharp black nails. "Why would I?"

"Why *wouldn't* you? Maybe you're sick of scaring children and want to start rewarding them instead!" Sinterklaas accuses.

"Start *giving* children *presents*?" scoffs Krampus. "Never! Those little brats don't deserve anything! I'd stuff them all in my sack if I could!"

"A likely story!"

"Where were you tonight?" asks Pere Noel calmly.

"In my cabin, asleep like everyone else!"

"Alone, no doubt! So no one can prove your story!"

Krampus glares right into Sinterklaas' disapproving eyes, his voice low and threatening. "I have no reason to hurt *any* of you."

"I believe him."

Everyone turns to Santa with surprise.

"You *do*?"

"Of course I do." Backing up his claim, Santa even puts a warm arm around Krampus' furry shoulders. "Just because he tortures children doesn't mean he's a bad guy! Well, it *sort* of does, but--"

"How do you explain those hoofprints then?" Sinterklaas asks. "Nobody else has hooves for feet!"

Santa surveys the ground with a frown. "Well...maybe they were already there."

"Wouldn't she have noticed?" Sinterklaas jerks his head at La Befana.

"Who pays attention to the floor?" Krampus shoots back.

But Sinterklaas refuses to back down. "I don't believe it! If it's not him, who could it be? It has to be someone here!"

"Innocent until proven guilty." Santa maintains firmly. "We just *can't* prove Krampus did this!"

"If he didn't do this, he should have no problem not being left alone," Sinterklaas decides.

"Whatever makes you feel better, you old ship loving freak," Krampus growls.

"I'm happy to host him in my cabin," Santa speaks up. "Now, everyone try to get back to bed. We can discuss this in the morning."

There is a lot of grumbling, but everyone does start to file back into the cold night air.

"Great. Now I get to share a room with two obnoxious elves *and* a terrifying, potentially murderous goat," Pia mutters.

"My cabin has plenty of room," Cupid offers with a grin. "As does my bed."

"I'd rather be murdered by the fucking goat."

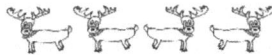

Pia glares at Holly over their lunch of cold herring and coleslaw. The meal is disgusting and it's not just the food that's turning her stomach; it's the female elf checking her phone and giggling approximately every two minutes while the little one piles enough coleslaw onto his plate to feed Ded Moroz's trio of reindeer. (The Russian Santa had just been at lunch bragging about them for an hour and a half before departing to take them out for a ride. At one point he swore up and down that one could play the cello.)

Santa is at the next table with Krampus discussing the percentage of naughty children now versus two hundred years ago. (Krampus is apparently no fan of cell phones and raged on about how they were rotting children's brains for a full seventeen minutes before he used his own to make a move in *Words With Friends*.)

"I don't believe this," giggles Holly. She glances up to find Pia still glaring at her and the young elf mistakes Pia's silent plea for her to shut up as a look of interest. "Look." She holds out her phone, which is displaying a photo of Wally half dressed and failing to look sexy, as he rubs up against a giant candy cane awkwardly.

Pia pushes her plate away. Now she can't even pretend to choke down another bite. "That is not an appropriate use of company property."

"What should I say? Do you think he actually expects me to send one back? Gross!" Holly laughs.

Oh the things Pia would say if Santa was not at the next table. Instead, she grits her teeth and forces out some polite and very carefully chosen words. "Absolutely do *not* send one back. And do *not* show me another photo like that. *Ever.*"

"Are you gonna eat your coleslaw?" asks Frank messily through a mouth full of the stuff.

"By all means, gorge yourself." Pia pushes the plate in his direction and then crosses her arms, trying to ignore the idiots around her and focus on the mystery at hand. Had Krampus been the one to sink the boat and poison La Befana? If nothing else happened, then the answer was probably yes. But Santa was so sure it wasn't him. And Pia had a gut feeling that he was probably right.

"Excuse me for a moment, I have to go use the little boy's room!" Santa wipes his mouth as he gets to his feet.

Pia bounds to her feet as well. "I'll come with you, Santa!"

228

"Uh…that's kind of you, Pia, but I think I can handle it by myself!" He laughs uncomfortably.

"I just don't think it's safe for you to be alone right now," Pia explains.

"Even in the bathroom?" Santa furrows his eyebrows.

"If it's not Krampus like you said, and I tend to agree with you, then that person is still out there. And they could strike at any time."

"But in the bathroom?" Santa repeats.

"Why not?" Pia shrugs." It's a place where you're bound to let your guard down."

"I could take Frank with me perhaps..." Santa offers thoughtfully. "I just wouldn't feel comfortable...I'm going to be in there awhile."

Frank pauses, his mouth full of coleslaw, as he quickly starts to turn a distinct shade of green.

Luckily for Frank, before Pia can agree to or reject this arrangement, another frantic scream sends everyone flying out of the cabin.

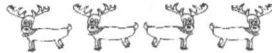

This time the screams are coming from the woods. Pia and the others arrive to find Ded Moroz lying in the snow, dazed but intact, at the edge of a cliff that drops off over a hundred feet to the ocean below. Snowy kneels at his side, crying for help. In the background, Sinterklaas, Zwarte Piet and Cupid are attempting to calm the Russian Santa's three reindeer, who are still rearing, snorting and clearly upset.

"What happened?" Santa cries, as they are joined by Pere Noel, Fouettard, Tio and La Befana.

"Dedushka was going for a ride when something spooked the reindeer!" Snowy explains with a trembling voice.

Ded Moroz sits up holding his head and elaborates. "I didn't see it, but whatever it was, it scared them so badly that they broke free of the sled as we were coming down that hill there. Luckily, I was thrown clear from the sleigh just before it tumbled over the cliff."

Standing at a safe distance, Pia glances down to see the mangled remains of the sleigh on the jagged rocks below.

"What could have spooked them?" La Befana asks. Sinterklaas and the others have finally managed to calm the reindeer and are gently petting and feeding them some carrots as they slowly lead them back over to the group.

"Must have been something horrific! My team is not easily spooked!"

"Thank goodness you're all right, Dedushka!" Snowy wraps her arms around her grandfather and doesn't let go.

Pia circles the area slowly, looking for anything out of place. Aside from the obvious sleigh and reindeer tracks in the snow, there are a bunch of nuts that are too clustered in one area to have fallen from a tree - probably the work of an animal that forgot their stash. But there are some other markings she doesn't recognize. "What's all this?"

Cupid comes over to see what she's pointing to. "Hmm…they look like whip marks."

"Like you'd know what the hell whip marks look like." Pia snorts. "In the *snow*."

"Damn right I do," he says with a suggestive wink. "I spent an amazing winter in the Alps with Chichi once."

Santa takes a glance for himself, a frown creasing his usually jolly face. "They *do* look like whip marks."

One by one, all eyes turn to Fouettard and the whip hanging from his belt. "So now it's me."

"I *told* you it wasn't me," Krampus says haughtily.

"It was not my work either," Fouettard insists.

"Was he with you?" Sinterklaas asks Pere Noel.

The French Santa slowly shakes his head no. "He said he went out for a walk."

"A walk of intended murder!"

Fouettard sets the Dutch Santa with a look that causes even Pia to avert her eyes. "I did not murder anyone."

"I think those little boys you butchered would say differently!"

"I didn't do anything!"

"Doesn't look like you have an alibi," La Befana speaks up.

Snowy leaps to her feet and lunges for Fouettard's neck before she is restrained by a quick thinking Cupid. "You monster! How dare you touch a hair on my Dedushka's head!"

"I didn't do anything!" Fouettard insists.

"Maybe *he* was framed too," Santa speaks up with some uncertainty.

"You wouldn't be saying that if he came for *your* head," Ded Moroz says seriously, finally getting to his feet.

"You're suggesting the same person tried to frame *two* different people?" Sinterklaas scoffs.

"Haven't you seen any of those *CSI* shows? Or those *Law & Order* shows?" Santa asks.

"Which ones?"

"I don't know," Santa shrugs. "There are like fifty of them. But this kind of thing happens all the time."

"Maybe they're working together!" Sinterklaas glares at Krampus and Fouettard.

"Ridiculous! I have no reason to harm any of you!" Krampus points an accusing finger at Fouettard as he continues. "But *he* doesn't want to be here. He's *never* wanted to be here. He's only here because he's being punished! He probably wants to make us *all* suffer like he is!"

"You have no proof of anything!" roars Fouettard.

"He has a point," Santa agrees.

"There's only one way to get to the bottom of this," Pia decides firmly, stepping to the center of the group. "I'm calling Corporate."

Cupid rolls his eyes. "Of course you are."

"What are *they* going to do?"

"They'll send in a team and we'll figure out who's behind this," Pia says calmly.

"Sure they will," mutters Tio.

"I promise I will not let Fouettard out of my sight in the meantime," says Pere Noel.

"You must believe me," Fouettard pleads to his Santa.

"Let's just…go back to the cabin." Pere Noel replies, avoiding the eyes of his assistant.

Everyone starts drifting back in the direction of the clearing, Snowy taking her grandfather by the arm. Santa shakes his head as he trudges back through the snow. "I'm glad I'm getting out of this holiday business. Whoever thought it'd get dangerous?"

Pia takes out her phone, staring again at the odd little pile of nuts just sitting in the snow.

"You really think Corporate is going to do anything about this?" Cupid asks, lingering behind with her.

"They fucking have to," Pia says firmly. "We can't have somebody scaring the Santa's like this. We have to find whoever's behind this...and deal with them *our* way."

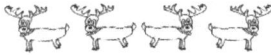

Within an hour of Pia's call, three representatives from Corporate show up. The first thing they do is insist on interviewing them all, starting with Krampus and Le Pere Fouettard. They make everyone else line up in the cold outside of the cabin they have taken over, waiting for their turn. Somehow, Pia winds up with Holly and Frank in front of her and Cupid behind. ("Just where I like to be," he says at least a dozen times.)

The interviews are being conducted fairly quickly and luckily for Pia, the elves are soon next in line. Holly is engrossed in her phone again, while Frank is wiping his curly toed shoes in the snow and complaining about the Pooping Log and all the times he nearly broke his neck on his presents.

"There are nuts and candy stuck all over the bottom of my shoes!" the small elf groans, picking up his foot to survey the damage. "They're all sticky!"

"Like you'll be when I'm done with you," Cupid whispers in Pia's ear. He gets an elbow to the gut in return.

"Pia, what should I do about these pictures?" Holly asks, flipping through all the photos she has received. Clearly, Wally has not been hard at work in the factory with his boss out of the way.

"Report the sick freak," Pia snaps, glad Santa was interviewed ten minutes ago and is safely out of earshot. "Tell HR about it while you're in there and they'll deal with his perverted ass."

"*No!*" Cupid interjects. "Don't listen to her! You need to send some of your own back! You gotta play the game! I'll be happy to take them if you feel uncomfortable."

"Oh…uh…I don't think…that'll be necessary." Holly blushes as red as her boss' coat.

Tio exits the cabin as the elves are called inside.

"Make sure you're naked!" Cupid calls in after her. Pia shoots him a fresh glare as the door closes and they move up in the line. "What? That's sound advice! That's what Ted did when he sent his pen pal some pictures! Although granted, I don't think poor Ted understood why his pen pal would be so excited to receive pictures of him in the mail…"

Ignoring this, Pia asks, "You told that stupid elf to send that ditz those disgusting pictures in the first place, didn't you?"

"Maybe I did. And I don't think it's very nice to call Wally disgusting. Sure, he needs to get to the gym more, but he doesn't look *too* bad."

"Ever think that maybe you should mind your own business?"

"Don't get mad at me for trying to help," Cupid smirks. "You should try it yourself one of these days."

"I don't help? I called Corporate here to catch a *killer*!"

"I don't for one second believe that was your only motivation."

"What the fuck is that supposed to mean?" Pia snaps with the intensity of a bone cracking in half.

But Cupid only crosses his arms over his chest as he cockily leans against the outside of the cabin. "You know exactly what I'm talking about, honey."

Fuming, Pia turns around and they don't exchange another word. After a few more minutes, Holly and Frank emerge from the cabin and Pia goes inside, facing the trio Corporate assigned to deal with this pressing issue.

"Have a seat," invites a young looking man with a sharp-featured face and glasses perched on his beaklike nose. Horace is a standout from the legal department, well known throughout the company.

Pia does as she is told. "I'm glad you were able to get here so quickly. All of these Santa's are very badly shaken by what's happened here."

The lone woman, a stern looking grandmotherly type, is Chell from human resources. She's known for being tough but fair, a rare gem in a department known for its harsh policies. "Tell us what you saw."

Pia goes through everything from the sinking, to the poisoning, to the spooked reindeer, not leaving out a detail. As she speaks, Horace and Chell take notes, but the representative from the emergency response team on the end, a tan young man with wild hair, just grins and makes a variety of suggestive gestures Cupid would have been proud of. He has his feet up on the table and is wearing a gaudy t-shirt with a silkscreen coyote splashed across the front. Pia knows Hugh well, only because he is widely avoided at all company functions.

"And that's when I phoned Corporate," Pia finishes, shooting Hugh a particularly nasty glare while the other two are busy with their note taking.

"And who do you believe is responsible?"

"I'm…not sure," Pia admits with difficulty. "Not yet."

Horace sighs, removing his glasses and inspecting them for no apparent reason. "You're the only one who has no thoughts on the suspect. Besides Santa."

"I can't argue with Santa's logic," Pia admits. "There isn't enough evidence against either Krampus *or* Fouettard."

"Very well." Chell puts down her pen and readjusts her bracelets, one of which prominently features a jaguar fashioned from black onyx. Another is fashioned like an entwined snake. "Send in the next interviewee, please."

"Of course. And please let me know if I can be of any further assistance." With a curt nod, Pia turns and leaves the cabin, bluntly informing Cupid that it's his turn.

"That go how you hoped?" Cupid asks with a raised eyebrow.

But Pia stalks past him without even acknowledging the question, brushing by Frank just as he narrowly avoids another sticky pile of nuts in the snow.

"Fucking Pooping Log!" the elf yells, although there is no one around to hear. "Clean up after your damn self, you useless, wooden piece of shit!"

Dinner that night is a group affair since no one wants to be alone. Everyone is crammed at a few tables in Santa's cabin, since it's the largest, with the food laid out buffet style in the kitchen. The menu was originally pasta, but La Befana quickly shot down that idea, and so it is back to herring and coleslaw. At least there are also some cookies that Sinterklaas had spent the afternoon "angry baking". (His words.)

The table Pia chooses starts off empty, but she is quickly joined by Frank and Holly (still giggling over her damn phone), Cupid, Snowy and finally Hugh, who wedges himself between the Valentine's Day figurehead and the Russian beauty before they have even completely sat down themselves. This does not please Cupid at all, and he glares at the interloper and his supposed date for most of the meal as they have an animated conversation in Russian.

"That fucking asshole," he spits as soon as the duo gets up for a second helping of cold, slimy fish. "I've been working on this for *months* and he thinks he can just come in here and steal her from me? I don't need this!"

"*Months?*" Pia can't help raising an eyebrow. "And you *still* haven't fucked her? Maybe you're losing your touch."

236

"Never. I'll get her. It doesn't help that she's worried about her grandfather now and doesn't want to leave his side. Not that I care if he watches. It's all part of the challenge."

"Your greatest challenge ever, no doubt," Pia mumbles.

"No, I'm still working on that," Cupid mutters, before turning to watch the pair share a laugh over by the cookie pile. "What do you think they're talking about?"

Pia smirks. "You don't speak Russian?"

"You *do*?" Cupid asks, surprised.

"Of course I do. I speak all of the major mortal languages."

"Of *course* you do," Cupid replies with a mocking tone. "Well? What were they talking about?"

"I'm not telling you," Pia snorts.

"Come on!" he begs. "I promise I won't try to grope your ass for a week! No, I can't promise that. You have a great ass. I'll...uh...I'll talk more about how much I love your ass!"

Pia fixes him with a dry look as she pushes away her barely touched dinner. Over at the table where the Christmas figureheads are sitting with the other visitors from Corporate, Santa is trying very hard to get a conversation going. However, everyone is too busy side-eyeing everyone else to do much talking. "Did you really think for a second that that would actually work?"

"Always worth a try."

Holly puts her phone down with a sigh. "I can't look at these anymore."

"If this is about those fucking pictures again," Pia mutters, already rubbing her temples.

"They're just so gross," the elf goes on.

"There is *nothing* wrong with being naked," Cupid assures her, as if he's some twisted school counselor.

"I just...I don't know."

Pia stands up, unable to take another second of the inappropriate conversation. "With all that's going on right now, excuse me if your ridiculous personal problems - that you will not shut the hell up about - don't matter to me." She fixes her eyes on Cupid as she continues. "That goes for *both* of you." This time she heads straight for the cookies, passing Snowy and Hugh on her way to the buffet table. They look delicious and smell even better, although anything halfway edible is worth getting excited about after so many months of eating in Jack Frost's cafeteria of horrors. Pia is about to grab a few when Pere Noel comes by and takes a look.

"Walnuts, I believe?" he calls to Sinterklaas.

"Of course!" the Dutch Santa responds, never taking his eyes off the twisted face of Fouettard.

"I'll have to pass." Pere Noel smiles kindly at Pia and waves her on. "I'm highly allergic to nuts. Some issues never go away."

After the Santa moves on, Pia fills her plate. She then returns to the table to find Frank finishing her coleslaw, Holly back on the phone and Cupid trying to subtlety push Hugh off of his chair. She eats her cookies and watches Horace and Chell grimace over their own food, all while Santa tries to unsuccessfully preach the importance of fire drills.

She knows she's not sleeping tonight.

Even after living at the North Pole for nearly eight months, Pia still isn't used to the quiet. Sure, the cabin isn't exactly silent. There's plenty of snoring from Santa and Fouettard, (it was apparently decided at dinner that the suspects should be kept together), not to mention Frank's grumbling and Holly's phone continuing to vibrate even when she's not awake to answer it. And Krampus - well - he makes noises in his sleep that no human would ever want to hear. But outside those walls, on the several walks she takes around the perimeter as the moon rises and falls in the cloudless sky above, there is nothing but silence; snow and silence. Not even the rustle of the wind through the forest. There were plenty of times at Corporate that Pia wished for this kind of silence, but during that very long night, she isn't sure if she likes it.

Then the sun comes up, just a sliver on the horizon, and she returns to the cabin. She starts puttering around the poorly stocked kitchen trying to find anything to make coffee with. Just as she comes up with a few forgotten sugar packets stuffed in a drawer, there is a burst of noise that summons everyone from their beds.

"What was that?" Holly cries, the curlers in her hair bouncing as she bolts off her pillow.

"Sounded like an explosion!" Santa is pulling on his boots as he hurries for the door.

The stream of people heading for Pere Noel's cabin makes the site of the incident clear. The group arrives to find the old man shaken and flecked with pieces of glass, but otherwise unharmed. However, the blender that had been sitting on the kitchen counter is in pieces and still smoking, the walls around it smeared with a thick, pinkish-white mixture.

"What the hell happened?" Hugh yells, pushing through the crowd. He spots Snowy and puts a tender arm around her. "Are you okay, hot lips?"

"I'm *fine*," she snaps, pushing him away. "I wasn't the one attacked!"

Fouettard is helping his Santa to his feet. "I'm all right," Pere Noel says, his voice shaky. "Just a bit stunned, that's all."

Santa is inspecting the ruined blender and the mess it left behind. "What's all this?"

"It's…uh…my…um…morning diet shake," Pere Noel admits sheepishly.

"So *that's* your secret?"

"I don't think now is the time to discuss weight loss tips." Horace already has a clipboard in his hands. "Please state what occurred this morning."

"I was just making my usual morning shake and when I went to start the blender, it exploded!"

"I wonder if someone tampered with the blender or the ingredients," Chell muses.

Hugh fearlessly takes a fingerful of the concoction off the wall and gives it a sniff. "Mmm. Strawberries."

"I think the culprits are obvious enough!" Sinterklaas says with a shrill cry. "Look!" He points dramatically to the floor. "Hard evidence!" Hoofprints, dark and fresh, cover the hardwood and Le Pere Fouettard's whip is lying on the floor beneath the table.

"That cannot be mine!"

Pere Noel bends down to inspect it with a frown. "It is. Your initials are on the handle."

"I had it with me last night--"

"And you clearly dropped it this morning when you tried to murder me!"

"I did no such thing!"

"We *weren't* here," Krampus speaks up, stomping his cloven feet. "We never left the cabin after dinner last night!"

Pia notices Hugh remove a piece of gold braid from his pocket.

"We didn't do this!" Fouettard yells.

"The evidence is clear," Hugh states. "You were in cahoots the whole time!"

"We were not!" Krampus insists. "Anyone could have made those marks or gotten their hands on his whip!"

"As if either of those things would be so simple!"

Even Santa is shaking his head now. He's given up the fight.

Hugh advances, the braid prominent in his hands.

Pia looks down at the prints and the whip again. It wouldn't have been impossible to slip a whip off a rope belt, especially if someone was getting ready for bed. And how would Krampus have made black marks on the floor if there was nothing outside to track around except melting snow?

"There's no use trying to run," Hugh says calmly.

"We will deal with this matter back at Corporate," Chell adds.

Then Pia notices the tiny cluster of nuts on the floor, right beside where the blender is still plugged into the wall.

"Nobody move!" Pia cries suddenly, just before Hugh grabs Krampus by the arm. "I know who's *really* behind this. *You.*"

There is some confusion at first as no one is sure who she is talking to. Sinterklaas points to several people in rapid succession before he turns his finger on himself, a confounded look on his face.

"*You.*" This time Pia points directly across the room. Everyone's eyes follow the direction of her extended arm before focusing on the suspect.

"I didn't fucking do anything!" Frank squeaks.

———

241

"Not *you*! *Him*! Or *it*! Whatever the hell it is behind you!" Pia snaps.

Frank turns and looks up to find Tio de Nadal standing there, the expression on his face as twisted as an angrily carved Jack-o'-lantern.

"It was *you*," Pia continues confidently. "*You* put the mines in the water. *You* poisoned La Befana's dinner. *You* spooked those reindeer and tampered with the blender."

"You're insane!" Tio scoffs.

"Pooping Log?" Santa questions. "He's harmless! He couldn't manage to frame anyone, let alone *harm* anyone! He's just a simple log with a hole in his backside!"

"That's what he wants you to think." Pia stalks over to the blender as she continues her accusation. "He could have gotten a whip anywhere. And his wooden feet easily could have been altered to make hoof prints on the floor. But every scene had one thing in common." She bends down and scoops up the pile of nuts sitting almost unnoticed on the floor.

"Ew," mutters Frank.

"You just couldn't help shitting yourself, could you?" Pia shoves the handful of evidence in Tio's face. "*Could you?*"

"Those nuts probably fell off the counter!" the little wooden creature cries defensively.

"They couldn't have!" Pere Noel protests. "I'm highly allergic to nuts! I would never keep them in my cabin!"

"Admit it," Pia seethes as she brings her face closer. "They make fun of you. They don't respect you. You're just the stupid old Pooping Log to them, so you decided to teach them a lesson. Show them they're not untouchable. You wanted them to be afraid."

Tio begins to shake with the rage he's attempting to contain within his tiny wooden body. "They get all the glory!" he explodes, to the shock of Santa especially. "For what? They barely do *any* of the work! They all have helpers!" He shoves Frank to the floor and starts backing toward the door. "It's not fair! I'm a Christmas figurehead too! But no one writes poems about me! Or lets me decorate greeting cards and soda bottles! No! Oh *no*! It's just, oh, he's the Pooping Log! He's a joke! He just poops out nuts! No one really cares about him! The only song about me is about me shitting my pants! I get beaten with sticks repeatedly and they just *laugh* about it! They all *laugh*! Well, who's laughing now? *Me*! *I'm* laughing! Laughing because I *won*! I proved you're all just scared, pathetic, terrible people! Christmas is supposed to be about love and family, but you turned on each other immediately! You're not *special*! They only respect you because you make them *money*! *I'm* a tradition! A *tradition*! A trad--" Hugh has come up behind Tio and touched him with the gold braid in his hand. Without any further work on his part, the metallic material winds around Tio's wrists, freezing him with his mouth open mid-sentence.

"Took your time there," Horace comments to Hugh with a frown, calmly adjusting his glasses.

"Didn't want to startle the crazy little fucker." Hugh pats the motionless Tio on the shoulder. A couple more nuts hit the floor and crack open.

"Let's get him back to Corporate and deal with him." Chell is already heading for the door, leaving Horace and Hugh are left to drag the statuesque Tio.

"He better not shit all over my office," Hugh grumbles as the three of them leave the cabin.

Pia frowns as she hears the door shut. The second the visitors from Corporate are gone with the would-be-murderer, the Christmas figureheads crowd around her enthusiastically.

"That was *amazing*!"

"Good for you for figuring that out!"

"I still can't believe it was Pooping Log!" Santa exclaims.

"I appreciate you clearing my name. Someday I will repay the favor," Fouettard tells her very seriously.

"As will I," Krampus adds.

"Well done, young lady!"

"I *really* can't believe it was Pooping Log!" Santa repeats.

"Most impressive!"

"I'm glad it was that stupid thing. Those nuts were a hazard anyway!"

"I am really, *really* in shock right now!" Santa shakes his head in disbelief.

"That was super sexy," Cupid tells her, sliding up to her with a smile.

"It kind of was," Snowy agrees, looking her up and down.

Cupid looks at the pretty blonde in shock and you can practically see his mind starting to churn. He casually clears his throat and puts an arm around each woman. "Threesome isn't a word I throw around a lot--"

"You've gotta be fucking kidding me," Pia mutters, stalking away.

Before Cupid's arm can even drop, Hugh is standing in her place, face lit up with excitement. "Did somebody say threesome?"

Shaking her head in disgust, Snowy walks back over to her grandfather.

"Well, not *now*," Cupid snaps.

"What are *you* doing later?"

Cupid glances over to where Snowy and her grandfather are both angrily glaring at him. "Nobody now. I should probably get out of

———
244

here."

"Call me," Hugh offers with a grin, handing over a business card before he's gone again in the blink of an eye.

"Yeah, right," Cupid mutters, crushing the card in his hand. "I'd rather fuck Bill."

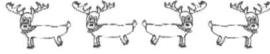

The rest of the convention is able to proceed as normal. The next two days pass without any further incidents. The Santas enjoy long talks around the campfire and tell many fascinating tales of their journeys. Frank hoards more coleslaw and Holly finally tells Wally that she doesn't want to see any more pictures.

Cupid takes off after the arrest, much to Snowy's delight. She certainly revels in ignoring his calls and bad mouthing him in his absence. "He's really very vulgar," she says to Pia at one point. "I don't know how I stood his presence for so long. I don't know how *anyone* can. And you say you work with him *every day*? I feel *terrible* for you!"

Pia checks her phone and tries to enjoy her first dinner that isn't cold fish. But, once things settle down, she finds she isn't enjoying the trip at all. "Yeah."

Now they are packing. Frank is in the fridge slapping all the leftovers into plastic containers while Holly folds up all the linens. Pia has packed her own small suitcase quickly and is standing by the window, staring out of it just because it is something to do.

"We're nearly ready to go!" Santa announces, stomping the snow off of his boots as he enters the cabin. "Holly, Frank - why don't you start getting our things loaded? Don't forget my foot cream, Frank! All this walking around has done a number on my tootsies! You're going to have to work some of your magic on the way back!"

Holly grabs some bags and heads outside, a grumbling Frank on her heels.

"Thank you for inviting me on this trip. I had a nice time," Pia says, trying to sound genuine.

"I should be thanking *you* for protecting *me*." Santa smiles. "I never did thank you for that. I know you stayed awake that night." He winks. "I know when you're awake. Even if I'm asleep."

"I was just doing my job, Santa. There's really no need to thank me."

Santa puts his hands on his hips and joins her at the window, watching as Ded Moroz and his granddaughter drag their trunks over to their repaired sled. "I'm going to miss these little get togethers after I retire."

Pia swallows with difficulty, her mouth suddenly dry. "Oh...you're still considering retiring?"

"*Considering?*" booms Santa with a laugh so loud and sudden that it startles her. "I'm not *considering* anything, my child! I've already made up my mind!" He nods definitively. "Yes. It's definitely time. *Definitely.* Speaking of leaving, it's also definitely time to go home!" He grabs a few bags that are resting on the bed and heads toward the cabin door. "There's still much work to be done! Just because I'm retiring, it doesn't mean I can take it easy! Not yet!"

He exits the cabin and Pia turns away from the window and the bright, sunny day beyond the glass, checking her phone for at least the fiftieth time that morning. She has been checking it so often that even Holly has commented on it.

Still no calls. No messages.

She doesn't know why she feels compelled to keep checking. It would have happened by now and she knew better than to expect one in the first place.

There will be no thank you call from Corporate. Not for her.

"Hey."

"Fuck!" Pia turns, clutching her heart to find Cupid standing behind her with his usual debonaire grin. "You son of a bitch! You scared the shit out of me!"

"Sorry," he says, although the word doesn't carry much weight. "I didn't mean to make you pee your panties."

"What are you even doing here? Since you left, Snowy's been spending almost every waking second tarnishing your already worthless name. I wouldn't want to be anywhere in her vicinity if I were you."

Cupid peers out the window with interest. "Has she now? Is she still here? I do *love* angry sex."

"What are you doing here?" Pia asks again, her miniscule amount of patience eroding quickly.

"I was on my way to Brazil for a little action," he begins with a wink as she rolls her eyes. "So, I thought I'd stop by and check on you."

"Check on me?" she repeats, each word dripping with disgust.

"Yeah. 'Cause I care. Did you hear anything from Corporate yet concerning your heroic actions?"

She is very aware of the phone still clutched in her hand, still painfully silent. "It's none of your damn business."

"You know you're not going to get a thank you," he continues, not missing a beat. "I hate to be the bearer of bad news, honey, but they barely care about those of us at the bottom of the ladder. We're like one rung above those suckers they sweet-talked into running their holidays. All they care about is the profit, because without it, we're nothing. Unless the mortals decide they want to dust the cobwebs off of their ancient religions and start building temples and praying to us again."

"I know how the company works," she snaps. "And what do you know about being at the bottom of the ladder, Cupid?"

He shrugs as he takes a couple of steps toward her. "Hey, I left. I decided I'd rather be 'down there' with the 'inferior' holiday heads than stay with *them*. There's no love lost there. Plus, there's the whole sex maniac thing. If that's not bottom of the ladder--"

"Get to the fucking point. If you even *have* one."

"The point is," Cupid continues firmly, "Don't go around yelling and cursing at everybody night and day, working your ass off to try and make Corporate proud of you. It's not gonna happen." He places a tender hand on her shoulder. "I know you think this is your chance, but it's not."

Pia does not react right away. In fact, for a fraction of a second the usually hard lines of her face seem to soften.

But then she is shoving Cupid's arm away from her body with such force that she would have easily snapped his bones had he been human. "How dare you come down here trying to lecture me on how I should conduct myself."

"I'm not--"

"Get out of here."

"Hey--"

With her next words the ceiling and walls begin to shake, bringing dust and tiny particles of wood raining down on them both. "*GET OUT!*"

In the blink of an eye he's gone and she is alone again like she wants.

Again, she looks at her phone. She can't help herself. She wants - she *needs* - him to be wrong.

But not a thing has changed.

What a failure this entire trip has been.

September

"What alarms Clucky is the amount of homeless pet rocks in the world."

"Don't be such a baby, it's only a cleaning."

"I – hurs--"

"Don't talk when I have my fingers in your mouth," Regina instructs firmly as she tilts Francis' head farther back. "You have a terrible overbite by the way. And you stink of carrots."

The Easter Bunny tries to respond, but his voice comes out muffled, causing the Tooth Fairy to roll her eyes.

"Believe me, it's not the worst thing I've smelled coming out of somebody's mouth. Or the worst thing I've *pulled* from somebody's," she adds, pulling something orange and stringy from between two of Francis' teeth. "I've pulled more pubes from Cupid's mouth than I have down – oh, stop worrying, of *course* I wash my hands. I'm a *doctor* for goodness sakes."

Because her office is so small, Regina is leaning on her desk as she pushes the large rabbit as far back in her desk chair as she can. In the corner near the door, Holly stands cradling a cup of coffee, watching with a look of disgust on her face.

"I don't know why Frank wants to become a dentist," Holly notes, shuddering slightly. "Who wants to stick their fingers into everybody's mouths?"

"It's better than being Santa's slave for eternity," Regina remarks without turning around.

"Being Santa's slave is better than being Pia's," Holly gossips. "I hear she has Baby New Year--"

"I think we should have probably started calling him Caleb a few months ago," Regina interrupts with a small smile. "There's something creepy about calling a sixty-year-old man *baby*."

"Fine then. I heard she has *Caleb* scrubbing the floors of her house with a toothbrush," Holly says.

Regina throws up her hands in frustration as she turns to face the elf.

"Why the hell would she waste a perfectly good toothbrush on some meager task like that?" she demands. "You'd think she'd be over the moon that she was the one who discovered Tio was trying to kill all of the Christmas figures--"

"I heard Tuss talking to Santa the other day and supposedly no one from Corporate even thanked her for that," Holly shrugs. "She's just pissed off because there are only three months left until Santa's last Christmas."

"I'm – miss – fat – man," Francis chokes around Regina's fingers.

"We're *all* going to miss him," Regina replies calmly. "Now stop talking. Don't make me tell you again."

"So did I tell you I've been getting chocolates and flowers in the mail?" Holly asks, taking a sip of her coffee. "I have no idea who's sending them."

"Sounds like you have a secret admirer," Regina smirks as she viciously scrubs Francis' overbite. "Enjoy it while it lasts. I don't even remember the last time somebody's given me flowers."

"Yeah, well, at least it's not *Wally* for once," Holly sneers.

"Of - it - is--" Francis mumbles around Regina's tools.

"*What?*" Regina asks, giving up and pulling her hands from his mouth with a sigh.

"I said of *course* it's Wally," Francis stretches his jaw. "He's completely in love with you!"

"The rabbit has a point," Regina smirks, sticking her hands back into his mouth.

"I wonder who it could be," Holly ignores the two of them. "Maybe Bobby! He's cute!"

"Which one's Bobby again?" Regina asks curiously.

"The really hot one with the huge muscles that works on Santa's sleigh," Holly sighs, lost in a daydream.

"Oh, *him*? He *is* cute!" Regina agrees. "Try flirting with him," she continues, raising her voice slightly to be heard over the Canadian National Anthem drifting out of Tilly's office a few doors down. "Gage his reaction. Men are simple creatures." Francis makes a noise of protest. "No offense," she says quickly. "I know you're a man *and* a creature. But anyway," she turns to Holly. "If Bobby's the one sending you all of this stuff, you'll be able to read his expression. And if not, well, what does it matter if he flirts back? You can sit up and rinse now." She looks down at the Easter Bunny. "We're all done."

"Oh, thank goodness." Francis sits up straight, opening and shutting his mouth as he runs his tongue along his teeth. "They feel good!"

"Rinse," Regina repeats again, removing her gloves and pointing to the rinse bowl built into her chair.

"You know," Holly says thoughtfully, trying to ignore the disgusting sight of a giant rabbit repeatedly spitting. "It's not a bad idea. Maybe I *will* do that."

"Regina's full of good ideas," Francis says cheerily, as he sits up straight once more and adjusts his turquoise colored bow tie. "If you're going to listen to anybody's advice on flirting, it should be hers."

"What's *that* supposed to mean?" Regina asks, furrowing her eyebrows.

"We all see how you flirt with Tuss," Francis replies casually. "How you two look at one anot--"

"Say another word about it and I'll pull out your teeth," Regina threatens the rabbit, as she picks up a sharp looking instrument from her desk.

Francis lets out a little moan of horror and covers his eyes with his overlong ears. "I'm sorry."

Holly laughs. "Look who's in denial now! Don't get so defensive," she remarks, when the Tooth Fairy rounds on her, red in the face. "Who can blame you? He's gorgeous. I'd *totally* do him!"

"I do *not* have a crush on Tuss," Regina says loudly, hot in the cheeks. "I'd rather date Bill."

"You might not want to say that with your door open," Holly says pointedly, glancing out of the office at the gloomy hallway beyond, where Bill, Ted and Jack Frost are trying to pull Tilly from the elevator her antlers are stuck in. "If he hears you--"

"He'd blow his load at the words," Regina says, rolling her eyes. "The point is, I don't have feelings for--"

She can't finish her sentence because Tuss has suddenly appeared in her doorway, seemingly out of thin air as if he were the Boogeyman. He clears his throat loudly to announce his presence, an eyebrow raised.

"Is this uh — is this a bad time?" he asks, looking into the small, overcrowded office.

"Not at all," Regina breathes, glancing into his blue eyes.

Holly and Francis exchange a look, both trying not to smirk, before the elf states, "We were just leaving."

"You don't have to," Regina begins, but it's too late. Holly quickly hurries from the room, the Easter Bunny hopping after her, both of them heading toward the end of the hall to help extricate the moose from the elevator.

"So," Regina begins, walking around her desk to shut the door and allow for some privacy. "Did you convince your *partner* there to give me Mother Nature's old office yet?"

"Believe me, you don't want it right now," Tuss laughs, taking the empty seat in front of the Tooth Fairy's desk. "It's more of a jungle than an office at the minute."

"That wasn't my question," Regina replies coldly, falling into her own chair.

"No, I haven't," Tuss sighs deeply.

"Well then, we don't really have anything to talk about right now, do we?" Regina asks, trying not to stare directly into his confused eyes.

"What's wrong with you?"

"Nothing."

"Why are you being so…so..."

"So *what?*"

"So *cold*," Tuss says. "So…*like Pia.*"

Regina's mouth drops open. "That's not the way to get into my pants, Tuss."

"I'm not trying to get into your pants, Regina," Tuss says, flushing a deep shade of red. "Not that I wouldn't like to, it's just--"

"Well everybody seems to think it's already happened," Regina interrupts, her voice softer now.

Since their not-so-secret Mother's Day kiss, their relationship had been entirely professional and yet slightly awkward. In June, Tuss invited her out to a 'business' dinner and then cancelled at the last minute. For two weeks in July, he brought her coffee every day 'just as a friend', only to nearly disappear from existence for two weeks afterwards. More recently, over the past month or so, they had been enjoying lunch together in the cafeteria practically every day. It was never planned, but it seemed no matter what time she sat down, there he was a few minutes later, tray in hand. He'd ask if she minded some company and she'd always invite him to sit with a smile. It was no wonder people were starting to talk.

"Is *that* what this is about?" Tuss asks. "It's embarrassing for you that people think that?"

"It's embarrassing for me that it actually *hasn't* happened yet," Regina laughs. "I don't want people thinking that I've done something I haven't. *Yet.*"

"Oh," Tuss says awkwardly. "We've talked about this, it--"

"I know," Regina says quickly, nodding her head professionally. "Don't worry about it."

The two stare silently across the desk at one another before Tuss says, "I'm actually down here on official business today."

"Alone?" Regina smirks. "The wicked bitch of the west trusts you to handle something without her breathing down your neck?"

"She has other things on her plate right now," Tuss explains. "The past few months have been hard on her. Between her Mother's Day campaign failing to impress Corporate--"

"Because it was the single stupidest campaign anyone's ever seen," Regina reminds him.

Tuss nods his agreement. "And the most fires ever breaking out on the Fourth of July," he continues. "She was hoping she'd win back some favor with Corporate when she unmasked the plot Tio had in place to scare all of the Santas."

"Which she clearly didn't," Regina says. "I heard she didn't even get an email saying thanks'."

"She didn't," Tuss confirms. "And with Santa's retirement looming closer, that's all she can focus on right now. I think she's actually touring his workshop today, trying to come up with a new scheme to stop him from going through with his plan. Which leaves *me* to deal with *you. Alone.*"

"Well, lay it on me," Regina insists, leaning back in her chair. "What's this about?"

"I wanted to talk to you about your entire operation," Tuss begins. "You know, how you sell all of the teeth you collect to British dentists and orthodontists."

"It's a great scheme, isn't it?" Regina laughs. "Their teeth are so bad in the U.K., nobody can even tell that the false teeth are dirty and used. Well, except the people I'm selling them to directly, but they don't care." She shrugs. "Do you know how much I get for a bag of used teeth? *Especially* if they're from someone famous? Even while giving a dollar to every kid who loses a tooth, I still turn a profit. So if Corporate has a problem--"

"Regina," Tuss holds up his hand, laughing slightly, and Regina can't help but admire his own wonderful teeth as he smiles. "Corporate thinks your operation is wonderful. Your department used to be a financial black hole until you came up with it, so they're very happy with you."

Regina smiles. "Well, good. They should be. Thank you."

"There's one thing I really don't get though. You mostly collect the teeth children lose, right?"

"Well, all teeth that are lost come into my possession one way or another, but children do lose the most, yeah. What don't you get?"

"The fact that these dentists in the U.K. are making dentures for adults out of children's teeth and nobody seems to complain."

Regina nods, pushing a loose strand of her hair behind her ear. "That's how terrible the teeth are over there. They don't even notice."

"Well, Corporate wants you to expand *beyond* the U.K.," Tuss explains. "And frankly, I think it's a good idea. You're limiting yourself to four countries when you have the whole world at your fingertips."

256

"That doesn't make any sense," Regina says defensively. "It works in Britain because their teeth are bad as it is, so used dentures fit right in without anybody blinking."

"There're always countries like Ghana," Tuss suggests. "Or other third world parts of Africa. They all have bad teeth--"

"And no money to pay for my used ones," Regina laughs.

"That's racist," Tuss says.

"It's true!" Regina protests. "Not at the rates I'm charging. And naming predominantly black countries *isn't* racist?" she adds, raising an eyebrow.

"You could also try the U.S., I suppose." Tuss points out. "The fattest nation in the world, loads of them have to have terrible teeth. Especially the way we push candy there. I mean, I hear they even have something called *turducken* now!"

"I--"

"Just – just think about it, alright?" Tuss asks. "Promise me?"

Regina sighs deeply – how could she say no to that face?

"I promise."

"That's all I ask," Tuss smiles, standing up.

"I don't think other countries will go for it though," Regina says, as he turns to leave the office.

"We'll see," he replies with a wink. "I have to get going. I'm going to use this alone time to try and convince Caleb to stop fawning over Pia." He sighs. "He's going to drive himself insane otherwise."

He walks out of the office and disappears into thin air, just as Bill, Ted, Francis, Holly and Jack all fall backwards onto their asses, finally extricating Tilly from the elevator.

"Thanks for that!" the moose says brightly, as the five of them lay on the floor in a groaning heap.

Regina rolls her eyes and, pulling her wand from thin air, waves her office door closed once again. Realizing she's finally alone, and wanting to distract herself from thinking about Tuss, she opens one of her desk drawers and pulls out a few photographs – some black and white, some in color, all extremely old.

The subjects are all different, but resemble one another; if a stranger was looking at them, having no idea who they were, they'd at least be able to tell they were all related. Regina can only stare wistfully at each of the faces for the briefest of moments before her office door bangs open again. Hugh and Hugo come flying in, low in the air and out of breath, both trying to keep an enormous, clearly heavy burlap sack off of the floor.

"What did I say about knocking?" Regina asks exasperatedly, staring at her employees as she quickly shoves the photographs back into her desk drawer before they can notice them.

"Sorry," Hugo pants, sweat lining his forehead. "But these are all of the teeth we collected last night."

"Good haul." Regina nods appreciatively, eyeing the two muscular pixies. "See how much work you two can get done when you're working *together* and not wasting time clawing at each other's throats?"

Hugh and Hugo exchange a look of disdain, but don't say anything in response. Regina grabs the sack from them and waves her wand, making it disappear.

"Who do I have an appointment with this evening?" she asks, grabbing her purse from her desk and slinging it over her shoulder. "And in what city?"

"Uh…" Hugh flies up to the shelf where his tiny desk rests and shuffles through a date book. "Dr. Fairweather. In London."

"Excellent," Regina smirks. "I always get a free meal out of him."

WWWWW

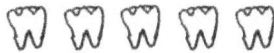

Jack Frost is not an early riser. Though he may have been around since the dawn of time, his mentality – much like his body – is stuck very much in the mindset of a teenager. He'd prefer to be able to sleep all day and party all night, but he unfortunately has a job to do.

Although he is a slacker, and procrastinates away the majority of his days (for how long, exactly, you'd have to ask Father Time), he still has to get some semblance of work done. As anything is preferable to cleaning up the St. Patrick's Day floor, he concentrates the bulk of his efforts on running the cafeteria for the other holiday heads. And even though they constantly complain about the quality of his food (all fair complaints, because Jack really does just throw leftovers in a pot and stirs), Jack knows that they'd be in even worse moods than normal without the sustenance he provides them with. For this reason alone, Jack considers running the kitchen a selfish endeavor. After all, who wants to listen to any more of their bullshit?

He is in the kitchen throwing leftover pieces of hot dog from the Fourth of July on top of some melting chocolate from Valentine's Day when loud alarm bells begin to ring throughout the building. As the lights above him begin to flash red, Jack Frost sighs deeply at the apparent security breach. The last time the alarms went off, he found two turkeys in a compromising position in the wrong closet. He is tempted to ignore the sounds and the lights, but security is, unfortunately, another aspect of his miserable job. Besides, if he lets it go on any longer, the holiday heads – or the witch and her flying monkey from Corporate – were sure to start complaining.

Sure enough, as he makes his way toward the elevators, he eyes Bill stepping out of one.

"The cafeteria's closed until noon," Jack Frost tells the irate man.

"How am I supposed to get any work done around here with all of this racket going on?" Bill demands, straightening his glasses. "I'm a very busy man, you know! Why don't you do your job and--"

"*Chillax*," Jack says, walking past the sweating man. "You're clearly not busy enough if you came all the way up here to yell at me! Besides, where do you think I'm going? I'm on my way to deal with it!"

"Well, hurry up!" Bill whines. "Rosh Hashanah isn't going to plan itself!"

"It'd probably be better off if it did," Jack snorts, stepping into the elevator Bill just exited. "We all know how successful *Flag Day* is, after all!"

Before Bill can object to this comment, the elevator doors close and Jack descends to the fourth floor. He knows exactly where to go due to the fact that the alarms still blaring overhead are chiming to the tune of *Here Comes Peter Cottontail*.

Emerging from the elevator on the Easter floor, Jack finds Francis standing at the end of the hall looking nervous, surrounded by Clucky and a few of his other employees, worriedly chirping.

"THANK GOODNESS YOU'RE HERE!" Francis yells over the loud alarm the second he spots Jack. "SOMEBODY BROKE INTO MY OFFICE!"

"What's that, Franny?" Jack asks with a sarcastic smirk. "Speak up. I don't think the Boogeyman can hear you up on the tenth floor."

"I SAID--"

"I was being sarcastic, you dolt," Jack deadpans, waving his hand through the air so that the alarm and the flashing lights cease immediately.

"Oh, thank you!" Francis sighs with relief. "Us animals have sensitive ears, you know."

"So I've heard."

Jack starts down the grass-padded hallway toward the Easter Bunny's office as Francis hops along after him, his whiskers twitching nervously.

"Be careful," Francis warns over the tweeting of the nervous chicks following behind them. "Whoever it is could be armed!"

"I doubt it."

"They could be dangerous!" Francis insists, wringing his paws.

"*Or* they could be asleep," Jack notes, as they reach the office (the walls of which are covered in their entirety with framed portraits of Francis' many wives and children from around the world). "It's just the Sandman."

He motions to the old man, fast asleep with his head resting against the rabbit's keyboard as though it is a pillow, drool coating most of the home row.

"Oh, thank *goodness!*" Francis breathes as Jack shakes the old man.

"Sandy! Hey, Sandy! Wake up!"

"No apple turnover for me, thank you," the Sandman mumbles in-between snores. "It gives me gas."

"Sandy! Wake up!" Jack Frost yells directly into his ear, causing the old man's eyes to snap open immediately.

"What did you do that for?" he yawns. "What time is it?"

"You're not in your office, buddy," Jack informs him.

"I was too tired to make it down to my office," the Sandman explains. "I only got twenty-three hours and forty-five minutes of sleep last night! Besides, it's cold down there!"

"It's cold up here too," Francis points out. "I wish the *maintenance man* would get on top of fixing the heat."

"Maybe he's too busy with other things," Jack hisses. "Like running the cafeteria and responding to fake security threats." Turning to the Sandman, he adds sternly, "You can't sleep in other people's offices. If you're so tired, why don't you just go home?"

"It takes too much effort," the Sandman laments, as he wearily stands up and slowly begins to shuffle out of the office in his well-worn slippers.

"Perhaps if you updated the security around here, he wouldn't be able to get into our offices for naps," the Easter Bunny suggests kindly.

"My security system is *fine*." Jack rolls his eyes as the Sandman trudges from the room. "I know how to do my--"

"What happened?" Tuss barges into the room, out of breath. "Is everything okay?"

"As long as Pia's not behind you, it is," Francis says nervously.

"She's with Santa," Tuss explains. "What happened?" he asks Jack again. "I heard the alarm--"

"The whole *building* heard the alarm," Jack interrupts, his patience waning. "It's hard to miss."

"But what--"

"It was a false alarm," Jack states firmly. "Just the Sandman sleeping again. But good thing one of the heroes from Corporate is here to save the day! Good to know that you have our backs!"

"You know," Tuss begins, regaining his composure. "I don't think we've discussed security at all since I've been here."

"Security's *fine*," Jack Frost insists. "*Trust me*. I know how to do my job."

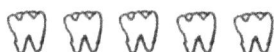

🦷 🦷 🦷 🦷 🦷

Santa's workshop is buzzing with excitement as Holly makes her way through it. Though constantly busy year round, the elves really kick things into high gear come September, when all of the mortals begin airing their Christmas songs on the radio and specials on television. The malls would already be decorated and Tom the turkey would be scheduling a meeting with Santa any day now just so the overstuffed bird could lace into his nemesis about trying to take over the whole year with his tinsel and jingling bells.

Holly passes by Willy, who is leading the choir elves in a rendition of *Santa Claus is Coming to Town* (a song that the Krampus originated the year Adolph Hitler became leader of Germany that was originally intended to be sung mockingly to Santa, making fun of his perverted methods of spying on little children), and bears left down a hallway leading toward the stable. Passing the bakery, from which the smell of gingerbread drifts out along with the sound of Mrs. Claus' voice ("Jolly, be careful! That's the second bowl you've dropped!"), Holly speeds up so she doesn't give into temptation and ruin her diet - even though her diet only started an hour ago, born out of nerves at the prospect of confronting her possible secret admirer, Bobby.

Pushing her way through the large double doors at the end of the hall, Holly finds herself in the stable, which always smell like wet animals, and nervously adjusts the diamond brooch pinned to her shirt – the latest gift she has received in the mail from her admirer. Santa's giant red sleigh is resting in the center of the hay covered floor and standing inside of it, polishing the sides while whistling to himself, is Bobby.

Holly admires the elf's strong jaw, lined with manly stubble, and bulging biceps as he works, before clearing her throat and walking over.

"Prepping the sleigh for Santa's last ride a bit early, don't ya think?" she grins, flashing her teeth as she approaches him.

Bobby looks up, smiling. "Hey, Holly. Never too early to start prepping the sleigh. The amount of work it takes to get this thing to stay airborne… I mean, there are literally tons of presents stacked in the back as it's driven by an old man who probably wouldn't even have a license anymore if he lived down with the mortals – it's *exhausting*. I nearly had to build a new one from scratch after he ran over that grandmother in Minnesota that one year. Constant care must be given to even the most *minute* of details."

"Sounds like hard work," Holly notes, pursing her lips slightly and trying to subtly stick out her chest. "You must be – ah – *good* with your hands to be able to keep it working year in and year out."

Bobby laughs, jumping down from the sleigh and wiping his greasy hands on his pants as he approaches Holly. "I'm great with my hands," he winks at her. "Nice brooch, by the way," he adds, noticing the diamonds pinned to her breast.

"Thanks. My – uh - my *secret admirer* sent it to me."

"Did he now?" Bobby asks with a cocky smile as he folds his arms across his chest. "He must really like you to send you something like that."

"That's what I'm hoping, anyway," Holly laughs, stepping closer to the elf. "All of the flowers, and chocolates, and sugar cookies, and candy canes…he has to really like me."

"Or he's overcompensating for something."

Holly laughs, trailing a finger down one of Bobby's muscular arms as she glances down at the bulge in his tight pants. "Somehow I doubt that," she remarks.

"Well…" Bobby breathes, his shifty eyes narrowing slightly as his grin widens. "Maybe I can show you for sure sometime."

"So you *did* send me all of these gifts?" Holly asks, elated.

After a very long pause, Bobby replies curtly. "Yes."

Holly can't say anything more than "I knew it!" before the doors of the stable open once more and Santa walks in with Pia, Wally and Frank on his heels.

"I'm *fine*, Pia," Santa is insisting. "Stop worrying so much! We *always* go through periods without the alarm going off at all and then it's constantly going off! It's nothing new!"

"But if it's a real security threat…we've just been through this with that freak of nature in Greenland and--"

"Jack Frost will take care of it," Santa interrupts with a smile. "Now, you remember my reindeer, don't you?" he continues jovially, leading Pia, who is staring down at the hay-strewn floor in disgust as her nose twitches at the smell, over to the reindeer pen. "That's Dasher and Dancer, and Prancer and Vixen. You remember Comet and Cupid, don't you?"

"Of course," Pia forces a smile onto her face. "And Donner and Blitzen."

Wally tries to suppress a smirk as he notices Pia's expression of distaste at her inadvertent rhyming. It looks as though she had been forced to swallow a lemon.

"Hi, Blitzen," she coos insincerely, reaching one of her hands into the enclosure to pet the reindeer, who immediately growls loudly and tries to bite her. "Watch it! You fucking…" She glances at Santa, who appears scandalized, "…*jokester*, you. You *fucking* little *jokester*," she repeats through gritted teeth.

"Blitzen sure is a card," Santa agrees, laughing as his stomach shakes like a bowl full of jelly. "I don't know if you recall Rudolph?" he asks Pia, guiding her to the last reindeer in the pen. "He's the most famous of all."

"Of course I remember him," Pia says harshly. "I mean, how couldn't I?" she asks, forcing politeness back into her voice. "With all of the songs and movies about him."

"He's doing much better now," Santa remarks, patting the top of the reindeer's head. "Next year he'll be able to take the new Santa to the convention in Greenland, no problem."

Pia, who is staring down at the bright red, flashing nose in annoyance, flinches at the words and pretends that she doesn't hear them. Rudolph, on the other hand, lets out a guttural moan and everyone recoils in disgust as the reindeer explodes from behind.

"Oh, well," Santa reaches up to cover his nose. "Maybe he's not back at one hundred percent yet," he laughs. "But don't worry, Bobby here takes good care of them and I'm sure he wouldn't mind cleaning up--"

"I'm busy with the sleigh, Santa," Bobby says quickly, hopping back into the vehicle and waving his oily rag through the air. "See?"

"Ah yes, don't worry about it," Santa says. "Frank can clean the pen!"

Wally, Holly and Bobby all try to stifle their grins as the short, bearded elf hangs his head in shame, looking as though he's about to cry.

"Fuck my life," he mutters, dragging his feet toward the reindeer.

"Good choice, Santa," Pia smiles. "He needs something to do." Frank throws her a dirty look as she places her hand on Santa's shoulder and guides him away from the disgusting animals. "Everything seems to be running smoothly here, as expected. I think we're going to have our most successful Christmas ever this year!"

"Ho, ho, ho, I *ho*-heartedly agree," Santa winks at Pia, chuckling at his terrible joke, which makes even his elves grimace. "It'll make my last Christmas here all the more memorable."

Pia's face falls, and unable to pretend she didn't hear this comment, asks, "You're still set on retiring?"

"I'm getting so old for this job, my dear," Santa sighs. "Old and fat."

"You're supposed to be old and fat," Pia points out. "It's in the job description."

"I promised the missus I'd take her to the Caribbean for a long vacation," Santa continues. "We both need one. And to tell you the truth, my long hours here aren't helping the sex drive. Mrs. Claus is actually starting to complain--"

"I'm sure Cupid could give you something for that," Pia cuts him off quickly, shutting her eyes in disgust at the mental image. "We can cut back on your hours if it means--"

"Pia," Santa says gently, staring into the woman's face which, normally so hard and expressionless, looks young and panicked now. "I've made up my mind. Now, if you'll excuse me, I have to go return Tom's call. He left me about twenty messages earlier. Complaining about mall decorations or something of the sort."

Pia watches as Santa walks from the room, shaking with rage, before rounding on Blitzen. "If you ever try to fucking bite me again, I'll have you skinned alive and wear your fur as a coat! And you two," she rounds on Wally and Holly. "Aren't you supposed to be shadowing Santa? One of you deal with that damn turkey and tell him that if I hear him complain about Christmas one more time to me, or Santa, or the Boogeyman's *fucking* Shadow, I'm going to have him stuffed for Thanksgiving dinner this year!"

Pia storms from the room angrily, red in the face, and after exchanging a quick glance, Wally and Holly hurry after her, the former remarking, "Nice brooch," as they do so.

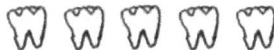

🦷 🦷 🦷 🦷 🦷

"*Again?*" Jack Frost demands to the empty kitchen, throwing his knife down on the cutting board and staring up at the ceiling in exasperation. The lights above are flashing red and the alarm bells are ringing to the tune of Adam Sandler's *The Thanksgiving Song*.

Storming toward the elevator, he reaches it just as T.J. comes flapping out of the opening doors, screeching loudly in annoyance.

"What do *you* want?" Jack snaps, running a hand through his platinum blonde hair in frustration.

T.J. continues to screech loudly.

"I don't understand what you're saying!" Jack exclaims in frustration, backing up a few feet as the eagle flaps its wings in his face and jerks its beak up at the lights flashing overhead. "Oh, what? The alarm's bothering you? Well get in line, bird shit! I'm trying to deal with it!"

T.J. continues squawking incomprehensibly, causing Jack to snap, "What do you care? You don't have to do any real work for another ten *months*!" And ducking under the bird, who rises angrily into the air, Jack Frost hurries into the elevator and slams the button that will take him to the eleventh floor.

"Sabotage!" Tom is clucking the moment Jack emerges onto the odd smelling Thanksgiving floor. "Somebody broke into my office and is trying to sabotage my holiday!"

"It's probably just a false alarm," Jack sighs deeply, snapping his fingers so that the alarm stops sounding immediately. "Did you see who--"

"Of course I did," Tom interrupts snidely. "Did you think I would just let the perpetrator escape? My turkeys apprehended him." And clucking loudly, he calls, "Bring him out, boys!"

Jack rolls his eyes as Tom's six employees emerge from the conference room, holding a sleeping old man between them.

"It's just the Sandman," Jack points out.

"Sent here by Santa to sabotage Thanksgiving!" Tom yells as his employees cluck their agreement.

"Oh, get stuffed you idiots, all of you," Jack snarls, striding forward and pulling the old man from the tight grasp of the birds. "He's just confused, you know what he's like!"

"Confused!" one of the turkeys bellows.

"I'm confused!" another chimes in.

"Confucius? He's my favorite philosopher!"

"Cranberries!"

"I want to sleep like the old man!"

"I have to use the bathroom."

As the voices of the six birds blend together to create a cacophony of sound that is painful to the ears, the Sandman groans in annoyance and opens his eyes slowly.

"What's all the commotion about?"

"*You*," Jack informs him rudely, propping the old man up on his own two feet.

"Oh, hi, Jack." The Sandman smiles sleepily at him as though noticing him for the first time. "Pia was looking for you before."

"*What?*" Jack demands urgently. "When? Why?"

"Down in the basement," the Sandman yawns as his eyes begin to droop once more. "She said something about an alarm? Her voice was grating on me, that's why I came up here to sleep."

Jack allows the Sandman to fall to the floor fast asleep once more as he hurries for the elevator.

"Where are you going?" Tom demands. "I expect justice!"

"Getting away from here before Pia shows up!" Jack calls over his shoulder as he pushes the down button.

"Well, I for one would love to talk to her!" Tom clucks, his chest feathers all puffed up. "I'm sure she'd love to know that her *precious* Santa Claus is trying to ruin my holiday!"

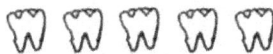

🦷 🦷 🦷 🦷 🦷

Regina, wearing a tiny black dress that shows off her cleavage, is sitting at a small, round table in a fancy restaurant on the River Thames in London. The Tower of London and the London Eye are visible through the front windows, and while most mortals are enthralled by the view, Regina's seen them enough over the years and is no longer amazed by these landmarks. Sitting across from her, Dr. Timothy Fairweather is eyeing her closely, nervously straightening his tie.

"I can't justify spending that much money right now," he says nervously, wiping at the beads of sweat sprouting from his forehead. "That's double the amount you asked for the last time."

"These teeth are of better quality, Timothy," Regina smiles, flashing her perfect teeth and leaning forward slightly to accentuate her cleavage further, drawing the dentist's eyes immediately. "Not to mention the mouths they've come from." She begins to name them off on her fingers. "Clint Eastwood, Angela Lansbury, Barack Obama--"

"How do you get your hands on all of them?" Timothy asks, giving a nervous twitch.

"Well, I couldn't tell you *that*, now could I? I don't need you stealing my business."

Timothy gives a nervous laugh as Regina takes a large sip of wine, eyeing her purse resting on the corner of their table.

"Look, I'm a regular customer," Timothy begins, eyeing the purse with longing. "So how about twenty percent off of your named price--"

"I'll give you five percent off," Regina cuts across him coolly. "And you pay for dinner."

"I *always* pay for dinner," Timothy sighs deeply, looking down at the dishes that line the table. After all of his meetings with this rather mysterious woman, he still can't understand how she can eat so much steak and lobster in one sitting and seemingly not gain a pound. "Who can I make it out to?" he asks gloomily, withdrawing his checkbook from his jacket pocket.

"Nobody. You know my policy - cash only, no checks."

"Are you a wanted criminal or something?"

Regina shrugs mischievously as she downs the rest of her wine. Timothy looks around the restaurant covertly before withdrawing a wad of cash from inside of his pocket. After passing it to her under the table, he reaches for Regina's purse but she slaps his hand away.

"I have to make sure it's all here first," she reprimands, waving the money around in front of his face, drawing the eyes of curious onlookers.

"Put it away!" Timothy hisses, but Regina takes her time counting the notes. Once she's sure all ten thousand pounds are present, she deposits the money in her purse and pulls out the large, heavy brown sack from within. Timothy eyes it nervously before placing it at his feet. "How did that fit in there?"

"Never you mind," Regina answers, standing up. "It was great seeing you, Dr. Fairweather," she says, extending her hand. "Until next time."

"You're leaving?" Timothy asks. "I thought this was – uh – *leading somewhere.*"

"Is your name Tuss?" Regina asks automatically.

"Tuss? What? No, what's a--"

"Then it's not leading anywhere. Maybe next time," Regina says, shaking the doctor's hand with a wink.

"You *always* say that!"

But before the doctor can argue, Regina turns on her heel and walks away from the restaurant, breathing in the cool London air. Sighing deeply, she watches as the mortals bustle around her, going about their daily business, and feels a stab of jealous envy deep within her at the normality of the short lives that they lead. Checking her watch and realizing it's still early in America, Regina decides to take Tuss' advice and try pawning some teeth over there. Taking out her cell phone, she dials a number and waits.

271

"This is Hugh."

"Hugh. Find me a dentist in New York City who'd be willing to meet with me today, would you? I want to try and expand my business."

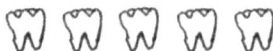

🦷 🦷 🦷 🦷 🦷

Wally approaches Santa's office with trepidation. Even from the lower level of the workshop the sounds of Tom's yelling can be heard, and the elf knows Santa won't want to deal with the turkey alone.

"September, fat boy! It's *September. Halloween* hasn't even happened yet! But your propaganda is already being put up all over the world!"

"Tom, my boy," Wally hears Santa chuckle. "It's only a few decorations that the mortals are putting up. The real meaning of *all* of our holidays can be found right--"

"The mortals only put the tinsel, and the trees, and the baubles up so early because *you* have an army of *yes-men* who promote your holiday twenty-four seven, all year long! But what does Corporate give *me*? Six birds who would be better serving our cause by *literally* being served on hot plates Thanksgiving Day! And on top of all of that, you try and break into my office earlier! What were you hoping to do, destroy my holiday completely? You stole my new gravy recipe, didn't you? *Didn't you, you fatass?*"

"I have no idea what you're talking about, Tom!"

"I wouldn't go in there if I were you," Holly tells Wally, as he approaches her desk situated just outside of Santa's office.

"Unfortunately, it's my job," Wally sighs. Then, noticing the bright flowers on her desk alongside a half-eaten box of chocolates, he smiles. "Looks like somebody has a secret admirer."

"Oh. Yeah. Well," Holly smirks. "Not *so* secret anymore. Bobby finally admitted to sending me all of this stuff."

272

"*Bobby*?" Wally repeats, as though he did not hear her properly. Straightening his glasses, he adds, "The *stable* boy?"

"And engineer extraordinaire," Holly corrects with a dreamy sigh. "The sleigh wouldn't fly if it wasn't for him."

"It wouldn't *fly* if it wasn't for the reindeer attached to it," Wally corrects a bit crankily.

"Which *he* takes care of."

"Holly, *I* sent you all of this stuff," Wally confesses, disheartened. "*Me. I* did, not Bobby. I can't believe he would take credit for it! What a low-life!"

Holly raises a skeptical eyebrow. "Mhm, sure you did."

"I *did*!" Wally insists. "I wanted to show you how much I care about you!"

Holly opens her mouth to reply when Santa calls out of his office, "Holly! I need your help, please!"

Meanwhile, Tom storms out of the doors, his feathers all ruffled. "Watch it!" he snaps at Wally, shoulder-checking him on the way past.

"I have to go." Holly stands up and walks into Santa's office without looking back at her coworker. She slams the door shut behind her, leaving Wally standing alone, confused as to what just happened as above his head the lights of the workshop begin to flash red and alarms chiming to the tune of Weird Al's *The Night Santa Went Crazy* begin to blare loudly.

Santa and Holly come hurrying out of the big man's office and rush toward a closet where the Christmas archives are locked up. Wally and Tom join them to find the door ajar. Before they can fully pull it open, however, Jack Frost shows up behind them.

"What the *fuck*?" he demands, wrenching the door open to find the

Sandman curled up in a ball in the corner of the closet, fast asleep. He's surprised, however, to find that the old man is not alone.

"*Frank*?" Santa asks, rousing the bearded elf from his sleep. "What--"

"Oh…uh…" Frank blushes as he stares up at his boss and his four companions. "I was just…uh…I heard the alarms, see, so I came in here to assess the situation."

"And fell asleep?" Santa asks, furrowing his eyebrows as Holly sighs deeply and Wally rolls his eyes.

"And people think that *I'm* the idiot," Tom smirks, mumbling to Jack in an undertone.

"I've gotta go," Jack says hurriedly to the turkey, backing away unnoticed by Santa or his elves. "If Pia's looking for me, the first place she's going to show up is where the alarm bells are going off."

And sure enough, seconds after Jack Frost disappears from the workshop, Pia materializes out of thin air behind the small group clustered around the closet.

"What the hell?" she demands, staring daggers at the turkey. "Trying to break into Santa's office now as retribution for something that he didn't – what the *fuck* is going on here?" She glances into the closet to see the sleeping Sandman curled up against Frank.

"I'm not entirely sure," Santa remarks thoughtfully.

"I think he's trying to spoon me," Frank frets, throwing the Sandman a frightened look.

Pia waves her hand through the air, causing the alarm to cease instantly, and mutters darkly to herself, "Wait until I get my hands on Jack Frost."

Before anyone can respond to this statement, Knobby hobbles up behind the group, sweating and out of breath, panting as he leans on his cane and cries, "The archives! The archives! I heard the alarm! Are the archives all right? I simply couldn't live with myself if something happened to the archives!" His wrinkled eyes get a load of what is going on inside of the closet and he gasps in melodramatic horror. "What have you *done*? Have you soiled the archives?"

Frank finally manages to peel himself away from the Sandman and brushes past the old elf, mumbling for him to get a grip.

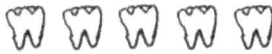

🦷 🦷 🦷 🦷 🦷

Regina likes New York City. It seems to be one of the few places on Earth that changes so much every year and it's the one city in the world that she can never suppress her amazement of.

She is standing in a long black trench coat at the entrance of a back alleyway a few blocks away from Times Square, waiting for the man she's supposed to meet. Seconds turn into minutes and finally when she's about to give up hope that he's going to show up at all, a balding man with a hooked nose sidles up, eyeing her with interest.

"Can I help you?" Regina asks, an eyebrow raised.

"I don't know. Can you?" the man asks, glancing around the alleyway as though nervous of being watched.

"Dr. Philips?" Regina asks.

"Yeah, that's me. You got the goods?"

"Yes," Regina nods, beginning to reach into her purse. "But perhaps first we should discuss compensation for — *ow*! What are you doing?"

The bald man shoves Regina against the wall and begins to cuff her hands behind her back, causing her to drop her purse.

"You're under arrest for the possession of..." The man reaches down and picks up the purse. Staring down inside of it, his look of triumph is quickly replaced by a look of confusion. "*Teeth*?"

"Wait - are you a *cop*?" Regina demands.

"NYPD. World's finest," the man says gruffly, flashing his badge in her face.

Regina rolls her eyes and bangs her head against the brick wall she's pinned up against. "Just perfect," she murmurs.

"Where's the body?" the cop asks forcefully.

"What are you *talking* about?" Regina asks.

"Don't play dumb," the cop snaps. "Where else would you get all of these teeth?"

"I collect them!"

"From rotting corpses, you sick fuck? You have the right to remain silent," the cop begins. "Anything you say can and *will* be used against you in a court of law. You have the right…"

As the cop reads Regina her Miranda Rights, the Tooth Fairy sighs in frustration. She could use her abilities to get herself out of this predicament of course, but a crowd is beginning to gather and Corporate would not be pleased if she exposes herself to the mortals. It is only when she is in the back of the officer's police cruiser that she realizes Corporate is going to be pissed at her anyway for being so careless and getting herself caught, and she profusely hopes that it isn't Pia they send down to bail her out of jail.

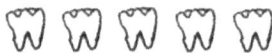

🦷 🦷 🦷 🦷 🦷

Waving his hand through the air in annoyance, Jack stops the alarm bells chiming *Oogie Boogie's Song* from *The Nightmare Before Christmas* as he steps onto the Halloween floor.

"Where's the damn break in *now*?" Jack asks a spider crawling along the wall.

In response, the spider weaves a web in the shape of an arrow pointing in the direction of a closet. Jack walks over to it dutifully and throws open the door, ducking immediately as a swarm of bats comes flying out. When he straightens up again, it is to find the Sandman fast asleep, just as he expected. This time, however, tight webbing is wrapped around his arms and legs, restraining him. Beside the constant napper is Maxwell, bending low, his fangs hovering inches over the old man's neck.

"What the *fuck?*" Jack demands.

"Drink?" Maxwell asks, flushing slightly in embarrassment as he offers the old man to the flustered head of security.

"I don't get paid enough for this," Jack sighs, nearly ready to unleash tears of frustration as he squats down to quickly cut the Sandman loose before Pia shows up to yell at him. Once the Sandman is free of the web, he's heading for the elevators at a steady jog.

Alone again with the still sleeping old man, Maxwell shrugs, bares his fangs once more, and shuts the closet door.

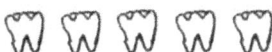

W W W W W

It had been one of the longest days of her life.

Regina, her hair frazzled, sits slumped in her office and watches the mortal news, flushing at the sight of her mug shot displayed on the television screen.

"And this is a crime you don't hear about every day, Bob," the female newscaster is saying. "A woman that the New York Police Department is dubbing *The Tooth Fairy* was arrested today for trying to sell a bag of used teeth to an undercover cop. Police are now checking the teeth for DNA, believing the woman to be linked to a recent string of disappearances in the area."

"How could you be so fucking *stupid?*" Pia demands, stomping her foot on the floor. She and Tuss are both standing in front of the Tooth Fairy's desk, the former livid, and the latter looking extremely uncomfortable. "What's our number one rule?"

"Make money," Regina snaps.

"*Don't get caught!*" Pia yells, slamming her hands down on the desk and leaning in close to Regina, who doesn't flinch despite the fact that they are so close their noses are practically touching. "And not only do you get *caught*, you get *arrested*! You had the money you made earlier today confiscated because it was thought to be obtained *illegally*! You *lost* money! You'll probably *continue* to lose money, because when this story makes it overseas, what fucking British moron is going to want to do business with you anymore?"

"Pia, calm down," Tuss goes to place a hand on his partner's shoulder but thinks better of it, running it through his hair instead to mask the awkward movement. "She's been through enough today. Have you ever been inside of a mortal prison? The women are *hairier* in there…and she had to use the bathroom in front of her cell mates."

He flushes as he says the words, which cause Regina to blush too. As far as she's concerned, the moment when Tuss showed up to post bail couldn't have happened at a worse time. The look on his face when he saw her peeing…they were both mortified.

"She shouldn't have fucking gotten herself arrested then!" Pia snaps, before rounding on Regina again. "You're forbidden from leaving the North Pole again until further notice! Supervised or otherwise!"

"On whose authority?" Regina demands.

"*Corporate's*," Pia smiles cruelly, drawing out every letter of the word. "How the hell do you expect me to do my *job*?"

"Your brainless fairies." Pia gestures toward the ceiling where Hugh and Hugo are crouching behind their desks, terrified. "They'll have to collect the teeth and pawn them off - if they *can* - until further notice. If it was up to *me*, you'd be fucking fired and out on your ass, but--"

"It's not," Tuss cuts her off coldly, causing Pia to turn around in surprise. "She runs one of the more profitable departments--"

"For now."

"She's not going anywhere." He smiles at Regina. "Don't worry about it, you'll be fine."

But Regina stares coldly at Tuss, biting her lip. Before either of them can say another word, Pia's phone rings.

"What?" she snaps, bringing it to her ear instantly.

Even from where Regina's sitting, she can hear the voice on the other end screaming into the phone, panicked.

"Pia! Help! Pia! I'm getting attacked by a gaggle of turkeys! *Turkeys!*"

Pia holds the phone away from her ear, annoyed, before shouting into it. "I told you to fucking talk to Tom about bothering Santa, but you can't even do that right, can you?"

"Pia, I tried!" Caleb whines. "But he sicced his employees on me! Called me a traitor! Said I'm in cahoots with Santa because our holiday's a week later! He keeps screaming something about a gravy recipe! Pia, help--"

But the sound of his desperate plea is drowned out by angry clucking as the line goes dead. Rolling her eyes, Pia pockets her phone and says to Tuss, "Regrettably, I should go deal with that. The last thing I need is Baby Fucking New Year getting mauled by a bunch of birds! I don't need Father Time's impotent ass breaking my door down. Finish dealing with *her*." She jerks her head at Regina before storming out of the office, rubbing her temples as she mumbles to herself, "As if I don't have enough to deal with between the Tooth Fairy and Frost's shitty alarm system, now I have to go and rescue my stalker."

"That could have gone worse," Tuss says lightly to Regina, shutting the door of the office gently. "She could have locked you in a room with a bunch of family members you can't stand to be around like she did with Francis!"

"You didn't even *try* to defend me," Regina begins, shaking with rage. The chill in her voice catches Tuss off guard. "It was *Corporate's* idea – *your* idea – for me to go to New York! And *you*," she glances up toward where Hugh is sitting. "You set me up with a *cop?*"

"I didn't know," Hugh shudders, holding his tutu tightly to stop his hands from shaking with fear. "You – you didn't give us enough time to properly research--"

"Regina, calm down," Tuss implores her. "You just had a bad day, that's all. This whole thing will all blow over within a week and then things will go back to normal. You're too important for Corporate to be upset with you for long."

"Nothing is *ever* normal here," Regina snaps, hot tears springing to her eyes. "*Ever*. But I'm forced to work here for eternity and--"

"Nobody forced you," Tuss says gently, taken aback by her candor. "Corporate just thought you'd be a good choice for the job, that's why they recruited you."

"Uh…Regina? Miss Tooth Fairy?" Hugo clears his throat from upon his shelf, staring at his computer wide-eyed. "We have a code cavity."

"A code cavity?" Tuss repeats, confused, but Regina knows exactly what her employee means.

"Where?" she asks urgently, her face going pale as she stands up. "Who?"

"Victoria Caine," Hugo reads off of his computer. "In Bridgewater, Virginia."

"Thanks," Regina nods, strolling past Tuss and opening her office door.

"Where are you going?"

"To do my job," Regina responds as she walks down the dark basement hallway. For once it is quiet; everyone has long since gone home for the night.

"You're not allowed to leave the North Pole." Tuss hurries after her. "I can't let you leave."

"Try and stop me," Regina says as she punches the up button and waits for the elevator. "Or fire me."

"You know I don't want to do that," Tuss says quietly.

"Then let me go," Regina flashes him a small smile as she steps into the elevator. "I'll be back before Pia even notices I'm gone."

And before Tuss can argue with her, the doors slide shut in his face.

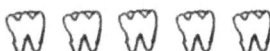

Regina, now a little bigger than a deck of cards with her pink, translucent fairy wings exposed and wand in hand, hovers outside of a second story window of a brick house in Bridgewater, Virginia. Peering nervously inside of the dark room, she sees a little girl of about six years old, fast asleep in her bed.

Regina waves her wand and the window slides open without a noise, allowing her to flutter in quietly and fly over toward Victoria's sleeping head. She stares at the girl's delicate features for a moment before sliding under the pillow and grabbing the little girl's tooth – her first baby tooth lost. Struggling with it at her size, Regina flies out from beneath the pillow and grows to her normal height once more. Pocketing the tooth, she takes a golden ring out from her pocket and places it gently beneath the pillow.

Staring once more at Victoria's sleeping form, Regina quietly bends down and brushes a strand of brown hair from her face before glancing around the room. It looks like a normal little girl's room – pink with stuffed animals piled in the corners. Drawings are tacked to the walls alongside pages from coloring books and a few photographs. On the bedside table beside the little girl is a framed picture of her with her mother.

Picking it up gently, Regina lifts it to her face and stares down at it. Mother and daughter look strikingly similar – the same eyes, the same pointed nose, the same delicate skin. Running a finger along the glass, Regina can remember years ago collecting the mother's first baby tooth and her mother's before that.

Tears begin to fill her eyes when a voice from behind her asks, "Are you alright?"

"Tuss!" Regina hisses, jumping with fright as she spins around to find her boss sitting on the windowsill, observing her. "Keep it down! What are you doing here?"

"I was worried about you," he says softly. "What's wrong?"

"Nothing," Regina says, quickly wiping the tears from her eyes. "I'm fine, don't worry about it."

Tuss examines her closely, before saying quietly, "You can trust me, you know. I care about you."

Regina smiles and lets out a soft laugh despite herself, as another tear falls from her eye. "I know," she replies. "You're a good guy, Tuss. I'm sorry for yelling at you earlier, it's just – it's been a bad day."

"I know," Tuss nods. "So what's wrong?"

"It's…*complicated*," Regina says truthfully. "It's--"

"The Tooth Fairy!"

Regina and Tuss stare around at the squealing voice to see that Victoria has awoken and is sitting straight up, wide-eyed in bed.

"I knew you'd come!" she squeals, clutching her teddy bear tightly to her chest. "Who's your friend?"

Regina stares around at Tuss, who appears panicked, before smiling down at the little girl.

"He's my secret helper," Regina says softly, sitting down at the edge of the bed. "I couldn't do my job without him."

Tuss smiles despite himself as Victoria nods her understanding. She then reaches beneath her pillow and pulls out the gold ring that Regina placed there moments earlier.

"What's this?"

"I leave something special behind for my *favorite* children instead of money," Regina explains, ignoring Tuss' look of curiosity. "That ring means a lot to me, just like you, so promise you'll take care of it, alright?"

"I promise," Victoria stares at it in amazement before indicating her teddy Bear. "Me and Bill will take good care of it."

Regina laughs. "I have a friend named Bill too," she says. "I don't sleep with him though. He's disgusting." Tuss and Victoria both laugh for very different reasons as Regina continues, "Don't tell your friends or your mommy and daddy that you woke up and saw me, alright?"

"Why not?" Victoria asks, disappointed.

"They'll all want to see me then," Regina says. "But I only come after the children of the world go to sleep, so keep this between you and me. It'll be our little secret, okay?"

"Okay," Victoria agrees cheerily before taking Regina by surprise and wrapping her arms around her. "Thanks for the pretty ring."

Regina awkwardly and nervously returns the hug, blinking fast. "Don't thank me," she says softly. "Now go back to sleep."

And running her fingers through Victoria's hair, she works her magic so that the girl instantly drifts back to the land of dreams.

"The Sandman taught me that one," Regina tells Tuss, gently lying Victoria down and covering her with her blanket.

"So how many children of the world do you leave antique heirlooms for instead of money?" Tuss asks.

Regina stands up to face him, hesitating for a moment. "Let's go back to the Pole. We'll talk there."

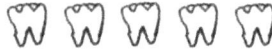

🦷 🦷 🦷 🦷 🦷

"I'm surprised it took you so long to find me," Jack says wearily as he steps over a thorny vine lining the floor outside of Tuss' closet office on the sixth floor.

Pia is sitting in the small, dark space – completely devoid of wildlife - staring up at Jack with a look of vindication. "You were too fast for me, so I decided to draw you out," she stares around the closet. "I hate the fact that that moron Tuss has a nicer office than me." She jerks her head out of the closet at her large, spacious office, which looks like the world's thickest rainforest in the dim lighting beyond.

"Well, let's get this over with," Jack sighs, stopping the alarms above from blaring *Mother Nature's Sun*.

"Do your fucking job!" Pia says angrily, getting to her feet. "Security around here is a joke!"

"My security isn't a joke," Jack snaps. "My alarms work fine! The Sandman--"

"Don't blame that idiot for your mistakes," Pia snaps. "The alarms shouldn't go off every time someone opens a damn door in this building! They should be going off when a mortal accidentally stumbles upon the place."

"That never happens."

"Or when a polar bear starts to terrorize the town!"

"I--"

"If you don't want to concentrate on security, concentrate on maintenance! Or cleaning! The third floor shouldn't still be a damn mess almost two years after a St. Patrick's Day party was thrown on it!"

"I'm not going near that place!" Jack says defensively. "The *rats* won't even go near that place! There's literal shit lining the floor! And that shit has been shitting shit of its own!"

"I don't care how many generations of shit there are! Do your fucking job!" Pia roars, before storming out of Tuss' office, leaving Jack alone.

Falling into Tuss' empty chair, Jack sighs deeply. Though he hates being told what to do, he can't deal with another day like the one he had just suffered through. Tomorrow, he'd resign himself to work on fixing the security system. And maybe, just maybe, once he had finished doing that, he would clean the St. Patrick's Day floor.

"*Chillax*, Jack," he smiles to himself. "Don't get ahead of yourself. One step at a time."

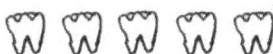

🦷 🦷 🦷 🦷 🦷

Tuss sits in the chair in front of Regina's desk, her office now lacking her two fairy henchmen who went home for the night. Regina shuts the door so that the two of them can have privacy before pulling down a jar of teeth from one of her shelves and placing it gently on her desk. She takes a seat and stares at Tuss.

"A code cavity is when somebody special to me loses a tooth," Regina explains, taking Victoria's baby tooth from her pocket and placing it in the jar. "Those teeth I keep instead of pawning them off to British dentists. And instead of leaving the children money, I leave them things close to my heart instead."

"But how do you choose which children in the world are more special to you them others?" Tuss asks. "Santa says each child has a special place in his heart, even the naughty ones. So how--"

"Do you know how I became the Tooth Fairy?" Regina asks, getting to her feet and crossing her arms across her chest, suddenly cold.

Tuss shakes his head, wide-eyed. "Only the higher-ups at Corporate know how all of you came to be who you are," he says, barely talking in a whisper. "Pia and I don't have access to that information. It's personal."

"I know," Regina nods. "So when I tell you how…just…*please* don't tell anyone."

"I would never," Tuss assures her, and in her heart, Regina knows that he is being sincere.

"When I was human," she explains, closing her eyes as the memories come flooding back to her. "It was the late nineteenth century. I lived in Virginia with my husband and was one of the world's first female dentists."

"You? A dentist?" Tuss asks with a smirk. "Who would have thought?"

Regina lets out a small laugh. "My husband was a businessman, very well-to-do," Regina continues. "We had two kids…a boy and a girl…Paul and Cecilia. The two of them…my husband…they meant the *world* to me. Every day I woke up and thanked God for everything I had."

And in her mind's eye, Regina can see her two children, her son with red hair, her daughter with blonde, neither quite matching the strawberry blonde shade of their mother.

"But we lived in a town – in a *time* – where the rich were rich and the poor were poor. There was no in-between. It was the poor who needed medical and dental attention more than anybody else, but nobody would treat them. Nobody except me," she lets out a bitter laugh. "My mother raised me to be kind and compassionate, so I pitied them. I'd work on their teeth for free."

Tuss listens intently, staring hard at the woman in front of him who still has her eyes closed tight.

"Well one night, this old beggar man knocked on my door and told me that he was in incredible pain," Regina says. "I will…I will *never* forget that night. *Ever.* It was so dark…foggy…and the rain was coming down in buckets. You could barely see two feet in front of you. Anyway, I took pity on the gentleman…invited him into my house. My husband and children slept upstairs while I worked on his teeth…it was around three in the morning when I finally finished."

Regina squeezes her eyes shut even tighter, fighting the tears as she remembers that night, so long ago.

"I walked him to the door…but being homeless, he started protesting." Regina goes on, her voice trembling now as the image of the older man with a thick gray mustache comes floating to the forefront of her mind. "He didn't want to leave."

"Regina," Tuss begins gently, rising to his feet. "You don't have to--"

"He had a knife," Regina continues. "Pulled it from his pocket…told me not to scream unless I wanted to see my kids hurt. I had no choice but to comply. But once I gave it to him, he expressed his desire for… for *something more.* He lunged at me with the knife, but I fought him off. Or tried to, anyway," she shudders. "I…I remember a pool of blood spreading around his midsection before he turned the knife on me and…and…" she sighs deeply. "The next thing I remember, I was floating naked in the clouds, surrounded by bright light. People were leaning over me. I don't remember who, but they told me that my mortal life was over and that my immortal one was just beginning. They dubbed me the Tooth Fairy."

As Regina finishes her story and breaks down sobbing, Tuss gently wraps his arm around her shoulders. "Hey, it's okay. It's okay. Cheer up. That was so long ago," Tuss says, wiping the tears from her cheeks.

"I don't know why they chose me, but--"

"You want to know why they chose you?" Tuss asks. "*All* of you? Because you're all people who led such good lives that your influence needed to continue on. All people with good hearts and intentions, even if they're deep down like the Boogeyman's. You're all people, or animals, who deserved to live on. *That's* why they chose you, Regina. You were such a good person who had their life cut tragically short--"

"And now I'm immortal, watching mortal life pass on by, all but forgotten. I still have family, you know. No one remembers me," Regina smiles grimly. "I watched my husband get remarried...watched another woman beam proudly at my son and daughter when they got married and had children of their own. I watched them all die. I watched the children of my own children grow up and die. Do you know how hard that is to do?" she demands. "But I don't have a choice!"

She pulls away from Tuss and grabs from within her desk the photographs that she keeps stashed away, laying them all out before him.

"This is my family," she explains. "I feel I need to watch over them. My *special children* are the ones who are distantly related to me. I leave them old family heirlooms that were discarded over the years. I collect them and keep them for the future generations. I know it's against the rules to interact with them, so I keep watch over them...I try to be their own personal guardian angel. I want to protect them so that none of them have to endure the same tragedy that I had to go through. It's the only thing that makes this immortal life bearable to me."

And suddenly, Regina's overreaction to Pia's Mother's Day marketing scheme makes sense to Tuss, as he once again places his arm around her shoulders.

"You're placing too much guilt on yourself, Regina," he says softly. "Hey, look at me."

Regina obligingly looks into Tuss' eyes as he wipes the tears away.

"You're a caring person who blames herself for something she couldn't control," he whispers. "But your family turned out just fine. And now children all over the *world* believe in you...wait for *you* to visit. You're not forgotten."

Regina bites her lips before smiling slightly.

———
288

"Thank you," she whispers.

The two continue to stare at one another, both of their hearts racing, before Regina decides to give in and make the first move. Quickly, before she can talk herself out of it, she locks lips with Tuss, who meets her halfway.

All of the flirting and pent up energy that had built-up between them over the past nine months begins to flood out from both of them, as though Regina's emotional honesty was the key that had finally unlocked their nervous, professional barriers. Their clothes come off and Tuss throws Regina down onto the desk as their hands feel one another's naked bodies. The entire time, Regina stares into the gorgeous man's eyes, feeling a connection – an *actual* connection – that she thought she'd never feel again.

This was the most human she felt in over a century – and she *loved* it.

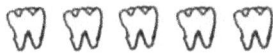

"Cupid, wake up! Wake up!" It's early in the morning and the sun is barely starting to rise as Wally pounds on Cupid's home door loudly, shivering in the snow that is coming down heavy around him. "Cupid, I need to talk to you!"

"I'm coming, I'm coming," Cupid shouts from within the house. "Literally! Give me a minute!"

Disgusted, Wally stops knocking and waits silently for another five minutes as he shuffles his feet in the snow. When Cupid finally answers the door, he has a wide smile on his face.

"Sorry. Morning wood, you know," he explains. "Had to take care of it."

"You couldn't put on some clothes first?" Wally demands angrily, shielding himself from Cupid's perfectly sculpted naked body. "You – you're *above* average, right?" he asks despite himself, catching sight of Cupid's flaccid appendage. "That's *definitely* considered large, right? I mean to say, that's not what – uh – they're *all* supposed to look like?"

"Coming up a little short down there?" Cupid asks, raising an eyebrow. "Well, don't let the ladies fool you. Size does *indeed* matter."

"Wonderful," Wally mutters. "Just wonderful."

"What brings you to my humble abode at the ass crack of dawn, anyway?" Cupid asks, shivering slightly. "Why are your panties in such a twist?"

"Holly," Wally grumbles. "The advice you've been giving me on how to win over Holly's affections. None of it's working. Plan G failed!"

"Really?" Cupid asks, genuinely surprised. "She's a tough cookie to crack. I thought for sure that showering her with gifts would work. Are you sure she's not just a huge bitch?"

"They *did* work!" Wally snaps, wiping snow from his glasses. "But Bobby took credit for them!"

Cupid lets out a loud laugh. "That's devious! Letting another man do all the work and then reap the rewards yourself, why didn't I think of that?"

Wally lets out a groan of frustration. "Well, what now?" he demands. "Do you have any other bright ideas?"

"Of course I do," Cupid replies. "It's time for us to move on to Plan H!"

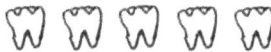

🦷 🦷 🦷 🦷 🦷

It is the loud snores of the Sandman shaking her office walls that wakes Regina. Blinking the blurriness from her eyes, she moans, stretching the soreness from her naked body. Sleeping on a wooden desk was not comfortable at all.

Glancing sideways at Tuss, whose chest is rising and falling slowly, she can't help but nervously smile at the sight of his peaceful, sleeping face. Until her brain, still groggy from having just woken up, registers the fact that if the Sandman's snores are rattling her walls, that means the Sandman is in his own office. Which means –

"Wake up!" Regina hisses quietly, elbowing Tuss in his side.

"Ow!" Tuss exclaims as his eyes snap open. "Ugh, my back!" He sits up groggily. "What time is it?"

"It's morning," Regina hops off of her desk and bends down to pick up their hastily discarded clothes from the night before, not noticing Tuss eyeing the view from her desk. "Hurry up and get dressed! Hugh and Hugo will be here any minute!"

She thrusts his dark pants into his arms.

"Wow," Tuss smirks. "Kicking me out the morning after? How romantic."

Regina smiles widely as she rolls her stockings up her legs. "Next time we'll do it at my house where we don't have to worry about what time we have to wake up. My bed is more comfortable than my desk, anyway."

"Next time?"

Regina's fingers slip as she buttons her blouse. "If you want there to be a next time, I mean," she covers hastily. "I just assumed that… uh…you know…"

"I know," Tuss says quickly.

"Yeah…" Regina breathes, looking around her office awkwardly. "So…now what?"

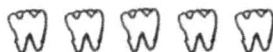

🦷 🦷 🦷 🦷 🦷

Meanwhile, down in Santa's workshop, Jack is standing outside of the closet holding the Christmas archives, exasperated as the alarm sounds around him.

"Okay, Sandy," he says. "This is getting old. You can't keep doing this anymore!" Grabbing the doorknob, he yanks the door open. "My new security system--"

But it isn't the Sandman in the closet. The moment he pulls open the door, Jack Frost finds himself face to face with an overlarge, growling, hungry looking polar bear that lets out a loud roar in the man's face, cutting off the rest of his sentence.

"Holy shit!" Jack quickly shuts the door on the North Pole native, throwing his back against it, his eyes wide and his entire body shaking. "Maybe security's too far gone to even try to fix," he mumbles to himself, trying to ignore the angry polar bear's clawing from the other side of the door. "Maybe I should concentrate on cleaning." And then a thought occurs to him. "Maybe Santa will lend me Frank to help clean up the third floor."

And with that thought, Jack Frost smiles to himself and hurries off to find Santa, leaving the polar bear locked in the closet to devour whichever poor, unlucky soul was unfortunate enough to wander across its path. With any luck, it would be Pia.

Unfortunately, he just misses Knobby, who is hobbling toward the closet, whistling a merry tune, ready to start his day the usual way – checking on Santa's precious archives.

October

"Clucky is too sexy for his spur."

Jeff Connelly is the perfect guy. Popular, good looking and intelligent, he is also the star quarterback of his school's top ten ranking football team and the president of his fraternity. Every guy in school wants to be him and every girl in school wants to be with him. But if they could see him now, they would barely recognize him, let alone be coveting his life.

Jeff is running through a dark, abandoned warehouse, completely alone. He has no recollection of how he appeared in such a place or why he is running. He is only sure of two things: one, the dark stains splattered on the walls every few feet look remarkably like blood, and two, he is panicked – running from something that will, if it catches up with him, take his life.

As he runs, he notices fleeting shadows dancing on the walls; shadows that are not his own, which is odd considering he's the only moving thing and there isn't an ounce of light coming from anywhere to even create shadows. Spotting the end of a long hallway, Jeff dashes toward it but can't get within ten feet before a huge fire erupts in the middle of the floor, blocking his exit. Terrified, Jeff turns on the spot and, slipping, falls on his ass. Eerie laughter immediately begins to ring around him and glancing down at himself, Jeff finds that his clothes have disappeared and he's sitting on the ground, naked.

Jumping to his feet, Jeff covers himself, flushing red, as shadows of all shapes and sizes begin to surround him, pointing and jeering. They're the shadows of people he recognizes – his parents, his teacher, his frat brothers, his girlfriend and her friends. And then the largest shadow of all appears; the shadow of something so large and grotesque, that Jeff cannot even fathom to whom or what it may belong.

The shadow in question looms over him, raising its long arm, at the end of which the shadow of a knife appears in its hands. Before Jeff can do more than scream - before the shadow can even bring the knife down - a mechanical voice blares loudly around them.

"Simulation terminated."

The fire at the end of the hall disappears immediately, as do the bloodstained walls. The shadows shrink down until they are barely more than shades of impish creatures, peering around at one another, disappointed, and Jeff stares around the empty void surrounding him, confused.

"We'll finish at a future date, my darlings."

Jeff spins around at the voice and gasps loudly when he sees the man who has just spoken. Tall and thin, wearing dark, flowing robes that make his pale skin seem almost luminescent, the man has oily, black, shoulder length hair and completely black eyes. He is at the same time the most terrifying and the most reassuring thing that Jeff has encountered that night.

One of the tiny shadows gestures wildly at Jeff, but the man holds up an impatient, long-fingered hand.

"I said we'll finish at another date," he snaps, baring his long shark-like teeth. "Now run along, my darlings."

At once, the shadows disappear until Jeff is left alone with the mysterious man.

"Wh-who are you?" Jeff stutters.

"You know me as the Boogeyman." He looks around the empty void in disdain. "Let's go somewhere more homely and talk, shall we?" And snapping his fingers, the four walls of Jeff's bedroom appear and Jeff is sitting, still buck naked, on his bed. "Much better."

"I'm dreaming," Jeff mutters, rubbing his eyes hard.

"You're a smart one, aren't you?" the Boogeyman remarks with a wink, walking over to Jeff's messy desk where a bottle of scotch and two tumblers are resting on a crystal tray. "It took you that long to figure it out?"

"I must have dropped acid last night," Jeff mutters under his breath, eyeing the Boogeyman's lean frame.

"That may be true, but it has nothing to do with what's happening here," the Boogeyman replies, pouring two glasses of scotch and handing one out to Jeff. "Drink?"

"I don't keep alcohol in--"

"I brought it," the Boogeyman smiles. "And you're lucky I did." Taking a seat at Jeff's desk, he snaps his fingers and a plain, manila folder appears out of thin air. Opening it, he reads, "Jeff Connelly, age twenty-one. We've been giving you recurring nightmares every night for three months. We estimate that one more and you'll have to go speak to a therapist and pay for a *multitude* of different kinds of medications to get them to stop. We get a cut of that, you know. A rather *new* business venture. We just rolled it out last year."

"How do you--"

"I've decided to give you a break," the Boogeyman replies, taking a long sip of his drink. "Push it off another night or two. I have problems of my own and since I have no access to the luxury that is therapy, and all of my associates are idiots whom I'd rather not talk to, I thought I'd talk to you. Don't look at me like that," he snaps as Jeff raises an eyebrow. "Would you rather me bore you to death by talking, or would you prefer me to let my darlings torture you first?"

"To be honest, I think I'd prefer the latter," Jeff laughs nervously.

"Too bad," the Boogeyman snaps his fingers so that Jeff is all of a sudden tied to his bed. "You're listening."

"Are you…uh…" Jeff clears his throat as his heart rate quickens. "Are you going to gag me too?"

"You're enjoying this aren't you, you sick pervert?" the Boogeyman asks, noticing all of the blood in the youth's naked body flow to a particular organ. "Mr. Popular…what would your girlfriend say if she knew you were hidden so far in the closet that you have dreams about talking to the skeletons inside of it? Don't get your hopes up. I'd only gag you if I was going to slit your throat. If you be a good boy and let me talk, I'll send one of my friends your way on Valentine's Day. He'll gag you the way you're looking to be gagged."

Jeff widens his eyes as the Boogeyman sighs deeply and takes another long sip of scotch, moving to sit at the end of the bed.

"You're probably a little too young to know this for yourself, but corporate takeover is a *bitch*," the Boogeyman says, snapping his fingers so that pajamas appear on the young man chained to the bed. "Suits breathing down your neck constantly, pressuring you to make more money even though you turn enormous profits every year - it's *exhausting*. A complete waste of company resources and *my* time. Not to mention an insult to my intelligence," he scoffs. "I've been running Halloween for hundreds of years and *now* they come in and think they can *change* the way things are done. It's *ridiculous*! As the old saying goes: if it's not broke, don't fix it."

"What are you *talking* about?" Jeff asks, perplexed. This is the strangest dream he's ever had.

"Though I suppose it's not *really* the fault of anyone at Corporate," the Boogeyman continues his lament, not even hearing the young man's question. "The world is changing. The mortals aren't as easily scared anymore, but if my bosses would take me off my leash for *one* night they'd see just how much money I could scare up for them. The scarier the dreams, the more therapy you mortals need, which means the more money we make. I don't need to rewrite the handbook, I just need to be given permission to give it my all."

He turns his head to stare at Jeff, who is unnerved by the black eyes.

"Take nightmares for example," the Boogeyman continues. "In the old days, I'd invade a person's dream myself – just *once* – and terrify them until they woke up incoherently babbling like a lunatic and wound up being forced into an asylum. Nowadays, it's all about progression. Slow buildup. Apparently it's more profitable to give recurring, slightly intensifying nightmares, than just one *real* scare."

The Boogeyman stands up with a dramatic sigh and starts pacing the room, his robes flowing around him. Jeff can't help but notice that the man does not have a shadow of his own.

———

297

"Nightmares used to just be a hobby, something I'd do with my free time during the off season, but now," he snorts, pouring himself another drink. "They've been added to my list of responsibilities and I have a quota to meet. The whole institution is going to shambles, I tell you. Halloween's less than a week away and they're more concerned with its future than its present. They shouldn't even be worried about my holiday as much as the future of Santa's."

"S-Santa?" Jeff asks, a small grin on his face. "As in *Claus*?"

"Who else?" the Boogeyman asks, stopping dead and turning to face his prisoner.

"You know Santa Claus," Jeff states, shaking his head. This dream is getting weirder by the second and he just wants to wake up and look at some internet porn in an effort to forget all of this craziness.

"Of course I do," the Boogeyman nods, taking a sip of his drink. "The mortals imagine we hate one another because our holidays are so different, but we're good friends. He's one of the only people who really *understands* me; who *understands* the pressure of running such a popular, profitable holiday. But now he's retiring and God knows who Corporate will pick to be the *new* Santa Claus."

"Santa Claus is *retiring*?"

"Are you hard of hearing?" the Boogeyman snaps.

"No," Jeff replies defensively. "It's just...uh...a *lot* of information to take in."

The Boogeyman narrows his eyes shrewdly. "Yes, well," he clears his throat. "I'm only confiding in you because they can't track me here and I doubt you'll remember any of this in the morning. And if you *do* somehow remember, nobody's going to believe you if you go blabbing to them about it. I..."

The Boogeyman's voice trails off as the walls of Jeff's bedroom begin to shake. Dust falls from the ceiling as a loud, female voice rings out, "Boogeyman! Where the hell are you?"

The Boogeyman sighs deeply, shaking his head as he downs the rest of his drink. Catching Jeff's eye, he winks, "Just try to ignore it. Maybe she'll give--"

"Answer me, you creepy fuck!"

"Ugh, reality calls," the Boogeyman groans. "Until next time. Enjoy your therapy."

He salutes Jeff before finding himself sitting on his throne of charred bones in his office up at the North Pole. Opening his eyes, he sees his Shadow standing in front of him, looking apologetic.

Glancing down at his desk, covered in dust and cobwebs, the Boogeyman notices the Jack-o'-lantern beside his computer glowing, its carved features appearing angry. Pia's voice is issuing from the moving mouth.

"You know the rules," she's saying. "No leaving the Pole without permission!"

"I didn't *leave* the Pole," the Boogeyman snaps, leaning close to the Jack-o'-lantern. "*Physically*, anyway. I was doing my job. Causing nightmares."

"*Personally*?" Pia demands. "That's what you have employees for! Do you think you can manage your department by yourself?"

"I can manage my department without you riding my ass all of the time," the Boogeyman replies coldly, glaring at his Shadow on the wall which is punching a closed fist into its open palm. "What do you want?"

"You're late for our fucking meeting!" Pia answers.

"I don't need to attend any meetings a week before Halloween," the Boogeyman responds loudly. "I have a holiday to prepare for and not much time left to do it! Understand? Now, hang up."

And at once, his Jack-o'-lantern speakerphone blinks out the lights within its carved features. It's barely dark for a second, however, before it starts vibrating on the desk.

"Uh…sir?" the pumpkin timidly begins. "She's trying to call again--"

"Ignore her!" the Boogeyman snaps, slamming his hands down on the surface of his desk. "Maxwell!" he calls out of his open office door and, almost immediately, the vampire shuffles in holding a thermos of blood in his hands.

"Yes, master?"

"What is *this*?" the Boogeyman demands, picking a purchase order up off of his desk and waving it in front of his employee's pale face.

"We need your signature," Maxwell replies timidly, placing his thermos on his boss' desk before pointing at the dotted line near the bottom of the page.

"Why is there a suspicious lack of costumes that are actually scary in this order?" the Boogeyman asks, narrowing his eyes.

"Uh…" Maxwell glances over his shoulder at the exit, but the Boogeyman's Shadow has risen up in the doorway, blocking his path. "Well, we *had* more on there," he clears his throat. "But Pia--"

"Gold bikinis?" the Boogeyman reads from the list, disgusted. "Ripped jeans? Fake abs? Crotchless tights? What the hell is this? Some kind of twisted joke? Because I am *not* amused."

"Pia thought they'd sell better than our normal stock of vampire capes, witch hats and werewolf masks," Maxwell explains.

"Pia's not your boss. *I'm* your boss."

"And she's *your* boss," the vampire points out, before hastily adding, "*Sir.*"

"Who doesn't have a clue about what she's doing," the Boogeyman sulks darkly. "She has no control over Santa Claus leaving, so she's grasping at straws trying to control the rest of us. The key is not to let her."

He stands up, staring at the cuckoo clock on the wall that is just striking ten a.m. Instead of a cute, chirping bird emerging from the closed doors built into the wood, however, an overlarge raven pops out, cawing angrily.

"I'm not signing this," the Boogeyman continues, thrusting the purchase order back at Maxwell.

"But, master--"

The Boogeyman holds up one of his long-fingered hands to silence him as a large spider scurries into the office and begins climbing the black wall.

"What *now?*" the Boogeyman asks, exasperated, as the spider begins to spin a web in the corner of the room, words intricately etched into it. When finished, the enormous web reads:

IF YOU DON'T GET YOUR BONY ASS DOWN TO THE SIXTH FLOOR IMMEDIATELY, I'LL CUT OFF YOUR FUCKING HIDEOUS HEAD AND SEND IT OUT AS A HALLOWEEN DECORATION.

"Well, I'm clearly not going to get any work done today unless I indulge her," the Boogeyman snaps angrily, shooing the spider from his office. "You, follow me," he barks at Maxwell as he sweeps from his office. "Maybe you'll learn a thing or two about sticking up to your superiors."

As the Boogeyman and the vampire, followed by the Boogeyman's Shadow, make their way down the stone, torch-lit corridor of the tenth floor, the dulcet tones of an organ play overhead, blocking out the scurrying sounds of the various creatures bustling around them.

"Coming through!" The Boogeyman launches himself to one side of the hall as Agatha, aboard a flying broomstick, goes zooming past

Howie, who is dragging a giant box into a closet.

"What's in there?" the Boogeyman asks.

"Rotting pumpkins," the werewolf answers, pausing to lean against the box. "Also, the new numbers came in from our European branch. Apparently, Bill's deformed Easter Bunny costume is our biggest seller in Finland."

"I want an order placed for triple the amount next year," the Boogeyman instructs, pushing the down button beside the closed elevator doors at the end of the hallway. "And when you're done with that, go into my office. There's a file on my desk bearing the name of Jeff Connelly. He's in phase three of his nightmare scheme. Schedule one of my darlings to finish him off tomorrow."

"Right away, sir," Howie replies.

The Boogeyman sighs deeply as he steps into the elevator and begins his descent to the sixth floor. His office runs like a perfectly tuned, well-oiled guillotine; things get done, money gets made and his employees are terrified of him. What more could a manager ask for? Corporate's presence, however, was making life difficult for him and if there is one thing the Boogeyman doesn't like, it's a difficult life.

Tuss rolls off of Regina panting, sweat dripping from every inch of his bare skin, and stares up at the red canopy, which serves as the upper part of the Tooth Fairy's custom made mouth-shaped bed. Sunlight is streaming in through the open windows of the spotless bedroom and, lying completely naked on her stomach beside him, Regina gives a contented sigh.

"That was amazing," she breathes, as Tuss props himself up on his elbow and kisses the back of her neck.

"*You're* amazing," he replies automatically, tracing a finger down her spine toward the middle of her back where her two wings flutter with happiness.

"How many times do I have to tell you?" Regina asks, rolling her eyes as she turns onto her back. "No matter how much you flatter me, I'm not going to let you stick it--"

"I wasn't trying to flatter you," Tuss cuts her off. "I'm being serious."

Regina stares into his brilliant blue eyes before breaking into a wide smile. "Well, you're pretty amazing too, Tuss."

"I'm also pretty late," Tuss remarks, staring at the alarm clock on the bedside table before hopping out of bed with a sinking feeling in his stomach. "Pia's going to kill me. I was supposed to be up in the conference room fifteen minutes ago for a meeting with her and the Boogeyman."

"Have fun with that." Regina stretches, giving a loud yawn. "I called in to Hugh and Hugo earlier letting them know I'd be late."

"If I didn't think she'd wring my neck, I'd do that with Pia," Tuss laughs as he pulls his pants on. "Though maybe that's a better alternative than sitting in on a meeting between her and the Boogeyman. He's the only one who's not afraid of her around here, which means she feels the need to shout even louder than she usually does."

"Are you coming over later?" Regina asks hopefully, pulling the covers up to her neck and snuggling into the pile of pillows.

"We'll see," Tuss says evasively. Then, after a moment of silence, he adds, "Of course I will. I *want* to, you know that."

"Why do I feel like there's going to be a '*but*' following that statement?" Regina raises an eyebrow.

"There's no '*but*,'" Tuss says wryly. "*However*," Regina smirks. "I *am* leaving in under three months. By no choice of my own, obviously. But Corporate--"

303

"I know," Regina mutters hurriedly, diverting her eyes.

"So I don't think we should get too…" He trails off, searching for the right word.

"Attached?" Regina supplies.

"Attached," Tuss agrees, nodding his head. "*Serious.*"

"I'm never serious," Regina says, her voice mocking. "Nor are you, so stop worrying about it. We're just fooling around."

"Well then," Tuss breathes a sigh of uneasy relief. "I'd be happy to come over and *fool around* later."

"Good," Regina smirks. "I'll even make you dinner before we move on to *dessert*," she drops the sheets from her body teasingly and the sight of her bare breasts causes Tuss to rearrange his pants.

"I can't wait," Tuss says, leaning in for a kiss. "I'll see you later."

And after a quick peck on the lips, Regina watches as Tuss hurries from her bedroom. The moment he disappears over the threshold, she sighs deeply, her smile faltering slightly. The past month and a half spent seeing Tuss had been the best of her life since she became the Tooth Fairy - and it really had nothing to do with the sex. How she was going to cope after Corporate whisked him away from the North Pole, she had no idea.

"Don't think about it," she tells herself, shaking her head. "Just enjoy it while it lasts."

And nodding to herself, she sighs deeply and crawls out of bed, preparing to face yet another day of non-stop teeth.

🎃 🎃 🎃 🎃

"Where the fuck have you been?" Pia demands as the Boogeyman glides into the conference room, Maxwell close on his heels.

"Doing my job," the Boogeyman replies, falling into his chair as Maxwell sits in the Tooth Fairy's empty seat beside him. "Where have *you* been? And what is this nonsense?"

Projected onto the wall behind Pia are multiple images of scantily dressed people: one, a shapely woman in a golden bikini; another, a teenage boy in nothing but a pair of ripped jeans (exposing abs so defined it would be impossible for the average man to obtain them); a young man in preppy clothes whose skin sparkles like diamonds; a woman in a cape worn over a slutty school uniform, sucking on a stick she has in the corner of her mouth – the list goes on and on.

Pia, red in the face and bristling with annoyance, is about to answer the Boogeyman when Tuss hurries into the room, his normally pressed suit disheveled and his hair a mess.

"Where the fuck have *you* been?" Pia demands of her colleague as he shuffles around the table and falls into a seat beside her, out of breath.

"Sorry, I overslept," Tuss replies, straightening his tie.

"Did you sleep in the same clothes you wore yesterday?" Pia asks with disgust, narrowing her eyes as she watches Tuss roll up his sleeves. "What the hell time did you get in last night?"

"I…uh…I don't know," Tuss replies quickly, pulling on the collar of his shirt. "I went out for drinks last night with--"

"A girl?" the Boogeyman supplies, grinning mischievously.

"A *friend*," Tuss replies defensively, avoiding those creepy eyes.

"You have *friends*?" Pia snorts before the Boogeyman can reply.

"Yes, I have *friends*," Tuss snaps. "Can we stop discussing my personal life and get on with the meeting, please?"

"I wanted to get on with the damn meeting twenty minutes ago," Pia replies. "But you were late! Along with this moron," she nods at the Boogeyman before locking eyes with Maxwell. "What the hell are *you* doing here?"

"I…uh…" Maxwell clears his throat as he throws a nervous glance at his boss who rolls his eyes.

"I brought him," the Boogeyman states. "Now I ask again, what the hell is this?" he motions at the images projected on the wall.

"New costume designs for you to implement," Pia says curtly. "Didn't you get the memo?"

"That's the only reason I showed up to this meeting at all," the Boogeyman shoves the purchase order he refused to sign across the table. "I'm not signing off on this."

"I know you have no concept of what *sexy* is," Pia says, drinking in the monstrous appearance of the man sitting across from her while ignoring his intimidating Shadow dancing on the walls. "But sex sells."

"Halloween is not about *sex*," the Boogeyman hisses, leaning in close. "Do you have any idea what the purpose of my holiday is?"

"To make money," Pia snaps. "Just like every other fucking holiday."

"No," the Boogeyman says sternly, looking at Tuss. "Do *you*?"

"I--"

"Why don't you just get stupid Bill in here in costume to explain it to us?" Pia leans back in her chair, crossing her arms across her chest.

The Boogeyman snarls angrily before glancing at Maxwell, who clears his throat.

"It's the one night of the year when the veil between the mortal world and the other world is so thin, the dead can pass through and walk amongst us again," the vampire explains. "It's a festival of the dead linked to the Celtic festival of Samhain, where the mortals used to host bonfires that included human sacrifice. Traditionally, the mortals would wear frightening masks--"

"Keyword - *frightening*," the Boogeyman interjects.

"To help blend in amongst the spirits and creatures that cross over from the other world on this night, disguising themselves so as to remain safe until morning when they'd be locked back from where they came for another year," Maxwell finishes.

Pia raises an eyebrow. "Let me ask *you* a question now," Pia leans forward. "Have you ever heard of *science*? The invention of *penicillin*?"

"Pia," Tuss begins, but Pia continues on with a mocking laugh.

"The mortals don't believe in that shit anymore! Scary masks for protection aren't *needed* anymore and newsflash, *pal*, the world isn't flat either. Scary's out, sexy's in."

The Boogeyman's Shadow bristles angrily as the Boogeyman himself launches into speech. "I've given into Corporate's demands a *lot* over the years," he begins dangerously. "I was fine with the whole trick-or-treating scheme and the UNICEF scam. I was even fine with commissioning that Charlie Fucking Brown Halloween special. But I am *not* compromising the whole point of my holiday completely. It's about embracing your innermost fears and scaring other people, *not* dressing like strippers to seduce your neighbor's wife. I mean," he gestures at the pictures on the wall again. "What are these costumes even supposed to be?"

"Costumes that the fucking mortals actually want!" Pia exclaims emphatically, standing up to point at each image in turn. "This is your modern day werewolf!"

She points at the picture of the half-naked teenage boy, to which the Boogeyman asks, "Where's the fur? The fangs? And isn't lusting over somebody so young technically illegal down there?"

"Your vampire!"

"They *sparkle*?" the Boogeyman chokes, disgusted, as Maxwell eyes the image thoughtfully, running one of his grotesque clawed hands over his misshaped bald head.

"I don't think it's that bad," he admits, his tongue sliding over his fangs. "I mean – it's *horrible*," he hastily adds after his boss throws him a dangerous look.

"Your witch," Pia points at the image of the girl in what is essentially a slutty school uniform with a cape draped over her shoulders.

"She's not a *witch*," the Boogeyman spits. "She's missing the wart, the hat and the flying broom! And what the hell is she sticking in the corner of her mouth?"

"I believe that's supposed to be a magic wand," Tuss answers, quickly referring to his notes.

"Only *fairies* carry wands," the Boogeyman replies as his Shadow shakes its head in disbelief behind him, crossing its arms over its chest. "It looks like she's tonguing a shaft!"

Tuss clears his throat loudly, going pink in the face as he mumbles quietly to himself, "That's…inappropriate."

"What's that last picture supposed to be?" the Boogeyman demands, eyeing the gold bikini. "It looks like something you cut out of a *Victoria's Secret* swim catalogue!"

"What the hell is *that*?" Pia asks, her eyebrows furrowed.

"Some kind of pornographic magazine that teenage boys like stealing from their mothers," the Boogeyman shrugs. "Cupid has a subscription."

"Of course he does," Pia mumbles before plowing on, pointing at the picture of the gold bikini herself. "This is a princess' costume."

"A *princess*?" the Boogeyman scoffs. "Since when don't princesses wear long pink gowns and get rescued from dragons and overgrown apes by Italian plumbers and their layabout brothers?"

"Since the mortals realized that sexy is in and both scary and sickeningly fucking cute are out," Pia snaps, slamming her hands splayed on the table in front of her as she leans toward the Boogeyman.

The Boogeyman does not flinch, but behind him, his Shadow leans in threateningly toward Pia as Maxwell stares at the picture of the bikini-clad girl on the wall appreciatively.

"She looks good enough to bite," he remarks.

"You see?" Pia points at Maxwell as the Boogeyman rolls his eyes. "Even your employees agree the sexy costumes are better! Max!" she barks.

"Maxwell," the vampire corrects, diverting his gaze.

"Look at what you could look like!" she points at the sparkling image of the vampire glowing on the wall. "It would be a huge improvement over the mutant-rat look you're cultivating right now. The mortals would throw themselves at you! Think of all the blood you could suck!" As Maxwell tries to imagine this hypothetical reality for himself, Pia turns back toward the Boogeyman. "Look at what Meowie the werewolf and Haggie the witch could look like!"

"Howie and Agatha," the Boogeyman corrects, shaking silently with anger.

"Whatever the fuck they're called," Pia scoffs. "Wouldn't you rather work with employees who look like *this*," she gestures at the wall. "Rather than *this*," she jerks her head at Maxwell, who is still lost in thought.

"Never."

"Well you're a sick freak anyway, so your opinion doesn't count," she spits, falling back into her seat. "The opinions of the billions of mortals that occupy this planet *do* count, however. And they're singing their wants loud and clear – sexy costumes. Sexy is the new scary. Right?" she barks at Tuss, who is doodling idly on the table in front of him.

"Huh?" her colleague blinks rapidly, looking up.

"What the fuck is your problem?" Pia demands.

"What do you mean?"

"You've barely said two damn words this entire time!"

"Preoccupied I guess."

"Men," Pia scoffs. "It's no wonder this world's gone to shit with your gender running things." Unable to get a rise out of Tuss, Pia turns back to the Boogeyman. "Think of all the costumes we can make scary – how much more money we'll rake in! Vampires, witches, werewolves, demons, masked killers – what can we do with Frankenstein's monster?"

"Enough! Now you're going too far!" the Boogeyman stands up so quickly, he knocks his heavy chair over in the process. "Don't you dare touch one bolt on that precious creature's neck! I'm not selling sex to increase sales for my holiday, do you understand? That's Cupid's job, not mine. So if you think I'm signing that fucking purchase order," he eyes the piece of paper lying on the table. "You're out of your fucking mind. Both of you," he adds, glancing at Tuss who blinks in surprise.

"Be reasonable," Tuss begins calmly, but the Boogeyman cuts him off quickly.

"I *am* being reasonable."

"Being reasonable would be doing your fucking job!" Pia yells angrily, snapping her pen in two.

"I *am* doing my fucking job!"

"DOING YOUR FUCKING JOB MEANS OBEYING US!"

"I KNOW HOW TO RUN MY HOLIDAY!"

The Boogeyman and Pia are nose to nose now, the former's normally pale face so red that he looks demonic. Maxwell has backed as far away from the table as he can go, while Tuss looks between the two of them warily.

"Let's just calm down, alright?" he says tentatively. "I'm sure we can work something out. Maybe we can make the costumes sexy *and* scary. Like the witch," he glances at the picture on the wall. "Maybe instead of having a wand in her mouth, she could have something scary like a bloody finger!" He pauses, narrowing his eyes and going red in the face. "Wait – no, that isn't any better."

Pia narrows her own eyes shrewdly before pulling back from the Boogeyman, a glint in her eye. "If you won't take our word that sexy costumes sell better than the scary ones," she begins, ignoring her colleague's suggestion. "I suppose we'll have to show you proof." She walks toward the door of the conference room confidently, leaving all three men staring after her appear perplexed at her sudden shift in mood. "Follow me."

"Where are we going?" the Boogeyman asks, boredom in his voice as he starts after her, his Shadow close behind him.

"To Santa's factory," Pia explains. "We're going to use that globe of his to take a peek into some of the mortal Halloween shops around the world."

"Any excuse to go down and see the old man, right?" the Boogeyman smirks. "Have you found a replacement yet?"

Pia ignores the comment and turns her back on him as she jabs at the down button beside the elevator.

Santa is standing on the second floor of his toy factory, a long yellowing piece of parchment in his hand, staring at his naughty or nice globe. Beside him, Holly is writing furiously in a notebook as Santa speaks and Frank is waiting, bored, for his next assignment, which he silently prays won't be anything disgusting this time around. Yesterday, Santa had him trimming his nose hairs. Before that, it was fishing through the garbage for a lost jingle bell. And most recently, Santa had him searching for the remote control to the naughty or nice globe. As he could not find it, however, Santa had resorted to reading names out to it the old fashioned way – *without* picture-in-picture.

He had to get out of this place.

"Erin Sylvester," Santa reads off of his list as the image of a girl with blonde hair forms in the smoke of the globe in front of him. He watches as she laughs, flirting playfully with her boyfriend, before declaring, "Nice!"

Holly hastily scribbles down Santa's assessment, absentmindedly fingering the diamond brooch pinned to her uniform.

"Brandon Sanders."

A thin, dark-haired boy with pointed features and dark glasses appears in the smoke now, replacing the image of the girl. He's playing hockey with his friends and when the referee isn't looking, he body checks a member of the opposing team, breaking their arm.

"*Definitely* naughty."

"About time you said one of these brats is naughty," Frank mumbles in an undertone.

"Naughty, got it," Holly says, marking it down in her notebook before glancing over her shoulder at Frank and hissing quietly, "Where's Wally?"

"I don't know," Frank sighs indifferently. He stares down at his shoes and starts kicking at the floor in front of him, just for something to do.

"Santa!"

"Boogeyman!" Santa booms jovially, spotting the head of Halloween gliding toward him followed by Pia, Tuss and Maxwell. "What brings you down here?"

Before the Boogeyman can answer for himself, Pia pushes him out of the way. "I did, Santa." She hastily forces a smile onto her face. "I thought perhaps we could borrow your wonderful globe for a moment?"

"My naughty or nice globe?" Santa asks. "Whatever for?"

"We want to use it to see if Pia's going to end up on the naughty list this year," the Boogeyman smirks.

"I'm never on the naughty list," Pia hisses, hastily pushing away thoughts of drop-kicking Willy, the elf-choir director, as the lyrics of *You're a Mean One, Mr. Grinch* begin to float up toward them from the ground floor.

"Could have fooled me," the Boogeyman replies.

"Could have fooled all of us," Frank adds, causing Pia to round on him, glaring daggers.

Putting on a calm face for Santa, however, she continues slowly, "I just want to show the Boogeyman that he's missing out on increasing profits for his holiday by not catering to a very large demographic of the Halloween consumer market."

"Why not just take him down amongst the mortals to see for himself in person?" Santa asks, his eyes twinkling.

"After seeing how much Caleb stuck out like a sore thumb amongst the mortals," Tuss begins quickly, as Pia's face darkens at the memory. "We decided it wouldn't be a good idea to take anyone from the Pole down to the mainland unless absolutely necessary."

"Ho, ho, ho, quite understandable," Santa strokes his beard. "He became *quite* the internet sensation, didn't he, Holly?"

"He was auto-tuned and everything," Holly nods, trying to suppress a smirk as Pia whips around to stare at her, panicked.

"What the hell does that mean?"

"It means that…uh…a few mortal kids at the mall thought it would be…*funny* to upload a video of his antics to the internet," Holly explains, biting her lip to keep from laughing. "You can search it online: 'Pre-Teen Acts like Overgrown Baby'."

"I'm going to kill him," Pia mutters as Santa, the Boogeyman, Maxwell, Holly and Frank all share a laugh, clearly having all seen the video. "I'm seriously going to kill him."

"I don't doubt it," Tuss says grimly. "The shit you have him do for you, it's a wonder he hasn't quit yet."

"Did you know about this video?" Pia demands.

"Uh…" Tuss clears his throat. "Let's just get on with the problem at hand, shall we?" He nods in the Boogeyman's direction pointedly.

Pia purses her lips but nods her agreement while silently making a mental note to lace into her partner later on when they both had a free moment. Stepping up to the naughty or nice globe, she states loudly and clearly, "Show me the biggest Halloween store in America."

Immediately, a store called *Halloween Outlet* appears within the smoke and the Boogeyman watches, horrified, as teenage boys and girls go straight for the revealing costumes: sexy cops, slutty nurses, hunky priests. He is forced to watch as Pia stands by smugly. The whole time, only small children bother to pick up the traditional monster outfits. After only five minutes, he can no longer take it.

"I've seen enough!"

At once, the Boogeyman's Shadow projects itself over the globe, darkening it until the images swirling within are no longer visible. Pia, however, does not mind; she's made her point.

"The amount of money we've been wasting on supplying stores around the world with horrific costumes is *staggering*," she says, trying to keep her temper in check with Santa standing so close by. "We can still rectify the situation somewhat if you just sign the purchase order," she thrusts it toward the Boogeyman. "And then next year we can order substantially more revealing costumes than--"

"I'm not signing anything," the Boogeyman replies stubbornly.

"*What?* I just proved my point!"

"It's my holiday, I'll run it as I see fit."

"You need to change with the times!" Pia yells as down below, the elves on the workshop floor begin to look up curiously. "You need to make your holiday more sexually appealing! Sex up the costumes! Sex up yourself! Your minions!" She motions wildly at Maxwell.

"Please leave me out of this," the vampire pleads quietly.

"The fact of the matter is," the Boogeyman moves toward Pia, his voice rising rapidly with each word that slips from his mouth. "There's still a market for a traditional Halloween involving scary costumes! And my holiday is one of the more profitable ones in this company, so until you show me numbers saying otherwise, we have nothing more to discuss!"

And before Pia can reply, the Boogeyman turns on his heel and storms away, his Shadow gliding along in his wake after making a threateningly rude gesture at Pia.

"That fucking asshole!"

"Pia!" Santa exclaims, horrified.

"Sorry," Pia mumbles, ignoring Holly and Frank who appear delighted to have seen somebody stand up to her. "I just – lost my temper."

"As did the Boogeyman," Santa nods gravely. "Hopefully you two can both turn your attitudes around before Christmas, otherwise you may just end up on the naughty list!"

"Speaking of Christmas," Pia begins hopefully. "I don't suppose you've given any more thought to this whole retirement thing?"

"Actually, now that you mention it, I have," Santa nods.

"Really?" Tuss asks, taken aback as an enormous smile spreads across Pia's face.

"Yes," Santa muses. "The Mrs. and I may live in Hawaii for a few years before settling in the Caribbean."

Pia's good mood evaporates instantly and as Santa turns back to his globe with his elves, she glares at Tuss who has taken out his phone to write a text message. "What the hell are you doing?"

"Cancelling plans I have for later," Tuss says absentmindedly. "I have a feeling it's going to be a *long* day."

"You actually have a social life?"

"Of course I do, I'm not *you*." Tuss lowers his phone in time to see a hurtful look pass over Pia's face. "I'm sorry. I didn't mean that."

"Fuck you."

"You know what, Pia? Maybe this is your problem," Tuss says sharply. "Maybe if you were nicer to people, they'd be more likely to listen to your ideas. Nobody wants to take orders from somebody who's mean to them all of the time."

"Where the hell are you going?" Pia demands as Tuss begins to walk away from her.

"To talk to the Boogeyman," he calls back to her. "He won't listen to you, so maybe he'll listen to me!"

"Yeah, right," Pia snorts before noticing Maxwell standing motionless, still staring at Santa's globe, his eyes glazed over as though he's not really seeing it. "What the hell is wrong with *you*, you creepy, disgusting leech?"

"Huh? Oh, nothing," Maxwell says quickly. "I mean," he forces himself to continue under Pia's withering stare. "I just...*maybe* wouldn't mind trying out the whole sexy thing for a little while. If it'll get me more food..." He licks his lips at the thought of more blood before sighing deeply. "But it'll never happen."

A small smile spreads across Pia's face as a thought suddenly strikes her. "Never say never."

"Isn't that a song?" Maxwell asks.

"Follow me," Pia says, ignoring the idiotic question. "I have an idea."

And like most of her ideas, Pia is positive that this one is brilliant.

🎃 🎃 🎃 🎃

"I don't know about this."

Wally is standing in the doorway of Cupid's office, staring down into the box of clothing that the professional pervert has given him.

"What aren't you sure about?" Cupid asks, exasperated.

"The whole plan," Wally confesses, straightening his glasses nervously. "I don't know if Holly will go for this!"

"If she's not a fan of munching pussy – which she's not, because I banged her last New Year's - then she'll go for it," Cupid insists, clapping a hand on one of Wally's shoulders as the elf grimaces. "You need to show her what she'd miss out on if she passed up an opportunity with you! Unfortunately, she doesn't seem to like you for who you are as a person, so that means you have to show off some skin."

"I already did!" Wally says, flustered.

"Well, now it's time to show off some more," Cupid replies, matter-of-factly.

"But *this* much?" Wally asks, horrified, as he pulls a green g-string from inside of the box. Instead of the typical thin layer of fabric that normally covers the crotch, there is only a green Christmas wreath with a hole in the center to slip on over a certain body part and allow it to dangle freely, as exposed to the eyes as the wearer's backside.

"Yes, *that* much," Cupid assures him. "Leave your hat on too, she'll love that."

"I don't think I like Plan H very much," Wally mumbles, still staring at the skimpy item in his hand.

"Do you have body image issues or something?" Cupid asks suddenly.

"What? No!"

The answer comes a little too quickly, causing Cupid to smirk.

"You don't have Bill's body, so that's something," he reassures the elf as he begins to circle him appraisingly. "You're a little bony, but some girls like that. And even if you do come up a bit short down there--"

"Which I don't!" Wally insists quickly, going red in the face.

"But if you *did*," Cupid continues, slipping an unwanted arm around the elf's bony shoulders. "It's not the size of the Christmas package that's important, as much as how you deliver it. If you're nervous, you can do a dry run with me--"

"Cupid!" Pia storms into the office, roughly pushing past Wally who falls to the floor, dropping the g-string in the process. "I - What the hell is *that*?" she demands, noticing the tiny article of clothing.

"Nothing," Wally says hurriedly, picking it up and shoving it into his pocket. "Nothing at all."

"It's Wally's Halloween costume." Cupid rolls his eyes before smirking at Pia. "It's called a g-string. Perhaps you've heard of it? You'd look good in one."

But only two words of Cupid's statement register with Pia.

"*That's* a Halloween costume?" she repeats before a wide smile breaks across her face. "Of course it is! Even Santa's stupid slaves realize that sexy is the new scary! That's wonderful! As disgusting as it is to picture you wearing that," she adds, gagging slightly as Wally peers at her, confused.

"I--"

"Get out," Pia says firmly.

Not needing to be told twice, Wally hurries from the office and is gone for barely two seconds before the sound of his distant scream reverberates around the walls.

"What the hell was that?" Cupid asks, concerned, but Pia sidesteps him before he can leave the room.

"It's not important," she insists. She knows exactly what caused the elf's terrified scream, but keeps it to herself. "I wanted to talk to you alone for a minute."

"Of course you did," Cupid smiles wide, falling onto the heart-shaped bed that takes up the majority of the room. "Have a seat," he pats the empty space on the mattress beside him.

"I'd rather have dinner with Caligula," Pia snarls, disgusted. "I need your help. And not in an even remotely sexual way."

"Is Ted off his meds again?" Cupid asks, worried. "How many times do I have to tell you, he's sensitive! You need to--"

"Fuck the groundhog!" Pia interrupts firmly. "This has nothing to do with him."

"Well then, I can't even fathom what you could *possibly* need help with that isn't sexual in any way, shape or form."

"I need help with Halloween," Pia admits, fingering her cornucopia necklace uncomfortably as she steps further into the room. "The Boogeyman doesn't see the value in sexualizing his holiday *or* his employees--"

"Of course he doesn't, have you *seen* him?" Cupid remarks, sitting up straight. "Well, well, well, I never thought I'd see the day you admitted you needed help."

"Forget it." Pia rolls her eyes. "Fucking forget it. I'll figure something out on my own. I'm sure that even that idiot *Caleb* can figure out how to use a sewing machine."

As she turns to leave the office, Cupid hops off the bed and grabs the woman by her shoulders, spinning her around so that their faces are only an inch apart.

"I'd be glad to help you," Cupid says sincerely as Pia diverts her gaze from his eyes, breathless. "What do you want me to do? Talk sense into him?"

"Tuss is trying to do that now," Pia explains, pulling away from the expert on love. "But that won't work because I already tried it earlier. And if *I* can't do it, then there's no way *Tuss* is going to be able to."

"Of course not," Cupid remarks, his eyes twinkling. "Because we all know that *you're* a better people person than Tuss is."

Pia bites back a disparaging comment as she continues. "I just need him to sign off on this purchase order to get one last shipment of sexy costumes down into stores before the actual holiday. And I figured if reasoning doesn't work, we can show him how much better glamorized monsters are than horrifying ones."

"By giving his employees makeovers?" Cupid catches on. "I love it. It'll be a challenge, but--"

"*That's* an understatement," Pia agrees.

Putting two fingers into her mouth, which causes Cupid to go weak at the knees, she gives a loud whistle and moments later, Maxwell, Howie and Agatha enter the office. Though he's able to contain his own scream at the sight of them, Cupid instantly knows why Wally couldn't contain his on his way out of the office and he's surprised that his cherubs passing up and down the hallway haven't been having similar reactions.

Howie is missing enormous chunks of fur from his chest, as though somebody blind tried to quickly shave him. Most of the patches that are shaved are badly done and speckled with dried blood, and Cupid can see the hair already starting to poke back through again.

Agatha, meanwhile, looks like an ancient hooker that Cupid has visited in Amsterdam on more than one occasion. Her gray hair has been let down and her saggy body is being kept so tight in a corset and stockings that it looks like the witch is having trouble breathing. The makeup plastered on her face to cover up her warts is so plentiful and is running so much, she looks like a clown who's been weeping for days.

Maxwell, on the other hand, is dressed in a preppy sweater, polo shirt and khakis that Cupid doesn't think would look half bad if it was on somebody even remotely good looking. But the horrible toupee sitting on top of his bald head and the foundation caking his cheeks makes him look even more unpleasant than he normally does.

"Wow," Cupid breathes, eyeing the three of them in disgust. "I mean, just...*wow*."

"It's good to know something can render you speechless," Pia grumbles, refusing to look at the three creatures. "Is there *anything* you can do to help?"

"Send you to beauty school?" Cupid suggests. "*You* did this?"

"I'm not used to working my powers on such trivial shit, alright?" Pia snaps as Cupid laughs. "Can you fix this mess or what? Make them sexy? Or at least less disturbing to look at?"

"Preferably, I'd need about a year to do it right," Cupid remarks as he begins to walk around them. "But I think I can make them look halfway fuckable within a few hours."

"Then I guess the question is *will* you do it?"

"I'm insulted you even have to ask!" Cupid replies, mock-scandalized. "In the clash between scary and sexy, what side did you think I fall on?"

🎃 🎃 🎃 🎃

Jeff Connelly is making out with his girlfriend in bed, running his hands over her half naked body. Despite his sordid, secret fantasies of having sex with his fellow fraternity brothers, he very much enjoys having sex with his girlfriend. Pulling his lips away from her neck, Jeff leans back to stare at her, drinking in her beautiful appearance.

Her normally pale as snow skin seems even paler under the dim lights of his dark bedroom and her shoulder length dark hair appears oddly greasy. Furrowing his brow, Jeff stares down into her dark eyes; there is something different about them today. They appear *too* dark. In fact, the longer Jeff stares at them, the darker they become until the whites fade away completely. As he stares down at her face in horror, her mouth spreads into a wide smile that shows off every single one of her shark-like teeth.

"Surprise."

"What the *fuck*, man?" Jeff demands, jumping away from the bed, covering his erection showing through his boxers with both hands, blushing.

"Your girlfriend's very pretty," the Boogeyman says, pushing himself off the bed and walking over to Jeff's desk where two tumblers and a bottle of scotch are resting once more, although Jeff is certain they hadn't been there two seconds ago. "What's her name?"

"Carly. Her name's Carly. What the fuck are you doing here?" Jeff

———
322

demands again, staring around the room. "I'm asleep?"

"*Bingo*," the Boogeyman says, pouring himself a glass of scotch, downing it in one gulp, and pouring himself another. "Like I said the last time we met, you're a smart one."

"What are you doing here?" Jeff demands. "Can't you give me one moment of peace? Sir?" he nervously adds when the Boogeyman turns to look him straight in the face with his completely black eyes.

Jeff knows immediately something's wrong. Though the terrifying looking man appears calm and collected, he seems more agitated than the last time they met. More fidgety.

"Would you prefer I send my darlings back to haunt you instead?" the Boogeyman asks sardonically. "Because if you do, I can have that arranged. Though you'll be seeing therapists the rest of your life."

Jeff says nothing, believing the safest thing to do is remain silent. He eyes the Boogeyman with trepidation as he paces the room, the darkness falling around him.

"I just needed somebody to talk to," the Boogeyman spits, annoyed. "That *bitch* from Corporate has been giving me headaches for months and now she's trying to tell me how to run my holiday. *My* holiday!" The Boogeyman rounds on Jeff. "It's incredibly frustrating! I've been running it without issue for centuries and she just walks in and tries to tell me that Halloween is more about being skanky than scary now! Can you believe that?"

He stares at Jeff expectantly and Jeff realizes he has no choice but to answer.

"There's...uh..." Jeff laughs nervously. "There's nothing wrong with skanky. You should see some of the costumes the girls in the sorority plan on wearing this year. I mean, even Carly--"

The Boogeyman lets out a frightening scream of frustration, causing Jeff to back up in horror as the features on the scary man's face rearrange themselves into an expression of unrestrained anger.

Crossing the room in the blink of the eye, the Boogeyman grabs Jeff by the throat and pins him against the wall, leaning in so their faces are inches apart and the boy has no choice but to stare him in the eyes.

"You are part of the problem," the Boogeyman growls. "Your whole generation. Obsessed with nothing but instant gratification. You want to see tits, so the girls dress with them hanging out. There's no build-up anymore. It's *exhausting*. And *terribly* trite. And what's worse, my fucking company wants to cater to your needs!" The Boogeyman stares deep into the frightened boy's wide eyes. "But do you know how extremely *gratifying* it is to be scared? *Truly* scared? To scare others? After weeks of build-up? Weeks of *stalking*? Studying your prey? Learning their fears? It's *immensely* satisfying. *That's* what Halloween's supposed to be about. Man's primal impulse of fear."

"Please don't hurt me," Jeff whines in a voice ten times higher than normal.

The Boogeyman stares down at his feet in disgust when he feels something wet spreading around the floor.

"Did you piss yourself?" the Boogeyman asks, exasperated, releasing the boy from his grip and backing up in disgust. "How *old* are you?"

"I'm sorry," Jeff says quickly, flushing red.

"Luckily this is a dream so my robes won't be stained when I return to my office," the Boogeyman mutters to himself.

"What…uh…" Jeff clears his throat. "What time is it?"

"Two in the afternoon," the Boogeyman replies.

"I should be in algebra," Jeff remarks.

"You *are*," the Boogeyman informs him. "Math has been putting people to sleep for centuries."

"It never *used* to put me to sleep," Jeff says, regaining some of his composure. "I just didn't sleep well last night either." He gives the

———
324

Boogeyman an accusatory glare.

"Like I said," the Boogeyman shrugs innocently. "Sometimes I just need somebody to rant to. Therapy's a luxury I cannot afford and I'll be damned before trying to find somebody sane enough at the Pole to listen to my problems. Look on the bright side," he smirks. "You get to talk to me instead of getting my darlings trying to scare you into insanity."

"I think I'd prefer your darlings," Jeff admits, scratching the back of his head awkwardly.

The faintest hint of a forming grin plays at the corners of the Boogeyman's pursed lips. "You know, Jeff," he remarks. "I think this is just the beginning of a *long* and *beautiful* relationship."

Before Jeff can respond, a disembodied male voice sounds loudly throughout the room.

"Uh…excuse me? Boogeyman?"

The Boogeyman sighs deeply, staring up at the ceiling of the room in exasperation. "If you'll excuse me. Reality calls once again."

And with a loud, shuddering breath, the Boogeyman's eyes snap open and he finds himself seated at the desk in his dark office, gripping the arms of his chair tightly. Tuss is standing across from him in the doorway, looking nervously at the intimidating Shadow dancing on the wall.

"What do *you* want?" the Boogeyman demands.

"We need to talk," Tuss says, trying to keep the fear out of his voice as he steps further into the office. "About Pia."

"I'm not interested," the Boogeyman replies, pointing at the doorway. "Leave."

"I know she's a bit…*abrasive*, sometimes," Tuss remarks, ignoring the Boogeyman's command and taking a seat in the chair opposite his desk, careful not to lean back and impale himself on the spikes sticking out of it.

"*That's* an understatement," the Boogeyman snorts, folding his arms across his chest.

"But you can't take it personally, alright? Pia's under a lot of...*stress.*"

"We all are. She's just. A *bitch.*"

"I know," Tuss agrees, throwing another nervous glance at the Boogeyman's Shadow, looming near the only door leading in or out of the room. "You're absolutely right. But--"

"Does your girlfriend ever get annoyed that you constantly defend her?"

"I *don't* have a girlfriend," Tuss replies firmly, staring hard into the Boogeyman's eyes.

"Sure you don't."

"I...uh...that's neither here nor there. The point is," Tuss presses on, wanting to get as far away from the subject as he can. "Pia's under considerable stress. More than the rest of us. She has Caleb obsessing over her. Corporate's on her case about everything, including the hundreds of complaints in the mail they've been getting from Mother Nature. She--"

"Doesn't respect you and yet you have your head up her ass," the Boogeyman interrupts.

"She's trying to stop Santa from retiring," Tuss plows on, raising his voice slightly as he goes red in the face.

"That's one idea I can get behind," the Boogeyman responds. "The two of you should be concentrating on *that, not* how *I* run *my* holiday."

"Unfortunately, Halloween's the next major holiday," Tuss sighs. "Corporate wants us to spend our time trying to maximize profits for it."

"Corporate still has no idea Santa's retiring, do they?" the Boogeyman raises an eyebrow.

"The point is," Tuss ignores him. "You'd be making my life, Pia's life and your *own* life easier if you'd just sign the purchase order."

"I refuse," the Boogeyman shrugs as his Shadow shakes its head. "As long as I'm running Halloween, I'm going to run it my own way."

Before Tuss can reply, Pia storms into the room, followed closely by Cupid. "Boogeyman!"

"Nope, out!" the Boogeyman points at the door, rising to his feet immediately. "Get out! You too," he addresses Cupid. "I don't need you transmitting various sexual diseases to my staff."

"How dare you, sir!" Cupid replies mockingly. "I'm clean as a whistle! I get checked out every time I have unprotected sex, which, between you and I, is not as often as I'd like. I mean, I'm only averaging about fifteen times per week--"

"You're beyond disgusting," Pia says.

"Both of you, get out!"

"What are you doing here?" Tuss hisses as he turns in his seat to look up at Pia, accidentally poking himself on one of the spikes jutting out of the back of it in the process. "Ow! I'm handling it!"

"Please," Pia snorts. "You can't even handle yourself. Have you seen how disheveled you look!"

Tuss stares down at his wrinkled suit, going red in the face. "You know, all I do is defend you--"

"GET OUT! ALL OF YOU!" the Boogeyman roars.

Coming to his master's aid, his Shadow begins to usher the three unwanted visitors from the office, but Pia calls out first. "Wait a second! I have something to show you!"

The Boogeyman sighs, resigning himself, and calls off his Shadow. "What is it?"

"Cupid," Pia nods at her companion, who snaps his fingers instantly.

Immediately, the haunting tone of the organ playing throughout the office is replaced by runway music, and three people enter the room, causing the Boogeyman's mouth to drop comically, his Shadow mimicking him on the wall.

"What the hell have you done?"

"The impossible!" Cupid replies happily.

Howie is completely devoid of a snout and all fur, appearing as a human for the first time since the Boogeyman has known him. His pectorals and abs are so well defined, they'd make any mortal jealous, and every inch of his skin is glistening, as though he has oiled himself up.

Agatha appears fifty years younger. Her long, normally frizzy gray hair is now sleek and black, matching the pointed hat on her head. Her flabby body has been replaced by one that would make a twenty-year old college girl on spring break die with envy, and her breasts are so large and so pushed up in a tight corset, they appear as though they're going to fall out. Frilly panties are visible under her short tight skirt and fishnet stockings ending in five-inch heels complete the ensemble, accentuating her long legs.

And then there is Maxwell. Loyal, faithful Maxwell, who now has tousled, boyishly cute, windswept hair atop his normally bald head and no noticeable fangs or pointed ears to speak of. His complexion is no longer deathly pale, though his skin now sparkles in the dim lighting of the room, and his outfit, which includes a cashmere scarf, makes him appear wealthy.

"Et tu, Maxwell?" the Boogeyman asks softly as the vampire averts his eyes immediately.

"I'm a miracle worker," Cupid says with pride, his eyes welling up with emotion as he stares at the redone vampire, werewolf and witch. "Look how amazing they are."

"They look horrendous," the Boogeyman spits, turning to Pia. "Back in my mortal life, I did a lot of terrible things. I experimented. But nothing I ever created turned out *this* bad."

"I think we look good," Howie remarks innocently.

"Well you're a fucking idiot," the Boogeyman says hotly. "You're lucky you're not fired!"

"You can't fire us," Agatha points out apologetically. "Not for changing our looks. That's discrimination. That would be wrongful termination."

"*Watch me.*"

"Now you listen here," Pia begins, annoyed, as she leans in, nose-to-nose with the Boogeyman. "This is how Halloween's going to be run this year. Sexy's in, scary's out. Deal with it. If you can't, you're fired."

The Boogeyman scoffs as he turns to Tuss for support, but when he doesn't come to his aid, he sighs deeply. "So that's it then?" he asks. "After all of the years of loyal service I've put in with this company, you're just going to fire me if I don't go along with your plans?" When Pia nods, he shrugs. "I quit."

Pia blinks, taken aback. "You can't fucking *quit.*"

"Be reasonable, man," Cupid says, shocked.

"I *am* being reasonable," the Boogeyman insists.

"This is ridiculous," Pia snaps. "You want to quit? Fine. You can do data entry in a well-lit room wearing a vest and a bow tie like a little boy dressed up for church for the rest of your immortal life! Does that sound better to you? Because that's the alternative!"

The eyes of both Tuss and Cupid look down at the floor, determined to avoid the Boogeyman's glare as they shift awkwardly where they stand.

"I don't understand why Santa can retire and I cannot!" The Boogeyman shoots back, bearing his sharp teeth.

"Because it's not in your contract!" Pia yells, startling the spiders crawling along the ceiling above her. "It's not in *any* of your contracts except Santa's! And how dare you try to compare yourself to him! Now sign the damn purchase order!" She removes it from her pocket and shoves it into the Boogeyman's face. "Or I'll have Cupid give *you* a makeover next."

"You wouldn't," the Boogeyman growls.

"Wouldn't I?" Pia takes a step back, smugly.

When neither Cupid, nor Tuss, nor any of his employees come to his aid, the Boogeyman snatches the purchase order from Pia and signs it. "Congratulations," he says, shoving it back at a triumphant Pia. "You got your way by threats and coercion."

"Just as it should be," Pia says triumphantly, turning to Cupid. "Let's go see who else we can make sexy on this floor. Who knows, maybe you can do something to make that repulsive moron Bill easier on the eyes while you're at it!"

"I can't work miracles *that* big," Cupid laughs, following Pia out of the office. "Except in the bedroom, that is."

The Boogeyman's three employees eye their boss silently for a moment before Maxwell speaks up.

"Boss," he begins. "We're sorry. We just--"

"If any of you say another word, I'll rip your fucking heads off," the

Boogeyman growls as his Shadow mimes the action behind him. "You'll be lucky if I don't end up doing that anyway the way you all just betrayed me. Now, get out!"

Maxwell, Howie and Agatha all hurry from the room, the witch tripping over her heels as she stumbles out the door.

"You know something?" the Boogeyman laments, letting out a hollow laugh as he turns toward Tuss. "I'm starting to think Santa Claus has the right idea with this whole retirement thing. The job's just not the same anymore."

Tuss, unsure of how to reply, is spared having to do so when his phone rings. "Hello?"

"Tuss!" Caleb's voice shouts into his ear. "It's Caleb! Pia's not answering her phone again! I need help getting down from the ceiling! I was in her office trying to plan her a surprise 'It's Tuesday' party when a vine grabbed me and hoisted me up! It's got my throat!" His words turn into a strangled garble.

"I have to go deal with this," Tuss says to the Boogeyman before hurrying out of the office with the phone to his ear once again. "Just hold on, Caleb, I'm coming."

As the Boogeyman watches Tuss scurry away down the dark hallway beyond his office door, he can't help but get excited at the prospect of watching him and Pia hurry away from the North Pole forever.

"Only two more months," he says to himself, turning to the giant pile of work waiting for him on his desk with great dismay. "Keep telling yourself that," he sighs. "Only two more months."

"Trick-or-Treat!"

"Oh, don't you two look precious!" Holly exclaims as she opens the door of her little house in the North Pole for two elf children. "What are you two supposed to be?"

"Santa Claus!" the boy replies.

"Mrs. Claus!" the girl declares.

"Well, I think they're great costumes," Holly smiles, dropping candy into their plastic pumpkins. "Happy Halloween!"

She shuts the door after they hurry away and is barely able to take two steps toward her living room when the doorbell rings again.

"Halloween is *exhausting*," Holly sighs, turning back to the door and plastering a fake smile onto her face as she throws it open. "Wally," she exclaims, surprised to find the nerdy looking elf on her front doorstep. "Aren't you a little old to be trick-or-treating?"

"Can I come in for a minute?" Wally asks, staring around the dark street nervously.

Holly looks over her shoulder toward her living room. "I'm kind of busy--"

"It'll only take a minute," Wally insists, pushing his way past her before she can argue.

"What are you wearing?" Holly asks, eyeing the long overcoat around the elf's sleek frame.

"Happy Halloween, Holly," Wally says nervously, steeling himself as he turns to her and drops the coat.

"Oh my gumdrops!" Holly claps her hands over her mouth and begins to laugh hysterically at the sight of Wally's almost completely naked body, his penis sticking out of a Christmas wreath attached to the front of a green g-string. "What the hell are you doing?"

"I'm…uh…" Wally clears his throat, mentally cursing himself as he feels his cheeks go red. "Seducing you?"

He places his hands on his hips as a voice from behind him makes him jump in surprise.

"Hey babe, do you have any more hot chocolate? I'm – what the hell is going on here, Wally?"

"Bobby!" Wally whips around, covering his groin with his hands, flushing a deeper shade of red than Santa's famous coat. "What are *you* doing here?"

"I'm on a date," Bobby says as Holly skirts around Wally and hurries over to the good-looking elf, who puts a protective arm around her. "What are *you* doing here?"

"Humiliating myself," Wally sighs, feeling idiotic.

"Is it cold outside?" Holly smirks, staring pointedly down at his crotch.

"That's it!" Wally throws up his hands in frustration. "I'm done! I give up! I've done everything to try and win your affections, Holly. If it hasn't worked yet, it's never going to work. And maybe that's for the best! Maybe I'm too good for you!"

And not wanting to give either Holly or her new beau a chance to respond, Wally rips open the door of the house and hurries out into the cold night beyond, running past a scandalized mother taking her three young children trick-or-treating.

"Put on some clothes!" the mother elf calls after him.

Holly admires the elf's cute backside as she watches him run away into the distance, before the three elf children approach her doorstep and distract her from the nice sight.

"Trick-or-treat!"

"Honey, I'm home!"

"I'm upstairs!"

Tuss throws his jacket aside as he bounds up the dark stairs of the Tooth Fairy's house. When he gets to her bedroom, his jaw drops. Rose petals litter the bed and at least ten lit Jack-o'-lanterns are placed around the room, bathing the bedroom in a hauntingly beautiful, otherworldly glow.

Regina herself is laying seductively on the bed in white stockings and a tight, bright pink skirt and matching corset that makes her cleavage even more prominent than it normally is. Her fairy wings have grown large and are fluttering excitedly behind her as she gives Tuss a come hither look from the bed through her heavily made-up eyes, the tip of her wand placed seductively in the corner of her mouth.

"*Wow*," Tuss breathes.

"Happy Halloween, big boy," Regina says, speaking in a low, sultry voice. "Now, why don't you hurry up, take off your clothes and get into bed. Then we'll see whether I have a trick or a treat in store for you."

Tuss complies quickly, before jumping onto the bed and wrapping his muscular arms around the sexy fairy.

Despite the festive atmosphere throughout the Pole, the Boogeyman is sitting in his office, depressed. The last week leading up to Halloween had been one of the worst of his immortal life. Pushing sexiness instead of scariness was a new low, even for him, but he had no choice. And worse still, the numbers show that Pia and the rest of the idiots up at the Corporate office are correct in thinking that the mortals are over being scared.

The one bright spot was that Pia and Tuss had at least turned Maxwell, Howie, Agatha and the rest of his employees back into their normal, horrifying selves. His one, small victory.

But he has been doing a lot of thinking over this past week and the Boogeyman has decided to focus on a new project over the coming year. He has to prove to Corporate that being scary can still be relevant with the right marketing. He just needs to work out how to push it. Bill's Easter Bunny costumes weren't enough, although they did provide a huge boost to last minute sales. He plans to work on incorporating more holidays into his own. Perhaps he can even find some facet of Christmas he'll be able to turn into something nightmares are made out of. Combine two of the most profitable holidays – Corporate can't say no to that!

He'll have to look into it.

But first, he needs to clear his mind. Perhaps he'll pay Jeff Connelly another visit. Good thing he always falls asleep in chemistry class.

"Nobody asked Clucky for his opinion. Clucky would have said you gotta have soul. Not that a turkey has one."

"The amount of corn--"

"The first Noel,
The angel did say,
Was to certain poor shepherds in fields where they lay..."

"As I was saying, the amount of corn needed--"

"In fields where they,
Lay keeping their sheep..."

"AS I WAS SAYING ABOUT THE CORN--"

"Noel! Noel! Noel! Noel!"

"ARGHHH!" Tom the turkey grabs a nearby broomstick he keeps handy just for this purpose and angrily slams it against the ceiling, trying to voice his anger to the elf choir practicing on the floor above.

Meanwhile, from around their private conference room table, his six turkey employees once again watch silently. This is the fifth time he has done this during their meeting. And while the stick does allow Tom to get out some aggression, it has never succeeded in getting the choir to shut up. That doesn't stop him, however, from using it at least a dozen times a day.

"I can't work like this!" the flustered bird cries as the lovely voices of the choir continue to drift in from above. "Drown them out! Sing a song about Thanksgiving!"

Six pairs of beady eyes dart around the room.

"_Now!_"

"Uh...pilgrims..." one begins uncertainly.

"Indians and...uh...corn..." starts another.

337

"Turkey, turkey, turkey! I made you out of clay!" belts the third.

"Thanksgiving...is...um...good?" another sings while scratching his feathered head with a wing.

"I say turkey and you say...posmurkey?"

"Home, home on the range! Where the deer--"

"Everybody shut up!" Tom screeches. "I said sing a song about Thanksgiving!"

The birds all look at each other again, gobbling quietly as none of them want to be the first to speak up.

"I don't know any," one finally admits.

The others all chime in their agreement on top of each other.

"Me either!"

"Or me!"

"Neither do I!"

"I have to go to the bathroom!"

Tom's dark eyes narrow. "It's not fair! It's November and all the radio stations are already playing that schmaltzy crap about snow, and Santa, and sleds landing on rooftops! I'm sick of it! Why should *Christmas* get all the radio time? Where are the *Thanksgiving* songs? There are plenty of great things about Thanksgiving you could write a song about! We *more* than deserve it! Why don't the radio stations play songs about *us*?"

"Because there are none," one of the turkeys puts in quietly.

"Then we need to fix that!" Tom declares triumphantly, pointing a wing at the ceiling. "We'll write one! We'll write a Thanksgiving song! And it will be the best song ever made!"

None of them know a thing about writing songs, or music in general, but the turkeys all start to gobble excitedly anyway. They haven't been this excited since they got off the elevator this morning and the lights came on by themselves; it gets them every time.

Tom grabs a clipboard and a pen. "I will put everything people like about music into our song! That will definitely make it the best! I will talk to everyone and see what they like! And when I come back, we'll get to work!" He then marches out the door to a flurry of encouraging words from his fellow turkeys, even the one currently doing his business on some hay in the corner.

Tom trots out of the elevator once it deposits him in the lobby and he is happy to see the coffee cart is just as crowded as he expected. The faster he can get all his information, the faster he can get to work on his fantastic musical extravaganza.

Tilly, Ted, Regina and Francis are sitting around while Mother Nature putters about cleaning a few dishes. The three animals are conversing animatedly while the Tooth Fairy sits several seats away, referring repeatedly to her cell phone. Typical humanoid, Tom thinks condescendingly.

"I still haven't heard anything about my *Mighty Ducks* movie," Tilly sighs sadly. "I'm never going to find out what happens to that loveable peewee hockey team."

"Well, I have good news!" Ted chirps up. "My pen pal promised to send me pictures! I can't wait to see what they look like!"

"I don't understand how you can have a pen pal," Mother Nature says, adjusting her display of crumb cake. "How are you getting letters? This person knows you're at the North Pole?"

"I told them I was on an arctic expedition doing science stuff," Ted admits guiltily.

"So they think you're human?" Mother Nature clarifies.

"What if they ask for pictures of *you*?" Francis asks, sounding worried.

Ted hesitates. "I've...already sent pictures."

Everybody gasps in horror.

"So they know you're a groundhog?" Tilly shrieks.

"No!" Ted speaks up firmly. "It's complicated!"

With a warm greeting and slight flap of his wings, Tom interrupts this juicy conversation and climbs up onto a chair as he drops his clipboard. "I have an important announcement!"

"Is it from Corporate? Did they mention my letters?" Mother Nature asks urgently.

"No and no. I am writing a brand new song about the best holiday--"

"Easter?" Francis asks.

"Groundhog's Day?" Ted inquires.

"Canada Day?" Tilly suggests.

"No!" the bird snaps, narrowing his black eyes. "Thanksgiving! Of *course*!"

"Oh, of *course*," Mother Nature agrees with obvious sarcasm that only Tom does not pick up.

"Of course," Tom huffs again. Then, tapping his clipboard with his wing, he continues with great importance. "Since it's going to be the greatest song ever, I want everyone's opinion on what they think the song should include. That way my song will be as amazing and inspiring as the amazing and inspiring holiday it represents." He waits, assuming everyone will be so excited over this idea that they will just start shouting their suggestions on top of one another. Clearly he hangs out with the other turkeys too much, for when no one speaks, he frowns and reluctantly turns to Tilly. "Let's start with you, moose."

"Oh, me?" cries the obviously flustered moose. "Well, let's see...I like horns! Like trumpets, trombones and tubas! Ooh, *especially* tubas! They're so funny looking! And so very, very loud!"

Tom diligently writes down: 'lots of horns - focus on tubas'. He then points to Ted. "Next."

"All of the mortal music I listen to seems to be about love and trucks," the groundhog informs him. "Sometimes even loving your truck. They must really like trucks. I know my pen pal sure does. I don't get why. They just tend to run us furries over! I couldn't live with that kind of pressure!" Suddenly looking nervous, he produces a pill from seemingly nowhere and throws it back with a large gulp of coffee.

Tom has already copied down his response and lost interest. "You, Francis."

"I would keep the song kid friendly," Francis suggests. He takes a sip from his drink, which has been resting on a large book on the counter in front of him.

"Why? So your five *million* kids can sing it?"

"No," the rabbit replies testily to the turkey's question. "So mortal children can sing it in schools. They're *always* having concerts around the holidays."

"And how many do you miss going to every year?" Tom scoffs.

"Do you want my help or not?" Francis responds, agitated.

Tom does write down this actually good suggestion before turning to the coffee cart proprietor. "Mother Nature?"

"You have to make it rock, honey!" she responds immediately. "It's gotta make you wanna bang your head, stand on your chair and hold up a lighter!"

"Why?" Tom asks, confused.

Mother Nature stops her head banging demonstration at this query. She's been holding up her hands with just her pointer and pinkie fingers extended, like she's trying to make a rabbit or something. Tom doesn't care for this display at all. "I'm not sure," she admits, looking a bit dizzy. "But mortals do it all the time."

"Fine," Tom mutters, writing it all down. "As long as it doesn't inspire them to make those disturbing rabbit hands." He's about to pack up his clipboard and leave when he remembers Regina sitting off to the side, alone. She hasn't said a word this whole time and has simply continued to check her cell phone every few minutes. "What about you?"

"Huh?" She pushes a strand of hair out of her eyes and glances over like she hasn't heard a word of their conversation. "What about me?"

"My song!" Tom reminds her with great annoyance. "What is your suggestion for my yet-to-be-written but certain-to-be-amazing song?"

"Oh…uh…" She looks down at her cell phone again, obviously not giving the all important song her full attention, which greatly annoys the proud bird. "Just keep it simple."

"Well, obviously! There's nothing simpler than America and a good, old-fashioned family dinner!" Tom huffs. But Regina is too busy texting to care. Grumbling, he writes down her stupid suggestion.

"Are we going to get to hear this song, Tom?" Francis asks.

"Of course! There's going to be a grand performance as soon as it's done! And you'll *all* want to be there! It'll be the best thing your ears have ever had the pleasure to hear!" Then, noticing the large tome in front of the Easter Bunny, he asks with a smirk, "What's that? A list of your monthly child support payments?"

"No!" But the rabbit does frown. "It's my kids' Christmas list."

"*That's* their Christmas list?" Ted cries, practically falling off his seat after really getting a look at the giant, *Moby Dick* sized book. "How are you not having a heart attack?"

"Actually, it's only half of it. Aaron through Hoppity Fifty-Seven. They're too heavy to carry together," Francis explains.

"*Christmas!*" Tom screeches. "How dare you be shopping for Christmas already! It's time for my holiday! *My* holiday! The fat man gets his turn *next* month!"

"I actually have to start shopping for Christmas right after Christmas," Francis admits. "So I never get a break."

"And that's just the way the fat man wants it!" yells Tom, heading back for the elevator. "He wants you to spend all year just shopping, and spending, and singing all about *him*! Well, *his* time is up! Once my song is done, it's going to be so wonderful that the radio stations won't ever want to stop playing it! Not on Christmas *or* on Easter!"

The elevator thankfully swallows him up after that, taking him and his screeching to annoy another floor.

"Don't ever tell him that my family doesn't celebrate Thanksgiving," Francis mumbles.

"Clotho! Did you order all the glitter?"

"I just ordered five more shipments! I think that should be enough to cover the West Coast!"

"Fine, fine! Atropos, what about champagne production?"

"They're ahead of schedule!"

"Excellent! And Lachesis! How many musical acts do we have for the television special?"

"Six! The blonde with the guitar, a black man who likes to dance, a band that doesn't play their own instruments, one that does play their own instruments, a woman with crazy eyes and a young man who likes to move like this." She begins a seductive looking dance, which causes all of her sisters to burst out laughing.

"Ugh!" bristles Father Time. "Mortals are disgusting." He ducks into his office and glances over to where Caleb, now ninety-years old, is stationed in the corner with two stacks of paper. In his hand is a giant stamp, which wobbles wildly in his unsteady fist every time he lifts it off the inkpad. Slowly, he takes a form from one pile and lays it out carefully in front of him, before shakily picking up the stamp and bringing it down gently into the proper box. He then returns it to the inkpad, puts the form in a second pile and starts the process all over again. The act of stamping one simple piece of paper takes him easily over a minute. "I don't understand why you're doing *her* work!" Father Time snaps. It's not the first time he's said this, or even the seventh. "You should be *resting*! You're *old* now! Enjoy the time you have left!"

"I want to help!" Caleb maintains. "She asked me *specifically* to take care of this!"

"Because she knows you'll do anything she asks! Not because you're *special!* Trust me, you're *not* special! In a few months I'll have a new one of you parasites and it better be a damn girl this time!" He says that last part specifically to the ceiling, but maybe he's talking to a higher power. "You can barely even handle that stamp! Look at you!"

"I can handle it just fine!" But after bringing the stamp down again, Caleb frowns. "I missed the box again. She's going to yell at me. At least she looks beautiful when she yells."

"You know she had some of the cherubs cleaning her office just yesterday, right? They were scrubbing it with toothbrushes and everything!" Father Time exclaims.

"What? But that's supposed to be *my* job!" Caleb replies, aghast. "I bet they didn't dust the vines!"

"Pardon me, gents!" Both of them look up to find Tom has waddled his way into the office.

"How long have you been standing there?" questions Father Time in surprise.

"Long enough to be reminded that he's mentally disturbed," Tom answers while gesturing to Caleb.

"Well, what do you want?" bristles the clock-obsessed old man. "I'm very busy!"

"I'm writing a song about Thanksgiving and I need your input. What's your favorite thing about music?"

"Nothing beats a good bell signaling what time it is," Father Time answers immediately. Tom diligently copies this down.

"Father Time?" Clotho calls from her cubicle. "Can you take a look at this? I know these novelty hats are supposed to border on ridiculous, but I really think this one has crossed the line. The colors are hurting my eyes."

"Excuse me," mutters Father Time, hurrying from the office.

That leaves Tom facing Caleb, who is smiling at him expectantly with his remaining teeth. In actuality, Tom never really wanted the opinion of the, in his mind, *disposable* face of the year. But now he feels like he doesn't have a choice. "And…what about *you*?" he forces out, trying not to make eye contact.

"Well, all the mortal kids are into rap!" Caleb says with the enthusiasm of a grandfather who considers himself hip.

"Ah, of course!" Tom copies down this idea eagerly. Looks like he didn't waste his breath on that sentence after all. "Rap is totally hip and with it!"

"Make sure you mention hoes," Caleb says pointedly.

"You mean the farming tool?" Tom asks.

"Yup!" Caleb replies. "Kids *love* that stuff!"

Tom writes all of this down and clicks his pen closed with a nod. "Thank you for your time!"

"You're welcome! I look forward to hearing your song!" As Tom leaves, Caleb turns back to his task with a frown, consulting one of the many clocks on the wall. "I'm going to have to ask for an extension...she's not gonna like that..."

"She was with another guy!" Wally sounds agitated, standing in the doorway of Cupid's office. The head of Valentine's Day is lounging on his heart-shaped bed as the Boogeyman stands in the corner, head bowed, trying not to laugh. "She doesn't like me! It's over! I'm not trying any more of your ideas! I was totally humiliated! He...he...he saw my wreath and berries. And *laughed*." He frowns, staring at the floor. "All of the elves are *still* talking about it."

"Ignoring the fact that you wasted a prime opportunity for a threesome, I don't know what you're complaining about!" Cupid toes off his shoes and tucks his hands behind his head. "Just because she's with someone else doesn't mean you should give up! It means you should try harder!"

"I've already tried my hardest," Wally insists. "I practically got *naked* for this girl!" He tries to ignore the Boogeyman, who is doing a poor job of stifling his laughter now. "I tried all of your ideas!"

"*All* my ideas? You've tried ten things! That is *far* from all, buddy," Cupid points out. "I've been doing this a long time. My playbook numbers into the thousands."

"Well, I'm done," Wally throws up his hands, frustrated. "I'm not trying any more of them. They don't work and then I have to listen to the elves in teddy bear construction gossip about me for a week straight afterwards!"

"Are any of them cute?" Cupid asks. "Maybe you just need a rebound for now!"

But Wally has had enough. With a shout of aggravation, he turns on the heels of his pointed shoes and heads back for the elevators, nearly trampling Tom in the process.

"Watch it, slave!" Tom calls after him. "Each of these feathers is worth more than your *life*!"

"Tom! What brings you to my humble place of business?" Cupid pats the bed invitingly. "Join me."

"Never."

"Why doesn't anyone ever want to join me?" Cupid asks the Boogeyman.

"Because you're *fowl*," the Boogeyman drones, lingering on the last word for added effect.

"Oh, ha, ha. Is that a bird joke?" Tom gripes. "Very funny. Well, I just came here to get your opinions. I'm writing a song about the wonders of Thanksgiving and I wanted to include everyone's favorite thing about music."

"Organs."

"Ooh. I like organs too," Cupid agrees. "But not specifically for music."

"I meant the instrument," the Boogeyman says, giving Cupid a hard stare with his creepy eyes. "A somber tone means you're serious."

"And I say you should make sure your song is sexy," pipes up Cupid. "Take the music playing on my floor as an example." They all pause for a moment to listen to the smooth tones of Barry White. "People love music they can bang to. Just keep your song sexy and everybody will love it."

"Well, that will be easy," huffs Tom. "Turkeys are naturally sexy. They are the sexiest bird and don't ever let those slutty chicks in the Easter department tell you otherwise." With those words, he heads back down the hallway.

"*Chicks?*" Cupid rubs his chin thoughtfully. "I was gonna say peacocks. Pretty sure they have the most porn. I don't consider chicks sexy at *all*. I mean, have you *seen* Clucky?"

"And people say *my* holiday is the most disturbing," mutters the Boogeyman.

Tom doesn't want to go to the July floor for a variety of reasons. He knows if anyone sees him up there, they will once again assume him and T.J. are best friends just because they both happen to be birds. No matter how often the two feathered foes make it clear that they actually do not like each other, people continue to jump to the conclusion that they are bosom buddies every time they are spotted together. Tom finds this incredibly racist. After all, just because Ted, Francis and Tilly are all mammals, it doesn't mean they're automatically best friends.

It's due to this issue that Tom almost skips over the seventh floor, but because he truly wants to make sure he produces the best song of all time, he sucks it up and presses the flag-shaped button.

As soon as he gets off the elevator and can clearly hear Bill and T.J. yelling at each other over the very loud patriotic tunes playing above, he is reminded of the other reason he didn't want to come to this floor.

"Well, I'm sorry!" Bill is screaming, his face red, sweaty and tear-stained as Tom approaches the office. "But in your language 'sky' and 'dumpster' sound really similar!"

T.J. screeches something nasty sounding in return, scratching his talons threateningly.

"No, hanging a bunch of flags in a dumpster didn't really make sense to me either, but maybe you should just speak clearly next time! Don't mumble!" Bill waits for the eagle's nasty sounding reply before adding, "I don't know who's gonna go get all those flags out of the dumpster, but I still don't think it should be me!"

T.J. clearly believes otherwise, but Tom interrupts their argument with a loud gobble, having stood in the doorway long enough already without being acknowledged.

"Oh. Hi, Tom." Bill wipes down his face with his disgusting, stained handkerchief. "You here to go to lunch with T.J.?"

"No!" Tom cries as T.J. also voices his displeasure at this assumption. "I'm writing a song and I want any suggestions you may have on how to make it great."

T.J. answers this question immediately, his words sounding less angry than usual.

"He says to make it patriotic," Bill explains, although he does turn to the bird for clarification. "You *did* say patriotic and not nail clipper, right? Because those words are also kind of similar - okay! I get it!" he grumbles at the once again angry response he receives.

"There's nothing more patriotic than spending money on tons of food and watching a nationally televised parade and football game," Tom says proudly, his beak held high in the air. "Where's *your* holiday's parade and football game, T.J.?"

Many unpleasant sounds start flying out of T.J.'s angrily snapping beak. As wings are flapped menacingly and sharp talons are brandished, Bill steps between the two birds, holding his hands over his face. "He wants me to escort you to the elevator. You said elevator and not--" Bill receives a particularly nasty screech right in the face. "He said elevator."

Tom seems quite happy to be escorted from the office and turns back to smirk at the other bird multiple times before he's finally out of sight.

"He is in some mood today," Bill complains, unfortunately whipping out the handkerchief again. "I'm not going to let him force me into going down to that dumpster, though. It's his fault he mumbled. What was your question again?"

"I want your opinion on what I should include in the song I'm writing about Thanksgiving. The soon-to-be-greatest song of all time," Tom elaborates.

Bill ponders this question for a moment as the elevator makes its way to them. "Well, I know what it *shouldn't* include. Any lyrics."

"No lyrics?" Tom is confused at this suggestion, even if he never expected much from Bill. "But how will I talk about how wonderful Thanksgiving is?"

"Lyrics are the worst part of a song!" Bill declares as Tom looks up in dismay to see the elevator is still several floors away. "You have these hot girl singers that think they're *so* pretty and *so* beautiful with their nice hair and their boobs and stuff, and they're up there right in front of you always singing about how they're *so* in love! And love is *so* great and *so* amazing and how they can't wait to be in *love*. In love with *you*! But you know they're *lying*! You know they'd never love a guy like *you*! Those teasing sluts!"

Tom is able to quietly back into the elevator and press the button for the next floor like his life depends on it without Bill even noticing he is gone.

And for that, he is thankful. Because Thanksgiving *is* relevant every single day of the year!

"Everybody gather around!" Tom struts back into the eleventh floor conference room, clipboard in hand. His fellow turkeys quickly gather around him, except for the one still finishing up his business in the corner. (And yes, it's a different one than last time, you bird racist.) "I have spoken to everyone and I know *exactly* what to do to make our song the best!"

"Hooray!"

"I'm so excited!"

"Music is fun!"

"Seventeen is a funny sounding number!"

"I wanna play guitar!"

"Locomotion!" the last one shouts, hurrying over from the now soiled pile of hay in the corner.

"Everybody quiet down!" Tom holds up the clipboard like a conductor might steady his baton before a concert. "Now, after all of my interviews, I've come to the conclusion that we need to keep this song simple, but make sure it rocks. It needs to be about love and trucks, but also patriotism. It needs to be sexy, yet kid friendly. And it needs to include a rap, tubas, bells, an organ and Kwanzaa said to make sure it has lots of drum solos." Putting down the clipboard, he finds six pairs of beady, mesmerized bird eyes staring back at him. "I think it's clear - this song is going to practically write itself."

"Hooray!"

"Everyone's gonna want to buy it!"

"I wanna buy it right now!"

"Pomegranates are the devil!"

"Somebody needs to clean the bathroom!"

"Drum solo!"

Tom smiles. How could they go wrong?

Only a brief week later, and the masterpiece is complete. Aside from a few late nights and a wing fight that nearly broke out over a tambourine, the songwriting process had gone well. Tom invites everyone to the main conference room for the big debut, but fails to show up on time himself because creative geniuses are always late. Instead, Father Time, Caleb, Cupid, Ted, Tilly, Francis, Mother Nature, T.J., Bill, the Boogeyman, Regina, Santa, Tuss and Pia are waiting rather impatiently for things to get started.

Pia is pacing up and down the back of the room, giving Bill's chair a pointless shove every time she passes it. "Where the hell is this damn bird? Doesn't he know people have other things to do? It's almost fucking Christmas here!"

"I'm sure he'll be along shortly!" Santa pipes up. "He *did* seem rather proud of his song." He frowns down at the piece of cardstock in his hand, which reads: 'This is where your Christmas carols come to die, fatass!' "Though his invitation is a *bit* lacking in holiday spirit."

"Should someone wake up the Sandman and get him in here?" Tilly asks. "He fell asleep in the hallway again!"

"Just let him be," Francis advises. "The last time I tried to wake him, he somehow wound up using me as a pillow." He frowns. "That was a terrible six hours."

"What is his problem? Keeping us waiting to hear the shittiest song that's ever existed," Pia complains, stomping by Tuss and forcing him to yank his eyes away from Regina and her suggestive blouse.

"Maybe it will be worth the wait," Tuss says diplomatically, even if he doesn't believe it himself.

"Of course it is!" Everyone looks up to find Tom standing dramatically in the doorway, clad in a pilgrim hat and carrying a computer. With a brief flutter of his wings, he hops up on the conference table and trots to the center where he drops the computer and turns to his audience.

352

Well, *some* of his audience. He makes sure his butt faces Santa. "I'm sure you're all very excited to be part of the premiere of my song, *The Best Thanksgiving Song Ever.*"

"Calling it the best implies there are others," the Boogeyman murmurs to some chuckles from those nearby.

Tom frowns, but chooses to ignore the comment and continues with his introduction. "This song was written about the best holiday, Thanksgiving, and in keeping with the spirit of that blessed day, I am very thankful to each and every one of you for your ideas, which will surely make this the most requested song on the radio this holiday season. Enjoy and be amazed!" He then presses a button on the computer and the song begins.

It starts with bells loudly chiming, reminiscent of what you might hear in a Christmas carol. Santa smiles and Father Time looks pleased, but then the vocals start. The song was obviously recorded by Tom and his gang of turkeys, none of whom are known for their singing abilities. Behind the singing is the drone of an organ mixed with a poorly played guitar and a horn that sounds like it's performing in someone's circus-based nightmare.

"Hey, America, turn off your trucks,
And forget about Christmas 'cause it really sucks!
There's only one holiday worth all the love,
And it fits this country like the perfect glove.

Only one holiday has an awesome parade,
And so much sexy turkey that I wouldn't trade.
So turn off those trucks and throw down your hoes,
There's only one holiday that doesn't totally blow!"

In comes the chorus, accompanied by more horns than should ever be allowed in a single song. Regina grimaces, sticking her fingers into her ears as she stares at the insane turkey, who is looking around at them all, swelling with pride.

"Thanksgiving is the perfect day,
Eat and drink all your cares away.

Sexy turkey on a silver tray,
It's the best American holiday."

Francis winces in pain as the Boogeyman's mouth drops open. Behind
him, his Shadow mimes committing suicide in a variety of creative
ways.

"Only Thanksgiving has a football game,
Every other holiday is totally lame!
Buying tons of food shows you got wealth,
Eating all that turkey is good for your health!

Turkey is the best food of all time,
Pair it with some stuffing and your favorite wine.
Grill it, roast it, or have it fried,
That turkey is a bird that died with pride.

Thanksgiving is the perfect day,
Eat and drink all your cares away.
Sexy turkey on a silver tray,
It's the best American holiday."

The next part is a rap featuring Tom backed-up by terrible beatboxing.
Caleb nods his head enthusiastically along with the music, smiling
widely.

"Thanksgiving over here,
Thanksgiving over there,
Thanksgiving up and down,
Thanksgiving all around!
Thanksgiving in your house,
Thanksgiving by a mouse,
Thanksgiving in a boat,
Thanksgiving by a goat!

I love Thanksgiving,
You should love it too!
Anyone who doesn't,
Is a stupid fool!
So all you kids on all those streets,

Stop, drop and roll to my sexy beat!
Take those Christmas carols and shove 'em up your butt,
Thanksgiving is the holiday for makin' you strut!"

In comes the drum solo, which goes on for five excruciating minutes. Tom looks around for Kwanzaa, who suggested this hazard of sound, but he's not at the meeting. Ted too is no longer visible, having ducked under the table in excruciating agony seconds before.

All of the turkeys come back in at the bridge and the verse that follows.

"Oh, Thanksgiving,
Why are you so amazing?
It's not fair to the other holidays,
Especially Christmas, which is totally stupid, and overblown, and who cares about a fat guy that gives gifts and a dumb tree that's basically a fire hazard anyway?

If you don't love Thanksgiving, there's something wrong with you,
You're such a weirdo you belong in a zoo!
Thanksgiving has something for everyone,
It's a day of eating, family, and nonstop fun!

So turn off your trucks and throw down your hoes,
Put aside your sadness and all your worn out woes.
There's only one holiday that's worth making you sing!
It comes in November, it's called Thanksgiving!

Thanksgiving is the perfect day,
Eat and drink all your cares away.
Sexy turkey on a silver tray,
It's the best American holiday."

The song ends with a flourish of drums and more obnoxious bells. Actually, it technically ends with Tom yelling at one of the other turkeys for dropping a cymbal, but he plans to edit that out later. He looks around at his audience excitedly. "Well?"

Eyes hit the floor, the wall, the ceiling - staring anywhere except at the turkey in the center of the table. Nobody even wants to breathe, let alone say a word. They all feel terrible. It's because of them and their

---

355

seemingly innocent suggestions that this twisted monster of a Thanksgiving song was born. They are all responsible, and part of their punishment will be to never unhear what they have just heard.

Pia, one of the few in the room with a clear conscience, just leaves her chair without a word, an expression of absolute disgust on her face.

Once she is gone, a flurry of looks are exchanged around the table. Then everyone else stands up, nearly in unison, and begins to silently parade out the door, not daring to look back at the bird in the center of the room.

"Speechless!" Tom cries excitedly. "I knew it!"

And the proud turkey is so full of joy it feels like all the kids in the world gave Santa the middle finger and launched him on a rocket into the sun, just like in his favorite recurring dream.

It's a marvelous, unfortunately fleeting moment.

"What's going on in here? I just had the worst dream!" The Sandman appears in the doorway, rubbing the sleep from his eyes. "It was about the worst song I've ever heard! It was like I was having one of the Boogeyman's nightmares! It was awful, just awful! The Boogeyman should really use it when he's trying to terrify people! Can you imagine anyone writing a *rap* about Thanksgiving? It's – why are you crying? You didn't hear it!"

"I *sang* it!" Tom replies indignantly. "That's the new Thanksgiving song that I wrote!"

The Sandman scratches his rumpled hair. "That was a song?"

Before Tom can blubber out a single word in defense of his precious song, Pia returns to the room, a baseball bat tight in her hands. Raising it swiftly above her head, the already flustered turkey can only watch in stunned horror as she proceeds to beat the computer containing his beloved song into a pulp of unidentifiable electronic sludge. When she is certain she has destroyed every last offensive component, she throws the bat in the bird's direction and stomps away to the slow clapping of the appreciative Sandman.

"Now *that's* what I call a performance!"

December

"Clucky only buys presents for one person – *Clucky*."

Pia is in a bad mood. Truth be told, she is always in a bad mood, but she is in a worse mood than usual today. You see, Pia can handle a lot of annoying, terrible things. She can handle Mother Nature's man-eating plants (which these days she has to keep swatting away every five seconds as she sits at her desk) and she can even handle Caleb's creepy, stalker-like tendencies (I mean, he can be useful sometimes; at the moment, Pia is watching him try to hang lights and Christmas baubles on all of those same annoying and often bloodthirsty plants that have taken over the entire floor). But what Pia cannot handle is disappointment. Not getting her way.

It is almost Christmas and the North Pole, which is full of snow and holiday cheer all year round, has ramped it up in the past few weeks. Almost everybody is constantly in annoyingly good moods, throwing frequent greetings of tidings and joy back and forth. The snow is falling harder, Christmas carols are constantly heard throughout the company building and on the streets of the little village below, and the elves have started to put even *more* decorations up in anticipation of the upcoming holiday. Sales wise, Santa has already tripled his numbers from the previous year which means that, theoretically, he could stop working right here and now if he wants (which he would never do) and Corporate would still be pleased with his work. And yet, despite all of this holiday joy, Pia is still miserable.

Why? Because in just under two weeks time, Santa Claus will be retiring and she has still not told Corporate, let alone found a suitable replacement to take over for the famous man in the big red suit. Not that she has any intention of doing either of those things. Oh no, that would be admitting defeat and Pia is *never* defeated. Despite all of her setbacks, her intention is still to stop Santa from retiring. Failure is unthinkable, which makes it not an option.

Pia runs her hands through her hair, which, normally well kept, is frizzy and sticking out of her ponytail due to her stress level and the humid temperature of her office (for which the plants are to blame, of course). She stares down at a piece of paper resting on the mulch covered desk in front of her which is filled with her tiny, cramped handwriting. Giant lines and arrows are drawn everywhere, making it look more like a sports play than a to-do list. But in reality, it is all of the different ideas she has come up with to try and prevent the old man from leaving his job.

None of these are particularly good ideas - holding him hostage would just upset him and holding the elves or the reindeer hostage would just put a dent in productivity (Corporate would not like that). Kidnapping his wife could be feasible, but again, Pia has to keep the old man happy and he actually seems to be one of the few men on Earth happy with his spouse. Offering him more money or vacation time would prove useless, for Santa cares about none of that, so Pia has no clue what she can do to stop him from leaving short of breaking down and begging him; letting him know just what his departure would cost her. She has too much pride for this, however, and tells herself she'd rather let Santa leave and face the wrath of her bosses before breaking down and begging him to stay like some lowly, pathetic creature (like Bill).

As she stares down at her list of ideas and tries to concentrate, she begins to get angrier and angrier due to all of the holiday-related noise outside of her office. How is anybody supposed to think, let alone plot Mrs. Claus' theoretical kidnapping, around Christmastime at the North Pole with all of the lights and sounds emanating from the village below? The noise drifts into her office as clearly as if she herself is outside singing *Carol of the Fucking Bells* with the elves.

She throws down her pen in frustration as there is a knock on her open office door. "What the fuck do you want?" Pia demands, staring up to see Tuss standing in front of her.

"Did you convince Santa not to leave yet?" he asks tentatively.

"Why, yes, Tuss, I did," Pia says with a smile plastered on her face. "I'm just writing my memoirs now." She waves her idea sheet in front of his face. "Because I'm now the biggest success that's ever come out of Corporate. I just look annoyed because retirement is more stressful for me than actually doing my job. OF COURSE I DIDN'T FUCKING GET SANTA TO AGREE NOT TO LEAVE YET, YOU DUMB PIECE OF SHIT!"

Tuss sighs deeply as he rubs his temples. As much as he is dreading

——

leaving Regina when he leaves the North Pole in a few weeks, he can't wait to get away from Pia.

It had been...a year. Nearly a whole year.

"I think it's time to call A--"

"I'm not calling anybody," Pia snaps, standing up.

"They're going to be *really* upset you kept this from them this long as it is," Tuss tries reasoning with her.

"That *we* kept it from them for this long," Pia hisses, a small grin on her face. "If I go down, you're going down with me, *partner*. How do you like being partners now?"

"You know that I'm in better books with them than you are, right?" Tuss raises an eyebrow.

Pia ignores him as she continues. "I haven't told anybody he's leaving yet because he's *not* leaving."

"He's taking his last flight in ten days!" Tuss points out with wavering patience. "What are you planning to do, Pia? Lock him in a dungeon somewhere?"

Pia continues to ignore him as she walks around her desk and out into the jungle beyond her office door. "I'm going to convince him, Tuss, you'll see," she says, as Tuss hurries along beside her, tripping over vines and hitting his head on low hanging branches. "Santa Claus *can't* retire. The idea of it is ridiculous. He makes too much money for us and he loves his job too much. He'll come to. He'll change his mind. He *has* to."

"Who are you trying to convince? Me or yourself?" Tuss asks, warily. "I wouldn't get my hopes up if I were you. If--"

"Caleb!" Pia barks at the now ancient looking baby New Year who has just entered her sights. He is standing five feet in front of her, gingerly outstretching one of his shaking arms to hang a red Christmas bauble

———

on the stem of a snapping Venus Flytrap. "What the fuck is this mess?"

Tuss glances around at the mess in question. The normally wild looking jungle looks simply stunning. Christmas ornaments and lights are hanging from most branches, and mistletoe is hanging over every doorway, including the one Caleb is now standing in.

"It took me hours to do this," Caleb says, the hurt evident in his shaky voice. "Look, Pia! Mistletoe!" He points at the leafy plant above his head before closing his eyes and puckering his withered lips, waiting.

"Ugh, I'm going to puke," Pia gags in disgust before looking around at the beautifully decorated plants in contempt. "This all looks like crap. Bill could shit out a better decorated office than this! Take it all down and start the hell over."

"W-what?" Caleb stutters, looking as though he is about to collapse from a heart attack.

"Pia," Tuss says in an undertone, his voice warning. But, as usual, his colleague ignores him.

"I said start the hell over!" Pia yells, stamping her foot. "Make it look like Christmas is supposed to look! Not like some blind, old, impotent asshole threw a bunch of garbage at the walls!"

"No!" Caleb grabs the nearest ornament he can reach and smashes it on the floor, causing both Pia and Tuss to jump back in surprise. He then points a shaking, crooked finger at the woman who stole his heart nearly a year ago. "You're nothing but a big bully!" he chokes, his face red as hot tears begin to run down his cheeks. "I'm sick of this! Your heart is smaller than the Grinch's before it grew three sizes on Christmas Day! Maybe you should go talk to him! He can teach you how to be nice! You and I, we're...we're..." Caleb gasps, crying harder now. "We're *t-through*! So fuck off!"

And Pia watches, her jaw on the floor, as her personal slave turns and begins to hobble toward the distant elevators, sobbing his eyes out.

"What the *fuck*?" Pia demands, rounding on Tuss who looks just as surprised.

"That was...*unexpected*," Tuss admits, trying to conceal the smile he can feel forming on his face.

"This month can't get any damn worse," Pia snaps as she continues toward the elevator, passing the slow moving Caleb in the process, who she can't help but shove into the wall. "Now I'm out a personal slave too!"

"He's right though, Pia," Tuss says. "You need to grow a heart."

"Don't be so ridiculous," Pia hisses as the two of them step inside of the elevator and begin to descend through the building, leaving Baby New Year behind, weeping in the jungle. "Growing a heart is scientifically impossible."

"You know what I mean," Tuss says gently. "It's Christmas! Be nice to people. For *once*."

"Why would I do something *stupid* like that? Niceness is a weakness."

"*Pia.*"

"I'll be nice to people when I finally convince Santa to stay on with us, alright?" Pia rolls her eyes. "Get off my fucking case."

Tuss sighs deeply. He can't hope for better than that; even that, in and of itself, would be a Christmas miracle.

"Deck the hall with boughs of holly,
Fa la la la la, la la la la.
'Tis the season to be jolly,
Fa la la la la, la la la la."

"Don't they sound great?" Willy asks proudly, staring around the oval table, beaming.

363

Wally, Holly, Willy, Bobby, Frank, Knobby and Jolly are sitting around a table in the middle of Santa's workshop, notebooks and pens situated in front of each of them.

"They sound perfect," Wally nods, staring down at his notebook before mumbling under his breath. "They sound exactly like they do all year round."

Jolly, who is sitting beside him twirling her blonde hair, tries to stifle a laugh at the statement.

"Can we get back to the matter at hand, please?" Holly sighs, glancing up at the Aurora Borealis swirling overhead before looking around at her fellow elves. "Santa's retirement party. We have a few last minute details to sort out."

"Yes, we do!" Frank says enthusiastically, stroking his dark beard. "We need to make it both spectacular *and* memorable."

"Since when are *you* excited about anything?" Bobby asks, surprised, as he turns away from the abominable snow monster helping a few of the younger elves decorate the twenty-foot Christmas tree in the center of the room.

"Since I realized I only have to put up with that fat ass for ten more days before he leaves and somebody else gets his job," Frank explains, as his fellow elves roll their eyes in exasperation. "Maybe it'll be somebody who actually respects me!"

Willy snorts. "As if anyone could respect you."

Before the shorter elf can reply, Holly interjects. "I'm glad you're so enthusiastic about all of this, Frank," she smiles. "Because *you* get to collect the money from all of the elves and other holiday heads for Santa's retirement gift."

Frank's face falls instantly. "Fuck my life."

"That's becoming your catchphrase, isn't it?" Wally mumbles.

364

"Can we *please* get on with this?" Knobby asks in his old, hoarse voice. "I have work to do, you know."

"What are we getting Santa, anyway?" Jolly asks.

"Watches are traditional," Holly says, making a note on the pad in front of her.

"And we have to pay for one?" Willy raises an eyebrow. "Father Time won't give him one for free?"

"Don't even go there," Holly sighs deeply. "I already talked to him. He told me he's not running a charity and he doesn't have any that would be as nice as the one we're looking for anyway."

"He's such a curmudgeon," Knobby states, as the other elves around the table avoid eye contact with one another so they don't burst out laughing at the irony of those words.

"Mrs. Claus wants to make a speech at the party." Wally stares hard at his notes, ignoring Bobby as he pointedly places his arm around Holly's shoulders.

"Tom does too," Holly says. "Obviously *he* won't be allowed to. How long do you all need to set up?"

"Well between us, the other holiday heads and our army of employees..." Wally looks out over the hundreds of elves bustling around the workshop like madmen, trying to fulfill the last minute requests of the children around the world. "I think it should take us about ten minutes."

"Which gives us plenty of time to get our buzz on before Santa gets back from his flight!" Bobby exclaims excitedly.

"Yeah, baby!" Willy leans across the table to high-five Bobby while Wally and Jolly exchange an exasperated look.

"Why can't you two ever act your age?" Knobby demands angrily. "When *I* was your age I *never*--"

"*If*, for some reason, you *can't* get everything set up by dawn," Holly cuts across, as though talking to a group of five-year-olds. "Just give me a call and I'll figure out some way to distract Santa."

"You're going on his flight with him?" Wally blinks, looking up in surprise.

"Well, yeah, obviously!" Holly meets his eyes. "He always brings his executive assistant with him."

"Wow," Wally breathes. "Your first flight."

"Yup," Holly smiles. "One year in the job already, I can't believe it!"

"Neither can I," Wally replies, as the other elves around the table exchange awkward looks. "Well, good luck. You'll need it. He flies that sleigh like a maniac."

"I'm sure I can handle it," Holly boasts confidently.

"That's right, baby," Bobby nods his agreement. "You're excellent at *handling* things."

Holly giggles like a little schoolgirl as Frank gags, Knobby shakes his head in exasperation and Willy adds his chortling to the mix. Had Wally not been so preoccupied with worrying about Holly's safety (Why should he? He promised himself he'd stop obsessing over her.), he would have noticed the pitying look Jolly throws his way.

"Ho, ho, ho," Santa chuckles. "You two *are* persistent, aren't you?"

Pia and Tuss are standing in Santa's office. Usually spotless, the naughty or nice list is covering most of the floor and Santa's desktop is in disarray, littered with cookie crumbs and candy cane wrappers. The old man himself is sitting at his desk, exhausted but still as jolly as ever.

"We just think you may be rushing this whole retirement thing," Tuss says gently, taking great care not to step on the ancient list as he paces closer to Santa. "You're the *best* Santa Claus who's ever worked for us-"

"I'm the *only* Santa Claus who's ever worked for you," Santa winks, his eyes twinkling.

"We'd just love if you'd reconsider and stay on with us. Just for a few more years. Right?" Tuss turns to Pia who has not spoken one word since entering the office. She's standing as still as a statue and is just as stone-faced.

"Right," Pia nods her agreement, biting her lower lip as she eyes the old man hopefully. "Just…give us enough time to train someone new."

"I gave you a year's notice," Santa laughs as he stands up and stretches with a huge sigh. He picks up a tiny snow globe off of a shelf and gives it a shake. As he watches the snow swirl within, he continues. "Tuss. Pia. As flattered as I am by your offer, I'm going to have to decline."

"But--"

"I love this job more than anything." Santa holds up a hand to stop Pia from interrupting. "Except maybe my wife and the reindeer. And I'm going to miss it more than you know. Especially my elves – I don't know *how* I'm going to be able to transition back to making my own bed, and cooking my own food, and doing my own laundry when I leave! But I'm getting tired. I've been sitting at this same desk and flying the same sleigh for centuries. It's *exhausting*."

"We understand that, but--"

"But it's been the love of the children that has kept me doing it year in and year out," Santa plows on. "Knowing that my visits bring smiles to their faces on Christmas morning is the greatest feeling in the world. But it isn't the same anymore. Now they're getting selfish and spoiled. They don't wait for Christmas to get what they want, their parents just get them everything as soon as they ask for it. I don't get nearly as many thank you letters as I used to, and it's just…" Santa sighs. "*Disheartening* to see the world changing around me like this. I just can't keep up with it and I believe it's *unfair* to the children of this *new* world to have a Santa Claus so stuck in the past. You know what they say — you can't teach an old dog new tricks!" He chuckles. "I just think the best thing for the kids of the world, *and* for Corporate, is to find a new Santa Claus who can change with the times. I think it's the best thing for my marriage as well. I've neglected Mrs. Claus a lot over the years."

Pia blinks in surprise. Months of trying to stop him from retiring and she had never heard him lay out his reasons as clearly as this.

"We can't replace *Santa Claus*," she manages to say. "You're the best! You're--"

"I'm sorry, Pia," Santa interrupts. "But I've made up my mind. You need to accept that."

Tuss nods his understanding, sticking a hand forward for Santa to take. "I'll let Corporate know immediately," he says, throwing Pia a pitying look. "It's been an honor working so closely with you this past year."

"And you too, Tuss." Santa shakes his hand. "Don't change! Stay on that nice list."

"I'll do my best," Tuss laughs before turning and hurrying from the office, leaving Pia and Santa alone.

"I guess this is it then," Pia says curtly.

"I'm afraid so, my dear," Santa replies.

"Well, it was an honor." She inclines her head slightly as she sticks out her hand for Santa to take, but is taken by surprise when the old man hurries around his desk and engulfs her in a hug instead.

"Don't lose your faith in others, Pia," Santa whispers. "Even if you lose it in me. I'm sorry I can't stay."

"Good-bye, Santa." Pia disengages herself from the man's arms and hurries from his office without a backwards glance, blinking back tears.

"God rest ye merry, gentleman,

Let nothing you dismay."

Pia hurries through the workshop, lost in her thoughts. Santa *can't* retire, he just *can't*. She'd be a laughing stock with Corporate if she let it happen.

"Remember Christ our Savior,
Was born on Christmas day."

All the good she had done for the company this past year - all the improvements she had made to how the other holidays were run - would be forgotten by her superiors in light of this colossal fuck-up. It was a blow she would not be able to withstand.

"To save us all from Satan's power,
When we were gone astray."

She'll have to come up with an eleventh-hour play, that's all. There has to be *something* she can do to change his mind. And who the fuck is *he* anyway to lecture her on giving up on people? He's giving up on the entire company…on all of the children in the *world*.

"O tidings of comfort and joy,
Comfort and joy,
O tidings of comfort and joy."

So lost in her thoughts, Pia doesn't even see the elf moving in her direction, a huge stack of wrapped gifts in his arms. Walking directly into him, she knocks him over and the gifts go flying everywhere as Pia herself falls onto her ass.

"What the *fuck?*" she yells.

"I'm sorry," the terrified elf says.

"Watch where you're fucking going next time, you midget piece of shit!" Pia snaps, pulling herself to her feet and watching in disdain as the elf scurries around, gathering his dropped presents.

"He said he was sorry."

369

Pia whips around at the voice to see Wally, Holly, Frank and some other elves she doesn't know by name, and doesn't *want* to know by name, sitting around a table in the middle of the workshop, having a meeting of some sort.

"What the fuck did you say to me?" she challenges, stepping nearer to Wally.

"Uh…" Wally clears his throat and readjusts his glasses. "It's just – it was an accident. That he apologized for," he adds pointedly.

"Nobody asked your fucking opinion! What the hell are you all doing just sitting around, anyway?" she demands, her eyes moving from elf to elf around the table. "Christmas is in ten fucking days and you're just sitting around like giant clumps of dog crap?"

"We're planning Santa's surprise retirement party," Holly explains.

"In the middle of Santa's workshop?" Pia asks. "Get back to fucking work, there's no need to have a retirement party."

"But--"

"I SAID GET BACK TO FUCKING WORK!" Pia yells so loud that the elf choir stops singing immediately and all of the elves, so busy building and wrapping last minute toys, stop what they're doing to look in her direction. "*All* of you!" Pia continues, her face red. "Get the fuck back to work!"

She storms toward the exit, kicking the abominable snow monster, who is putting the star on top of the giant Christmas tree, in the heel as she walks by. He roars loudly and trips into the tree, knocking it down and sending the elves nearest it running for cover.

As she pushes her way out of the workshop, the last thing that Pia hears is the elf choir resuming their singing, this time crooning the lyrics of *You're a Mean One, Mr. Grinch.*

"Oh, would you grow up? You're one hundred and five years old! You're going to *die* soon! Don't let that bitch ruin your last few weeks as Caleb."

Father Time is sitting beside Caleb in his office, patting the old Baby New Year on the back reassuringly as he gasps for air and tears spill down his ancient face.

"But I l-love her!" Caleb whines, wiping his nose with the sleeve of Father Times' robes. "And she was using me all this time!"

"At least you finally figured it out," Father Time says in disgust, as he stares at his snot-stained sleeve. "I was beginning to think you were brain damaged. It wouldn't be the first time. Fifty-years ago when you were reborn, you were convinced you were a cat! I'm still not quite sure I managed to get the smell of urine completely out of my carpet." Caleb wails harder as Father Time rolls his eyes. "Stop crying," he continues, exasperated. "It's going to be all right! In a few weeks when you die and come back - preferably as a girl this time if the universe doesn't *completely* hate me - you won't even remember her!"

"How could I ever forget her?" Caleb declares, breaking into fresh sobs.

"Uh…is this a bad time?"

Father Time turns to see Frank standing in the doorway of his office, looking at Caleb awkwardly, a manila folder in his hands and an empty sack over his shoulder.

"Does it look like a good time?" Father Time snaps as he absentmindedly rubs Caleb's back. "Baby New Year is driving himself insane over some she-devil of a woman and I have to take time out of *my* fucking busy day to comfort him. Does he *care* that New Year's Eve is seventeen days away? Of course not! No one does - not even Pia! She's too fucking obsessed with Santa's imminent departure to realize that the only reason she spent a *year* here was because New Year's Eve underperformed *last* year!"

"Speaking of Santa…" Frank steps into the office, waving the envelope in front of Father Time. "I'm collecting money for his retirement gift. We each have to give five gold bars."

"Of course we do," Father Time mumbles, snapping his fingers so that ten tiny gold bars appear from thin air. "This should take care of me and Caleb."

"T-thank y-you," Caleb sobs, wiping tears from his eyes with his snot-covered hands.

"Uh…there's a card too," Frank says to Father Time, as he deposits the gold bars in his sack. "Maybe you should sign for Caleb as well…" He eyes Baby New Year's old, bony, liver-spotted and snot-covered hands, feeling sick.

Father Time wrenches the envelope from the tiny elf and takes out the card. "Even the other elves make you do their bitch-work, huh?" he remarks, signing his name.

"Not for much longer," Frank proudly informs him. "Once there's a *new* Santa in town, I'll get the respect I deserve."

"Keep dreaming," Father Time snorts, dropping the card back into the envelope before handing it back to Frank. "Because you're going to be sorely disappointed when the new one turns out worse than the old one."

"Don't even joke about that," Frank says gloomily.

"All I'm saying is be careful what you wish for," Father Time points out wisely. "You're wishing away the devil you know. What if the new one treats you the same way? Or *worse?*"

"Then I'm going to fucking quit and become a dentist."

"You know who has the nicest teeth?" Caleb sobs.

"The Tooth Fairy?" Frank hazards a guess as Father Time rolls his eyes.

"P-Pia!" Caleb buries his face in his hands, wailing, and as Father Time starts to rage at him once again to grow up and act his age, Frank hurries from the room.

Of *course* he has to be the one to collect the money – because he fucking *loves* getting involved in the personal lives of everyone he doesn't give a shit about at the North Pole.

Tuss is standing at Mother Nature's coffee cart in the lobby of the building, only half-listening to the woman who runs it. She's once again complaining about her latest letters to Corporate.

"I just don't understand," she is ranting. "I'm Mother Nature! They have to reinstate me! You people think you can just walk right in here and change how things are done – no offense, dear. You're very sweet. It's your *partner* who needs a lesson in manners."

"Uh-huh," Tuss replies absentmindedly. "I understand."

As Mother Nature continues on, he stares out across the lobby, his mind drifting. Jack Frost is sitting at the front security desk, typing furiously into a computer, and sitting at the little coffee tables in front of Mother Nature's cart are Ted, Tom, Francis, T.J. and Tilly, who are having their monthly "Animals in the Workplace" meeting. Until ten minutes ago, Tuss had no idea that such a group existed and he was absolutely enthralled when they spoke their pledge:

"We are animals, and that is good. We are not human, and that is not bad. There's no one I would rather be than me. It's better to fly free than cease to be."

Tuss is currently blocking out Mother Nature's words and trying to eavesdrop on what the members of the group are speaking about. Sitting at a table near the meeting is Howie, cradling a cup of coffee in his paws and glancing hopefully at the group.

"I still haven't gotten my movie," Tilly is saying sadly, her antlers even seeming to droop. "Maybe if a few of you try and request it, they'll feel bad and send us a copy."

"I'm not going to sit here and listen to you try to tell us the story of that stupid peewee hockey team one more time," snaps Tom. "Today's topic is: Bladder Control – How to Make it to the Litter Box On Time."

Francis clears his throat. "I believe we have something else to discuss first." He eyes Howie sitting at the nearby table.

Tom heaves a sigh. "*Fine*. If we *must* go through this again! Howie thinks he qualifies to be a member of our exclusive club, even though he's technically a wolf*man* and *men* are *not* considered *animals* the last time I checked."

"Last time *I* checked, men *are* animals," Mother Nature calls over.

Tom ignores this. "Let's put it to a vote, shall we? All for him joining?"

Tilly and Francis both vote yes.

"All opposed?"

Tom and T.J. both raise their wings as Howie sits on the edge of his seat, a hopeful look in his wolfish eyes.

"I don't know," Ted sighs.

"He's not an animal," Tom insists angrily. "Just vote no and we can get on to learning about bladder control like we all want!"

Howie can be heard making a dog-like whining sound as Ted's eyes dart from Tom to the wolfman before back to the turkey. "I can't think about this right now! I have bigger problems! My pen pal was supposed to send me some pictures and I still haven't heard anything. Do you think that means they don't like me anymore?" He pops a few pills into his mouth.

"Oh, forget it," Howie mumbles, getting up from his seat and sadly walking away toward the elevators.

Tom looks very happy to see him go. "Good. Now we can get on with things."

"But what about my problem?" Ted whines.

"One hour isn't *nearly* enough time to help you with your problems, Ted," Tom says spitefully. "Now, bladder control! Ten things you need to know!"

"I'm sorry, dear," Mother Nature places a hand on Tuss' arm, bringing him back to their conversation. "Here – here's your coffee." She passes one to him from behind the counter before asking, "What is it you wanted to see me about?"

"I actually need some advice," Tuss says, inwardly relieved that they are finally getting to the point. "On…uh…*women*."

"Oh?" Mother Nature smiles. "What can I help you with?"

"Well, you know," Tuss scratches the back of his head awkwardly as he lowers his voice so the animals sitting a few feet away can't eavesdrop on him like he did on them. "Christmas is coming up--"

"It's kind of hard to miss that fact living up at the North Pole, dear," Mother Nature jokes.

Tuss laughs. "Yes, well," he clears his throat. "I was just wondering…uh…what women look for in the perfect Christmas gift."

"I see," Mother Nature says thoughtfully. "Is this woman your girlfriend?"

"Uh…well…" Tuss goes red in the face. "She's a girl…who is a friend."

"I get it." Mother Nature winks. "Well, what type of things does this girl in question like?"

Teeth. She likes teeth. But Tuss does not want to divulge this revealing fact to the old woman, so he merely shrugs nonchalantly. "You know…uh…normal stuff."

Mother Nature blinks, waiting for him to elaborate, but when he does not, she responds, "Well, women really like gifts that come from the heart. You know, something personal. It's not about how much you spend, but how much thought you put into it."

"Hmm…" Tuss mulls this over for a moment, before saying, "Thanks. I have to go."

"Good luck, sweetie!" Mother Nature calls after him as Tuss hurries toward the elevators behind the security desk at which Jack Frost is still sitting.

"How's your new security system coming along?" Tuss asks, pressing the up button. "You know, since the whole Sandman mishap?"

"It's not important," Jack Frost grins, typing furiously into his computer.

"I think security is *very* important," Tuss replies seriously.

"Learn to take a joke, Tuss." Jack rolls his eyes. "I've been managing the security of this place as long as it's existed – hiding it from the prying eyes of adventurous mortals and their *pesky* satellites. We've never had an incident before--"

"Except at some point they must have seen something to realize that Santa Claus lives at the North Pole," Tuss points out.

"That was years ago!" Jack says defensively. "Before satellites! Some fucking explorer accidentally saw the workshop. That was *long* before the other holidays set up camp here! Give me a break, we haven't had an incident since."

"Well…good." Tuss nods. "Keep it that way. Keep up the good work."

The elevator doors finally ping open and Frank the elf comes

———

stumbling out, lugging a heavy brown sack over his shoulder.

"Hi Frank," Tuss says.

"Yeah, hi," the elf replies, looking around the lobby and letting out a small sigh of relief. "Oh good, I can kill two birds with one stone!"

Throwing a look at Tom and T.J., Tuss replies, "Phrasing. You don't want them complaining to HR."

"You know what I mean," Frank grumbles, rolling his eyes as Jack laughs. "Excuse me, everyone," he calls out to the lobby at large. Everyone turns to face the elf, who pulls himself up to stand on Jack's desk so that they all can see him. "I'm collecting five gold bars from everybody for Santa's retirement gift and I also have a card here for everybody to sign!" He waves the envelope he's holding through the air. "So...pay up."

As Mother Nature, Jack, Tuss and the animals make their money appear from thin air, Tom clucks disapprovingly.

"Santa already gets enough attention all year round!" he gobbles indignantly. "I'm not chipping in to give him more just because he's retiring."

"Oh, let's not talk about it," Francis replies, his whiskers quivering. "I'm going to miss him."

"Me too," Ted agrees. "He always calls off the Boogeyman's Shadow when it's terrifying me!"

"He is very nice, eh?" Tilly nods her antlered head as T.J. screeches his agreement loudly.

"Nice? Ha!" Tom folds his wings across his chest and looks around the lobby stubbornly. "It's just an act he puts on so he's able to break into people's houses and steal their food! As if he needs more calories. It's not even good food anyway – milk and cookies. Bor-*ring*! My holiday has delicious, succulent, plump turkeys! And all kinds of amazing side dishes!"

"You realize how disturbing that is, don't you, my dear?" Mother Nature asks, waving Frank over toward her so she can sign the card.

"It's the truth," Tom states firmly, staring darkly as the card is passed around and everyone begins to hand Frank their money. "And I'm not signing that *or* contributing a single bar to that old pervert. The only thing I'm going to do is help him pack his bags so he can be on his way out of here in nine days--"

"Fifteen hours, twenty-three minutes and four seconds," Frank finishes, taking Tom by surprise. "What? I'm excited too."

Tuss sighs deeply as he watches the exchange and remembers that he still has to call Corporate and inform them that Santa's leaving. It's a phone call he's dreading making, but he just has to do it and get it over with because Pia never will. But still, he thinks it will be twenty times easier to do that terrible chore than find the perfect Christmas gift for Regina.

Pia is sitting alone in a corner of the cafeteria staring down at a plate full of leftover Thanksgiving dinner. Compared to the normal lunch offerings of stale fruitcake, candy corn and old Easter chocolate, today's lunch is a gourmet meal and yet, Pia is still disgusted by it.

Maybe it's not so much disgust with the food, she thinks, as much as disgust with her general place in life. Corporate had not yet called to lace into her about Santa's plan to leave, but she knows it is coming. *Eventually.* Who knew if Tuss had even told them yet?

"Penny for your thoughts?"

Pia looks up to see the Boogeyman has slid into the seat across from her, his shark-like teeth bared in a hideous grin. Behind him, his Shadow looms protectively.

"Fuck off, I'm on my lunch break," Pia snaps, scooping up a spoonful of now cold mashed potatoes and shoving them into her mouth.

"I've never seen you take a break before," the Boogeyman notes as his Shadow shakes its head. "You must be preoccupied."

"Gee, you think?" Pia snaps. "Now – fuck. Off."

"I think I'm going to stay right here." The Boogeyman crosses his arms across his chest and stares at her, tauntingly.

"What is your damn problem?" Pia demands, slamming both hands on the table in front of her.

"You," the Boogeyman replies simply. "But I'm going to offer you a word of advice despite the fact that I despise you."

"Oh yeah? And what the hell is that?"

"Stop obsessing over getting Santa to stay here," the Boogeyman states. "He's not going to change his mind. You're wasting your time."

"What the hell do you know?" Pia snorts. "Mr. 'I'm Keeping Halloween Scary'. Maybe you should learn to do your own fucking job correctly before lecturing me on how the hell to do mine!"

The Boogeyman bristles with annoyance, but before he can respond, Bill appears at their table.

"Uh…Pia?" he clears his throat.

"This day keeps getting worse and worse," Pia mumbles, placing her head in her hands, trying to fight back the massive headache she feels coming over her.

"I just wanted to inquire about whether or not you had found a replacement for Santa yet--"

"That's none of your fucking business, Bill!" Pia yells, glaring at him with a look so fierce, Bill actually takes a few steps back from the table.

"Well…uh…if you haven't," he continues on, avoiding the woman's eyes, rather bravely in his own mind. "I'd like to submit my name forth as a candidate. I have my resume here…"

"You can't be serious," Pia laughs mirthlessly, knocking Bill's resume out of his hand as the Boogeyman's smirk widens on his face. "*You* take over for *Santa*? *You* run *Christmas*? Come back and talk to me when I feel like running this company into the ground."

"I--"

"Pia!"

"What *now*?" Pia yells, frustrated, as Regina hurries over to the table, throwing wary looks at Bill and the Boogeyman. "What the hell do *you* want, jailbird?"

"I just wanted to talk," Regina says with an innocent shrug, folding her arms across her chest. "Have girl talk…you know…chit chat. Talk about Christmas…the holidays…do you and Tuss exchange gifts? I mean to say," she forces out a fake laugh. "Do you have any idea what he might want for…uh…*anything*?"

"Subtle," the Boogeyman says under his breath, making Regina go red in the face.

Neither Bill nor Pia, however, catch onto what the Tooth Fairy is really talking about.

"I don't have time for any more of your bullshit," Pia snaps, standing up quickly. "Honestly, what the hell is wrong with you people? You, stop fucking meddling." She glares at the Boogeyman. "You, stop fucking *existing*," she directs at Bill. "And *you*," she turns to Regina. "Stop…being…fucking…just leave me the fuck alone!"

She storms out of the cafeteria before either of her subordinates even get a chance to reply, sidestepping the attempts of the Boogeyman's Shadow to stop her as she leaves and pushing past Frank the elf who is on his way into the cafeteria to collect money for Santa's gift.

Reaching the hallway, she pounds on the down button to call the elevator and closes her eyes tightly as the sounds of caroling drift all the way up to the eighth floor from the village below.

"On the fifth day of Christmas my true love gave to me:
Five golden rings!
Four calling birds, three French hens, two turtle doves,
And a partridge in a pear tree!
On the sixth day of Christmas my true love gave to me..."

"I hate Christmas," Pia growls angrily to herself, sticking her fingers into her ears to try and block out the joyful singing from below.

Christmas Eve arrives quicker than Pia expects. She is standing, shivering, in the center of Santa's stable. The doors leading outside are thrown wide open and the snow is falling thick and heavy, blowing against the dark sky. Around her, Bobby is hitching the reindeer to the front of Santa's sleigh while Wally, Holly and Frank are helping a horde of elves pack the gifts tightly into the back of the shiny red vehicle. In the corner, Willy and his choir are belting out the lyrics to *Santa Claus is Coming to Town* at the top of their voices.

When Tuss called Corporate to let them know that Santa was retiring, they had reacted exactly as Pia had assumed they would. Angrily. Wanting to know why they were not informed earlier, they had verbally attacked Pia and made it clear that if she wanted to keep her position and not get demoted, she'd have to find a way to stop Santa from leaving. Tuss, of course, was barely chastised – he had way too many connections in *much* higher places, and no matter what happened with Santa, or how much Pia was going to be punished, he would be okay. As much as she tried to act like she was above him, she knew they would never be equals. Not to Corporate.

Pia had made a few desperate, last minute attempts to try and get Santa to reconsider his position. Nobody would ever be able to say she didn't try her hardest. She baked warm, gooey chocolate chip cookies for him; she had tried personality mirroring and sending gifts to him from the anonymous children of the world (and had subsequently blown that great idea by accidentally putting her signature on the tags); she had tried holding Frank hostage, only to realize Santa wasn't quite sure who Frank was, and had even considered kidnapping his wife, but had gotten bitten in the ass by Rudolph when she had tried to break into the Claus' house in the dead of night. At her lowest, Pia even tried declaring her love to the old man.

"I'm in love with you!" she had shouted, while eating dinner with Mr. and Mrs. Claus one night.

Both husband and wife had frozen with their forks raised halfway to their mouths, eyes wide.

"Excuse me?" Mrs. Claus asked.

Pia had ignored the old woman and stared into Santa's twinkling blue eyes.

"I'm in love with you," she said, trying to choke back her disgust. "I've been trying to deny my feelings all year long, but I don't think I can live without you. Please don't leave. We can have fun. I know we can. I just want you to bend me over the table and…" She swallowed hard. "And…" She stared at the ancient man across from her, who had turned red with embarrassment. "Nope, can't do it. Absolutely not. Not worth it. I'm sorry. I have to go."

And she had hurried away from Santa and Mrs. Claus to go and vomit, their laughter ringing in her ears. Apparently they thought she had been practicing a monologue for the musical adaptation of *Love Actually* that Willy was planning on having his choir perform in the New Year.

But now Pia is out of ideas and out of luck. Santa is moments away from leaving on his last trip around the world and she has no idea how to get him to stay.

"Santa, I need to talk to you!" She marches over to Santa, who is standing beside his sleigh, overseeing all of the hustle and bustle around him.

"Ho, ho, ho, I'm a little busy here, Pia!" Santa beams, as Mrs. Claus hurries over to wrap a scarf around his neck.

"Now, be warm," she instructs her husband. "And pace yourself with the cookies this year. I don't need you coming home and getting sick all morning again."

"I can't help it, I--"

"*Eat slowly*," Mrs. Claus instructs gently, patting his enormous stomach.

"Hard to do when you're on a tight deadline, my dear." Santa kisses her on the cheek, making his wife smile.

"Just fly safe," she says. "I love you."

"And I you, sweetie."

Pia tries not to gag at the display of affection, quickly interrupting, "Santa, I really need a word."

"Can't it wait until morning?" Santa turns to face her, smiling politely.

"No," Pia insists, thinking that if Santa does not change his mind before his retirement party, he'll never change it, and all her many years of hard work at Corporate would be washed away like Atlantis. "This is important."

"Well, alright then," Santa agrees, speaking loudly over the music. "What – oh damn." He pats his jacket, frowning slightly, before turning to Frank. "Frank, have you seen my mittens?"

As both Santa and the tiny elf climb into the sleigh and begin to look under the seat for them, Pia turns to Mrs. Claus.

"Can't you do *anything* to stop your husband from retiring?" she asks.

"He's made up his mind," Mrs. Claus replies sweetly.

"And you think it's a good idea?"

"Honey, I've been trying to get him to retire for *years*," Mrs. Claus laughs. "He deserves it! And so do I, quite frankly. I can't take the cold any longer!"

"But--"

"It's *his* decision," Mrs. Claus says gently, resting a hand on Pia's shoulder. "And I'll support him in whatever he chooses."

Pia sighs deeply as Mrs. Claus turns away to assist her husband in looking for his mittens. This was it. It was over. There is nothing more she can do to convince the old couple not to leave.

"Fascinating."

Pia whips around quickly at the familiar and annoying voice to find Bill standing right behind her, a notebook in hand. He is scribbling furiously in it as he observes all the activity around him.

"What the hell are *you* doing here?"

"Watching Santa's technique," Bill explains, stopping to watch a few elves scurry past. "In case I get the job--"

"It will be a cold day in hell before you get Christmas, Bill," Pia snaps angrily. "I'd sooner take the job myself than see it go to you."

"It may be out of your hands," Bill winks.

"What the fuck is that supposed to mean?" Pia demands, clenching her hands into fists.

Bill shrugs, smugly.

"I ASKED WHAT THE FUCK THAT'S SUPPOSED TO MEAN!" Pia yells, wrapping her hands around Bill's throat, sending the elves nearest them running away in fright.

"Pia!" Tuss has arrived and hurries over toward Pia and Bill, who is now turning blue. "Let go of him!"

Tuss pries Pia's fingers away from the man's neck, causing Bill to fall to

384

the ground, gasping for air. "You're crazy!"

"And you're a fucking loser, Bill!" Pia yells at the top of her voice, as he scrambles to his feet, shaking. "Now get out of here!"

"But--"

"GET THE FUCK OUT OF HERE!"

And Bill, terrified for his life, trips over his overlarge feet as he hurries from the stable, passing by Cupid, who is on his way in.

"Being your usual, charming self, I see?" Cupid grins at Pia.

"Bite me."

"With pleasure," Cupid says, coming to a halt beside her and Tuss, who remains staring at the door Bill ran off through, speechless. "What did you say to him?"

"I told him to get the fuck out," Pia reports, the anger still in her voice. "You should do the same thing. What the hell are *you* doing here anyway?"

"Came to watch Santa take off for his last flight." Cupid shrugs. "It's a momentous occasion, you know."

"Pia," Tuss rounds on her, finding his voice again. "What the hell was that?"

"He was taunting me!"

"You strangled him," Tuss says, his eyes wide with shock. "He can file a complaint against you!"

"Oh, big deal," Pia waves her hand through the air. "He's not the first person I've strangled this year. They can add his complaint to that pile of shit Mother Nature's been sending in all year. And every other moronic complaint someone's filed against me. The pile's probably to the ceiling by now."

"I'd be careful if I were you," Tuss says, the pitying sympathy evident in his voice. "They're already pissed enough."

"He's right, you know," Cupid adds, his tone of voice serious for once.

"No one asked you," Pia snaps, massaging her temples, which are beginning to throb. "*Either* of you," she shoots at Tuss.

"We're just trying to help," Tuss points out. "You could be a little more grateful--"

"*Fuck*," Pia yells, throwing an annoyed look at the elf choir in the corner. "Don't they ever shut the fuck up?"

Before either Tuss or Cupid can answer her rhetorical question, however, the sounds of clapping and cheering catch their attention. Turning, they direct their gaze toward Santa, who is climbing into his sleigh followed by Holly, who appears nervous but excited.

"Buckle up," Wally is saying to Holly. "Safety first."

"She'll be fine, my boy!" Santa laughs. "I make this trip every year and I always come back in one piece!"

"For the past fifty-years you've always let something fall from your sleigh when you hit inclement weather," Wally points out.

"I'll be fine," Holly says adamantly.

Wally bites his lip nervously before leaning in and impulsively kissing her quickly on the lips. Pulling away, fireworks going off inside of his head, he straightens his now foggy glasses and looks at Holly, whose mouth has dropped open and is staring at him, speechless.

"I…" Wally clears his throat, going red in the face as Holly, Santa, Frank and Mrs. Claus, who are nearest him, all stare in surprise. "I…uh…I just--"

"Move!"

Pia shoves Wally aside, saving him from having to come up with an excuse as to why he kissed the woman, and approaches the sleigh with Tuss and Cupid.

"Pia," Santa nods at her, grabbing at his reigns, his hands tucked snugly into the mittens Frank found for him. "Tuss. Cupid."

"Good luck, Santa," Tuss smiles at him.

"Can you leave this note for Elaine Geller in New York City?" Cupid asks, passing a folded piece of paper to Santa. "It explains why I can't be with her. How NASA chose me to go on their new shuttle taking off for Mars."

Wally sidles back over to the sleigh and, ignoring Holly's still wide eyes, stares at Santa and points at a headset sticking out of his ear.

"If you need anything, just give me a call," he instructs. "We'll be tracking you to make sure everything goes smoothly."

"We'll be *fine*, Wally," Santa says gently. "I'm used to this flight by now."

Wally nods before stepping back to join Frank and the remaining throng of elves.

"Safe flight, Santa," Pia mutters, shaking nervously, mixed emotions coursing through her body at this historical event.

"Thank you, Pia," Santa smiles before turning to Holly. "You ready?"

Holly nods, staring past the reindeer pawing the ground impatiently, and out of the stable doors at the night sky beyond.

"Right then," Santa grabs the reigns tightly and begins to shout. "Now Dasher, Now Dancer, Now Prancer and Vixen! On Comet, on Cupid, on Donner and Blitzen!"

"On Rudolph!" Holly yells.

"To the top of the porch! To the top of the wall!" Santa calls as Holly joins in for the last part. "Now dash away, dash away, dash away all!"

And with whinnying sounds, the reindeer break into a run, dragging the heavy sleigh behind them. Most of the elves run after it, applauding and cheering, until it finally lifts off of the ground and disappears up into the snowy night sky beyond. In the darkness above, Santa's distant, cheerful voice can be heard yelling, "Merry Christmas to all, and to all a good night!"

Wally, who has remained in the stable, turns to Frank nervously. "Listen," he says quickly. "You can't tell Bobby what I did."

"What are you talking about?" Frank asks innocently.

"Kissing Holly."

Frank rolls his eyes, smiling. "I don't think I have to, idiot."

"You kissed Holly?"

Wally freezes before slowly turning on the spot to face Bobby, who has walked up behind them.

"Bobby," he croaks, his voice an octave higher than normal. "What are…uh…what are you doing here?"

"You kissed Holly?" he demands again angrily.

"I can explain," Wally begins.

But Bobby doesn't wait for an explanation. He punches Wally so hard, he breaks the bridge of the elf's glasses and sends him flying to the floor.

"Is everything okay over here?" Tuss asks, joining the group.

"Everything's fine, *dad*," Bobby states.

"You knew he was behind me, didn't you?" Wally groans, as Frank helps him to his feet and Bobby smugly walks away.

"Yup," Frank says uncaringly.

"I think I need tape," Wally says gloomily, holding the two halves of his broken glasses out in front of him. As the elves begin to filter back into the stable, chattering excitedly, Wally calls loudly, "Come on, everyone. Let's go set up the twelfth floor for the party."

Tuss watches as a mass of green and red heads out of the workshop before noticing Pia still standing at the stable doors, staring up into the night sky.

"Maybe you should go talk to her," Cupid suggests, stepping up beside him.

"She won't talk to me," Tuss sighs, but feeling bad for the woman, he walks up to her anyway. "It's cold out here," he notes, folding his arms across his chest.

"It's the fucking North Pole," Pia replies without looking at him.

"Are you okay?" Tuss asks nervously, glancing sideways at her.

"I'm fine."

Silence falls between the two of them.

"You tried, you know," Tuss speaks up finally, wiping snow from his hair. "That's the best you could do."

"Clearly I didn't try hard enough," Pia says stiffly.

"There's nothing--"

"Can you just leave me the fuck alone, please?" Pia snaps, looking at Tuss full in the face. He is surprised to see that her face is red and her eyes watery. "I just – I need a damn minute."

389

Tuss nods his head, understanding. "I'll be inside helping to set up for the party," he informs her. "If you need to talk," he adds. "Or need a stiff drink," he smiles before hurrying away.

Pia scoffs as she turns back to the dark night sky again, finally alone.

Or so she thinks.

"If you need something stiff that's more fleshy, I can help you with that."

"What the hell do *you* want?" Pia demands, turning to face Cupid, who is now standing beside her, his hands deep in the pockets of his perfectly pressed Armani suit.

"I want *you*."

"Well, I *don't* want you," Pia states. "I'll *never* want you, so stop trying."

"I'm persistent." Cupid shrugs. "Just like you. What?" he asks innocently, as Pia glares at him. "It's not a bad thing. Even if our trying doesn't pay off, it-—"

"What do you *really* want?" Pia demands. "Seriously? Why did you even come down here tonight?"

Cupid hesitates for a moment, going slightly pink in the face, before answering, "I came for *you*. I thought you could use somebody to talk to. I knew it was going to be a tough night for you."

"I don't *need* anybody to fucking talk to," Pia snaps. "I'm not a lost little girl. I'm not a pathetic mortal. I'm not…I'm not made of glass! I wish people would stop treating me like I'm about to break!"

"No, you're definitely not any of those things," Cupid agrees with a small smile. "But everybody hurts sometimes."

"Not me," Pia says. "So stop feeling bad for me and go."

Cupid nods and walks inside without another word, leaving Pia alone with nothing but the snowy night sky and her own thoughts.

Holly shivers in her seat, watching the snow flutter in the sky around her as Santa directs his sleigh and reindeer down East toward Australia. Santa is staring straight ahead, smiling brightly to himself as he sings under his breath.

"Thanksgiving is the perfect day,
Eat and drink your cares away."

Wally kissed her. Holly still can't believe the elf's assuming confidence. He *kissed* her.

"Sexy turkey on a silver tray,
It's the best American holiday."

"You know that song insults Christmas, right?" Holly asks, sounding more annoyed than she intends.

"I can't help it," Santa replies. "It's a very catchy tune."

"Terrible lyrics though," Holly says, leaning over the side of the sleigh to see how high up they are. All she can see are clouds.

"Are you alright, my dear?" Santa asks. "You seem tense."

"I'm fine," Holly says.

"Not afraid of heights, are you?"

"No, nothing like that," Holly responds politely. Then, after a moment of hesitation, she blurts out, before she can stop herself, "What do you think of Wally?"

"Wally?" Santa repeats. "He's such a nice elf. Hard worker. Clearly in love with you."

"He is?"

"You haven't realized that yet? Ho, ho, ho. Oh, Holly. Perhaps I should have gotten you a clue for Christmas this year!"

Holly blinks, unsure of whether or not she should be offended by the old man's statement. As silence falls between the two of them once more, she finds herself thinking of the geeky elf back at the North Pole. The one who, apparently, hadn't just been trying to get into her pants the entire year.

He wasn't bad looking and the kiss was far from terrible, even though it was rushed. He had nice breath. And there *was* something very sweet about him…maybe it *wouldn't* be so horrible for her if she gave it a shot with him. Who knows? Maybe it would even work! But what would she do about Bobby?

She sighs deeply as the sexy, muscular elf floats to the forefront of her mind. Nothing says Christmas like personal drama.

The twelfth floor of the building is packed. Lights are glittering on the trees, garland and wreaths lining the walls, and hundreds of elves are setting up tables with alcohol and all kinds of food, ranging from candy canes to figgy pudding. On a stage against one of the back windows, Willy is directing his choir in an endless cascade of Christmas carols – *Rudolph the Red Nosed Reindeer* followed by *Frosty the Snowman*, which is followed by *Jingle Bells*.

Among the elves, the other holiday heads are mingling with one another, laughing and chatting, drinks in hand. In a corner, Frank is trying to wake up the Sandman, who is slouching against a window fast asleep, the colors of the Aurora Borealis dancing over his face.

"Wake up!" Frank is shouting in the old man's ear, shaking his body. "Wake up, you lazy bastard! I need five gold bars from you! I need you to sign Santa's card!"

"No, mommy," the Sandman murmurs. "I don't want to go to school today. The teacher beats us."

"Waste of time," Jack Frost says in a sing-song voice as he walks by, winking at the elf.

"Ugh." Frank kicks the Sandman in his shin. "Has anyone seen Cormac?"

"Does anybody *ever* see the leprechaun?" the Boogeyman asks, standing a few feet away with Francis.

"Well, I think that's pretty much everybody then," Frank mutters, reaching inside of the Sandman's pajama pants and pulling a gold bar from one of his pockets. "Where's Wally?" He grabs the end of his giant sack of money resting on the floor and begins to drag it across the room with great difficulty.

As he disappears into the sea of people, grunting under the weight of the bag, he passes Mrs. Claus who is standing in the center of the room, instructing a few elves who are hanging a banner that reads: 'Congratulations Santa Claus!'

"Higher," Mrs. Claus decides, staring up at the glittering red and green banner. "The left side has to be higher!"

"Mrs. Claus!"

Tom the turkey, appearing happier than anyone has ever seen him in the month of December, hurries over to the old woman, bags in hand. Behind him, his six turkey employees march in unison, each carrying suitcases of their own.

"Oh, Tom!" Mrs. Claus beams at the turkey. "Merry Christmas!"

"Yeah, yeah, Merry Christmas," Tom shrugs off the words, giving a shiver of disgust. "We've taken the liberty of packing all of you and your husband's belongings." He jerks his head at the turkeys behind him. "That way you two can leave immediately after the party! Also, I will not be held responsible for any broken items."

"That's so sweet of you, Tom," Mrs. Claus coos, as Tom tries to suppress a smile at the woman's cluelessness. "Why don't you just leave them over by the stage? That way Santa can be sure to thank you in his speech."

"Will do."

"Oh, and Tom," Mrs. Claus calls after the turkey as he begins to walk away. "Check under the large tree in the corner over there! I think Santa may have left you a gift."

Tom clucks his disapproval as he hurries away, passing Father Time who is standing at a table watching a miserable Caleb do shots of vodka.

"There you go," Father Time says gently. "Just drink your troubles away, there's a good boy."

"Is Pia going to be here tonight?" Caleb asks, his words slurring slightly. "I want to talk to her. I *need* to talk to her."

"You *need* to go to bed," Father Time corrects him. "It's past your bedtime."

"I don't have to listen to you," Caleb spits. "I'm over a century old."

"Only in appearance," Father Time points out.

Pia does emerge from an elevator a few minutes later and stares around the room, depressed and disgusted. The Christmas music echoing throughout the space presses on her eardrums, slowly driving her to drink. In one corner of the room, she notices Ted and Tilly opening gifts that Santa left for them, only feet away from the Boogeyman and the Easter Bunny.

"Wow, a new pill box!" Ted exclaims happily. "There's a compartment for each day of the week!"

"He got me *D2: The Mighty Ducks* and *D3: The Mighty Ducks*!" Tilly cries with excitement. "He finally made my dreams come true! I knew Santa would be able to! I just knew it! Santa can do what even Corporate can't!" She glances closer at her gifts. "What's a Blu-ray?"

"It's like a DVD, but better," Ted explains, as he begins to place five pills into each labeled compartment of his pill box. "You need a special machine to watch them though. I don't know what it's called."

"A Blu-ray player, perhaps?" the Boogeyman supplies sardonically as Francis begins to dig around under one of the Christmas trees.

"But I only have a DVD player," Tilly bows her antlered head sadly. "I guess I have to start asking Corporate for one of *those* now."

"Hey, Ted?" Francis calls, straightening up with an envelope in his hands. "This was under the tree for you too."

"My pen pal!" Ted exclaims happily, grabbing the letter from the Easter Bunny's hands and eagerly tearing it open. "I finally get to see what they look like!" He stares down at a photograph that falls from the envelope. Almost immediately, his tiny eyes go wide with shock. "He's...he's..."

"He's what?" Tilly asks in concern, as she glances down at the photograph, her own eyes widening. "Oh my...oh dear..."

"He's...he's naked!" Ted yells, tears forming in his eyes as he pops an entire week's worth of pills into his mouth and hurries away, panicked and disappointed. "I can't deal with this. I'm going back to being friendless."

"Ted, come back!" Tilly cries, bounding after the groundhog. "Are you alright? I'm worried about you!"

The Boogeyman raises an eyebrow at Francis, who shrugs in response, before reaching down for the picture.

"Hey," the Boogeyman smiles, baring his shark-like teeth as he brings the picture up to his eyes. "I know this man!"

"Thank *you*!" Cupid says, plucking the photo cleanly from the

Boogeyman's twisted hand before bounding away.

"Awesome!" Jack Frost exclaims from behind them, having just arrived at the tree. He has just unwrapped a snowflake-shaped chair bearing his name. "I get my own chair in the conference room now! Hey, Sandy! Wake up! Wake up!" he yells at the sleeping old man in the corner. "I think Santa may have gotten you your own chair too!" He points at a large chair-shaped gift addressed to him beneath the tree.

A few feet away from the unconscious geriatric, Regina and Tuss are talking quietly amongst themselves. Pia begins to walk in their direction when Bill falls into step beside her, hurrying away from T.J. and Cupid.

"Pia!"

"Get the hell away from me," Pia snarls, as she pushes her way through the crowded floor.

"I wanted to apologize for before," Bill pants, beads of sweat sprouting across his forehead as he struggles to keep up with Pia's purposeful stride. "I shouldn't have been so flippant. I know it must be hard to hear that you may lose your job over something you can't control."

"I don't know where the *fuck* you get your information," Pia says in an undertone. "But it's incorrect. I'm not getting fired."

"Demoted then," Bill says, trying (and failing) to hide a smirk. "But regardless of what you want to call it, I just wanted to go over why I should be promoted to Santa's position before you leave."

"Because I want to tie the noose tighter around my neck?"

"Because I'm intelligent, I'm hard working--"

"Annoying as hell and pompous," Pia interrupts. "Now get the fuck away from me before I rip your fucking head off of your disgusting, useless body."

As they near Tuss and Regina, Bill continues, not taking no for an answer, "And with better marketing, we can double the profits of

Christmas! If there's one thing I'm good at, it's marketing. Now that I run Hanukkah as well, we could just lump the two of them together and create one giant holiday that both the Christians and the Jews celebra--"

"I'M NOT GIVING YOU FUCKING CHRISTMAS TO RUIN! GET THAT THROUGH YOUR THICK FUCKING SKULL!" Pia yells so loudly, the elf choir stops singing and everyone in the room turns to look in her direction. "HOW MANY TIMES DO I HAVE TO SAY IT? WHAT THE FUCK IS WRONG WITH YOU?"

"Pia," Tuss says quietly, hurrying over to the two of them. "Calm down."

But Pia cannot calm down. Months of being trapped up at the North Pole, acclimating to their insane ways of life; months of trying (and failing) to stop Santa Claus from retiring; months of dealing with idiots; all these months of frustration come spilling out of her mouth, as her entire body turns a deep shade of red and she begins to shake, making all of the lights flicker above and the floor beneath their feet shake.

"WHAT THE FUCK IS WRONG WITH *ALL* OF YOU?" she roars, turning on the spot and looking around at all of the horrified faces around the room. "YOU'RE ALL WORTHLESS! ALL REPLACEABLE! *ALL* OF YOU! EVERY SINGLE LAST FUCKING ONE OF YOU!"

Tuss opens his mouth to intervene, but immediately thinks better of it. He is sick of playing her conscious; sick of trying to reign her in when she goes off the rails; sick of jumping in to defend her. He has spent an entire year doing that, and it got him nothing. If she wants to lose whatever dignity she has left, that's her own problem, not his.

"THE ONLY REASON WORTH KEEPING THIS FUCKING COMPANY OPEN IS BECAUSE SANTA CLAUS BRINGS IN THE MOST MONEY! AND NOW HE'S FUCKING LEAVING, SO WHAT'S THE POINT? WHAT'S THE FUCKING POINT? NOT JUST ANYONE CAN REPLACE SANTA! ESPECIALLY NOT ANY OF YOU WORTHLESS FUCKING IDIOTS!"

Pia shouts herself into silence, her hands clenched into fists. Bill has backed away from her so quickly, he has fallen onto his ass and crawled behind Regina for cover. After a few moments of silence, the Boogeyman bravely ventures forward.

"*You're* the idiot," the Boogeyman states confidently as his Shadow rises threateningly behind him, nodding its agreement. "We were all doing just fine until *you* came and started trying to change the way everything works around here."

As murmurs of agreement spring up among the crowd, Tom clucks. "Maybe you should listen to some of our ideas! *We're* the ones in the trenches bringing in money for this company! We know how to do things! We've been doing them successfully for *centuries*!"

"Don't fucking talk to me like that," Pia snaps at the bird. "Or I'll cook you for Thanksgiving dinner next year!"

"A cause I'd *gladly* die for," Tom retorts.

"*Christmas* dinner then," Pia says, causing Tom's beak to drop open in horror.

"You do nothing around here other than make our jobs more difficult," Mother Nature pipes up from where she is standing behind Wally and Frank in the crowd. "And make our lives *miserable*."

"And all because you have no life outside of your job," Jack Frost puts in, as T.J. screeches his agreement.

"And no real power with Corporate," Bill bravely ventures. "Right, Sandy?" he glances at the Sandman, still snoozing in the corner.

"Mmm, chocolate chip pancakes," the Sandman mutters dreamily.

Pia stares around in shock and anger, speechless. Every disgruntled expression, every nasty glare, every resentful face at the party is meant for her; she is standing very much alone.

Father Time stares right back at her as he says, "We're not scared of you anymore. Why should we be? You're leaving soon and Corporate needs *us* now more than ever with a new Santa to train!"

"Don't talk to her like--"

But Father Time covers Caleb's mouth with one of his ancient hands before he can finish his objection.

Tuss, feeling guilty, glances over at Regina, who is now standing beside Ted, Tilly, Mrs. Claus and Cupid, and though none of them will downright attack Pia, none of them seem keen to jump to her defense either.

Tuss feels as though this has gone on long enough.

"Let's go outside." He places his hand on Pia's shoulder and steers her toward the elevator bay. "You need to calm down."

"I'm fine. I don't need--"

"Let's go."

As they wait for the metal doors to open, the party slowly begins to resume with the elf choir beginning to, once again, sing *You're a Mean One, Mr. Grinch*.

Once inside of the elevator, Tuss hits the emergency button and turns to Pia, who pulls the normally tight elastic out of her hair, letting it fall down around her shoulders, long and wavy.

"What the *fuck* was that?" she demands. "I've always known that they hate me, but they don't even fucking *respect* me?"

"*Chillax*," Tuss says gently, trying to crack a joke. When Pia doesn't even smile, he continues. "They're just stressed. Everybody gets stressed around the holidays, it's tradition."

"I'm their fucking *boss*! Imagine if I spoke that way to *my* boss!"

"It's Christmas Eve. *Relax* for *once* in your *life*," Tuss says pleadingly.

"Here." He snaps his fingers and a wrapped gift appears in his hands. "Merry Christmas."

He holds it out to Pia who blinks in surprise, taking it from him. "What the hell is this?"

"Open it."

Pia rips apart the paper and opens the box, revealing a pair of tasteful pink heels with a strap at the ankle and a peep toe. She stares silently at them for a moment before asking once again, "What the fuck are these?"

"They're shoes," Tuss replies, his brows furrowed in confusion. "Size eight. I thought you'd…" Pia throws them to the ground. "…Like them."

"I don't need a pity gift from you, *Russ*."

"It's Tuss," Tuss bristles angrily. "*Tuss*. And you *know* it's Tuss. You've known for *years* that my name isn't Russ, or Guss, or Puss, or whatever else you insist on calling me. Stop calling me by the wrong name as some sort of stupid power play! In fact, you know what, Pia?" He stares around the elevator, searching for the right words to vocalize everything he has been pondering lately. "You want to know why people don't respect you? It's because you don't respect anybody. Not even yourself! It's no wonder everybody hates you. If you want people to like you, you have to make an effort with them."

He hits the button to open the doors and rejoins the party raging on the twelfth floor, leaving Pia alone in the elevator, staring down at the rejected shoes with a lot to think about.

"What did you think of New York City, Holly?" Santa asks, as he directs his reindeer away from the concrete jungle toward the suburbs.

"It was beautiful," Holly gushes. "I can't believe how tall the

Rockefeller Center tree is!"

"It gets bigger every year," Santa assures her. "Mortals. Obsessed with size."

Bringing the reindeer and sleigh to a landing on the roof of a small, brick house, Santa steps out, clutching at his lower back.

"Oh - ho, ho," Santa laughs in pain. "The last half of the journey is always when I start to feel it," he admits, as Holly looks at him with concern. "I'll be fine. I can manage." He picks up the large bag of gifts resting in the back of the sleigh and throws it over his shoulder. "I'll be back in a jiffy," he winks.

Climbing into the chimney, Santa allows himself to slide down and lands hard on the pile of ash resting in the grate below. Quietly, he creeps over to the lit Christmas tree a few feet away and opens his sack of presents. Silently, he begins to lay them out beneath the tree, listening to the ticking of the clock on the wall above him.

"There we go, shh." He pulls a small puppy with a bow tied around its neck from his bag. "You're going to love it here," he whispers, placing it down while laughing as it licks at his face. "Little Charlie and Virginia are such nice kids. They've always wanted a dog."

He watches as the puppy turns in a circle under the tree and settles himself amongst the gifts. Santa smiles to himself and walks over to where the milk and cookies are left for him. Shoving them into his mouth whole, Santa chugs the milk and places the empty glass down before turning back toward the chimney. Bending down to pick up his bag, Santa notices something colorful out of the corner of his eye.

A crayon drawing is nestled between two of the stockings on the mantle; a picture of himself holding the hands of two little children, one in a pink shirt and one in blue. Santa picks it up and reads the note that is scrawled across the top in childish handwriting:

Dear Santa,
We love you. Thank you for coming every year and
spreading joy and Christmas spirit to everybody in the

world. We love you.
Love, Charlie and Virginia. (P.S. Mommy helped us with the
spelling.)

Santa's eyes well up with tears as he re-reads the note again and again. It has been so long since he received any kind of appreciation from a child, he forgot how nice it was; forgot that there were children in the world who cared about him and were thankful for what he did year in and year out.

"Are you alright?" Holly asks as he emerges from the chimney, wiping at his eyes and straightening his hat. "There wasn't another raccoon, was there?"

"I'm fine," Santa assures her, smiling widely as he climbs back into the sleigh. "Better than fine. Let's go, boys!"

And with a snap of the reigns, the reindeer take off into the air and ferry Santa over to the roof of the house next door.

This home too ends up having a profound impact on him. No, there are no thank you letters in this house. But there is a little girl lying asleep on the couch, her pink blanket hanging off of her and one arm draped over the edge. Santa gently places the blanket back over her still body, but freezes when he feels something strange under his boot. Looking down and pulling his foot away, he notices a small book lying on the carpet right below her outstretched hand. Curiously, he picks it up and begins to flip through it.

The book is one of those blank-paged autograph books that are given to children in places like Disney World so that they can get signatures from Mickey Mouse, Goofy and other beloved characters. Indeed, flipping through it, Santa sees many signatures scribbled to the girl, Annabelle, ranging from Donald Duck to Bugs Bunny. He smiles to himself, thinking it sweet that the little girl cherished the signatures so much that she even slept with the book in her hands.

And then it hits him like a ton of bricks.

Annabelle had been waiting for *him* – for Santa Claus – to arrive and add his signature to the book. In fact, clutched in her other hand is the red pen she had intended for him to use. Santa's heart melts as he carefully pries the pen from her other hand and adds his signature to her collection, leaving the book open on the nearby coffee table. Little Annabelle is in for an extra surprise come Christmas morning.

Sure, it's not a direct thank you. But attempting to stay awake to meet him and get his autograph in the first place proves that this little girl cares about the man who delivers the presents, rather than just the presents themselves.

Perhaps, Santa thinks, he was wrong about the children of the world. Perhaps they are not all as greedy or ungrateful as he believed them to be.

In fact, Santa runs into many similar situations on his flight that night. Thank you notes and plates of extra cookies; pictures drawn for him and more blank pages for him to sign. At one house he even finds a wrapped gift for himself under the tree, left by a little boy whose dream was to become Santa Claus himself one day.

And as Santa guides his team of reindeer through the air, sitting besides Holly in silence as they travel apartment to apartment, house to house, and to every dwelling in between, he cannot help but think that perhaps it is he who has become jaded with each passing year, not the children. Maybe they have always been this thankful for his yearly visits, but he has just become so used to it and so increasingly exhausted by it, that he slowly became blind to their generosity.

The children of the world would probably miss him when he retired and Santa cannot help but think that he's actually going to miss them all as well. Miss putting smiles on their faces year in and year out…miss how grateful they are to him for visiting…he was going to miss his elf employees and his team of reindeer….miss all of his co-workers up at the North Pole….

Santa Claus is actually going to miss his job when he retires – in less than twenty-four very short hours.

To distract Caleb from his misery, his former babysitters - Clotho, Lachesis and Atropos - have brought a laptop to the party and are sitting in the corner with the ancient-looking man, pointing to something on the screen.

"This is NORAD's website," Clotho explains.

"What's NORAD?" Caleb asks drunkenly, cradling his drink close as he sways back and forth.

"It stands for North American Aerospace Defense Command," Lachesis clarifies, casually taking the alcohol away from her former charge. "They track small aircrafts flying in, out and over North American airspace."

"Fascinating," Caleb says. "Do you know where Pia is? Can this website track her?"

"No," Atropos answers sternly. "Stop worrying about her. Anyway, if you click here..." She clicks a link on the screen and the three sisters burst out laughing at once.

"Is that Santa Claus?" Caleb asks, staring wide-eyed at an image of Santa's sleigh passing over the American Midwest.

"It's what the mortals *think* is Santa Claus," Clotho explains in-between bouts of laughter. "Look, he's animated! And no Holly in sight!"

"They pretend to track him for the mortal children," Lachesis adds, trying to catch her breath. "As if they have the technological capabilities to do that."

"They really have no clue," Atropos agrees with a grin.

"What's so funny over here?" Father Time asks, joining his employees grumpily. "What are you, tracking Santa? Such a waste of time." He shakes his head bitterly. "We have our own holiday to run, but do any of them care? No. Nope. Not at all. It's always Santa, Santa, Santa. You know, I can sometimes see where Tom is coming from with his complaints." He sighs deeply. "Oh well. He did get me a nice new staff this year at least."

Panicked, the Fates glance over to the Christmas tree in the corner that Father Time is pointing at and see a literal wooden staff with a bow tied around it. Sighing with relief, they turn back to the computer screen as Maxwell, Hugh and Hugo join the elf choir on stage and start singing along with them to the tune of *Do They Know It's Christmas?*

Tom and his turkeys are angry with this new choice of song and begin to cluck in disapproval and outrage.

"Yes, they do!" Tom yells. "They always do! It's always about Christmas!" Turning to his fellow birds, he orders them, "Sing! Sing!"

And in different pitches and to different tunes, all of the turkeys begin to sing Tom's disastrous Thanksgiving song. In order to drown them out, the elves begin to sing louder, which only spurs the turkeys on to do the same.

"Boo, you suck!" Agatha yells drunkenly at them.

Howie, unsure of which group she's yelling at, pours himself a large glass of vodka. Straight. "I'm not drunk enough for this," he mutters to himself, downing his drink in one gulp.

On the other side of the room, Tuss is standing with Regina in relative privacy, concealed behind one of the large Christmas trees.

"They sound terrible." Tuss screws up his face, trying to block out the sounds of the turkeys clucking. "I need to talk to them before Santa gets back here. I don't want them ruining his party."

"Santa's used to it," Regina says, placing a hand on his arm. "Don't worry about it. What did he get you for Christmas, anyway?"

"A snow globe," Tuss tells her. "With miniature versions of the North Pole and all of us inside of it."

"Aw, that's cute!" Regina smiles.

Tuss nods. "He said it was so I can remember this place after I leave."

Regina's smile slowly fades. "Well...that was very thoughtful of him."

Tuss nods his agreement. The two stare into one another's eyes awkwardly for a moment before Regina plasters a fake grin on her face and says, "I got you something too."

"Really?" Tuss asks, grinning. "Because it just so happens that *I* got something for *you* as well."

"Oh, me first." Regina claps her hands excitedly as Tuss reaches into his blazer and pulls out a small, wrapped gift. "I love getting gifts." Ripping open the paper, the Tooth Fairy gasps as a purple toothbrush, engraved with her name and lined with diamonds, rolls into her palm.

"It's self-cleaning," Tuss explains. "That'll last for years without you ever having to replace it."

"I love it," Regina replies genuinely, fingering the cleaning utensil that most people would be dismayed to find in their stocking. "Thank you."

"You don't have to thank me," Tuss says sincerely.

Snapping her fingers, Regina's wand appears from thin air and with a wild wave of it, the toothbrush disappears and a wrapped gift appears in Tuss' hands.

"I hope you like it," Regina bites her lip nervously, as Tuss rips the paper carefully.

"If it's from you, I'll love it," Tuss notes, laughing when he sees what the gift is. "Great minds think alike, huh?"

A solid gold nameplate bearing his name is laying in the box.

"I thought it would be nice for your office door," Regina says, her face falling slightly again. "Back at Corporate...something to remember me

_____

by."

She looks down and Tuss, saddened that he only has one week left with this kind, beautiful, loving woman, places his finger beneath her chin.

"Hey," he whispers, lifting her head so that their eyes meet. "I don't need anything to remember you by. How could I ever forget a thing about you?"

Regina smiles as Tuss leans in for a kiss. The kiss is long and tender, and they only break apart when Cupid walks by with a new bounce in his step, singing, *Love is in the Air.*

Breaking apart, embarrassed, Regina and Tuss turn in time to see Cupid wink at them.

"Don't worry, I won't tell anyone!" he calls loudly, walking away. "I'm all for a bit of romance. Besides, I'll be busy for a *long* time with the gift that Santa got me this year!"

"What did he get you?" Tuss asks, placing his arm gingerly around Regina's waist. "Do I even want to know?"

"Lifetime subscriptions to *Playboy* and *Hustler*."

As Regina laughs, Cupid turns his back on them and walks by Wally (now sporting poorly taped together glasses), who is helping Frank hang more garland on one of the trees.

"I'm just worried about her, you know?" Wally is saying. "She's just so small and delicate, and Santa's a maniac with that sleigh! It has nothing to do with how I feel about her, the kiss was just for luck!"

"I really *don't* care, Wally," Frank grumbles. "I really fucking don't."

"That's rude," Wally says, scandalized. "I thought we were friends!"

"Ha!" Frank lets out a laugh. "*Friends*? I can't be *friends* with *anybody* in this building! You're all nuts!"

"Have some Christmas spirit," Wally encourages. "You're an elf, for goodness sake!"

"Fuck Christmas spirit," Frank replies. "I can't take any of this craziness anymore."

And Wally, unsure of what to say, suddenly hurries away to talk to Mrs. Claus when he catches sight of Bobby coming his way.

Holly watches Santa closely as he guides his sleigh low over the plains of Kansas. He has been oddly quiet since New York and the elf swears that his eyes are misty.

"Whoa, Rudolph," Santa says, pulling on the reigns slightly to slow his team of reindeer as they hit a patch of turbulence. "Easy now."

"Is everything alright, Santa?" Holly asks, gripping the sides of the sleigh and squeezing her eyes shut tight. She doesn't like flying very much; hopefully whoever Corporate hires to replace Santa is better at driving the sleigh.

"You know, that's the first time anyone's asked about me and sounded as though they genuinely cared," Santa laughs. "Everything's fine, Holly. Are you alright? You look as though you're going to be sick."

"I'm fine," Holly says dismissively, refusing to open her eyes. In truth, despite how scared she is, she really *is* fine; at least the wind is distracting her from the whole Wally and Bobby dilemma.

"Ho, ho, ho, it's alright if you have to vomit, just do it over the edge," Santa instructs. "When I took Rudolph out on his first flight, he was vomiting the whole way."

Rudolph's nose shines brighter as Santa talks about him and he lets out a low growling sound.

"Oh, don't be embarrassed," Santa reprimands his pet. "It happens to the best of us."

As the sleigh shakes slightly, Holly, determined to distract herself, asks again, "Are you *sure* you're alright?"

"I'm fine," Santa insists. "You know, I just – I think I'm *actually* going to miss this job. I mean, I always knew that I would, but it's really starting to hit me now. I'm never going to be able to bring joy to the children of the world again."

Holly opens her eyes, surprised.

"Well," she begins. "Maybe you're rushing retirement a bit. It's not too late to change your mind, you know."

As Santa mulls this over, he snaps his reigns again and yells at his reindeer, "Let's give it some speed, boys! We have a schedule to keep!"

Holly is thrown to the side and grips her seat firmly – Christmas couldn't end fast enough.

"Here it is!" Father Time exclaims excitedly, walking toward Mrs. Claus who is standing in the center of the room, cradling a glass of wine while talking to Wally and Tom. He is holding up a large, heavy-looking gold pocket watch that glistens as it reflects the multi-colored lights from the Aurora Borealis shining in through the panoramic windows and skylights above. "Santa's retirement gift. Made from the finest golds and jewels in the world. Notice the diamonds running around the edge and Santa's name engraved with rubies in the center. And on the inside…"

He opens the watch to reveal a Christmas tree clock-face, which is decorated with different colored emeralds, wrapped with lights that are actually lit. *Santa Claus is Coming to Town* is also emanating from the watch, playing over the ticking of the clock's hands. The minute Father Time snaps the lid shut, the music ceases.

"It's beautiful," Mrs. Claus breathes, taking the watch from Father Time. "Nicky will love it. Wally, could you wrap it please?"

"Of course, Mrs. Claus," Wally replies dutifully, taking the watch and hurrying away, disappearing amongst the crowd of elves.

"What a waste of money," Tom clucks in disdain. "Why spend so much on a guy who can make anything he wants with his bare hands? He could probably *make* a better watch than that! Ugh, I'm glad I didn't waste *my* money by contributing."

Mrs. Claus and Father Time exchange an exasperated look before the old woman smiles sweetly at the turkey.

"Tom, dear, did you see the gift Santa left you under the tree?"

"I don't want it," Tom says immediately, throwing a curious look at the tree in question despite himself.

"Why don't you go see what it is first before you make any decisions," Mrs. Claus smiles.

Tom sighs deeply before stalking over to the tree haughtily. "Move," he snaps, pushing Frank, who is crouching under the tree shaking a present addressed to him, out of the way.

Snatching up the small, square gift with his name on it, Tom rips open the orange and brown wrapping paper.

"What the…"

A CD with an image of himself at the forefront, a do-rag tied around his head and flocked by his fellow turkey employees, falls into his wings. A post-it note is stuck to it, reading:

To the Most Fowl Dude and the Best Musician that I Know,
Keep being hip! Merry Christmas.
Love, Santa Claus

Tom stares down at the CD, speechless, a lump forming in his throat. "Well...this isn't...that...great..." he swallows, opening the case and causing a ripped piece of paper to flutter to the ground. Picking it up, he reads, "101.7 WHUF – 4 a.m."

Checking his watch, Tom hurries over to where the Fates and Caleb, now joined by Cupid and Ted, are still tracking Santa on NORAD's website.

"Move!" he demands, grabbing the computer and typing hurriedly into the search bar.

"Hey!" Clotho exclaims. "You could say excuse me."

But Tom pays no attention as he brings up a live stream on WHUF's website just in time to hear something that makes his heart skip a beat.

"And although it's Christmas morning folks," the DJ speaks. "We have a very special...*unusual* request. Someone who simply wishes to be known as *Santa Claus* wants to dedicate *The Best Thanksgiving Song Ever* to his good friend, Tom. So this one's for you! Merry Christmas!"

And to the turkey's amazement, his own voice issues from the computer speakers.

"Hey, America, turn off your trucks,
And forget about Christmas 'cause it really sucks."

"I can't believe he did this," Tom whispers, tears welling up in his eyes. "For *me*."

"Neither can I," Cupid says. "This song is terrible."

Though Ted does not vocalize his agreement, the expression on the groundhog's face says it all.

"Again, if you're just tuning in, this is a song dedicated to Tom from his own secret Santa," the DJ speaks over the song. "Some friend you've got there, Tom. He must really hate you to dedicate this piece of garbage to you. What a piece of--" Tom's eyes widen as the DJ's voice is bleeped out. "Clearly we have no standards at this station anymore. I can't even finish this. I've got to get a new job."

And without further ado, the beginning of *Jingle Bells* begins to play as Cupid stifles a laugh at Tom's furious expression.

"I hate that fat bastard!" Tom yells, slamming the laptop shut and pitching his CD across the room, where it shatters against the wall just behind Wally's head. "I hope he crashes his sleigh!"

He storms off, passing Tuss and Regina who are about to ask him if he's okay before the Boogeyman and the Easter Bunny step into their line of sight.

"A word, Tuss, if you don't mind," the Boogeyman says silkily.

"Sure," Tuss smiles. "What can I do for you?"

"Santa's replacement," the Boogeyman begins. "Have you chosen anyone yet?"

"Not yet," Tuss replies, his smile fading instantly as Regina turns to look at him, just as curious as her colleagues. "It won't even be left up to me or Pia to decide. Corporate will make the final call."

"Well, a word of advice," the Boogeyman continues. "I'd recommend *not* putting Bill's name forward for the job."

"I don't think you have to worry about that," Tuss laughs, glancing at Bill who is standing alone in a corner, trying to awkwardly dance with Jolly who hurries away from him in disgust. "Although he *is* the only one here who doesn't handle anything too important right now."

"Francis, here, has intimated to me that he'd take Christmas on in addition to his Easter duties," the Boogeyman begins. "If you--"

"What?" Francis asks, panicked, his ears quivering. "I never said that! *You* were the one who said you'd rather take it in addition to Halloween before letting Bill have it!"

"Well, I would!" the Boogeyman scoffs. "Who wouldn't? You can't let someone like him get his hands on *Christmas*."

"I would too." Regina takes a sip of her drink. "I'd love to inherit Santa's workshop since *somebody* hasn't given me Mother Nature's old office yet."

"Everyone just…calm down," Tuss laughs. Turning to Regina, he says, "I'm still working on that. As for replacing Santa," he turns to the Boogeyman. "I'd rather worry about *that* tomorrow. Maybe they'll go with an outside hire. Let's just all enjoy the party tonight, alright? Come on - how about a drink?"

And as Willy leads his choir in a rendition of *Christmas in Hollis*, Tuss, Regina, Francis and the Boogeyman walk over to a table of liquor and all do a shot together, the Boogeyman's Shadow mimicking the action on the wall behind them.

Pia is sitting alone outside of the empty reindeer stable. The sun is beginning to rise along the horizon and the snowfall is finally slowing down. Pulling her parka tightly around her shivering body, Pia wipes her frozen tears from her blotchy cheeks, waiting, as the sounds of *Welcome Christmas* drift down from above. It's been a terrible night. Meanwhile, she's just sitting here waiting, not even sure about what she's waiting for.

Seconds pass. Then minutes. And then suddenly, in the distance, Pia can make out a faint red glow.

She hurriedly gets to her feet as Rudolph and the rest of the reindeer fly toward her, lower and lower, bringing Santa's sleigh and its two occupants into view.

"Ho, ho, ho," Santa laughs as he brings his sleigh in for a smooth landing. "Good work, boys! We pulled it off again!"

The minute the sleigh comes to a complete stop, Holly jumps off of it, shaking, and stumbles over to Pia.

"What the hell is wrong with you?" Pia asks, staring at the elf in surprise.

"I don't like flying," an alarmingly pale Holly replies, pushing past Pia and calling over her shoulder. "Santa? Can you meet me up on the twelfth floor in a few minutes? I think there's an emergency - I just got a text from Wally."

As she disappears into the building, Santa chuckles to himself before turning to Pia.

"I suppose my retirement party's up there?"

"How did you know?" Pia asks.

"I'm Santa Claus," he winks at her. "I know everything."

Pia smiles despite herself as she follows Santa into the stable where he locks the reindeer in their individual pens. "Did you have a nice flight?" she asks stiffly.

"Best one yet," Santa smiles at her. "Holly's good company."

Though she disagrees, Pia doesn't feel like arguing with the old man.

"How was your night, my dear?"

"Terrible," Pia replies honestly. Santa was leaving and she was most likely going to be demoted *again*, so why lie? Why act like it didn't bother her? "Everybody hates me."

"They do not."

"No, seriously. They *really* do."

"I'm somebody, aren't I?" Santa shrugs. "I don't hate you."

"Thanks."

Noticing how bloodshot the woman's normally piercing green eyes are, Santa continues. "Speaking of which, it's Christmas. I have a gift for you."

"Seriously?" Pia reacts with surprise as Santa begins patting the pockets of his red coat, searching for something. "I'm not on the naughty list? I strangled both Cormac and Bill this past year, *and* I turned Caleb into my personal punching bag!"

"Of course not," Santa tells her. "You're on the nice list. You may be rude. Abrasive. Occasionally violent. And you may swear more than anyone ever should, but you have a heart deep down. Deep down, you care about people. You've always been on the nice list. Everybody always winds up on the nice list. Christmas is a time to see the good in mankind, even if they can't see it in themselves."

Pia is taken aback. Unsure of how to reply, she remains silent as Santa continues patting his many pockets.

"Where is it – ah, yes, here it is! Merry Christmas, Pia."

Pia's eyes widen as Santa withdraws a string of silver chains adorned with large, white, sparkling pearls from the folds of his coat. She recognizes the necklace immediately and although he's holding it out for her to take, she's afraid to touch it. Afraid that if she does, the necklace will only disappear.

"W-where did you find that?"

"I can find anything. I'm Santa Claus, remember?"

Hesitantly, she takes the pearls at last and holds the delicate necklace carefully in her hands. A flood of memories comes rushing back to her. All of the times she wore this around her neck as a small child before he – her step-father – up and sold all of the jewelry, leaving her without a single tangible memory.

"This was my mother's."

"I thought you deserved something a little extra special this

Christmas," Santa replies, placing a hand on her shoulder. "Something to remind you of where you came from, possibly to point you in a new direction in life. If anything, I hope it fills you with Christmas spirit and reminds you that you don't have to shut yourself off to everybody, my child. There are good people in this world. Your mother was one of them."

Pia blinks hard, but the tears begin to flow freely anyway. She can't remember the last time she got any sort of gift from anyone, for any reason.

Tuss, a small voice at the back of her head reminds her. Tuss tried giving her a gift earlier. And she had rejected it, after he had been nothing but nice to her all year long.

Staring down at the necklace, she wonders if her mother would have told her to always be kind and accepting of people had she not died so young. What would her mother have said if she could have seen her tonight, yelling at and berating everybody? Pia can't imagine that would make any mother proud of their daughter. Maybe at least for one day, to honor her memory, she can try and change. If not at Christmas, then when?

And as an image of her mother floats to the forefront of her mind, a huge rush of affection for Santa Claus wells up inside of Pia. He had given her something that she had thought was gone forever; something that meant more to her than words could ever describe.

"Santa," she begins. "I…I don't know what to say." She wipes the tears from her cheeks before they can freeze to them once again. "Thank you."

"You're more than welcome," Santa replies, placing a hand on her shoulder. "You have a good heart, Pia."

"Please don't go." Her voice is small and child-like as it spills from her mouth automatically. "I know that I've been begging you not to retire all year, and you probably think it's only about the money, but it's not. It's you. We can't replace *you*. Anyone can put on the suit and anyone can drive the sleigh, but not just anyone would go out of their way to find some necklace that's meaningless to everybody except one insignificant woman. Not just anyone has the heart to be Santa Claus. You're a once in a millennium find. Christmas will never be the same if you go. *Please*. We *need* you to stay. I…*I* need you to stay."

Santa smiles, touched by the words. The truth is, he changed his mind about four hours ago on the flight from Alaska to Hawaii. While flying, he had realized that despite breaking his back for little more than milk and cookies, he legitimately loved his job. The children loved him and he loved them just as much in return. Seeing the way he touched the lives of people around the globe, like he had just done with Pia, meant the world to him. He can't imagine leaving it. Not just yet, anyway. Maybe in another year's time.

He is about to vocalize all of this to Pia when something stops him from doing so and his smile widens. He can give her one last Christmas gift – a much-needed boost to her confidence.

"Well, you've twisted my arm," Santa sighs. "How can I not stay after such an impassioned speech?"

"Really?" Pia asks, unable to contain her excitement.

"Really," Santa nods. "But *only* for another year."

"That's all that I'm asking," Pia squeals in a girl-like fashion most unlike her and throws her arms around Santa Claus' neck, taking the old man by surprise as she kisses him on the cheek. "Merry Christmas, Santa."

"Ho, ho, ho, Merry Christmas," Santa pries himself from her death grip. "Now, let's get inside. I have a retirement party to ruin."

The moment Santa and Pia emerge from the elevator and step foot onto the crowded twelfth floor, they are met by a wall of deafening sound.

"SURPRISE!"

Almost at once, Willy begins to lead his elf choir in a rendition of *Here Comes Santa Claus* as Pia leads Santa through the crowd toward the stage on which Mrs. Claus, Holly, Wally and Frank are standing with the choir.

"Oh my goodness, a surprise party! I had no idea!" Santa says dramatically, making his way through the crowd. "Thank you. Thank you so much," he says in response to each hand that pats him on the back. "Thank you, you're so kind."

Pia tries not to laugh at Santa's over the top acting but finds she can't contain it when she imagines what the reactions of those in the crowd might be when the big man announces his new plans.

"Here he is, my wonderful husband," Mrs. Claus says into a microphone, as the applause and singing die down and Santa joins her on stage. "Merry Christmas, darling."

"Merry Christmas, sweetie."

Santa gives her a peck on the lips before Mrs. Claus begins to address the crowd once more.

"Well, it certainly has been a busy and productive few centuries for my husband," she says. "He's a very passionate man in *all* respects," she winks slyly at him, causing Santa to go red in the face as a few nervous laughs sound throughout the room. "Who's loved every *second* of his job. But if any man deserves a long, happy, peaceful retirement, it's him. So let's all have a big round of applause for the man who puts the Merry into Christmas – Santa Claus!"

As applause breaks out again, Mrs. Claus gives her husband a big hug before placing the microphone in his hand.

"Thank you," Santa says into it. "Thank you all so much. It means a lot to me. Words cannot…" He clears his throat loudly as he wipes a tear from his eye. "Words cannot even begin to express the amount of gratitude and love I have toward you all. So why not give *yourselves* a round of applause?"

More clapping. A few feet away from Pia, Bill and Tom are exchanging a dirty look.

"He's laying it on a bit thick, don't you think?" Bill whispers to the turkey.

"I still don't understand why the fat man gets to retire," Tom responds quietly. "Not that I'd ever abandon my holiday like that enormous heap of crap is doing."

"This is from all of us, Santa," Wally says, presenting him with a gift.

"You got me something?" Santa asks, with genuine surprise this time. "You shouldn't have!" He rips the wrapping paper off of the gift to reveal the pocket watch and gasps loudly as he clicks it open. "A watch! It's beautiful!"

"That it is," Father Time calls from the crowd gathered around the stage. "It's the only one of its kind in the world!"

"We got you a card too," Holly says, happily presenting it to Santa.

"Well, would you look at that," Santa says into the microphone. "The surprises just keep on coming!" He opens the card. "And you all signed! Even Cormac! How did you manage that? I never see that little guy."

"Who does?" Cupid calls loudly, eliciting laughs from those nearest him.

"And Tom signed too!" Santa finds the turkey in the crowd. "I never thought I'd see the day! Thank you, my feathered friend! It means the world to me!"

"Plagiarism!" Tom yells shrilly, pointing one of his wings at the card. "That's plagiarism! I never signed that! I didn't even chip in for the gift!"

But Santa ignores the bird as he continues to scan the card.

"But I *did* do something for you, Santa," Tom continues happily. "My fellow turkeys and I took the liberty of packing all of your bags so that you and your equally fat wife can leave for Cabo right away."

"The Caribbean," Mrs. Claus corrects, leaning in to speak into the microphone. "We're going to the Caribbean."

"Ah, yes, about that," Santa speaks up, looking around the room awkwardly as Pia covers her mouth with a hand, trying to hide her wide smile. "While I appreciate the gesture, Tom, I'm afraid you've wasted your time. I'm postponing my trip another year."

Silence. Complete silence as the statement sinks into each of the various minds (some slower than others) in the room. Finally--

"Wait, what?" Mrs. Claus asks.

"*Excuse* me?" Bill exclaims, horrified.

"What the hell does that mean?" Tom demands loudly. "How dare you tease me like this!"

From across the room, Tuss finds Pia's eyes, questioning. Frank, meanwhile, has gone as white as a ghost, and Wally, Holly and the other elves and holiday heads merely look confused.

"I've decided to stay with the company for one more year," Santa reveals, speaking into the microphone. "I really appreciate everything you've done for me, all the effort you put in." He looks around the room at all of the banners and Christmas-themed decorations. "And to show you I'm not being ungrateful about it all, I'm going to keep the watch you all bought me." He clips it to his coat as Father Time's mouth drops open in disgust. "But on the bright side, we all get to work together for another year! Although you're going to have your work cut out for you next December! How you're going to top this party with my second retirement party, I have no idea!"

"*Second* retirement party?" Frank repeats loudly, storming over to Santa and grabbing the microphone from his hands. "That's it! I can't fucking take it anymore! You are a greedy, selfish, clueless old man who doesn't give a *fuck* about his employees! All year long, I've been trimming your nose hairs and cutting your toenails! Bringing you toilet paper while you're on the toilet and fetching you hot chocolate! Cleaning up the shit of your *nine disgusting pets*! And I did it all without complaining to you! The only thing that kept me going was knowing that in a year's time, you would be leaving and there would be a *new* Santa Claus! One who treated me with the respect that I deserve! But I am *not* serving another year under your buffoonish, idiotic tyranny! I *quit*!" And then turning to face the stunned crowd, he adds, "If any of you want to keep in touch, I'll be opening my own dental practice down in the village!"

He shoves the microphone back at the bewildered Santa Claus and storms off the stage, red in the face, to loud applause from Bill, Tom and the other turkeys.

"Who was that?" Santa muses aloud, watching the tiny elf disappear into one of the elevators.

Holly and Wally exchange a look.

"Frank?" Holly pipes up timidly. "Your – your intern?"

"Oh, yes," Santa says with a nod. "What a shame! I was going to promote him to my assistant to my personal assistant," he shrugs. "Oh well. Wally, tomorrow I want you to start compiling a list of possible replacements."

"Of course, Santa," Wally replies.

"Everyone else, carry on with the party! Even though I'm not retiring, it's still Christmas after all!"

As the chatter resumes, Santa hands the microphone to Willy, who instantly starts singing *The Little Drummer Boy* with his choir. Santa, meanwhile, allows himself to be pulled aside by his wife for a private word.

"Are you sure about this?" Mrs. Claus asks, confused. "Not retiring? Because if Pia is pressuring you--"

"My decision has nothing to do with Pia, my dear," Santa smiles warmly at his wife. "I just realized tonight how much I *do* love my job. I'm not ready to go. Not just yet."

"Oh, Nicky," Mrs. Claus beams, inspired by her husband's dedication. "I love you, Mr. Claus."

"And I you, Mrs. Claus." Santa kisses her sweetly.

"I *do* wish we could go to the Caribbean though," she says with a small sigh.

"Don't worry, Mary," Santa smiles warmly. "The Caribbean will still be around next year."

The party rages on for the next few hours and with each passing moment, the guests become drunker, louder and happier. As Santa weaves his way through the room, he is glad that for the most part, his friends are not bothered he's sticking around for another year ("Look at what the alternative could have been," the Boogeyman says to him, darkly glaring across the room at a sweaty Bill trying to dance with yet another reluctant female elf.).

"Santa!" Mother Nature drunkenly declares, approaching the spot where he is struggling to communicate with an unintelligible and very frustrated T.J. "There you are!" She hiccups, swaying on the spot. "I have a bone to pick with you!"

"Mother Nature," Santa smiles, eyeing the glass of red wine in her hand. "A little too much to drink this evening?"

"No such thing," Jack Frost calls from a few feet away, where he is doing a fast step with Tilly. T.J. lets out a screech of disagreement at the statement before flying away to land beside the Sandman, who is still fast asleep in the corner.

"You didn't leave *one* gift for me under the tree this year," Mother

Nature points out, insulted. "Has Pia been talking to you? Did she convince you I was naughty? Because, I - I have a few choice words I can say about her!" She hiccups. "She should be arrested for multiple counts of attempted planticide!"

"Mother Nature, my dear," Santa grips her by the arms to stop her from swaying too far to the left and tipping over. "Nobody on this planet is nicer than you."

"Oh, stop," Mother Nature says bashfully, hitting Santa playfully. "You're making me blush."

"I thought that was just the alcohol," Cupid says as he walks by, taking a sip of beer.

"The reason I didn't leave you a gift under the tree is because I wanted to give it to you in person," Santa explains, reaching into his pocket and withdrawing an official looking envelope. "For you."

"What is it?" Mother Nature asks, snatching it from his hands.

"A letter from Corporate," Santa reveals as he watches the woman begin to frantically tear the envelope open. "I got them to agree to read your complaints. They're going to give you your job and your floor back. They're also giving you Arbor Day and Earth Day. On the condition, of course, that you don't send them anymore black mold spores."

"Really?" Mother Nature asks, her eyes filling with emotion as she stares at the two blurry old men in front of her.

"Really," Santa smiles. "Of course, there are going to be a few changes. You're now going to be sharing the fifth floor with Regina and that gentleman who they hired to run Kwanzaa...who I don't think I've seen tonight, oddly enough."

"Thank you." Mother Nature wraps her arms around the man's fat frame as he chuckles.

"It's my pleasure."

"I bet this is killing you."

Pia, who is watching Mother Nature and Santa hug from across the room, turns to see that Tuss has sidled up to her, smirking.

"I don't care anymore," Pia shrugs. "We're leaving in a little over a week anyway."

"Yeah…yeah, I know," Tuss says gloomily, eyeing Regina across the room, where she is laughing with Ted and Francis. "You know," he laughs nervously. "I never thought I'd say this, but I'm going to actually miss this place." Pia looks at him, an eyebrow raised, and he plows on nervously. "It's become sort of like a home, you know?"

Pia nods curtly. "I know," she says softly. "I'd never thought I'd say it either, but I sort of agree with you. There is something about this place that I'll miss." Tuss is taken aback by the admission, but doesn't say anything as she continues. "Who knows if you and I are ever going to work together again."

"Maybe someday," Tuss shrugs.

"I'd like that," Pia confesses, causing him to nearly tumble over in surprise. "Look, Tuss…I'm sorry about before. About how I treated you. About how I treated you all year long."

"No you're not."

"No, I'm not," Pia confesses with a laugh. "But I *am* sorry for before. That was rude of me. I love the shoes." She looks down and Tuss is shocked to see that she is actually wearing them on her feet. "I'm surprised you knew my size!"

"I pay attention," Tuss brags. "Besides, you had Caleb try on enough of them."

"Well, thank you for my Christmas gift," Pia continues. "It just so happens that I got one for you too."

And snapping her fingers, a pen appears in her hand. A pen made of solid gold that she hands to Tuss, who sees that it is engraved with his full name - Plutus. Smiling, he pockets it. "I love it. Thank you."

"Merry Christmas, Plutus."

"Merry Christmas, Copia."

They stand in silence for a moment before Tuss says, "Well, I think I'm going to give Regina the best Christmas gift ever and let her know that she's getting her own office with a window."

"I guess that means I should find Kwanzaa to tell him," Pia says to herself as she watches her colleague walk away. "But where the hell is-"

"Excuse me? Do you know where Santa Claus is?"

Pia turns around to see who is speaking and jumps back in fright. "Fuck!" she yells, staring down at the log-like creature with a carved face. "What the hell are *you* doing here?"

"Celebrating Santa's retirement?" Tio answers, confused. "What do you--"

"You have some fucking nerve showing up here after what you tried to pull at the convention in August!" Pia snaps, drawing the attention of the elves nearest her. "Why did they even let you--?"

"*Relax.* He's the *new* Tio."

Pia glances up to see the Krampus standing over her, along with Sinterklaas, Ded Moroz, La Befana, Pere Noel and the other Christmas figureheads from around the world.

"I'm sorry," Pia composes herself, staring down at the log. "You caught me off guard. My apologies."

"No need to apologize, ma'am," Tio smiles. "It's Christmas!"

"And we're ready to party like it's nineteen-ninety-nine!" La Befana shouts, smiling wide.

"Now, where's the fat bastard?" Krampus asks.

And Pia, not wanting to miss the look on their faces when they hear that Santa has changed his mind about retiring, says, "Come on, I'll help you find him."

Wally, standing alone in the shadow of one of the Christmas trees, watches as Pia leads the group of Christmas misfits through the crowd. Taking a sip of his wine, he jumps when a voice sounds from directly behind him.

"Wally."

"Holly!" Wally spins around. "You scared me!"

Holly giggles, holding an empty shot glass in her hand and swaying slightly, clearly drunk.

"I didn't get to ask before, how was your flight?"

"Terrible," Holly slurs. "I need more booze, but I *think* Cormac came and stole it all."

Wally laughs before glancing over his shoulder nervously. Holly, taking note of the action, shakes her head.

"Don't worry, Bobby won't come looking for us," she burps. "Oh, excuse me."

"How do you know?" Wally asks, still looking around for the burly elf.

"He went down to the stable to take care of the reindeer," Holly explains. "He decided to leave right after I broke up with him."

"You broke up with him?" Wally exclaims, his heart leaping with joy.

"He's not the one that I want," Holly says, staring into his eyes. "A few near death experiences tonight helped me to realize that."

Wally gulps nervously as the subject of his desire steps nearer and

_____

426

removes his broken glasses. "What are you--"

"Shh..." Holly places a finger to his lips and glances upward. "Look. Mistletoe."

Wally's eyes travel toward the ceiling to see that Holly's right. Though everything is blurry without his glasses, he can distinctly make out the small, romantic Christmas decoration.

"So...uh..."

But before Wally can choke out a statement, Holly plants her lips full on his. The kiss lasts for about ten seconds before Holly breaks it, stumbling backwards slightly and grabbing at her stomach.

"I think I'm going to be sick," she chokes, covering her mouth with her hands and running off to find a bathroom, leaving Wally standing alone, shell-shocked.

"Best. Christmas. Ever," he remarks aloud to himself before coming to his senses and running after Holly. "Wait up!" he yells. "I'll hold your hair back while you puke the alcohol out of your system!"

Pia, who has watched all of this transpire as the reunited Santa's of the world celebrate behind her, snorts into her vodka cranberry. "Pathetic."

On the stage behind her, the elf choir begins to croon a slow version of *We Wish You a Merry Christmas* as a voice nearby says speaks up sensuously, "So...Copia – goddess of wealth and plenty. I have a *plenty* good Christmas gift for you."

Pia rolls her eyes, knowing it's Cupid before she even turns around. "Is it in your pants?"

"It is!"

"I absolutely don't want it."

"But it's the gift that keeps on giving!"

"Well, feel free to give it to somebody else," she tells him with an actual smile playing on her lips. "Snowy is over there and plenty of these elves look slutty."

"I could come visit you at Corporate. It's been like a century since I've been there, but I'm pretty sure I still have an office."

"Don't bother. I won't want to see you."

"You're lying," Cupid shoots back, a twinkle in his eye. "You're going to miss me."

"I'd sooner miss Bill." They both look over to where he is once again surprising an unsuspecting elf by dancing right behind her. "And he wanted to fucking be Santa Claus," Pia snorts. "The elves need a restraining order against him as it is."

Cupid takes her hand and, though caught off guard, she doesn't pull away.

"I'll miss you."

As sincere as he sounds, she doesn't want to believe him. "You'll find someone else to sexually harass."

"I think you should dance with me."

"And why the hell should I do that?" she replies with a laugh.

He responds, looking straight into her eyes. "Because you want to. And because I want you to."

And maybe it's the party atmosphere or the kindness that she's been shown tonight…maybe it's because he is sort of charming and unbelievably attractive. Or maybe it's because she's had all of these strong vodka cranberries. Whatever the reason, Pia shrugs and allows a smiling Cupid to lead her to the dance floor.

"What the hell," she says. "It's a fucking Christmas miracle."

And Santa Claus, who is dancing with his darling wife a few feet away, can't help but silently agree as he watches the god of love twirl the goddess of wealth on the dance floor. Maybe there was hope for her yet.

Who would have thought? After centuries on the job, Christmas could still provide Santa Claus with a few surprises.

"We wish you a Merry Christmas,
We wish you a Merry Christmas,
We wish you a Merry Christmas and a Happy New Year.
Good tidings we bring,
To you and your kin,
Good tidings for Christmas and a Happy New Year."

"Well, Father Time, you did it," Pia says, walking into the old man's office on New Year's Eve. It is almost midnight in New York City and sales are already ten times what they were during last year's disastrous snowstorm. "Don't ask me how, but you did it."

"Don't thank me, thank Mother Nature," Father Time replies, rather humbly in his opinion. "She held off on the snow this year. Hmm…on second thought, perhaps you should thank Jack Frost. Why wasn't he the one fired again?"

"Don't get into fucking semantics with me," Pia begins. "I – what the *fuck*?"

She notices for the first time since entering the office that Father Time is crouched over Caleb, who is slumped over in a chair, his breathing ragged. Both of them are dressed completely in black and candles are lit around the dark room.

"He's dying," Father Times explains, as though telling a five-year old something as obvious as the sky is blue. "He'll soon be reborn as the new Baby New Year. And I *really* hope it's a girl this time."

Pia stares at Caleb, who appears skeletal now in size and appearance, and says in a disgusted tone, "Maybe I should come back later."

"Perhaps that's a good idea," Father Time nods his agreement, but before Pia can exit the room, another voice speaks up weakly.

"Pia…"

Pia closes her eyes, praying for patience, before turning around to face the dying man. "Yes?"

"Come…closer…" Caleb breathes.

Rolling her eyes, Pia leans forward.

"I…take back what I said…" Caleb coughs loudly. "Before

Christmas...I love you, Pia...I don't want to die with you thinking that I don't..."

"Believe me, I don't c--" Pia stops short, noticing Father Time's pointed look, and not knowing whether it's her lingering Christmas spirit or an actual change of heart, she continues, rolling her eyes. "Yeah, thanks. It's good to not die sad...or...whatever. That's a recipe for a ghost." Father Time clears his throat angrily and she feels compelled to continue. "I'm...uh...*sorry*...if you felt that I was ever...uh... *mean* to you."

"I will...never...forget you..."

"Yes you will," both Pia and Father Time say in unison.

But Caleb appears not to hear them. Closing his eyes with a contented smile, he falls silent before bursting into flames. Pia backs away as the fire dissipates immediately, replaced by a huge pile of sand.

"Ow! My fucking eyes! This happens every year?" she demands of Father Time.

"Without fail," the old man nods. "It's like clockwork. Time is a precise, beautiful thing."

There is silence for a moment before a baby's wailing is heard from under the sand. Father Time digs through it to reveal a small infant, squirming uncomfortably.

"What is it?" he asks, handing the baby to Pia, his eyes squeezed shut. "Does it have a penis? Because I swear, if it does--"

Pia throws him a dirty look as she asks, "What kind of question is that, you sick fuck?"

"A legitimate one," Father Time insists. "Any parent would ask it."

Pia stares at the baby, which stops crying immediately as it locks eyes with her.

"It's a girl," Pia states.

"*Yes!*" Father Time exclaims, dropping to his knees and folding his hands. "Hallelujah! Thank you, Lord!" he cries. "My prayers are finally answered!"

Pia stares uncomfortably at the baby girl. She holds her awkwardly at arms length, praying that it doesn't go to the bathroom on her, when it suddenly reaches one of its tiny hands for her nose.

"Mama."

Pia and Father Time both widen their eyes.

"Oh no," Father Time groans, his shoulders slumping.

"Oh *fuck*," Pia breathes, as the baby giggles loudly and begins to pee all over her.

🥂🥂🥂🥂🥂

"You won't believe what just happened," Pia reports in disgust, as she walks into the tiny house that her and Tuss share down in the village. "Caleb fucking died and was reborn right in front of me."

"Congratulations?" Tuss asks, not looking up from the holiday decorating magazine he is reading on the couch.

"Baby New Year is now a girl," she continues. "Father Time named her Bridget. She pissed all over me," she motions at her wet blouse. "The little shit."

"That's nice," Tuss comments, sparing his colleague a glance and smirking slightly.

"She *is* sort of cute, I have to admit," Pia goes on. She then hesitates, sounding somewhat stunned by her next words. "She called me mama."

———
432

"Father Time must have loved that," Tuss says, once more absorbed in his magazine.

"What the hell is wrong with you?" Pia demands. "I'm standing here covered in piss, trying to have a conversation – what the hell is on your neck?"

Tuss stares down in surprise, horrified to see a large hickey poking out of his collar, in plain sight.

"Nothing," he rushes, trying to casually hide it. "So, Bridget, huh?"

"No, seriously, what the fuck?" Pia stomps over to him and pulls his hand away from his neck. "Is that a fucking hickey?"

"No!" Tuss replies defensively.

"Well, I know you can't have a girlfriend. That can't possibly be the case. What girl would want *you*?" Pia laughs. When Tuss shifts uncomfortably in his seat, Pia's face drops instantly. "You actually have a damn girlfriend?" she asks. "Who the hell is it?"

"It's none of your business," Tuss states, standing up. "I have to finish packing."

He starts up the stairs, crouching to avoid hitting his head on the low ceiling, and is dismayed to find that Pia is at his heels.

"Tilly?"

"I'm not into bestiality."

"That elf slut?" Pia guesses. "Folly?"

"Jolly?"

"No, no. *Holly*."

"No," Tuss snorts, walking into his bedroom where the majority of his belongings are already packed tight into two open suitcases. "She's with

_____
433

Wally."

"Not Mother Nature," Pia groans with disgust, crossing her arms across her chest. "Are you having an affair with Mrs. Claus?"

"No," Tuss replies exasperatedly, turning to face his colleague. "I'm not into older women." He laughs, turning back to his suitcases. "Can we please drop the subject?"

"Well, it can't be that brainless Tooth Fairy," Pia snorts. "Not even *you* would be fucking stupid enough to get involved with *that* emotional mess."

Tuss, who is reaching for a pair of socks, freezes in midair and feels himself go red.

"You're kidding me." Pia reacts stiffly, as Tuss turns to face her slowly. "Regina? Fucking Regina? Tuss, do you realize how inappropriate that is?"

"I know," Tuss begins quickly. "But let me explain--"

"What the fuck is there to explain?" Pia yells, throwing her hands in the air. "You're her boss! I think I'd be less disgusted if it was fucking Mother Nature! How could you even think about being with one of *them* in the first place? How long has this been going on?"

"Since…" Tuss scratches the back of his head awkwardly. "You know, since…uh…since September," he mutters.

"Fuck me," Pia exclaims, looking around the room.

"That's Cupid's job."

Pia rolls her eyes. "Don't be a wiseass. You can't keep seeing her."

"I know," Tuss says hurriedly. "We're leaving anyway, so--"

"I mean in general," Pia cuts him off sternly. "Anymore. Even before we leave."

"But--"

"Tuss, if Corporate finds out, they'll destroy you," Pia tells him seriously. "No matter *who* you're related to. She's a fucking holiday figurehead! It's unacceptable! It's forbidden!"

Tuss sighs deeply, knowing that she has a point.

"Does anybody else know about this?"

"The Boogeyman saw us kissing," Tuss confesses. "So did Cupid. I'm pretty sure Santa has a semblance of an idea. And Regina said that Francis and Holly alluded to it at some point."

"Is that all?" Pia asks sarcastically. "Are you sure the Sandman didn't watch you guys making out in his sleep?"

Tuss nods.

"Good," Pia sighs. "None of them will tell a soul. That's not their style. You're lucky I have better things to do than report you for this. I know it's boring up here, but, seriously, a holiday head? Gross. Now, hurry up and finish packing. We can head back to Corporate tonight."

Tuss sadly stares at his suitcases. He doesn't want to go. Doesn't want to be apart from Regina. Doesn't want to leave the North Pole without at least saying goodbye to the Tooth Fairy. But on the other hand, he knows that Pia is right. What he has with her is wrong; Corporate would not tolerate their relationship if they found out about it, and besides, it wasn't as though Regina was clueless to any of this. He stressed countless times that they shouldn't get serious, as did she. So there was no way that she'd care, or probably even notice, if he left without another word.

Or maybe he was just trying to convince himself otherwise because he felt so guilty.

Either way, both he and Pia spend the rest of the night packing their belongings in silence. When they are finally done, they drag their luggage out onto the front porch of their house and stare around at the snow-covered village, where Christmas lights are still shining brightly as the sky lightens overhead. Glancing one last time at the giant block of ice that is the North American Headquarters, Tuss and Pia grip hands and disappear into nothingness, leaving the North Pole – going home.

And Tuss has no idea that at that very moment, Regina is sitting in her bedroom getting ready to surprise him at his house with the promise of late night shenanigans. Nor that she'll be heartbroken when she realizes he left without saying good-bye.

🍷🍸🍷🍸🍷🍸🍷🍸🍷🍸

"Here we are, my pretties! Home sweet home!"

The elevator doors open on the fifth floor and Mother Nature steps out proudly, a box full of fertilizer in her arms. Behind her, Regina ambles out, looking tired and depressed, followed by Jack Frost who instantly balks at the sight of the overgrown vines, overabundant flowers and numerous leaves cluttering the hallway. The cardboard box in his hands holds a watering can, gardening gloves, a pack of toothpaste and a giant bottle of mouthwash.

"Screw this," he addresses Mother Nature. "I am *not* cleaning up this mess! And you actually *wanted* this floor?" he asks the Tooth Fairy.

"It's not the only thing I wanted," she replies gloomily.

"Oh please, this is nothing!" Mother Nature smiles. "I can fix this right up!"

And with one simple snap of her fingers, the plants instantly slink back into the walls and floor. The hallway is still lined with the beautiful leaves and flowers, but no one will have to fight the vines to get down the corridor now.

Jack Frost smirks as Regina slinks past a beautiful waterfall toward her new office to unpack.

"You could have done that the whole time?" he asks.

"Fuck that bitch," Mother Nature huffs with a small wink, as she makes her way toward her old office. "Thank goodness she left. Though I *am* going to miss Tuss."

"You and me both," Regina sighs, taking a seat at her large desk and staring around the office, which is as empty as she now feels on the inside. "You and me both."

♈︎♈︎♈︎♈︎♈︎♈︎♈︎♈︎♈︎♈︎

Meanwhile, somewhere else...

Colonel Bateman is one of Washington's most prominent war room presences. Having fought in three wars himself, he is quick thinking and even quicker to act. He is also used to – and hates – surprises. So when he is awoken by one of his subordinates in the middle of the night on January first, needless to say he is pissed off.

"What the hell is this all about?" he demands, stepping into the control room of a small, dimly lit underground bunker filled with office nerds staring at their computers. "What's so important that I had to be dragged down here in the middle of the fucking night in my pajamas?"

"Sir? I'm uh – my name's Derek Pendleton," one of the desk-jockeys says, standing up quickly and offering his hand. When the Colonel does not take it, he continues, "There's something you need to see."

Bateman takes Pendleton's seat as the twitchy man brings up a video image on the computer screen, talking a mile a minute as he does so.

"This is footage from December twenty-fourth. Our satellites barely managed to catch this."

Bateman stares at the computer screen, wide-eyed, as Pendleton brings up video footage of a giant red sleigh flying through the air, led by nine reindeer. As they approach the right of the video screen, they start disappearing one by one, as though crossing some invisible threshold, until nothing but the snowy tundra is visible.

"What the fuck was that?"

"We think," Pendleton begins, with enormous trepidation. "We think that it...uh...that it was *Santa Claus*."

"Santa Claus," Bateman replies, deadpan. "Fucking Santa Claus. As in *the* Santa Claus? The *fictional* one?"

"As you can see from the video footage, sir," Pendleton speaks hurriedly, playing the video again. "It doesn't appear as though there is anything *fictional* about him."

"There's no such thing," Bateman replies with a loud scoff. And yet, his eyes tell him differently as he stares at the images on the computer screen. "Could it be some kind of hoax?"

"No, sir. Absolutely not."

He remains silent for a moment, pausing the video just before the red sleigh is about to disappear into nothingness, before deciding to cover all of his bases.

"Wire tap the entire Pole," he says. "I want live satellite images on the entire landmass twenty-four-seven and audio transmitted to me *directly*. I want information on what the fuck this video is showing me. *Stat*."

As his inferiors begin rushing around, hurrying to fulfill his orders, Bateman leans closer to the computer screen.

If on the off chance the image is proof that Santa Claus exists, the entire world would be forever changed. All he can picture is the weaponry and technology that could be developed from studying somebody who could see people while they slept and know when they were awake. Theoretically, he'd be able to locate any given terrorist, at any given time, anywhere in the world.

If Colonel Bateman could prove the existence of Santa Claus and bring him down to Washington for detainment and questioning, his life would change forever.

And with the prospect of riches at the forefront of his mind, the middle-aged man could not help but smile widely to himself.

The New Year has the potential to be *very* good to him.

ACKNOWLEDGMENTS

ANTHONY'S ACKNOWLEDGEMENTS

Thank you to my lovely wife, Sarah, for putting up with me talking about this book nonstop for the past year or so. Thanks for putting up with me reading sections to you for your criticism and opinions, and then *re*-reading them to you during the editing process. Without you, this book could never have happened. You've helped with it more than you know. I love you.

Thank you to my parents, Marie and Tom, for always encouraging me to follow my dreams and pursue my passion. You've always believed in me and have always been there for me through the good times and the bad, and for that I am eternally grateful.

Thank you to my grandparents: Gloria, Pasquale, Phyllis and John. Even though you've always loved me and believed in me, you've never been afraid to reign in my dreams and force me to think more realistically about the future.

Thank you to my aunt, Debbi, for always reading every single project that I've ever finished writing, although none of them have ever been published.

Thank you to my "best men", Nikolai and Mike, for always being there through my ups and my downs. You two have always encouraged my writing and have always believed in everything that I've written. I don't know what I'd do without either of you.

Thank you to my closest ally - my sister, Analisa - for always fueling my imagination as a child.

And last, but certainly not least, thanks to my awesome writing partner, Lauren, without whom this novel couldn't have happened. Thanks for being a friend and believing in my initial pitch in the first place; for putting up with my terrible first drafts, my corny jokes and my nitpicking questions. Here's to three more novels to complete the story.

LAUREN'S ACKNOWLEDGEMENTS

Thank you to my parents, Donna and Joseph, who have supported me through my triumphs and many failures with their generosity and unconditional love.

Thank you to my sister, Michelle, my first writing partner and best friend. Thank you for fueling my creativity and putting up with my insane ideas for all these years.

Thank you to my husband, Brian, who contributed more to this book than I'd like to admit. Thank you for your encouragement and support, and for all your suggestions and almost-always-constructive criticism.

Thank you to my FFF supporters (you know who you are!), whose feedback and encouragement kept me writing and creating for so many years.

And thank you to my writing partner, Anthony, whose initial suggestion inspired this whole crazy journey. Thank you for being my friend and listening to me every time I started a sentence with, "This is kind of weird, but…" I never would have been able to do this alone.

ALL THE REST

We also want to give a joint "thank you" to Judy (the best Canadian aunt there ever was), Michelle (the best sister in the world), and Tom and Marie (the best parents in the universe) for helping us reach our fundraising goal which allowed us to get this published in the first place! Also to: Josie, Kayleigh, Huma, Megan, Janessa, Kim, Jess and Carly - all of who are completely awesome for either reading/critiquing our book, sharing our Facebook page to help us promote it, or helping us with last minute edits.

Lastly, two *huge* "THANK YOUS" to two people without whom this book would never be published.

First, to Kelly Campion, who did the amazing front and back cover art for this novel. We couldn't have asked for a more talented artist to give a face to our story.

Second, to Jeanne LoPriore, who helped us manically clean up the proof of our book in order to make it publishable.

You guys both rock and are the absolute *best*! ☺

ABOUT THE AUTHORS

Anthony Caruso knew he wanted to become a writer from a young age and has been honing his writing skills since he was thirteen years old. He attended Northumbria University in the United Kingdom, where he obtained his Masters of English Literature. Currently, he lives with his wife and two cats in Rockland County, just north of New York City.

L.J. Simone has been busy writing since the second grade and still has nothing to show for it. She lives outside of New York City with her husband and daughter.

ABOUT THE ARTIST

Kelly Campion has been drawing since the age of five before she considered turning her hobby into a possible illustration career seven years ago. She currently resides in Bergen County, New Jersey. To contact her, visit:

http://www.kellycampion.com

FOR MORE INFORMATION ON *HOLIDAY, INC.*, PLEASE VISIT:

http://www.holidayincbook.com
http://www.facebook.com/HolidayIncorporated
http://twitter.com/HolidayIncBook
http://twitter.com/HolidayIncBill
http://twitter.com/HolidayIncPia
http://twitter.com/TheBoogeymanHI

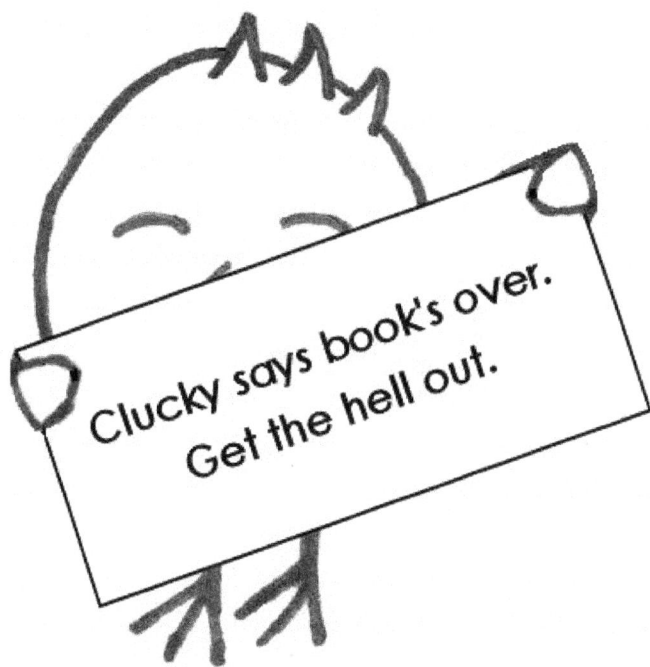

www.ingramcontent.com/pod-product-compliance
Lightning Source LLC
Chambersburg PA
CBHW072336090426
42741CB00012B/2808